PLANTATION WORLDS

MAAN BARUA

Plantation Worlds

DUKE UNIVERSITY PRESS
Durham and London
2024

© 2024 DUKE UNIVERSITY PRESS
All rights reserved
Project Editor: Liz Smith
Designed by A. Mattson Gallagher
Typeset in Portrait Text by Westchester Publishing Services

Library of Congress Cataloging-in-Publication Data
Names: Barua, Maan, [date] author.
Title: Plantation worlds / Maan Barua.
Description: Durham : Duke University Press, 2024. | Includes bibliographical references and index.
Identifiers: LCCN 2023040680 (print)
LCCN 2023040681 (ebook)
ISBN 9781478025610 (paperback)
ISBN 9781478020868 (hardcover)
ISBN 9781478027744 (ebook)
Subjects: LCSH: Tea plantations—India—Assam—History. | Tea plantations—Environmental aspects—India—Assam. | Tea plantation workers—India—Assam—Social conditions. | Elephants—Effect of human beings on—India—Assam. | Human-animal relationships—India—Assam. | BISAC: HISTORY / Asia / South / India | NATURE / Environmental Conservation & Protection
Classification: LCC HD9198.I43 A8437 2024 (print) | LCC HD9198.I43 (ebook) |
DDC 338.1/73720954162—dc23/eng/20240510
LC record available at https://lccn.loc.gov/2023040680
LC ebook record available at https://lccn.loc.gov/2023040681

Cover art: Paul Klee, *With the Wheel* (*Mit dem Rad*) (detail), 1923. Gouache, watercolor, pen and ink on paper laid down on the artist's cardboard mount, 6¾ × 9⅝ in. (17 × 24.5 cm). Private collection. © 2024 Artists Rights Society (ARS), New York. Photo credit: HIP / Art Resource, NY.

For Rana Uncle and Ben Jethai

Rana Partap Behal,
doyen of plantation labor history

Monisha Behal,
who has worked tirelessly for the women of Assam

CONTENTS

ix   Acknowledgments

1   **Introduction**
          Postcolonial Fauna

21   1   **Plantationocene**

64   2   **The Slow Violence of Infrastructure**

98   3   **Material Politics**

121   4   **Accumulation by Plantation**

147   5   **The Diagram of Connectivity**

185   6   **Decolonial Cartographies**

205   **Conclusion**
          A Reverse Déjà Vu

217   Glossary
221   Notes
257   Bibliography
289   Index

ACKNOWLEDGMENTS

This work has been possible only because of the kindness, warmth, and, at many a time, the camaraderie of my interlocutors in Assam. They have been anonymized, but each of them has been vital in shaping my understanding and apprehension of plantation worlds.

A number of people have been pivotal in helping me develop the ideas informing this work. Sushrut Jadhav has been a dear friend, encouraging mentor, and thoughtful collaborator; Sarah Whatmore has inspired a whole generation of scholars looking at worlds beyond the human; and Paul Jepson was not only extremely supportive in the initial stages of this work but also helped me find my feet in academia.

The fifteen years of research that have gone into this book began, formally, when I read for a DPhil in geography at the University of Oxford. A University of Oxford Clarendon Fund Scholarship made this possible. I also received generous support through a Felix Scholarship and a grant from the Harold Hygham Wingate Foundation. A European Research Council Horizon 2020 Starting Grant (Urban Ecologies: Rethinking Nonhuman Life in Global Cities; uEcologies, Grant No. 759239) provided space to develop ideas and opened up the time for bringing this work to conclusion. At a later stage, I have also benefited from a British Academy Knowledge Frontiers Symposium Seed Fund (Grant No. KFSSFKAW\100017) on Plantationocene Futures that created opportunities for discussion and exchange.

I have been invited to present this work at various forums, including the Freie University, Berlin; the Institute of Ethnology, Czech Academy of Sciences, Prague; the Université libre de Bruxelles, Brussels; the Liege Université,

Liege; ETH Zurich; College du France, Paris; the University of Canterbury, Christchurch, New Zealand; the Nehru Memorial Museum and Library, New Delhi; University of Exeter, UK; the University of Oxford, UK; the University of Kent, UK; the Open University, UK; Imperial College, London; and the Center for South Asian Studies, University of Cambridge, UK. Comments and feedback from the audience and workshop participants have helped refine my arguments.

Several archives and libraries have been vital for accessing historical material, particularly the Assam State Archive, Guwahati, National Archives of India, New Delhi; the Bodleian Library, University of Oxford; and the Centre of South Asian Studies Library, University of Cambridge. Aditya Ranjan Pathak and Raza Kazmi helped track down many files and references, for which I am immensely grateful. Achintya Kumar (Manju) Barua provided access to a rich repository of newspaper clippings from the 1990s, a crucial decade in Assam's environmental history. Dhananjay Katju and Damodar Baruah kindly shared archival material that went into writing this book.

Courtney Berger, executive editor at Duke University Press, was enthusiastic about this project right from the outset and has been instrumental in bringing this work to publication. I would also like to thank Laura Jaramillo, editorial associate at the press. Two anonymous readers of the manuscript were generous in comments and helped sharpen my arguments.

During the course of fieldwork, several people have been extremely generous with their time, insights, and advice. I am particularly grateful to Dhruba Jyoti Das, Nandita Hazarika, Bhaben Hazarika, Apurba Basumatary, Narayan Das, Scott Wilson, and Alex Zimmerman of the Assam Haathi Project; Jyoti P. Das, Niranjan Bhuyan, Amarjyoti Lahkar, Bibhab Kumar Talukdar, and Bibhuti Prasad Lahkar of Aaranyak; Rohit Choudhury; Dilip Gogoi; Jamesingh Hanse; Ruth Ganesh and Mary Powys of the Elephant Family; and Vivek Menon, Sandeep Tiwari, Rahul Kaul, Sunil Subba Kyarong, and Dilip Deori of the Wildlife Trust of India. Vivek's enthusiasm for elephant conservation remains contagious. Bhupendra Nath Talukdar, whose grasp of wildlife management in Assam remains unparalleled, has been a longtime mentor. I would also like to thank Pankaj Sharma, Pallav Deka, and Jayanta Deka of Assam's Forest Department for their counsel over the years. I remain indebted to the late Mark Shand, who was unrelenting in his support and who helped me at a difficult time.

My work has drawn liberally from the arguments of scholars of Assam and northeastern India. I would particularly like to thank those I have had the honor to meet or know personally: Sanjay Barbora, Pranav Jyoti Deka, Hiren Gohain, the late Amalendu Guha, Rajib Handique, Sanjoy Hazarika, Dolly Kikon, Mriganka Madhukaillya, and Arupjyoti Saikia, who helped immensely with historical sources and with whom I have had several conversations. All of their work has enriched my thinking. Conversations with several other people have deepened my scholarship, including Nitin Bathla, Uli Beisel, Sarah Besky, Shonil Bhagwat, Cristina Bogdan, Thomas Cousins, Gail Davies, Clemens Driessen, Josh Fisher, Tom Fry, David Gellner, David Goldberg, Ramachandra Guha, César Giraldo Herrera, Steve Hinchliffe, Tim Ingold, Ben Jacob, Nanda Kishore Kannuri, Premesh Lalu, Roland Littlewood, Nicolas Lainé, Jamie Lorimer, Rebeca Ibañez Martin, Prabhu Mohapatra, Ursula Münster, Mahesh Rangarajan, Steve Redpath, Stefan Schütte, Shaunak Sen, Narayan Sharma, Dilip Simeon, AbdouMaliq Simone, Nishant Srinivasaiah, Raman Sukumar, François Thoreau, Jonathon Turnbull, Thom van Dooren, and Tom White.

Anindya Sinha has been a dear friend and provocative collaborator, from whom I continue to learn. Tarsh Thekaekara's work has always been a source of creative energy. Sayan Banerjee and Dhruv Gangadharan Arvind provided comments on the manuscript and on chapter 1, respectively. The late Kamini Prasad Barua shared many insights on indigenous modes of brewing, which informed my analysis in chapter 3.

At my department in Cambridge, I have benefited from the intellectual generosity of Ash Amin, Matthew Gandy, David Nally, and Philip Howell. I would also like to thank my colleagues Bill Adams, Neil Arnold, Alex Cullen, Mia Gray, Mike Hulme, Emma Mawdsley, Clive Oppenheimer, and Tom Spencer. At the School of Geography and Environment at Oxford, where I began much of the research that went into this book, I thank Patricia Daly, Beth Greenhough, Richard Grenyer, Yadvinder Malhi, Derek McCormack, Linda McDowell, Giles Wiggs, Kathy Willis, and Rob Whittaker.

Taz Ahmed's insights have always been as sharp as his wit. Annelie Bernhart, Arnaud Brohe, Lydia Cole, Kate Fayers-Kerr, Carlo Ferri, Joe Gerlach, Adam Gilbertson, Sumon Gowala, Thomas Jellis, Ian Klinke, Jack Loveridge, Shubhra Nayar, Helge Peters, Bablu Saikia, Thomas Turnbull, and John Zablocki have been immensely supportive over the years, as have been Mallika Sekhar and Leela Jadhav, in whose home I wrote some of the earliest versions of these chapters. During the COVID-19 lockdowns in 2021, when much of this book was written, I had many interesting conversations with PN Ravishankar. Thanks go to my wider family: Rojita Borpujari; Ayon and Anuj Kapil; Monoranjan, Namita, and Nimisha Thakur; Rajan Dowerah; Sujoy Hazarika; Padmakshi and Pratik Patowary; and Vishal Baruah. My uncle Raj Baruah passed away before this book came into print. He would always ask when it would come out, and I am saddened by his sudden demise. My parents, Achintya Kumar (Manju) Barua and Moromi Goswami, have always been encouraging. Manju Papa's theories of life and politics in Assam have allowed me to see many things differently. Marthe Achtnich has given me the latitude to do what I love, and the recent arrival of Miraia has been a source of joy. This book is dedicated to Rana Behal, who has inspired many of us to think about plantations, and to Monisha Behal, who has inspired a whole generation of social workers in Assam.

An earlier version of the introduction appeared in *Environment and Planning D*. Portions of chapter 3 appeared as "Volatile Ecologies: Towards a Material Politics of Human-Animal Relations" in *Environment and Planning A*. Portions of chapter 5 appeared as "Circulating Elephants: Unpacking the Geographies of a Cosmopolitan Animal" in *Transactions of the Institute of British Geographers*.

Introduction
Postcolonial Fauna

Only the sound of feet sinking into mud interrupts the cicadas. Searchlights echo in the far distance, flashed by people who are awake, alert. Then that barely audible patterned sound, familiar to those who live in the edges of Assam's forests, softly pierces the humid air: the hollow grating of rice paddy being uprooted, muffled splashes of water as stalks are threshed to remove clinging earth, punctuated every now and then by low rumbles. This pattern repeats for about half an hour, but there is nothing to be seen. The sounds slowly retreat and then wither away. The landscape is momentarily still before the ringing of cicadas engulfs the wet September night.

The next morning, when I return, evidence of elephant presence is everywhere (figure I.1). The tracks of what appear to be a herd of four run through gardens and fields belonging to a community of tea plantation workers. A plot of rice paddy, grown for subsistence, lies trampled. The manicured

I.1   Earth/life: tracks of a herd of four. Photo by the author.

tea bushes of a plantation are unsettled, coated with a film of mud that has rubbed off from proboscidean bodies. Bricks from a demolished wall lie scattered, sparking the ire of the workers. "The elephants broke [into] seven or eight houses to get food," says Putru, a wage laborer from the Adivasi community in the Phulbari Tea Estate. "It is a regular occurrence. They no longer live in reserved forests but in and around the plantations. Raiding crops and breaking into the labor lines at night has become their habit." "It is like carrying out an eviction," adds Putru's neighbor Andreas. "The animals belong to the government, but we have to live with them. There is no alternative of moving out of here. With so many mouths to feed, what will we do?"

The landscape of Sonitpur in the northeastern Indian state of Assam, where this event unfolded, harbors what might be called postcolonial fauna, that is, fauna that has been historically transformed by colonialism as it altered landscapes and worked upon plant and animal bodies, giving rise to a fraught politics of earth and life.[1] Fissured into distinct settlements, with reserves for wildlife and spaces for people, earth becomes a terrain of contestation, underlined by a mass enclosure of land by tea plantations and forestry in the late nineteenth century that mobilized colonial capital and the toil of migrant labor brought to Assam to work under conditions of indenture. At the same time, the lively tracks of elephants unsettle enclosure by knitting forest and habitation, plantation and plot in new spatial combinations. In postcolonial India, elephants have begun to cultivate novel habits to adapt to this unprecedented change in their landscape. What emerges is a politics of dwelling, for elephants have become powerful vehicles for asserting control over enormous tracts of land. The rural poor liken the animals' forays into settlements to evictions. This is not a mere analogy, for elephants are inexorably caught up with violent expulsions the state continues to carry out in the name of conservation.

Postcolonial fauna are symptomatic of what scholars have termed a Plantationocene: an unparalleled transformation of the planet's landscapes through the racial and colonial exploitation of labor, leading to a dominance of monocrop agriculture and capitalist systems of production.[2] This book is concerned with the travails set in motion by plantations and the altered ecologies to which they give rise. It asks questions about habitability and what livability means amid immiseration and the routine violence that plantations spawn. It looks at how elephants and people make worlds in the face of unprecedented environmental change and how such worlds are sustained in spite of relentless dispossession. More importantly, it queries planetary transformations, not through a promontory viewpoint, and not solely from the Global South. It does so by looking and thinking from a region that is a South within the South.

But before delving into debates on specifying and categorizing environmental transformations and prior to outlining the argument of this book, I want to take the reader on a foray through the worlds of people and elephants, a foray that has been part of a large portion of my own life. I grew up in the landscapes I write about in this book, a region that I still call "home" and to which I return every year. This journey might give us a sense of what it means to inhabit landscapes fissured by colonial history and why a Plantationocene might be an alternative starting point for understanding planetary change. In light of an explosion of scholarship on novel natures and wildlife in the Anthropocene, some of which eschews colonial histories and summons the singular figure of *anthropos* or humanity as a whole as an agent of change, the worlds of people and elephants might enable one to slow down. They might create a slightly different awareness of how relations between earth and life are historically and politically molten.

I.2   Denizens of a Plantationocene: the SP04 herd in a tea plantation (*left to right:* Tara-4, Tara-3, Tara-1, and Tara-5). Photo by the author.

The Diagram of Enclosure

The elephant tracks encountered in the opening vignette are those of a herd of four bulls, named SP04 by a group of researchers who have been monitoring the animals' movements in Sonitpur. Led by Tara-1, the dominant *mukhna* or tuskless bull, SP04 is adept at raiding crops and breaking into houses to obtain stored food grain. The three other elephants in the herd are Tara-3, a subadult male approximately ten years old, whose small tushes suggest that he is likely to grow into a tusker, Tara-4, and Tara-5 (figure I.2). A fifth elephant, Tara-2, had left the herd before I commenced fieldwork with the Assam Haathi Project (AHP) team studying the elephants. The prefix *Tara* was derived from Tarajuli, a tea plantation where Dhruba Das, a member of the AHP, first identified them.

The movements of SP04 might be seen as boundary crossings of a particular kind: a transgression from areas demarcated as reserved forests to those spaces allocated for human settlement. This parceling of land in Sonitpur into the space for Nature and that for Society is underpinned by a colonial history, one that is vital for understanding the fraught politics of planetary transformations, giving rise to a condition that might be understood through the devastating effects of plantations when the analytical gaze is situated outward from locales such as Assam. In 1873, the newly formed colonial Forest Department in Assam brought large tracts of land under its control. Regulations under the Indian Forest Act of 1865 thwarted people's access to forest land, customary rights to farm were effaced, and grazing cattle or collecting firewood stopped.[3] The cartographic demarcation of reserved forests operated, in the Forest Department's words, with the logic of fencing "strictly what we could find really merchantable timber growth" while "[leaving] the rest to the uses of the local population."[4] Through enclosure, Assam's forests became sites for systemic revenue extraction. Guided by a quest to maximize profit, the Forest Department began rubber plantations in Sonitpur's forests, transforming heterogeneous stands of trees into monoculture. The cordoning off of forests continued well into the middle of the twentieth century. By 1950, the area of land under the Forest Department's control in the wider Darrang, the erstwhile administrative district in which present-day Sonitpur lies, more than doubled, constituting as much as 17 percent of its total area.[5]

Colonial attempts to control and order the Sonitpur landscape were fostered by the emergence of a new diagram of power.[6] A diagram is an informal dimension, a relation of forces akin to a map that organizes practices, distributes functions, and allocates resources, becoming coextensive with an entire social and ecological field. Power operates diagrammatically by creating new fields of visibility. Cartographic surveys, taxonomies of flora, and catalogs of valuable forest produce generated by colonial forestry gave rise to a luminous environment, one that visualized Sonitpur's jungles as a commercial resource (figure I.3). As an informal dimension, a diagram traverses the discursive and the nondiscursive, the formed and the unformed. New forest acts and legislations were the discursive elements of control, while material practices of boundary demarcation, the policing of certain practices and distributing bodies in space, were its nondiscursive elements. By making advanced claims on uncultivated and uninhabited land, colonial power worked on what was unformed. What resulted was a model of enclosure and the institution of a binary between forests and human habitation, a separation of Nature and Society that did not emerge from Cartesian conjectures but was constituted through colonial modes of governance and control.

The diagrammatic logic of controlling bodies and regulating people's practices was inherently about bringing the landscape and its denizens

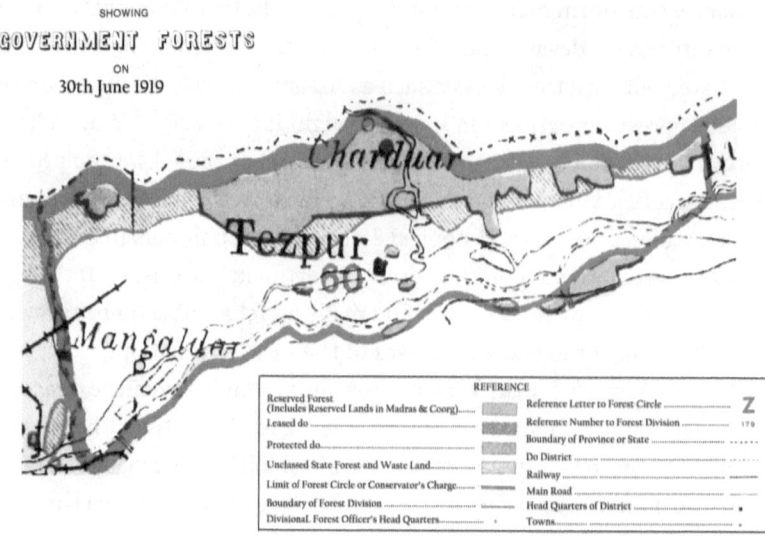

I.3 Enclosure: reserved forests set aside for commercial forestry in Darrang (now Sonitpur), 1919, upon which the contemporary map of elephant reserves is superimposed. Source: Bodleian Library, Oxford University.

into the realm of calculability and profit. The latter also extended to elephants. The colonial government sought to gain a monopoly over the elephant trade that had been in operation in Assam since precolonial times, run mainly by feudal estates and private contractors.[7] In 1873, as enclosures began to take hold, the Forest Department brought elephant capture "under more precise regulations." Every district in Assam was divided into *mahals* or leases for elephant capture, partitioned "according to the number of *poongs* or salt-licks in each."[8] Leases were sold annually by auction and, in addition, the government reserved a royalty of £60 per animal caught.[9] The government also retained the rights to purchase any animal over seven feet in height.[10]

In the eyes of the colonial administration, elephants were "distinctly a forest produce."[11] Like forests, the animals were visualized as and transformed into a resource for generating revenue. What began as regulation of elephant capture soon gave way to complete colonial monopoly over the elephant trade. In 1879, an Elephants' Preservation Act was instituted, whereupon no wild elephant could be killed, injured, or captured unless it was an act of self-defense or when the animals caused serious damage to settlements and cultivation.[12] This imperative was not based on ethical considerations. Rather, it had to do with the fact that elephants were living infrastructure that served as beasts of burden for the expansion and administration of empire. Elephants were mobilized to further colonial claims over territory and resources. Vast tracts of land were barred from being opened up for agriculture on grounds that they contained elephant populations that could be captured in the future.[13]

A significant outcome of enclosure was that it led to colonial ownership over elephants, giving the state the authority to dictate how modes of human-elephant cohabitation should unfold on the ground, irrespective of whether the animals inhabited reserved forests or dwelled outside them. The legacies of enclosure continue in the present day, reflected in people's association of elephants with the state. Furthermore, the diagram of enclosure introduced yet another schism in the landscape. The act of inhabiting a landscape was inverted into that of occupation,[14] whereby worlds are laid out in advance by a dominant authority to regulate bodies and govern access to resources. This found its fullest expression in the 1940s when, in spite of intense opposition, the Assam Legislative Assembly adopted a bill empowering the Forest Department to evict anyone found occupying forest land.[15] And yet, every diagram has "certain relatively unbound points, points of creativity, change and resistance."[16] Landscapes are never settled by power: certain points fall off and even challenge their spatial order.

Unbound Points

What is striking about SP04 is that it is an all-male group. The association of the four bulls is relatively durable: the animals have grouped together for a period of about three years. Asian elephant herds are typically matriarchal. Bulls born into matriarchal natal groups continue to stay in these herds until adolescence, after which they disperse and are predominantly solitary.[17] Loose associations sometimes form between bulls, where animals band together to raid crop fields at night and disperse during the daytime, a strategy elephants adopt to reduce the risk of human retaliation when venturing into people-dominated landscapes.[18]

Relatively stable all-male associations, however, are novel. Archival accounts of elephants in the Sonitpur landscape reveal how, throughout most of the twentieth century, crop-raiding bulls were predominantly solitary animals. For instance, in the early twentieth century, several bounties were offered for the destruction of solitary bull elephants that had been "doing serious damage to tea" and other crops in Sonitpur.[19] The colonial administration used the term *intruder* to describe such animals,[20] indicating how entrenched spatial binaries between forest and settlement had become. Offers by the government to keep the elephants' tusks provided incentives for licensed hunters to shoot animals declared rogues.[21] However, not all bull Asian elephants have tusks. *Mukhnas* or tuskless males—like Tara-1 of the SP04 herd—are common. In 1935, amid complaints regarding elephant depredation from tea plantations and farmers, the Forest Department introduced an Elephant Control Scheme. Approved and armed sportsmen were further incentivized by being offered a "free" tusker "for every corresponding *Mukhna* destroyed."[22]

What elephants might have made of bloody encounters with colonial sportsmen is difficult to ascertain from the archives, given their resolution and grain. Yet archival stories indicate how colonial hunting shaped proboscidean dispositions. Efforts to control elephants resulted in a number of wounded animals, inducing "an ugly temper" in animals that could not be put down.[23] As sentient creatures with a great capacity for memory, capable of recognizing individual humans and even distinguishing between communities based on odor and garment color,[24] one might contemplate whether some of the animals declared a problem were themselves products of violent colonial encounters.

Some cues specific to the Assam landscape are provided in the accounts of Frank Nicholls, a tea planter and *shikari* who spent fifty years in Sonitpur in the first half of the twentieth century. Nicholls describes how a "bad" tusker disrupted their attempts at cutting a path through a forest that lay in "exceedingly wild country." Seeing unfamiliar people in the forest, the "determined tusker" chased Nicholls's *mahout* "for three consecutive days." On another occasion, the same individual killed a man from an elephant-capture party whose attempt to strike the elephant with a knife was of no avail.[25] Nicholls put down the animal when it charged his elephant a few years later. The signs of past encounters on the animal's body were telling. It had the mark of the dead man's knife blow, as well as an "old bullet wound" inflicted by Nicholls himself.[26] The elephant's disposition was certainly shaped by past, painful encounters, and they probably had bearings on how the animal sensed transformations that were taking place in the Sonitpur landscape.

Shuttling between field and archive, ethnography and ethology, gives one a sense of how postcolonial fauna emerges. It is only in recent times that all-male herds like SP04 are being documented. The ethologist Anindya Sinha and his colleagues contend that such novel elephant "cultures" are a response to inhabiting peopled landscapes—milieus that are unpredictable and laden with risk.[27] The sizes of such all-male herds also tend to increase when elephants take to living in agricultural and plantation landscapes, a tactic of creating safety through numbers. Such novel behavior, Sinha and colleagues argue, is environmentally rather than biologically influenced.[28] Put another way, one could contend that such emergent elephant cultures are a response to inhabiting a Plantationocene, an adaptation to the upheavals of landscape colonialism set in motion.

Tracking SP04's movements with the AHP team is an activity of feet following quadruped soles. Tracking also animates a landscape's past. The herd leads us through different parts of Sonitpur: in Phulbari Tea Estate we see Tara-1 stand up, alert, as the other individuals rest, and a group of women pluck tea nearby. We move through the Harchora Tea Estate, established in the 1850s, with its long rows of labor lines housing its Adivasi workforce. As far back as 1911, elephants would arrive in Harchora "at night to eat the long succulent grasses" that grew by a small river SP04 wades through.[29] As with forest reserves, the emergence of tea plantations too proceeded through a violent history of enclosure. Colonial money capital was invested to grab land and initiate monoculture tea plantations in the 1850s, aided by extremely liberal grants from the colonial administration.[30] The first plantation in Sonitpur was set up in 1854 and, less than a decade later, nearly twenty thousand acres of land had come under the control of private plantation companies.[31] This transformation of landscape into monoculture was achieved through the toil of indentured labor, brought to Assam under the most despicable of conditions. Between 1863 and 1868 alone, over fifty thousand workers were, to use the colonial administration's expression, "imported" to Assam. As many as seventeen hundred people died en route.[32]

The movements of SP04 also enliven other elements of colonial pasts that coexist with a landscape's presents, known to animate bodies, human and other-than-human,[33] in their own, corporeal ways. The animals guide us into parts of the Balipara Reserved Forest where timber plantations from the 1870s still persist. The herd then ventures into localities we refrain from entering, as they are hideouts of secessionist rebels. When they resurface, we follow SP04 south toward Goroimari, a former elephant habitat requisitioned to build an air base in 1950.³⁴ Approximately forty to forty-five years old, Tara-1 was not born at the time. However, it is plausible that members of his erstwhile natal troop frequented such places. The tracks that the animals forge are thus not mere lines through blank space. They are replete with memories and other-than-human knowledge, gained through a perceptual engagement with landscape.

Elephants' apprehension of a landscape's topography and its durations, however, is very different from that of bipedal, and primarily ocular, humans. As Dhruba from the AHP remarks, "Elephants encounter the world sensually. We, on the other hand, do so intently." Elephants live in another sensory world of audition, olfaction, and tactility. They communicate over long distances and at low frequencies inaudible to the human ear. Such sound waves can travel up to almost 10 kilometers, covering an area of 300 square kilometers,³⁵ although their reach in forest and plantation landscapes is not always so far. Traffic and activities during the daytime also increase ambient noise. The auditory world of elephants thus shrinks and expands in tune with other rhythms of the landscape. Low-frequency elephant rumbles, however, travel even further through the ground. Elephants deploy their feet to sense these waves and to communicate over scales and distances not possible for humans when unaided by technology.³⁶ Through elephants' sensory and sentient worlds, the landscape therefore takes on another meaning: it becomes a medium of communication.

Tracking thus foregrounds how landscapes are not solely human arrangements. Their extent and shape are also folded according to the ways in which other bodies sense and apprehend the world. A map of SP04's movements shows how elephants' tracks unbind from the diagram of enclosure (figure I.4). As Dhruba explains, "We might designate specific reserved forests for elephants, but this is very different from the ways in which elephants apprehend their habitat. For all you know, elephants might consider 'our space'—settlements and agriculture—to be 'their space' as well." What is noticeable about SP04's movements is that they live predominantly outside protected areas. Such modes of dwelling strike at the heart of the contemporary imagination that elephants ought to inhabit spaces allocated to them: reserved forests, wildlife sanctuaries, and national parks. Female-led groups, on the other hand, venture into human settlements and crop fields but, unlike SP04, do not inhabit plantations and agrarian landscapes for prolonged durations. The all-male herd is a distinct outcome of a number of forces acting in conjunction: deforestation and the transformation of jungles

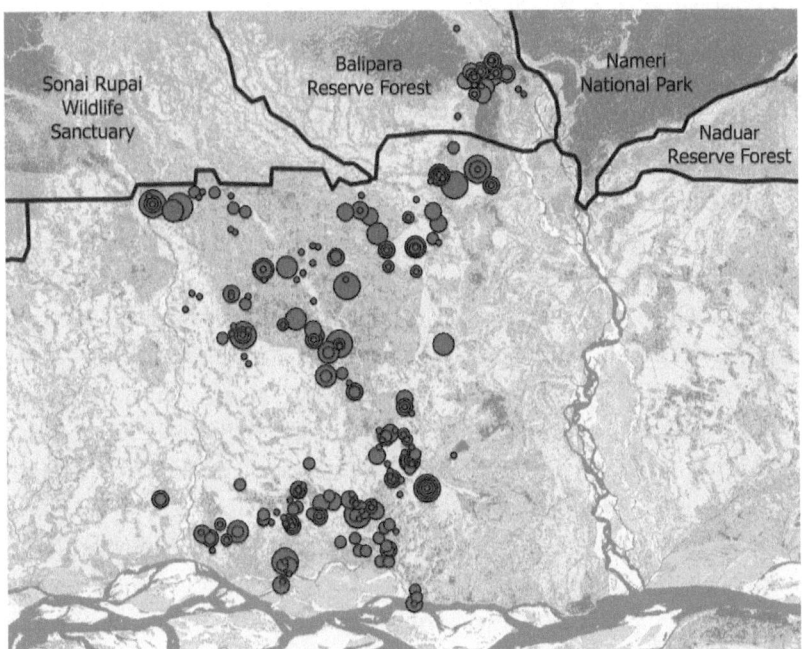

I.4   Unbound points. Map of SP04's movements, where circles depict clustered activity, much of which is outside protected areas (indicated by black line). Source: Assam Haathi Project, Ecosystems India and Chester Zoo; forest boundaries added.

into monoculture, the capacity of the animals to adapt, and the questions posed of them as they inhabit a landscape riven with frictions.

The Politics of Living Alongside

If the ecologies of elephants are altered by colonial and postcolonial reconfigurations of a milieu, there is also a distinct politics of living alongside these megaherbivores.[37] Dwelling with elephants is a fraught endeavor, particularly for rural Assamese peasants dispossessed by erstwhile forest enclosures and the plantation economy, as well as for the Adivasi tea plantation worker community, whose landholdings have always been meager given their history of migration and indenture.[38] Wide-scale deforestation of the Sonitpur landscape in the 1990s, which proceeded through informal concessions and opportunistic felling during moments of political turmoil, have further spurred elephant incursions into settlements and crop fields. Such incursions, imposing significant burdens on people, are skilled activities, learned by elephants through negotiations, observation, and emulation.

Like the AHP team, people who inhabit the landscape are also acute observers of elephant behavior. Many are familiar with SP04, although they do not have a name for the herd. Putru, whom we encountered in the opening of this chapter, recounts how "four elephants came at night and broke into the room" in which he was sleeping. "Not finding any food, they demolished my neighbor's kitchen wall, followed by a couple of other houses, only to come back here again." Living with his wife and young child, elephant presence poses significant risk for Putru's family: "I desperately tried to stop them, but they charge and will trample you! Their arrival is so sudden that there is not even time to light a fire. What will you do?"

A Plantationocene landscape is thus laden with risks, which both the rural poor and elephants have to negotiate. Vulnerabilities generated historically and those in the present are crucial in the formation of an all-male herd. For many adolescent bulls, venturing into new areas after leaving their natal group is not straightforward, especially when they lack knowledge of the risks a landscape poses. Between 2003 and 2016, Sonitpur witnessed 138 reported elephant mortalities, some of which involved deliberate electrocution and poisoning by people frustrated by depredation.[39] In 2001, an unprecedented death of seventeen elephants was reported in Sonitpur. Poisoning by pesticide was one identified cause. Reports suggested that "local villagers or tea garden labourers" did so in relation to "elephants causing destruction to crops, property and life on a regular basis."[40] Irate denizens of the village of Haleswar even scrawled the words "Paddy thief elephant . . . [bin] Laden" in Assamese on the body of one poisoned animal (figure I.5). The reference to Osama bin Laden, a household name in Assam at the time, was an allusion to the terror elephants were perceived to cause.

Elephants that inhabit Sonitpur are potentially living witnesses to such past events. As long-lived creatures, elephants sustain memories, including intimate knowledge of the places in which members of their group have died.[41] Older animals thus have a tacit grasp of the landscape, the opportunities it presents, and the risks it poses. Tara-1 is skilled in negotiating Sonitpur's patchwork of tea plantations, crop fields, and forests, having learned where not to venture, what not to touch or eat during the course of his lifetime. Tara-1 is also adept at finding sources of food and places of

I.5 "Paddy thief elephant... Laden," scrawled on the body of a poisoned elephant. Haleswar, October 2001. Photo: Sunil Subba Kyarong/Wildlife Trust of India.

safety. Being in the company of another skilled animal benefits younger individuals like Tara-3 who, over time and through cultivated habits and emulation, gain an expertise in dwelling in friction-laden landscapes.

As Dhruba tells me while inspecting a house damaged by the herd, SP04 has become proficient in accessing food grain stored in people's homes. "If you look at SP04's timings, there is always an 'element of surprise' in their raids," says Dhruba. "That is why they are successful. Led by Tara-1, they have become very clever. Seldom will you see them venturing into villages in the early hours of the evening when people are up and generally alert. They are likely to be chased out then." Such knowledge, gathered through trial and error, unsettles the idea that humans are the only knowing subjects of a landscape, just as it redistributes who or what apprehends and forges a living and livable milieu. Ethological studies of elephants reveal that individuals within a social group may derive significant benefits from the influence of an older leader, partly because of their enhanced abilities in making crucial decisions about threats.[42] Over the years the AHP team has been following the herd of bulls, Dhruba has noticed how Tara-3's skills in crop raiding and breaking into houses are becoming more attuned: "Tara-3 used to be a very aggressive elephant. Nowadays he has become calmer, and his technique of breaking into houses has begun to mimic Tara-1's: to do so causing minimal damage."

Many inhabitants of Sonitpur allude to this enskilment elephants have undergone. Echoing Dhruba's observations of SP04's decision making, Putru says these particular elephants are "unreliable." They turn up at unexpected hours and at any time of year, not during the fallow winter months alone. "None of them have tusks," he adds, clearly identifying the animals. "These individuals roam around in our vicinity, entering villages and breaking houses." Andreas, Putru's neighbor, whose house was broken into three times, discerns how they differ from "other herds that raid crops." "If you chase those animals, they leave the fields and go away. But not these elephants. They are obstinate and break houses." He further tells me that "entering homes has become [the herd's] habit," providing an astute insight into the transformation of elephants' lives and the rise of postcolonial fauna. "The elephants *know* what to do," says Andreas. "They have become just like humans."

These encounters are inherently asymmetrical, given that elephants are protected by the state. Colonial legislation now informs how certain people view the animals. "Anything that inhabits forests belongs to the government," says Putru, "elephants being one of them. The government has employed foresters. It is their duty to ensure that government animals do not venture into our fields and homes." Through the 1990s, the Forest Department undertook several, often violent, eviction drives in Sonitpur to resettle people who had encroached upon forest land,[43] actions legitimized by laws put in place in the 1940s. People invoke the violence of eviction to describe elephants' actions. "These elephants are government dacoits," remarks Preeti Bahadur, another Sonitpur resident. "Like the Forest Department, they carry out evictions in our villages." This comparison of elephant incursions with actions of the state reveals how a colonial past continues to operate as a duration, combining with the present in novel ways and bursting through to create fraught combinations and arrangements.

Preeti Bahadur in fact abandoned cultivating his vegetable fields due to elephant presence. Putru, on the other hand, contemplates moving elsewhere. "With a wife and child at home, I can't even travel anywhere," he remarks. "I would like to move out of here, but alternate options are very limited." Elephant presence has in fact resulted in erstwhile homesteads and gardens being abandoned (figure I.6). "Isolated homesteads become

I.6   SP04 grazing in an abandoned hamlet belonging to an Adivasi community. The patch is overrun by *Mikania*, a nonnative vine. Photo by the author.

unsafe for people at night," Dhruba remarks, pointing to how living alongside elephants is a fraught practice. "As a result, people shift elsewhere, usually to larger villages where they feel more secure." As the undergrowth takes over, these sites become proboscidean spaces once again: locales amid human settlement and plantations that reflect elephants' own ways, ends, and doings. Yet the emergence of such proboscidean spaces is contingent upon structural inequalities. The houses of the Adivasi community tend to be more frequently damaged by elephants, a phenomenon that is not mere chance or coincidence, but dictated by the fact that many, after leaving the plantations, settle down in the fringe of larger villages, near rivers and forests. Their dwellings too are seldom made of concrete and offer limited resistance to elephant incursions.

These transformations of landscape, underpinned by the colonial history of forest enclosure and the violent creation of plantations, draw attention to the multiple ways in which worlds are made amid the eviscerations and ruins of what one could call a Plantationocene. They point to the need for developing an alternate political ecology, one that recognizes both people and elephants to be immersed in overlapping histories of dispossession, erasure, and exploitation, histories that operate in tandem, which might have elements that are shared, but which are also replete with trajectories that diverge. Such manifold and situated histories can become starting points for imagining landscapes and inhabitation in other ways. A foray into the worlds of elephants and people in Assam also challenges grand narratives of planetary change. It situates environmental transformations in particular places—places on the planet that are not simply underdeveloped regions, the Souths within the Global South, but loci that are vital for grasping the dynamics and politics of earth and life. They furnish steps toward an ecology of a Plantationocene, an ecology that the chapters of this book seek to elucidate.

Plantation Worlds

This transformation of life and earth—the *bio* and the *geo*—and the ways in which they are underlined by a racial and colonial history, and whose legacies endure or recombine with other forces to forge a fraught postcolonial present, are this book's central concerns. More specifically, it aims to specify ecologies of a Plantationocene present, narrated through the lifeworlds of elephants and their relations with people, as well as the particular kinds of living and material worlds these relations summon. The lives of rural Assamese farmers and of the Adivasi community are at the center of this work. My endeavor here is not to write a history of plantations and colonial forestry, and neither is it an ethnography of labor on Assam's tea plantations. Rather, what marks out this book is its attention to a "plantation multiple," where plantation logics or the production of sameness, the violent exploitation of human labor and other-than-human work, the transterritorial circulation of biota, the generation of simplified ecologies, and the ongoingness of extraction and plunder proliferate and become extensive with a wider set of practices in a social and ecological field.[44] A further thread running through this work is elephant conservation in a Plantationocene, examining the various ways in which the postcolonial Indian state deploys the animal to govern large tracts of land. Through these avenues, the book looks at how worlds are made amid the eviscerations of plantations and ruins of a Plantationocene, a making where people and elephants also subvert, challenge, and deterritorialize plantation logics to forge other ways of inhabiting, along and against the grain of established order. This book is an outcome of longitudinal research conducted over the past fifteen years, but it also derives from a much longer engagement of having lived and grown up in the very rural landscape that I write about. I remain uneasy about and skeptical of the use of terms such as *field*, commonplace in the interpretative social sciences—especially those that have historically been caught up in projects of colonialism—for divisions between home and site of study, friend, neighbor, and interlocutor are in this case tenuously drawn. The same holds for the blurred lines between history and memory: many of the violent events of the 1990s—secessionist militancy, military intervention, mass deforestation, and incursions of elephants into settlement—described here were part of my childhood. This vantage point has allowed me to think much more carefully with duration. At the same time, the book's endeavor to think planetarity differently and to maintain some critical distance from terms such as *the South Asian Anthropocene* stems from my own experience of having grown up in what is the South within the Global South.

To this end, chapter 1 ("Plantationocene") builds on emerging work that queries themes regarding planetary change, altered forms and distributions of life, and ecological crises that emerge in their wake.[45] The emphasis of the chapter is not to intervene in debates regarding stratigraphic signatures or to propose yet another name for a new geological epoch. Rather, its aim is to recalibrate how and from where one grasps planetarity and global environmental change, taking Assam's riven landscapes and plantations as a point of departure. By uncovering histories through which a plantation multiple took hold, I show how colonial violence cemented divisions between nature and society, and exploited a resource frontier with devastating consequences for both people and other-than-human life. Many of these forces continue to operate in the postcolonial—or neo-colonial—present.

The preceding pages and chapters that follow draw from what could be called a more-than-human ethnography, in that the ethnographic orientation is directed toward transversal processes cutting across heterogeneous assemblies of people, animals, plants, spirits, and things, rather than the category of "species" and dyadic relations between people and other-than-humans that have become the staple of "multispecies" ethnographies.[46] If ethnography entails participant observation, a more-than-human ethnography takes both people and elephants to be observant participants of the same world both inhabit, a world that at times operates in common and at other times in tandem, where histories of enclosure, exploitation, plunder, and dispossession overlap but also diverge. This endeavor retrieves the ecology sometimes evacuated from political ecology. What emerges is an account of postcolonial nature that is material and affective, while recognizing that other-than-human agency is historically situated, emerging through specific channels. At the same time, a more-than-human ethnography recovers a politics of nature that is inexorably enmeshed with the dynamics of power, where bodies are redistributed for purposes of generating profit while unevenly distributing loss.

This book's commitments of working between field and archive, ethnography and ethology, are further expounded in chapter 2 ("The Slow Violence of Infrastructure"), which reads a Plantationocene through its infrastructure and vice versa. A central theme of writing on the Anthropocene pertains to the social, political, and economic effects of infrastructure. Picking up from the archival history of elephant conservation narrated above, I attend to the ecological consequences of populist agitations against colonial underdevelopment that Assam witnessed in the 1970s and 1980s. Mass political resistance to what was perceived as a form of neocolonialism by the Indian state and big bourgeoisie later developed into full-blown secessionist militancy. Infrastructure was a central pivot around which much of the demands of the Assam Movement—as the agitation was called—were organized. Later endeavors to meet these demands had cascading repercussions, conditioning habitability for both elephants and people. These repercussions manifest in the form of a slow violence upon the landscape's denizens, a violence that is gradual, accretive, and often out of sight, but not to those exposed to its harms.[47] By addressing ecological and political effects of infrastructure, the chapter develops a wider infrastructural ontology attentive to the travails of a Plantationocene's present and past. Such an ontology, the chapter argues, enables alternate readings of how infrastructures condition the ambit of human and other-than-human life, foregrounding questions of postcolonial history and livability sometimes occluded by interdisciplinary fascinations with infrastructure in the Anthropocene.

Chapter 3 ("Material Politics") examines relations between elephants and the Adivasi community in greater depth. Attending to uncanny and unexpected ways in which alcohol mediates relations between people and elephants, the chapter specifies a material politics of a Plantationocene. There has been a flurry of scholarship on the politics of matter in the Anthropocene, influenced by neovitalist and new materialist approaches.[48] These approaches strive to take matter seriously, not just as raw materials or commodities, but as forces that act and as potentials that direct sociopolitical outcomes. While it is tempting to see the rise of particular materials and the often toxic ecologies they create as outcomes of the Anthropocene, close attention to the history of how particular materials are produced points to other explanations. The chapter shows how plantation logics and a necropolitics of aiming to profit from the expenditure of Adivasi lives shapes the ways in which materials, in this instance alcohol, have agency in contemporary ecologies.

In lieu of a new materialist politics of matter, this chapter develops a material politics, where the actions of materials depend on their qualities rather than properties, where agency is configured historically and its expression is contingent upon regulation and practices of use. Matter and materials might seem synonymous to the reader, but I draw some crucial distinctions. Accounts of matter, particularly those espoused by new materialists, emphasize the property of things, residing within them and expressing themselves relationally. Materials, on the other hand, index qualities. The latter are continually produced and dissipated as materials cross osmotic bodies and leach into their surroundings.[49] Tracking materials through a more-than-human ethnography expands this book's wider argument that planetary transformations are situated and grounded events that do not affect *anthropos* as a whole but unevenly and unequally distribute harms.

To further develop a more-than-human ethnography attentive to transversal relations, the book then turns to vegetal life and the ways in which it forges habitability in the landscape (chapter 4, "Accumulation by Plantation"). The violence that followed the Assam Movement had a range of ecological repercussions, beyond those generated by infrastructure. Effects included mass deforestation in the region: an extralegal exploitation of resource frontiers that was to have devastating consequences for both elephants and the Adivasi community. Deforestation fostered the spread of *Mikania*, a nonnative plant that smothered forestry plantations and put tea estates out of production. Coupled with violent land grabs, deforestation set the stage for the further expansion of tea. I term this dynamic accumulation by plantation, a contingent, extralegal form of accumulation in which enrolling the vegetal agencies and attributes of plants also plays a critical role. Vegetal geographies and the dynamic of accumulation by plantation bring a whole raft of agencies and beings into specifying a Plantationocene and show how plantation logics are reproduced through heterogeneous pathways and at a number of scales.

The expansion of infrastructure and tea estates during the turn of the millennium depleted elephant habitat. In response, what has emerged is a new model of conservation, one that shifts from the diagram of enclosure, which is about governing populations within a reserve, to the diagram of connectivity that is about regulating mobility and modulating flows. Chapter 5 ("The Diagram of Connectivity") thus tracks this emergent paradigm of conservation in a Plantationocene, attending to its political and ecological consequences. Connectivity arises through conjunctions between biogeographic science, imperatives of conservation nongovernmental organizations (NGOs), and actions of the postcolonial state. It materializes in the form of wildlife corridors, some of which are being implemented through expulsions. Connectivity is laden with friction and meets opposition, particularly by those affected by its territorial imperative. The paradigm of connectivity also draws attention to the ways in which conservation is increasingly being scripted in the spatial idiom of infrastructure. The latter becomes a biopolitical technology for governing other-than-human life and, at the same time, draws conservation into ever greater proximities with capitalism. The diagram of connectivity reveals how force fields of power are rearranged, giving rise to new modes of territorial control in a Plantationocene.

Chapter 6 ("Decolonial Cartographies") attends to the ways in which coercive diagrams of a Plantationocene are challenged. Drawing on insights from Adivasi interlocutors, it attends to the ways in which people resist statist logics by invoking spirits, positing other ontologies of animals and an unbounded cartography that unfolds along tracks and trails. These forms of resistance deterritorialize colonial binaries and plantation logics, sometimes beneath the threshold of detectability, and are expressions of people's agency in a milieu of dispossession. Decolonial cartographies, I argue, point to world-making practices that generate other ways of dwelling alongside elephants and amid plantations, just as they brim with the potential of altering what it means to inhabit a Plantationocene. Together, these chapters draw attention to alternate ways of specifying planetary transformations and of understanding the politics of livability and dynamics of life on an altered planet. But to understand the wider importance and salience of this foray into the worlds of elephants and people, we might pause and ask: Why not the Anthropocene?

1

Plantationocene

After the Anthropocene

By the beginning of the twentieth century, Assam's landscape had undergone a dramatic upheaval. As we saw in the introduction, a petty trade in forest products was transformed into a global industry, accompanied by an unprecedented series of enclosures. Over four thousand square miles of land had come under the control of the colonial forest administration,[1] alienating the peasantry from cultivation, grazing, and other customary rights. One-fifth of Assam's geographical area was converted into tea plantations (figure 1.1), aided by surplus British capital and through the indenture of over three million people recruited from central and eastern India.[2] Plantation regimes extended to the enclosed forests in the form of commercial forestry. Aims to improve forests created a simplified ecology where each vegetal body coordinated only with replicas and with the time of the market.

1.1   Upheavals of landscape: newly established tea plantation in Assam, 1885. Source: Boileau Collection, Centre of South Asian Studies, Cambridge University.

Close to ten thousand elephants, twice the number surviving in the wild in Assam today, were captured,[3] forcibly torn from their eco-social modes of being and rendered into commodities for generating exchange value.

The multiple effects of such an alteration of earth (the *geo*) and redistribution of life (the *bio*) have become a pivotal concern of the social sciences. Calls for "putting life back" into the social and natural sciences have gained immense traction with the advent of the Anthropocene as a marker of our present times.[4] From engagements with biopolitics to metabolism, geology to multispecies worlds, life is now at the center of much academic attention and interdisciplinary rapprochement. What engagements with the Anthropocene in the humanities and the critical social sciences have sparked is the dissolving of the old (read colonial) settlements of Nature and Society, Science and Politics. The breakdown of these settlements has witnessed the erection of others: of a novel planet where "mankind" becomes a geologic force, a new Pangaea where human-induced circulation of biota runs geological history backward, and a global space where anthropogenic materials percolate into every pore of earth and life, from cells to continents.[5]

There has been significant investment in the Anthropocene, even a rush to specify what it means outside of the narrow confines of geological stratigraphy. From glib assertions that there may be "other Anthropocenes elsewhere,"[6] to nuanced and situated engagements reworking its colonizing tendencies, the Anthropocene is constantly evoked as a signature of our contemporary condition. It ushers in new ontologies and speculative futures in equal measure. Amid this clamor for specifying and diagnosing the Anthropocene, one cannot but help feeling what Eduardo Vivieros de Castro calls a "reverse déjà vu,"[7] a feeling that one inhabits a situation that appears new and unfamiliar while having been there before. Dismantling divisions between nature and society, human and natural history, biology and culture, has had a long-standing tradition in geography and anthropology, where academic labors of partitioning the study of life and that of earth has never been deeply entrenched.[8] As our foray into the worlds of elephants and people in the Sonitpur landscape showed, many have long refused these imposed divisions right from the outset. Yet Anthropocene thinkers sometimes write as though these are novel revelations.[9]

One debate that runs through much of this book is whether we are living in the Anthropocene, the "age of mankind" with its Eurocentric and technodeterminist vistas, or we are inhabiting another formation, shaped by colonialism and the relentless accumulation of capital, where human life and biotic assemblages—populations of interacting organisms in a particular environment—are riven and transformed through very specific pathways. At the heart of the matter lies this book's troubling of the figure of *anthropos*: humanity as an undifferentiated whole and agent of change, which gives the contemporary condition of the Anthropocene its name. In its more dangerous avatars, the driving force behind planetary transformations is even attributed to a Malthusian focus on population growth. These arguments about epochal change are nothing but a god trick: a view from nowhere that fails, even refuses, to locate transformations in racial and colonial history.[10]

The Anthropocene, in this sense, is a "colossal falsification."[11] The undifferentiated humanity centered in many strands of Anthropocene scholarship, whether these have to do with human agency and planetary tipping points, stratigraphic signatures, or radically altered distributions of life, serves to reproduce white supremacist claims to universal knowledge. Epistemological blinders in Anthropocene scholarship on the role of race and colonialism, as Janae Davis and colleagues argue, "are not simply academic oversights: They have implications for how we might envision (or fail to envision) just responses to global ecological change." The power geometries at stake, some of which were highlighted in the histories of colonial enclosure tracked earlier, are a reminder that the Anthropocene "is not the product of 'human nature,' or humanity as a whole, but rather the interrelated historical processes set in motion by a small minority."[12] What needs to be asked then, grounded through ethnographic and archival inquiry, is "why the Anthropocene?" rather than "why not?"

Several debates have come up with the meteoric rise of the Anthropocene as a marker and diagnosis of our present condition, and in this sense the term has been generative for fostering cross-disciplinary conversations. The first is an argument about geological periodization. When does the Anthropocene begin and what are its signatures?[13] A second thread involves understanding the Anthropocene as a project of scale, one that asserts "scalar enormity,"[14] evidenced through macroscopes and the dozens of graphs that show exponential increases in "human impact" upon the planet. A third conversation, following on from the Anthropocene's scalar assertions, revolves around planetary crises and environmental sustainability. Here, transformative agency is realized principally through technology-resource complexes rather than the interpenetrating relations of power, technology and capital. The fourth, as Jason Moore puts it, revolves within the West's university system and is concerned with conversations across the nature-society divide that the Anthropocene reinvigorates. Much of these are rife with "shallow historicization" that eschews understandings of the planetary "as a system of power, profit and re/production in the web of life."[15] Similarly, scale does not obey fixed ontologies: they are relational and emergent, crafted in practice, just as they are "outcomes of social, cultural and technopolitical processes."[16]

Yet these debates are important for social scientists, unless one wants to leave pressing questions about habitability and environmental justice in the hands of eco-modernists and the geo-engineers. In lieu of the Anthropocene and the singular agency of *anthropos*, Jason Moore, Andreas Malm, and Alf Hornborg, among others, propose the Capitalocene—a world ecology that is a world system and an ontological transformation, brought about through the vagaries of capitalism and its unending quest for expansion and profit.[17] The Capitalocene has emerged through primitive accumulation or the violent dispossession of masses, and it has arisen through a new world praxis: the production of cheap nature. Cheapening serves to reduce the working costs of capital, directly and indirectly, and it simultaneously treats nature as unworthy, not deserving of dignity or respect.[18] Cheap nature is both capital's ontological practice and the source of its expanded reproduction. As Marx and Engels evocatively remarked while describing planetary transformation in passages of the *Communist Manifesto* in 1872, "cheap . . . commodities are the heavy artillery with which" capital "batters down all Chinese walls."[19] Drawing cues from Marx's insights on underproduction and the idea that "the rate of profit is inversely proportional to the value of raw material,"[20] Moore sees the Capitalocene as a world ecology. Here, cheap commodities and cheap natures are often produced through means that are violent and extraeconomic, involving control, domination, and a revival of the scale of profit on a planetary scale.[21]

The production of cheap natures cannot be cleaved from the ravages of race and colonialism. One must draw connections between Moore's important conception of nature as cheap and the organization of a cheap, colonized workforce. Similarly, to ground planetary change, one needs to develop archival and ethnographic insights that look at transformations "from the standpoint of those who are made into 'cheap' objects of commerce," whose bodies are captured through enslavement and indenture, and whose lives are rendered disposable.[22] The mass enclosure of forest land and the speculative conversion of jungle into tea plantations, the uprooting of people to work under conditions of indenture and the concomitant capture and control of elephants outlined in the introduction create an opening in this direction. Many of the ecological consequences of this transformation, including the rise of postcolonial, as opposed to anthropogenic, fauna, are only becoming apparent now, over a century later and long after India acquired independence. This particular grounding of planetary change needs to be pushed further: toward ethnographies of a Plantationocene.

Plantationocene

Moving away from some of the falsifications of the Anthropocene, a number of scholars have looked to plantations and their enduring legacies as alternate loci to situate planetary change and understand ecological crises. Environmental modernization, homogeneity, and control crystalized on plantations. Resources extracted through colonial plantations underwrote the birth of industry and urban settlement. Plantations arguably provided the impetus, and even model, for the carbon-hungry mechanized factory production system sometimes referred to as an inflection point of the Anthropocene.[23] Maintaining a plantation system required more than capital. As Walter Rodney argues, what matters in plantations is not so much an abundance of capital as "having a labor supply of a particular type": labor must be "cheap and plentiful, and, even more important, the labour must be easily controlled."[24] The strategies for doing so included slavery and, in the instance of Assam's tea plantations, indenture. Forest and timber plantations on the other hand were places where imperial sciences of calculation, control, and profit, including botany, silviculture, soil science, and entomology, were practiced and furthered.[25]

While plantations themselves have long been the subject of study, the Plantationocene is a concept that has emerged only in recent times. It aims to redress some of the epistemological blind spots of the Anthropocene, whether to do with the racial and colonial origins of the latter's inflection points or world ecologies producing cheap natures. Collectively generated in a conversation between anthropologists and ecologists in Aarhus in 2014, *Plantationocene* is a term for epochal change stemming from "devastating transformation of diverse kinds of human-tended farms, pastures, and forests into extractive and enclosed plantations, relying on slave labor and other forms of exploited, alienated and usually spatially transported labor."[26] For others, the Plantationocene is "a concept grounded in life on the land and centered around the role of the plantation in sustaining a racialized elite, propelling colonial exploration, creating a core and a periphery, sanctioning forced labor, and shaping both the cultures we consume and the cultural norms we inhabit and perform."[27] From a socio-ecological perspective, each constituent of such monocrop production systems, including labor, land, plants, technology, and infrastructure, is caught up in mutual dependencies and becomes essential to the operation of the whole.[28]

The environmental humanities and multispecies approaches to the Plantationocene, notably those emerging from the conversations in Aarhus, have however been critiqued for sidelining core issues of race and colonialism.[29] Ecological disruption is emphasized over the violence of slavery or, in Assam's instance, indenture, which have been central to the construction of a new world order. As Davis and colleagues persuasively argue, "the current multispecies framing conceptualizes the plantation largely as a system of human control over nature, obscuring the centrality of racial politics." In its multispecies iteration the role of racial and colonial politics is minimized, leading to a "flattened notion of 'making kin'" and, as the fraught modes of inhabiting landscapes like those in Sonitpur show, they remain inadequate "for the creation of more just ecologies in the plantation present."[30]

In a similar vein, emerging scholarship on the Plantationocene has to engage with a wide variety of work that offers substantial critiques of the plantation mode of development. Katherine McKittrick, in her brilliant essay on plantation futures, argues that plantations are ongoing loci of racial violence and death, and their spatial histories are crucial to understanding the nature of power in the modern world. She asks, "What is at stake in linking a plantation past to the present? What comes of positioning the plantation as a threshold to thinking through long-standing and contemporary practices of racial violence?"[31] The work of Black feminist scholars is of immense value for thinking about not just plantations but the uneven racial and colonial contours of a Plantationocene, its enclosures and spatial divisions of landscape, as well as the quest to subjugate human and other-than-human life. As witnessed in the introduction, transformations of Assam's landscape through forestry and tea plantations were not an undifferentiated socio-ecological transformation, but one underscored by power-laden hierarchies and a motive to produce profit, sometimes from the disposability of life. The ways in which such colonial pasts act as durations, combining with the postcolonial present to give rise to new, fraught worlds, is a theme that I develop through this book.

Although questions regarding the origins of a new epoch are not my central concern, it is worth noting that a Plantationocene opens up alternatives to the Eurocentrism of the Anthropocene. A crucial point here is the date-oriented argument introduced by debates surrounding the Anthropocene and its origins. Such arguments, as the cultural theorist Sylvia Wynter suggests,[32] blot out different lines of reasoning. A date-oriented discourse elaborates existing hierarchies of scientific knowledge and human worth, but is "not a significant conceptual or cognitive departure" from "conventional reason." The quest to identify a singular stratigraphic point for the Anthropocene "is indicative of a form of epistemological reductionism that remains trapped within the strictures of a Eurocentric worldview."[33] Other, more critical scientific approaches take European contact with the New World as a historical background for an alternate starting point for the Anthropocene.[34] Such approaches offer up possibilities for foregrounding the ways "in which questions of race and the persistence of Eurocentric epistemologies play a much more significant role" in alterations of the planet.[35]

A Plantationocene, in the way I refer to it in this book and in relation to Assam's postcolonial ecology, exceeds the physical locus of the plantation. Rather, what is at work is a "plantation logic,"[36] a system or set of principles underlying the arrangement of elements that foster and operate via the violent "planting" of people considered subordinate in colonial and racial hierarchies as cheap labor to bolster crop economies, the transformation of land purportedly seen as belonging to no one to the services of a racial and colonial economy, and a deep dispossession and dehumanization of people. Plantation logics are about erasure and displacement, replacement and simplification, and are permeated by practices of extraction and exploitation. As upheavals of Sonitpur's landscape in the introduction has shown, a plantation logic goes beyond the tea plantation and its exploitation of indentured labor to permeate other fields of colonial endeavor. The fencing off of forest land for other kinds of monoculture led to a simultaneous dispossession of the peasantry who were put to work through contract labor. Forest villages were set up to ensure a steady labor supply so that forests could be turned into plantations, producing yet another cheap commodity: timber.[37] This profit-driven motive extended to other forms of life deemed exploitable. Elephants were rendered into "forest produce," while the same colonial economic rationale operated in their destruction and killing.

In effect, a plantation logic issues forth diagrammatically,[38] becoming coextensive with a whole social and ecological field. McKittrick hits the nail on the head when she proclaims that "the plantation is a persistent but ugly blueprint of our contemporary spatial troubles."[39] I use the term *diagram* as it creates new fields of visibility and connects different bodies, ecologies, and practices, enabling a coercive and racial plantation logic to proliferate.[40] It is replete with frontier orientations, bringing new spaces and their denizens into its fold, creating enclosures, indenture, and mass dispossession, and even treating these as normal. Diagrams morph, whereby a plantation logic is worked out anew in response to the problems and situations at hand. Through other connections and proliferations, yet other frontiers are opened up, denizens and resources are folded into the ambit of accumulation, and plunder continues. Hierarchies are sustained, albeit not in the same way as the older order. There is a different impetus of territorial control, one that produces the same binaries of "spaces for *us*," inhabited by "secular economically comfortable man and positioned in opposition to the under-developed impoverished spaces for *them*,"[41] where those considered inferior in a Eurocentric hierarchy of humankind are planted. Yet amid the proliferation of plantation logics, there are points of creativity and resistance. They unbind from diagrams of power and enable formulating possibilities for dwelling otherwise.

As scholars in the North American context have remarked, a "colour-blind conception" of a Plantationocene, symptomatic of certain strands of scholarship, "diminishes the deep history of Black struggle and the ways that attention to slave life can provide guidance for cultivating worlds that support multispecies well-being."[42] In a similar vein, accounts of landscape transformation and the rise of anthropogenic fauna in the Anthropocene that fail to look at questions of indenture and colonial and caste-based forms of oppression skew both cause and consequence of change. They leave us with an impoverished understanding of how more-than-human worlds are coconstituted and how they might be remade. This book's specification of a Plantationocene stems from an ethnography of the Adivasi community—former and current tea plantation worker communities. The lives and struggles of these communities, sometimes seen as ungeographic and left behind, become central to understanding how worlds are made amid dispossession, the expansion of resource frontiers, and the ecological crises they draw in their wake.

The plantation logics that I wish to specify and a Plantationocene that I want to ground take inspiration from a remarkable body of work on Assam's plantations. Notable here is the pioneering scholarship of Amalendu Guha, Hiren Gohain, and Rana Partap Behal,[43] whose insights on colonial and postcolonial political economy are of critical importance, not only for writing the plantation in Assam but for thinking a Plantationocene more broadly. Much of this work has also been somewhat relegated to the margins of what circulates as South Asian theory, partly because of the peripheral place India's northeast occupies in mainstream discourse. As Behal presciently remarks, "In most studies of Indian indentured labour in British colonial plantations, mention of the Assam indenture system does not occur even as a footnote reference." This is not just oversight or irony, given "the massive mobilization of millions of indentured labourers within British India who were recruited and transported to work in the tea plantations."[44] Rather, it shapes the ways in which one understands and specifies planetary transformations from the Global South and conditions how more just ecologies might be imagined. A failure to see the pivotal role of plantation logics and their diagrammatic morphing in shaping South Asian environments often results in a reproduction of the same Anthropocene discourse this book seeks to work against. While strands of South Asian theory such as subaltern studies have been field-defining endeavors in terms of writing history from below[45]—and this book draws liberally from these traditions—it is equally important to realize that these bodies of work have their trajectories and epistemic centers, just as this book has its own.

My endeavor is not only to evoke a periphery, which others have done convincingly,[46] but also to develop concepts in more transversal ways. Theory must be unparochial, and it must forge transversal alliances, but it cannot be a view from nowhere. Interrogating the Anthropocene through ethnographic work in Assam and from what is considered the margins of South Asian studies leads me to think with a Plantationocene. Guha and Behal's work, both of which are scathing critiques of imperial and nationalist histories, are of vital importance for grasping how Assam's plantations were not just regional phenomena. Plantations were, and continue to be, caught up in the production of a commodity that circulates worldwide: tea. As the anthropologist Dolly Kikon states, "rather than arguing that Northeast India is an exceptional or neglected region—a position propagated by experts, policy makers, and academics in India," one needs to challenge "taken-for-granted categorizations such as remoteness, unruliness [and] backwardness" deployed to specify places like Assam. The region, like others in northeast India, has to be reconceptualized "as an important location through which we can understand new forms of heterogeneity, citizenship, indigeneity, legitimacy and gender relations in contemporary India."[47]

I wish to push Kikon's provocative reasoning further. Regions such as Assam are critical not only for interrogating questions of nature in India, but for specifying and grounding world ecologies that proceed through the opening of extractive frontiers, the creation of plantations, and the rise of forestry regimes, aided by colonial capital and the violent exploitation of labor. Guha's and Behal's insights have been furthered by a vibrant body of historical scholarship on the politics, economy, and ecology of Assam's tea plantations.[48] Notably, the work of Arnab Dey and Namrata Borkotoky provides crucial insights into plantations' environmental pasts and the ways in which colonial plunder exhausted both labor and soil, giving rise to fraught, virulent ecologies.[49] In an analogous vein, Hiren Gohain's and Udayon Misra's poignant analyses of Assam's political economy vis-à-vis its relation to the Indian state, and Virginius Xaxa's luminary scholarship on

Adivasi lives, furnish avenues for understanding the neocolonialism that constitutes a Plantationocene present.[50] Together with other poignant ethnographies of South Asian tea plantations,[51] this critical body of writing on India's northeast provides rich openings for situating a Plantationocene and its racial-colonial world ecologies.

My formulation of an expanded plantation logic that becomes a diagram of a Plantationocene and its ecologies equally draws from Arupjyoti Saikia's and Rajib Handique's lucid specifications of how colonial forestry was developed in Assam.[52] Working within the rich tradition of South Asian environmental history and political ecology,[53] Saikia and Handique reveal how colonial power operated transversally, knitting different spheres of knowledge and intervention, giving rise to new forms of accumulation through dispossession. These endeavors of writing environmental histories are extended by lucid work on animal histories in the region.[54] Forest officers from Assam too provide insightful accounts of elephants in the region. Bhupendra Nath Talukdar's writings are crucial in this regard.[55] Furthermore, my formulation of a Plantationocene takes inspiration from scholarship on the more recent past, including expositions of how people negotiate frictions with wildlife, often in the backdrop of militarization and structural violence that, operates as a duration in the landscape.[56] Such violence also extends to resource extraction for building infrastructure, which, as scholars have argued, takes on a unique material politics in the region, whether in the colonial past or postcolonial present.[57]

The creation of Plantationocenic life, which lies at the heart of this inquiry, must be situated in place. In this work, I refer to "a Plantationocene" rather than ascribing to "the Plantationocene" as though it is a universal condition with one history, one humanity, and one world ecology. The latter is what one gets with heroic assertions by certain political ecologists that we are entering a "global more-than-life context."[58] As Gabrielle Hecht and Sophie Chao argue, an Anthropocene and a Plantationocene are not merely planetary: they have particular and differential manifestations.[59] The endeavor of archival and ethnographic inquiry must strive to hold the planet and places on the planet within the same analytical plane. Understanding a Plantationocene, or even an Anthropocene, as a scalar project "therefore requires treating scale reflexively, as both an analytic category and a political claim,"[60] where scale is made through practice, with multiple connections and disconnections. The act of situation is vital for a lot of work on planetary transformations, particularly those associated with the Capitalocene and a world ecology, which sometimes runs the risk of becoming distal or too overly general, losing the specificity of place and the difference they make to understanding planetarity.

Ecologies of a Plantationocene need to be gleaned through both the stories of people and those of other-than-humans with whom such ecologies are inexorably enmeshed. To this end, this book brings elephants, creatures long caught up in colonial endeavors of forest felling on plantations and timber operations in forests, and whose populations are pivotal to the postcolonial governance of land, onto center stage. Drawing ethnographic attention to other-than-human life, and how such life is enmeshed with those of Assam's plantation workers and rural peasantry, I offer up ways for understanding more-than-human worlds without replicating some of the blind spots of environmental humanities and multispecies approaches to a Plantationocene.[61] It is, however, important not to throw the baby out with the bathwater. Insights from multispecies anthropology and environmental humanities have queried the anthropocentrism of social theory and, as the introduction as well as other situated accounts show,[62] can be brought into more critical engagements with a Plantationocene's fraught, postcolonial ecologies.

The endeavor here is of taking other-than-human life, and people's knowledge of such life, seriously. Other-than-humans are not mute, and neither are they entirely reducible to being cultural constructs. Rather, elephants and other sentient beings are observant participants of the same world that people inhabit, with their own proclivities and knowledge of a landscape and its events. While caught up in fields of power, they respond and pose questions to power, unsettling attempts to order their lives and hone them in. A close attention to other sentient denizens of a landscape, I argue, renews ways for narrating which bodies slow violence acts upon, just as it enables retrieving other zones of habitability amid a fissured Plantationocene world.

Grand narratives are often not helpful for situating a Plantationocene. In the chapters that follow, I aim to foreground how worlds are made amid the fraught ecologies of a Plantationocene. Each chapter tells small stories and stories that are big enough, which shore up complex historical transformations and intersecting paths,[63] while keeping the edges open for other connections to be made. This book situates a Plantationocene in a landscape, patch, and plot. It works against the distal analyses of promontory views of the global that too easily erase difference and the unevenness through which planetary transformations unfold and proceed. While certain strands of Anthropocene discourse reduce other-than-humans to biomass or appellatives such as species, a feature of the chapters of this book is to grasp how alterations differentially affect other-than-human life and how they respond to upheavals of landscape. In effect, the chapters attend to a Plantationocene as a multiple: an ecology of relations and scales, never cleaved from the uneven and coercive effects of power. Grasping this multiple is crucial for understanding how power functions and how people and elephants dwell in a world fissured by plantation logics. It is to this multiple that I now turn, before outlining the individual chapters and mapping the course of the book.

A Plantation Multiple

Situating a Plantationocene requires examining how colonial and postcolonial diagrams of power worked upon a range of bodies and practices, violently bringing them into the ambit of accumulation. At hand, one could argue following Annemarie Mol, is a plantation multiple, in that plantations are more than one, working upon different socioecological fields, monopolizing resources, and subordinating law and government to plantation logics, but not fragmented into many.[64] This process is not uniform but proceeds through particular constellations and in historically specific ways. Drawing extensively on the work of a number of scholars, I want to provide a brief but synthetic and synoptic outline of how plantation logics operate. To do so, I revisit already established ground. In many ways, my exposition of plantation logics has already been preempted by Sanjay Barbora and Sarat Phukan's brilliant essay on Assam's environmental present. Barbora and Phukan draw attention to the ways in which this specific world ecology has been marked by decades of relentless resource extraction, not just by plantations, but by the oil and coal industry as well.[65] However, the act of revisiting can be generative. It prompts new forms of synthesis, particularly between three areas that concern this book—forests, tea plantations, and elephants—and the ways in which they have bearings upon one another in a wider story of a Plantationocene.

To this end, I first attend to stories of labor and the production of cheap natures. I argue that plantation logics proceeded through indentured and contract labor, as well as the unpaid work of other-than-humans. Second, I turn to questions of the production of space. As we witnessed in Sonitpur's landscape, a Plantationocene portends contentious spatializations of human and other-than-human life. This gives rise to a fraught politics of embodiment and dwelling. Third, I specify a plantation multiple as constituted by circulation, including the escalation and expansion of the latter as plantations begin to forge a world ecology. Fourth, I argue that the production of cheap nature in a Plantationocene gives rise to simplified ecologies. Here, human and other-than-human bodies are replaced, disciplined, and homogenized to maximize profit. However, as we shall witness, the very conditions for increasing profitability, resting on erasure and exploitation, give rise to virulence and ruin. These four themes are interrelated and have bearings upon one another. While not the only way of specifying a plantation multiple, they provide crucial insights into the making of a Plantationocene.

Labor, and Vegetal and Animal Work

Plantations mobilize labor in service to capital, often through a range of legal but also extralegal means. Nature is put to work by organizing production and markets through a cash nexus. Jason Moore's argument that world ecologies of capitalism rest on a tripartite division of work—"labour-power, unpaid human work and the work of nature as a whole"[66]—is particularly helpful for understanding what produces a plantation multiple. Conventional political economy often introduces an arbitrary distinction between the exploitation of nature and the exploitation of human labor power, placing them in two distinct realms of ecology and economy. A vital feature of a Plantationocene, on the other hand, is that both people and other-than-human beings are steeped in the same histories of accumulation and dispossession. A postcolonial political economy must therefore account for "extra-human work," or what could be called more-than-human work, but without resorting to frightening assertions that "plantations are just the slavery of plants."[67] At stake in a Plantationocene is the rendition of nature into "lively capital" through a violent expropriation of human labor and other-than-human work, put to the service of an "uneven racial-colonial economy" that "the plantation evidences."[68]

From its inception in early nineteenth-century Assam the tea plantation industry was intensely concerned with labor. Planters, aided by the colonial administration, realized that tea's profitability depended on labor being fixed and tethered to the plantations. Local Assamese communities were unwilling to become the cheap, plentiful, and easily controlled labor that a plantation demanded.[69] As Amalendu Guha shows, the state-planter nexus tried to coerce these communities into working on the plantations by raising land revenue taxes. This led to protests and even confrontations. The quest to mobilize the Assamese into working on plantations was by and large unsuccessful.[70] From the 1860s onward, on the back of a speculative tea boom, planters began bringing labor from other parts of eastern India. Many of these communities came from parts of Bihar, Bengal, Orissa, and the United Provinces, and had already been marginalized by colonial land revenue policies. These regions became hunting grounds for recruiters who transported people to Assam. Upon arrival, they were rendered into indentured "coolies," made to "reside and work under coercive strategies of labour control and 'clockwork' industrial discipline."[71]

The rapid expansion of tea plantations in the mid-nineteenth century was founded on the history of contracts between British-owned venture companies and the colonial Indian government, contracts that laid out the legal and political foundations for resource extraction. After the annexation of Assam to the British Empire in 1826, prospects of colonization of the province with the import of private enterprise and capital from Britain became one of the government's primary concerns.[72] It aimed to attract, through numerous concessions, a class of European planters, along with their capital, to Assam's "wastelands" and convert these into productive landscapes.[73] The government's overtures came to fruition only with the institution of tea plantations in the 1860s, when offers made to set up plantations on wastelands became even more lucrative.[74] Furthermore, as Guha argues, British private enterprise in mid-nineteenth-century Assam was not the outcome of laissez-faire policy: the heavy cost of early experimentation in Assam tea was entirely borne by the government. The expertise so acquired was handed over as "free gifts" to the Assam Company, the first enterprise to start growing tea on a large scale. Land provided to European planters was much more than mere sites: it contained all necessary housing material, including, in many instances, valuable timber.[75] Such government-assisted plunder constituted forms of primitive accumulation and, later, enabled venture companies to become multi-estate corporations.

The capitalist plantation complex in Asia, and particularly Assam, however, "differed from the much older Atlantic plantations in one important respect: it did not have a history of slave-based production."[76] This did not mean servitude went missing: it took on the form of indenture. Shortly upon arrival in the plantations, people were immobilized, planted in "coolie lines" resembling barracks, and cut off from the rest of the populace. Indenture meant that the worker was unable to withdraw his or her labor power, and it was held in place by legal provisions. A breach of contract resulted in criminal prosecution. European planters were even granted penal sanctions. They could arrest workers, capture runaways, and hold labor within the *phatak*, a private prison erected in the plantation.[77] As one observer remarked, notices describing runaway coolies posted on river ferries and railway stations "reminded one of *Uncle Tom's Cabin*."[78] Racial logics underscored this mode of producing cheap, plentiful, and immobile labor. Many planters considered workers subhuman and even likened them to animals. "Assam," one planter wrote in his memoirs, "imports . . . a number of curious and expensive animals known as Act I coolies."[79]

Continuing well into the twentieth century, until it was dismantled in 1926, indenture was "a new system of slavery."[80] Cheap natures of a Plantationocene were also produced through the toil of women and children. Women constituted almost 50 percent of the labor force but were paid less than men, while children were paid less than women. This was despite the fact that both men and women performed the same number of working hours. This unequal wage structure was legalized statutorily by the colonial state at the very inception of the plantation industry. Not only did it enable planters to keep the wage bill low; it pushed wages below the level at which labor power could be reproduced.[81] This was no trivial matter, given that by the early twentieth century, Assam employed more than half of all laborers working on South Asian plantations at the time.[82]

Labor-power was also vital for bolstering commercial forestry and timber plantations, but the colonial strategies of coercion followed a different route. The large-scale enclosure of land meant that villages had been pushed away from the proximity of forests. Obtaining a regular supply of labor for work in the timber plantations was a challenge the Forest Department constantly grappled with. In the early twentieth century, colonial forest officials settled parts of the peasantry in forest villages in order to create an accessible labor pool. In return for limited privileges, people had to offer their labor power to the Forest Department, a practice referred to as *begār* in Assamese.[83]

The peasantry took up *begār* largely because of a failure of Assam's agrarian economy and increasing pressure on land, the availability of the latter being already constrained by the expansion of tea plantations. Immobilizing the workforce, however, was a source of constant anxiety for the

Forest Department. It contended that if people were not granted greater access to forest resources, they might leave the forest villages. As a result, the Forest Department made concessions such as grazing rights. The profit-driven colonial forest administration, however, saw to it that revenue could be gained from every such concession. Significant fees for grazing were introduced. The main catch, however, lay in coercive stipulations: in return for concessions, every adult male member of a family had to work free of cost for the department for a period of ten days each month and were compelled to sell their labor power to the department for a further fifteen days in return for nominal wages. Widespread protests and the equation of this system with slavery led the Forest Department to tone down its practices in the 1930s. Over the years, as villagers settled in forest land, they gained loose forms of tenurial rights. In 1963, after Indian Independence, many of these forest villagers became "privileged tenants."[84] However, a push toward conservation in the 1980s led the Indian government to exercise exclusive rights over forests, further marginalizing the peasantry. New peasant movements that have arisen as a response are the manifestation of what has been almost two centuries of dispossession.[85]

It is within this field of violent expropriation of human labor that one needs to situate discussions of other-than-human work and the production of cheap nature in a Plantationocene. More-than-human work on plantations, whether it has to do with tea or commercial forestry, entails what Marion Ernwein and James Palmer call "vegetal work."[86] Vegetal work refers to processes of growth or the photosynthetic, metabolic, and reproductive activities of plants, which, from the standpoint of capital, convert nutrients and sunlight into carbohydrates and ultimately proteins in ways anthropogenic machines cannot yet duplicate. The category of *work* is not a shorthand for all of the activities of a vegetal being. Rather, plants' productive and reproductive activities should be regarded as vegetal work when the activity is intrinsic to the process of valorization for a particular economic sector, that is, when they are brought into the ambit of economic activity and when benefits to their own proliferation are absent or incidental. It is pointless to deploy the term otherwise.[87] The notion of work is important because it foregrounds the contingency of production regimes and underscores the regenerative work done by plants in processes of production.[88] Furthermore, the colonial and postcolonial economy of plantations rests on transforming life, and the time of life, into the time of work and into dead labor. Vegetal work becomes part of the dead labor embodied in the cheap commodities of a plantation economy, but it always proceeds through the simultaneous exploitation of human labor.[89] Failing to account for this milieu of work leads one down the wrong path, to the nauseating, ahistorical, and color-blind idea that plantations are just the slavery of plants.

Rana Partap Behal's analysis of Assam's plantation economy clearly expresses how the growth of the tea plant has bearings on human labor and work organization in the plantation. Once plants have been started in nurseries, usually from seeds, they are transplanted to the tea estates. The plucking of tea leaves commences when the plant is mature. A skilled activity, plucking is mainly performed by women, pointing to the highly gendered division of labor at stake. The manner in which the plant sprouts leaves, called "a flush," introduces "a very strong element of continuity" to the production process.[90] A week or two after the first flush has been plucked, a second one appears in the form of shoots growing from the axils of the tea bush, followed by a third flush, and so on. Plucking needs to go on almost continually from the time of the first flush in April or early May into the months of August or September. Pauses result in sprouts becoming mature, spoiling the quality of the tea, besides upsetting the plucking level and subsequent flushes. Vegetal growth thus creates a demand for the continuous supply of labor and influences work-time discipline on plantations.

During the dry winter months, tea bushes are pruned in order to prevent the plant from becoming a full-grown tree. A low leafy bush is maintained at a height of two to two and a half feet so that it is within the reach of a woman's hand while plucking.[91] The plant is not anthropomorphized but rendered "anthropo-ontogenetic,"[92] in that a vegetal body is grown such that it maps onto a laboring worker's body. One might see this as an anatomo-politics of the vegetal body,[93] whose motive is to suck living labor in a vampire-like fashion and convert it into dead labor. If pruning is not conducted during the winter months, the next year's crop is lost. The plant, therefore, must be prevented from becoming unruly, for which human labor has to be immobilized so that it is available all year round and the tea plant continually managed. To maximize productivity, dead and injured wood of the tea plant needs removal. Child labor was often used to clean the tea plant's stem, as children were able to reach under the low bushes.[94] In other words, plantations violently disciplined both people and plants, and their coercive design was about exploiting labor power to the hilt.

Extending plantation logics, I argue that capitalist accumulation also involved the violent expropriation of animal work.[95] Elephants were living infrastructure—beasts of burden subtending economic activity—for the colonial economy. They were also working bodies or, as one commentator put it, "trained labourers of enormous strength."[96] The expansion of tea would not have been possible without elephants, as indicated by accounts of how new plantations were set up.[97] This included initially surveying land on elephant back, before felling jungle on a few hundred acres of land. Labor, working under a foreman-contractor or *thikadar*, would be brought in to lop trees and clear the undergrowth. Tree stumps had to be removed in order to prepare the soil for growing tea, for which elephants and buffalo were deployed.[98] The unpaid work of elephants and buffalo was also essential for cultivating land with plows before planting tea,[99] and for uprooting tea bushes when new plants were put in place. Ropes tied to bushes would be attached to an elephant, and each animal was capable of pulling out two hundred bushes a day.[100]

"Without elephants," writes Hinson Allan Antrobus, the official historian of the Assam Company, "it was impossible to get about the country and supervise the scattered areas being cultivated."[101] Elephants enabled travel to remote plantations with no road network. "In Assam," writes one traveler, "*elephants* are *horses*, as these magnificent brutes are as essential to locomotion in some parts of the province, as horses are elsewhere."[102] In the nineteenth century, elephants were often "the only means of locomotion" on "average roads" of the province.[103] This made elephants a crucial conduit in connecting plantations and their products to wider networks of circulation and trade (figure 1.2). During much of the nineteenth century, elephants would be used to transport tea chests from plantations to the Brahmaputra River, from where they would be dispatched by steamer to Calcutta and onward to London.[104] Each elephant would have six chests strapped onto it, a mode of transportation viewed by planters as "a great saving of labour."[105] Certain plantations also had elephant carts for moving tea chests, although these were later superseded by bullock carts.[106] The deployment of elephants even extended to hauling factory engines and boilers over Assam's soft roads,[107] indicating the part played by the animal in the modernization of the plantation.

Elephants became agents in the transformation of landscape and were enrolled in the extractive apparatus that sought to exploit Assam's resources. They were, as Ursula Münster writes, part of the cheap labor essential for establishing monocultures of a Plantationocene.[108] In timber concessions and forestry plantations, elephants were used to roll large logs

1.2   More-than-human work and the forging of a Plantationocene. Using elephants to transport timber for tea boxes, c. 1897. This exemplary photograph of working elephants and their relation to tea was brought to wider academic attention by Jayeeta Sharma in her book *Empire's Garden: Assam and the Making of India*. While the Smithsonian Institution archives list the image as c. 1903 or earlier, the image was reproduced in the May 1897 edition of the *Strand Magazine* (see Lewis, "Elephants at Work," 560). Source: Photo lot 161, Emma A. Koch photograph collection relating to India, South Asia, and Australia, National Anthropological Archives, Smithsonian Institution.

through forests with their head and trunk. Once reaching a clearing, elephants were harnessed to logs in order to drag them to either rivers or railways on which timber would be transported.[109] Working elephants would receive transported logs at depots. Accounts state how the animals handled logs with great dexterity, often working together with one another and with "the least direction from their mahouts."[110] This pivotal role of elephants in resource extraction is testified by the Assam Forest Department's accounts. "These animals," wrote Gustav Mann, then deputy conservator of forests, "are not only most useful, but quite indispensable for timber work in this

Province, since manual labour is simply not procurable for it, and the nature of the forests, in consequence of the entangled undergrowth, rough broken surface or swampy deep ground, precludes the employment of carts and even buffaloes in nearly all localities."[111] In its initial days, the department even kept logs of the labor performed by its elephants, including "the nature of the work done, the amount of work accomplished, the hours during which the animal was working and its condition."[112] Elephants, as Nicolas Lainé poignantly argues, were part of the "labour collectives" deployed in extraction,[113] collectives that enrolled animal work of diverse kinds. As in clearing jungles for tea, buffalo were also used in timber operations, working to drag logs after elephants transported them "over rough and difficult ground."[114]

However, the deployment of other-than-human work in extractive labor collectives was in no way a smooth or settled process. We see flashes here and there of other-than-human resistance and a refusal to work. Elephants, a late nineteenth-century commentator writes, "don't need a trade union, every elephant being able to look after his own interests. A heavy trailing chain is sometimes fixed to elephants that are turned loose to feed in the jungle at night; this is in order that wanderers may be traced by the trail left by the chain in the jungle. Well it has been known that when an elephant has 'made up his mind' to bolt, *he has carefully gathered up the tell-tale chain and carried it for miles on his tusks!*"[115] Although this account is anthropomorphic, it reveals how, as sentient and knowledgeable beings, elephants could elide the demands made upon them by plantations and the forestry apparatus. On occasion, buffalo deployed in timber operations too would run away, sometimes making the animals, in the colonial government's view, "more bother than they are worth.[116]

The difficulties in enrolling elephants as working bodies are most evident when some animals come into *musth*—a condition in bulls when testosterone levels are elevated and which triggers aggressive behavior. Planters often referred to this as a state of the animal going "mad," and as a "disease," reflecting the threat they posed to plantation order.[117] "Nothing domesticated is safe," writes Ramsden, "from human beings to tame buffalo."[118] In 1893, one such elephant in the Jorehaut Company's Cinnamara Tea Estate chased a number of workers, wrecked a portion of the plantation superintendent's bungalow, "destroyed four thatched huts in the lines and broke the woodwork of some barracks."[119] The elephant then went into the tea factory, smashing doors and frames of machinery. It had to be ultimately put down, and the plantation incurred significant losses, both in terms of the value of the animal as well as in terms of the capital assets it had destroyed.[120]

Not only did elephants act as infrastructure for extraction, but they were also used to expand infrastructures of a Plantationocene. Notable here is the role of proboscidean work in Assam's railways, which were largely put in place to support the tea plantation industry.[121] The significant quantities of timber required for railway expansion were transported by enrolling elephants to work. "All supplies, tools and casings" for Assam's oil wells, another major extractive colonial endeavor, had to be carried from settlements to forest sites "by elephant, the sole means of transport to the site itself."[122] In certain instances, elephants acted as "railway engines," in that they hauled trucks onto the main line in sidings of the Assam Railways and Trading Company.[123]

As outlined in the introduction, the colonial administration exercised a monopoly over the elephant trade, first by regulating capture from reserved forests and later through the Elephant Preservation Act brought into force in 1879.[124] Elephants had become "a temptation" for planters. As they "cost virtually nothing to keep," many caught elephants to sell them. Planters even tried to exercise their right over elephants. The Assam Company management made arrangements with local *kheddah* operators to capture elephants, charging fifteen rupees "per cubit in height" for every animal caught.[125] The colonial state's claim of ownership over elephants put an end to such practices. However, their actions too can be likened to a process of primitive accumulation. Animals were torn from their ecological modes of being, disciplined, and rendered docile to work in its plantation regimes or hurled into the marketplace as living commodities for generating exchange value. Such accumulation went hand in hand with usurping indigenous knowledge relating to the capture, training, and upkeep of elephants, knowledge that the colonial government parasitized but did not itself initially produce.[126] Between 1868 and 1980, close to nineteen thousand elephants were captured in South Asia, of which close to ten thousand were in northeast India alone.[127]

Animal work thus constitutes a vital element of a Plantationocene's past and present.[128] Elephants' role as plantation infrastructure is now on the decline. Many animals are out of work, and this has all kinds of ramifications for the creature's future in captivity. Yet unlike machinery, elephants do not rust. Their obsolescence as infrastructure is now replaced by other kinds of work, some of which is conducted informally and often includes clandestine timber felling, creating conditions of precariousness for both elephants and their owners.[129] The transformation of frontiers into plantations thus creates surplus collectives: human and other-than-human lives that linger on and somehow subsist, reeling in the aftermath of the damage that has been done.

Production of Space

A further theme pertaining to a Plantationocene is its uneven spatialities. As the introduction shows, diagrammatic logics of mapping and demarcating space enabled tea plantations and the forestry regime to expand, a process that went ahead through the generation of enclosures. Historians have pointed to the common roots of both plantation forms in Assam's context. The discovery of wild-growing tea plants in the 1830s, Nitin Verma contends, led to some of the earliest proposals for taking possession of "natural" tea forests (figure 1.3). The idea stemmed from wanting to territorialize what was a valuable and exploitable plant. Such forests, Verma argues, were "proto-plantations," containing "the germs of a prolonged process of dispossession of the forest common."[130] Proto-plantations were those particular forests where commercially exploitable trees were clustered naturally, cheapening the costs involved in harvesting timber and other forest produce. Proto-plantations prompt us to think as to whether forests themselves were a source of primitive accumulation. The mapping of distributions of rubber in Assam's forests in the 1870s, which informed decisions on what to demarcate, reserve and enclose, and what to leave aside for the local populace, is a poignant case in point.[131]

The expansion of tea plantations, themselves enclaves, proceeded through substantial support from the colonial administration. In 1838, the Wasteland Grant Rules came into effect, framed primarily to make Assam's hinterlands attractive for planters with capital. These rules, furnishing long-term lease of land to applicants, "did not discriminate against indigenous inhabitants as such" but were "framed in such manner as to exclude them from all concessional grants in practice."[132] All grants had to be for one hundred acres or more, and applicants who did not possess capital worth three rupees per acre were barred. Under such circumstances, only Europeans had the means of availing themselves of concessions.[133] The Wasteland Grant Rules were revised in 1854, also on even more liberal terms.[134] This tempted planters to grab even more land, often in excess of what they could manage, stimulating a land rush in Assam and ushering in a Plantationocene.[135]

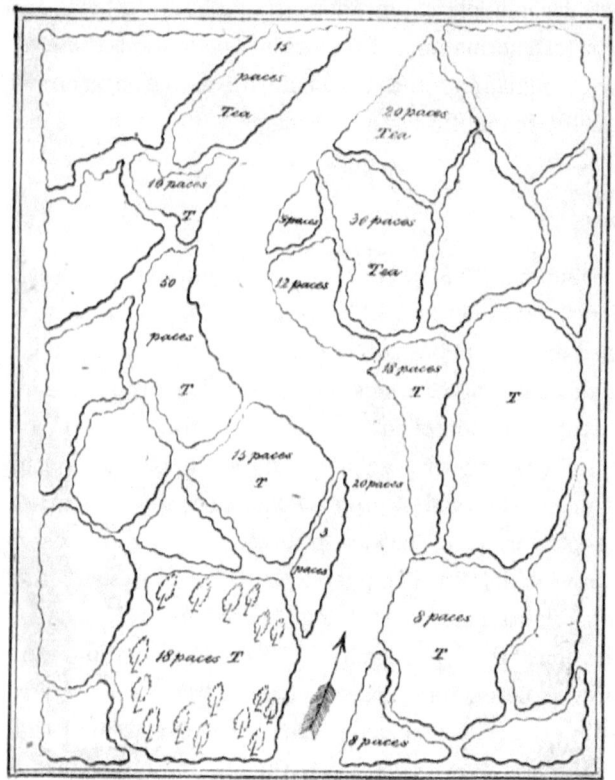

1.3   Proto-plantations. Map of section of Kahong River drawn by Robert Bruce in 1838, depicting "the little islands . . . covered with tea plants under shelter of . . . other trees." Source: Bruce, *An Account of the Manufacture of the Black Tea*.

In 1861, the state made even further concessions through fee simple rules, which granted freehold tenure, sparking what was to become a speculative boom in plantations. Land was sold at prices as low as two to five rupees an acre. Stipulated conditions such as evidence of the means to cultivate were removed so that the administration did not come across as a roadblock to industry. Planters did not have to pay revenue for the first two years, and increases over the next ten years were incremental. In contrast, Assam's peasantry had to pay a revenue of two to three rupees an acre to the colonial government. Proprietorial rights of planters were to remain intact at the end of the ninety-nine-year lease.[136] As Behal shows, this led to a "massive rush" for grants, and a plantation economy was ushered in through "reckless speculation, land-grabbing and over-extensions. . . . Money was invested in 'gardens' that never existed. Tea companies with or without land sprang up overnight and shares rose to dizzy heights. Lands were cleared without any consideration of their suitability for cultivation or availability of labour."[137] Exploiting social wealth while heralding a new mode of production, planters, to paraphrase Marx and Behal, had a "nicely mixed character of swindler and prophet."[138]

The industry went into a deep crisis in 1866 when the boom busted, but it recovered in the 1870s and continued to expand well into the 1940s. Land under planters' control rose from 54,000 acres in 1859 to a staggering one million by 1900, which included 27.4 percent of all of the temporarily settled areas in the Assam valley. Estimates from the early twentieth century show that planters contributed only 9 percent of the land revenue collected by the colonial administration. Furthermore, at no point in time until the mid-1940s did acreage under tea cultivation exceed 35 percent of the land in possession of plantations.[139] Together, they evidence the scale at which land had been privatized in Assam and the amount of power colonial capital wielded. Planters were "the biggest landlords in the countryside. . . . [They] usurped the grazing fields and encroached upon the *jhum* (slash and burn) rights of the tribal shifting cultivators. They even disrupted inter-village communications by fencing in portions of the existing public roads and denying the right of way."[140] The pressure on land induced by enclosures led to a decline in pastures. Under the Cattle Trespass Act of 1871, planters fined villagers when their cattle entered the tea estates, and this turned into matters of heated dispute between plantation management and neighboring villages.[141] In certain instances, plantations appropriated grazing lands. The government often excused them for doing so, issuing land deeds for encroached pastures.[142] These power geometries reveal why it is problematic to refer to the Anthropocene as the product of humanity as a whole. Planetary change emerges through historical processes of dispossession set in motion by a minority: a clique of white men.

A Plantationocene's spatiality emerges through tensions. As Hiren Gohain has argued, "plantations notoriously are enterprises of the 'enclave' type, and do not trigger development" in the wider landscape.[143] At the same time, plantations spawn their own economic zones where growth is bolstered along a plantation's transportation corridors.[144] In Assam, infrastructure for the plantation industry grew with substantial aid from the colonial administration, who invested public revenue to help planters. The government thus continually assisted in plunder through contracts, concessions, and "free gifts." The expansion of railways is a case in point. Railway mileage in the state expanded rapidly as demands for the transport of tea swelled. Construction of railways began in 1881; by 1891 coverage had reached 114 miles, and this increased more than sixfold to 715 miles by 1903. Not only did the railways penetrate into a resource frontier, making the extraction and commodification of Assam's nature possible,[145] but they also connected remote plantations with global markets. Inherently extractive,[146] these infrastructures gave birth to a modern industry, where resources from the region could circulate on the world stage. The plantation, one could argue, was structurally coded into such infrastructures: "The alignment of railways was done through the thinly populated submontane tea-belt with the obvious purpose of serving planters' interests. Old trading centres . . . and towns . . . were by-passed, thus allowing them to stagnate and decay," while "an organized trade in indentured coolie supply" recruiting "thousands of labourers" from "remote tribal tracts" became the infrastructure's mainstay.[147]

Infrastructures of a Plantationocene running through forest tracts created deep fissures in elephants' landscapes. Habitat was opened up and fragmented. Reports of elephants colliding with trains at night were not uncommon. The Nambor forest on the south bank of the Brahmaputra was one locality where numerous such incidents took place. In July 1901, a train ran into a herd of wild elephants, whereupon the engine collided with one animal, causing the front wheels to derail. The unfortunate elephant "had one of his back legs broken" and succumbed to injuries the next day.[148] Cases of collisions increased with the expansion of railways, as elephants were "to be found practically every night on the railway line."[149] Vital for the circulation of cheap commodities of a Plantationocene, the fraught effects of railways on elephants continue. Between 1990 and 2006, there were at least thirty-five incidents of elephant mortality due to train collisions in Assam.[150] In the past decade, there have been sixty-two elephant casualties.[151] Incidents occur when elephants venture into adjoining paddy fields in search of crops at night, and when gradients along tracks are steep, barring the animals from getting out of the way in time.[152] Recent studies seem to indicate that the conversion of Assam's tracks from narrow- to large-gauge rails in the late 1990s, coupled with deforestation, has increased collisions and elephant mortality.[153]

As an extractive apparatus, colonial enterprise also extended to commercializing mineral resources such as coal and petroleum, all of which were geared to whet a global appetite for commodities. The discovery of coal deposits in Assam in the early part of the nineteenth century was a matter of importance for the colonial government, for it opened up prospects of capital investments by London-based companies in the landscape.[154] It also came as a major boost for plantations' energy demands.[155] The newly formed Assam Railways and Trading Company Limited was not just interested in expanding railways; they invested in the exploration and trade of coal. The company acquired four collieries and began to excavate the mineral by recruiting labor from outside the province.[156] Even long after the formal end of empire, the deleterious effects of coal mining, injuring both earth and people, continue. Communities have been displaced; many have been exposed to toxins over long durations; and the enterprise has come at significant human cost.[157]

The colonial state also asserted an exclusive claim on petroleum, noticed in Assam as early as 1825, before the province was formally annexed to the British Empire. It was with the formation of the Imperial Geological Survey of India in the mid-nineteenth century that explorations for petroleum and coal became systematic.[158] Commercial ventures were underway in 1884, some of them initiated by the Assam Railways and Trading Company, which was granted a lease over thirty square miles for petroleum exploration.[159] Soon, the Assam Oil Company was formed. By 1904, the company declared a profit of £18,960.[160] Assam's oil fields attracted even greater attention after World War I generated a boom. Colonial structures of extraction were largely unaltered after Indian Independence, and oil became the subject of intense contention in postcolonial Assam. Viewed by certain sections of the Assamese "as a major example of Indian internal colonialism," the decades after Independence were marked by continual, sometimes violent, protests over rights to oil.[161] The issue became so contentious that it threatened India's federal structure and development paradigm.[162] The environmental legacies of these extractive apparatuses, which continue to "depend on obsolete technologies of extraction,"[163] have been devastating. These histories of material extraction are a crucial prelude to a slow violence that haunts Assam's Plantationocene, a theme I interrogate in chapter 2.

The uneven spatialities that constitute a Plantationocene are further amplified by the constraints plantations, as exclusive, enclaved enterprises, placed on the development of Assam's agrarian and urban economy.[164] Not only did tea plantations constrict the expansion of cultivation, but they encroached upon the peasantry's land.[165] Both the tea industry and the Forest Department were in constant competition with one another in their quest to gain control over Assam's land and resources. Soils in the dense jungles were more porous, with greater organic content, thus making them ideal for the cultivation of tea. The higher productivity of such soil meant that the competition between the Forest Department and the plantation industry over jungles was even more intense.[166]

Although a later entrant into Assam's landscape, the Forest Department gained control of over four thousand square miles of land by the mid-twentieth century, making it the largest land-owner in the region.[167] The department complained that tea plantations had "locked up" significant tracts of land, thwarting their entry into the ambit of revenue generation.[168] Much of this land in planters' possession remained uncultivated and without settlement until the middle of the twentieth century. Tree felling by plantations was also rampant. Estimates by Borkotoky suggest that by the mid-1920s, a staggering ten million trees were cut down by plantations in the Sibsagar district of Assam alone.[169] Erstwhile plantation labor that left the tea estates was also blamed for settling down in forest land and for driving it to exhaustion.

The tea industry on the other hand saw the Forest Department as a generator of obstacles. Planters opposed the creation of reserved forests, for they continued to apply for fresh land grants to expand plantations and settle labor.[170] As Dey shows, tensions between these two monopoly sectors, "one directed at forest capital, and the other at crop capital," expedited the demarcation of forests and the alienation of the peasantry from the land. Limited availability of internationally marketable timber like teak, a paucity of markets, and meager local demand "meant that the tea industry and its requirements was a primary customer—and 'creator'—of forest wealth" in Assam, notably through its large-scale requirements of wood for tea chests.[171] This quest to produce cheap nature through monocrop agriculture and indentured labor on the one hand, and monoculture forests and the exploitation of peasant labor on the other, generated the highly uneven and asymmetrical landscapes of a Plantationocene.

Plantation logics, understood as principles underlying the arrangements of bodies, materials, and flows in a (post)colonial landscape, where the ongoingness of plunder is diagrammatic rather than proceeding through reified spatial formations, continually mark bodies as "those without"—without history, land, or home, "without ownership of self." At the same time they forcibly secure people, resources, and circulations into the "geographic mechanics of the plantation economy."[172] The identities of the Munda, Oraon, Kharia, Bhumij, Santhal, and other communities brought to Assam, who are now referred to as Sah Janagusthi (Tea Tribes) or Adivasis, "were subsumed into anonymous 'gangs' and 'muster rolls.' Treated as a nameless mass, they were confined to depots during their journeys and planted in 'coolie lines' upon arrival in the plantations" (figure 1.4), where the indenture regime "identified labourers only using numbers and cancelled their names."[173] As plantation labor came from various parts of central and eastern India, and belonged to different ethnic communities, a new language—Sadani or Assam Sadri—was invented. Derogatorily referred to as *coolie baat* or "coolie tongue" by colonial planters, Assam Sadri is a link-language, enabling diverse communities to converse. The language now unites the community in Assam as Adivasis.[174] This book uses the latter term over "Tea Tribes," for most of my interlocutors referred to themselves as Adivasis and, as the poet Kamal Kumar Tanti scathingly asks, "Is there any community in this world named after a commodity?"[175]

Such histories of erasure echo Sylvia Wynter's observations of how, in the "New World," various African communities were converted "into a homogenous commodity, into a unit of labour power, . . . *not* in order to form societies, but in order to carry on plantations."[176] The rendition of people into nameless masses also had a spatial corollary: keeping people in place while tagging them as placeless, historically and in the present.[177] These logics extended to other-than-human denizens of the landscape and, as outlined in the introduction, their legacies continue to seep into the present. Animals' sentient inhabitation of the world is inverted into an act of occupation and, through a range of legislations and material practices, landscape is riven into spaces for Nature and those for Society.

Yet it is vital to account for the ways in which people, and also animals, pry open other spaces that do not conform to plantation logics. A central focus of this ethnography is to look at the lives of the Adivasi community, including those among them who were formerly tea plantation workers, to retrieve a different sense of place.[178] Almost seven decades of continuous recruitment of migrant labor sponsored by the tea industry resulted in a community that today performs what historians have called generational labor, with families continuing to work in plantations for over a century and a half of living in Assam.[179] As the anthropologist Sarah Besky has poignantly argued, plantations become sites of social reproduction.[180] At the

1.4   Uprooting and planting people. "Coolie" lines, c. 1897. Source: Photo lot 161, Emma A. Koch photograph collection relating to India, South Asia, and Australia, National Anthropological Archives, Smithsonian Institution.

same time, a large pool of people left the plantations and settled in tea estate land grants and in government land, usually in the vicinity of tea estates. Called *basti* or *faltu* labor, a term invented in the 1930s, many still work on plantations during the peak working season. They accept lower wages than settled labor and serve as a reserve army for the plantations.[181] Equally, many now cultivate their own plots of land and even grow tea. Attending to their lives and encounters with elephants is critical for positing other time spaces of a Plantationocene, just as they are important for retrieving other kinds of "subjectivity . . . outside the plantation landscape" while being mindful of how they are deeply implicated in the making of one.[182]

At stake in such an outside are not peacefully settled contact zones but "difficult encounters" that produce "untidy historically present geographies,"[183] difficult because living alongside elephants plays out over an uneven terrain, and untidy because simply wishing away a Plantationocene's binaries does not necessarily equate with a more just political project. Several scholars, drawing from Katherine McKittrick's reading of Sylvia

Wynter, foreground "the plot" as a space of resistance and self-sustenance for the dispossessed.[184] By dismantling the plantation's economy of scale, the plot "opens up important emancipatory possibilities."[185] These are helpful avenues for developing a countercartography of a Plantationocene. In subsequent chapters, I situate countercartographies ethnographically, attending to what they mean in Assam's context. I develop a vocabulary of tracks and trails as another spatiality of human and other-than-human creativity and openness through which some of the bindings of a Plantationocene might be undone.

Circulation

Just as "the *idea* of the plantation is migratory," generating "diasporic life" that is "knots" of "plant and culinary life, representational politics and practices,"[186] a Plantationocene too entails historically arrested and ecologically emergent forms of diasporic life. Historically arrested because plantations constitute frontiers repopulated by people, plants, and animals uprooted from one place and planted in another, often through dispossession and violence. Ecologically emergent because a Plantationocene gives rise to "a distinctive niche in world history,"[187] a niche that simultaneously produces novelty and ruin. Circulation is therefore key to understanding a Plantationocene as a scalar project, where power geometries dictate not only who moves and who does not, but where power is exercised in relation to movement and flows.[188]

The latter becomes crucial for bearing in mind the arrested histories through which a Plantationocene present has arisen. Assam's plantations were never attractive destinations for employment. The "coolie trade" flourished in part because it had become a lucrative business for recruiters and contractors as the demand for cheap, plentiful, and easily disciplined labor in the plantations grew.[189] False representation, corruption, and oppression of every kind were deployed to swell the numbers of contractors' recruits. There was no proper provision for food, water, sanitation, and medical care during passage. Its result was "starvation, disease and . . . mortality." The dire conditions even shocked staunch defenders of planters. One of them remarked that "the horrors of the slave trade pale before the horror of the coolie trade of Assam." The situation did not get better upon arrival in the plantations. "The weak, the halt, the maimed" were "rejected by the planters as useless" and "were turned adrift, to find their way, penniless, hundreds of miles to their village homes, or, more probably, to starve."[190]

The mobility of labor through which a Plantationocene arose thus involved a brutal planting of people in conditions of indenture, forced to live in isolation and cut off from the world outside plantations. At the same time, plantations and their quest to produce cheap natures created other forms of "diasporic life" that knotted plants and politics in often harmful ways.[191] The replacement of jungles with tea went hand in hand with the transport of an entourage of other plants to assist in the production of cheap nature.[192] These included, among others, *Grevillea robusta*, native to Australia, as a shade tree; *Crotolaria pallida*, originating in tropical Africa, as a legume for nitrogen fixation; and *Mimosa pudica*, native to the Caribbean and South and Central America, for the preparation of soil surface or producing tilth.[193] Experiments with nonnative plants to form heterogeneous collectives of other-than-human work continued well into the 1970s, all of which are examples of deploying life to accumulate capital from life.[194] In more recent times, such collectives are being forged through "organic" plantations, which serve less as alternatives and more as support for plantation economies.[195]

The infrastructures set up to bring labor to work in Assam and for the transport of tea also led to the unintended circulation of a large number of nonnative plants, some of which have now become "invasive,"[196] rupturing Assam's economy and making claims on its ecological future. One such plant that circulated through infrastructures subtending plantations and coded by plantation logics was *Eupatorium*, a weed that now grows extensively in elephant habitat and which has become a major conservation concern. Now referred to as *Chromolaena*, *Eupatorium* arrived with the import of railway sleepers in the early 1920s,[197] at a time when the Assam-Bengal railway line was connected directly to Chittagong port in what is now Bangladesh. *Eupatorium*'s spread was aided by the world ecology of a Plantationocene. In an early account of "foreign weeds" published in the journal *Current Science* in 1934, K. Biswas, curator of the herbarium at Calcutta's Royal Botanic Garden, observed that *Eupatorium* and other plants "hailing from tropical America" were becoming terrestrial pests in Bengal and Assam. They had taken a "particular liking for the Indian soil" and had the potential to "spread like wild fire in no time." "It is very likely," Biswas wrote, that *Eupatorium* "might have been introduced from the West Indies to India and Burma by seeds confined to the ballast heaps of Cargo boats calling at Singapore."[198] Responsible for the circulation of tens of thousands of species across the world each day, ballast tanks are akin to floating ecosystems. They have played a major role in transforming the distribution of life on earth and in the rise of the cosmopolitan ecologies of a Plantationocene constituted by flora that are no longer parochial but present the world over.[199] Interestingly, *Eupatorium* was welcomed by certain communities practicing swidden cultivation in the hills bordering Assam, on account "that its presence enables the soil to be cultivated at shorter intervals with the additional advantage that subsequent cultivation does not entail the felling of heavy tree jungle."[200]

Cosmopolitan ecologies are not always benign. "The forests of Upper Assam give an impression of . . . ruins," wrote A. K. Choudhury, a forest officer, in 1972 (figure 1.5).[201] Choudhury was describing forests and timber plantations completely covered by *Mikania micrantha*, a perennial climber from Central and South America that spread rapidly through Assam during the late 1950s. His equation of landscape with ruin is a deep reflection of the structures of vulnerability and protracted processes generating a Plantationocene present. "To ruin," as Ann Laura Stoler writes, "is to inflict or bring great and irretrievable disaster upon." Ruination is a destruction of certain kinds of agency. The effects of ruin "reside in the corroded hollows of landscape, in the gutted infrastructures of cityscapes and in the microecologies of matter and mind."[202] Plantation logics and the circulations they set in motion routinely bring about ruination. They persist, permeating the present and conditioning futures.

Specific pathways of *Mikania*'s introduction into Assam's landscape are uncertain. A popular story is that it was used after World War II to camouflage airfields,[203] while some people contend that it came to the region along with the fodder grass of mules used during the war. The Assamese name for the plant, Jāpāni Lota, meaning Japanese creeper, is an allusion to these origins, but they may be, as Choudhury remarked, "hatched out stories."[204] In all probability, it was used as a protective cover crop for tea. In a 1908 essay on "plant immigrants" in India, the botanist Paul Brühl described *Mikania* as naturalized in the forests of Assam.[205] The climber was already in use as an agent for suppressing other weeds in plantations in the Malay region and in Ceylon at the time. The climber's ability to grow quickly and smother vegetation deemed undesirable by plantations led to its recommendation for use as a cover crop.[206] By the early 1930s, *Mikania* had become "a familiar sight" in the Assam plains. "The spread of this climber,"

1.5 Ruin: the proliferation of *Mikania* in Assam's forests in the early 1970s. Source: Parker, "The Mikania Problem."

occurring on "shrubs, trees, bushes and marshy areas even over choked up tanks," Biswas warned, had to be kept under close watch.[207]

Mikania took on what Choudhury called its "malignant form" in the latter part of the 1950s.[208] The climber was absent in many of the timber plantations of Assam in the early 1950s but around 1956–57 had appeared in the Forest Department's sal plantations in western Assam, "actually killing off young trees." In 1958, *Mikania* had "spread in an alarming fashion and it was climbing up large mature Sal Trees and virtually smothering the forests." It soon began to spread to tea plantations.[209] While *Mikania* was locally present in the landscape, what led to the plant spiraling out of control was a major geological event: the Assam earthquake of 1950. With a magnitude of 8.6 on the Richter Scale, the 1950 Assam earthquake resulted in enormous landslides and caused a major upheaval of the region's topography. A significant consequence was aggravated floods in the Assam valley. The "inundation of vast areas of forest by flood (after 1950 earthquake)," writes Choudhury, created a conducive environment for the plant. It "helped the climber to flourish and spread menacingly."[210]

Mikania thrived in sites of commercial forestry, where trees were regularly felled to extract resources.[211] Conditions of a Plantationocene were thus particularly conducive to its proliferation. *Mikania* spread along big drains and rivulets, entering tea plantations and "virtually putting them out of production." The only effective means of control was uprooting by hand, a process that was prohibitively expensive and involved "large numbers of labourers when they [were] in heavy demand for normal cultivation, plucking and other work." Furthermore, "complete control" was impossible unless such labor was carried out consistently. The economic effects of *Mikania* were thus not only reduced production but a disruption of the continuity of the labor process that tea plucking demands. *Mikania* seeds, being windborne, made "reinfestation" from jungles neighboring plantations a common occurrence. The altered topography of Assam also continued to have an effect: floods carried "seed long distances," rendering efforts to contain the plant almost futile.[212]

Plantations, as diagrams of power, thus connect distal places through their infrastructures and create cosmopolitan floras through intended and unintended circulations. The power to guide and bring about circulations also begins to bite back. After years of trying to control *Mikania* through chemical and biological methods, the tea industry has still not succeeded. "Intensive weeding of *Mikania* has become necessary" in many plantations, and close to 20 percent of plantation labor in Assam is involved in weed removal. In tea estates "where weeding is not carried out intensively and regularly," "productivity and profitability are reduced drastically."[213] The effects of *Mikania* spill over into surroundings. Large tracts of forest taken over by *Mikania* have depleted habitat for Asian elephants. This potentially reduces forage for the animal and accentuates their reliance on agricultural crops.[214] The ecology of weeds has bearings on elephants of a Plantationocene,[215] just as it does on people. Abandoned plots, as we saw in the introduction, are not reclaimed by native vegetation but often overrun by *Mikania*.

Circulation and ruination are thus characteristic of a Plantationocene. The story of cover crops getting out of hand does not end with *Mikania*. In the late 1990s, *Mimosa invisa*, a plant from tropical America used for nitrogen fixation in tea plantations, spread into some of Assam's sanctuaries and national parks, causing significant damage to elephant and rhino habitat.[216] *Mimosa invisa* was recommended as a cover crop in tea plantations, on the grounds that it was "very beneficial in combination with Guatemala grass (*Tripsacum laxum*)," another nonnative plant from the Americas, "for soil rehabilitation."[217] Ruinous ecologies are thus not one-off events but continually produced in a Plantationocene. They unevenly distribute harms and work over long durations: colonial imperatives do not simply wither away but persist as forms of slow violence permeating ecologies and bodies.[218] The fraught ecologies we witness in Assam through *Mikania* manifest with other weeds in many plantation landscapes.[219] These circulations of biota entail both transplanting and mobilization, just as they involve creating ecologies where first nature and capitalist nature are mixed. Circulations become crucial to understanding the effects of power in a Plantationocene, which is never global, but unevenly juxtaposes planet and plot.[220]

Simplified Ecologies

Bodies and ecologies are disciplined in plantations. Although plantations were not necessarily sites where class, gender, and racial divisions were invented, they "were perfected there—strict hierarchies laid down, justified, and often internalized."[221] Katherine McKittrick's argument that plantations serve as geographical loci through which race is made known "and bodies therefore differently disciplined across time and space" is crucial to understanding ecologies of a Plantationocene.[222] The twin logics of producing cheap, plentiful, and immobilized labor and cheap, homogenized, value-generating nature proceeded through disciplining logics steeped in colonial and racial inequality and a quest to accumulate profit from life. They provide insights for building much-needed links between political economy and biopolitics, which Foucault hinted at in his early writings on biopower.[223] However, contrary to Foucault, such accounts cannot be from the viewpoint of a universal, abstract subject. They must account for the specific, gendered, economized, and colonized bodies subjected to discipline.[224]

The relentless push for increase in tea production in the latter part of the nineteenth century resulted in an intensification of the cultivation process, primarily achieved through manual labor. Mechanization of manufacture went hand in hand with a reorganization of the rhythm of work in the manner of industrial supervision. Labor had to be available at all times to sustain this production organization, and "this could only be ensured through residential compulsion of labourers." "Coolie lines" set up within plantations ensured that workers could be "easily mobilized from sunrise to sunset every day."[225] New forms of time discipline were imposed.[226] Sirens would go off to announce the working day. Planters flouted the legally stipulated nine-hour shift, making people labor eleven hours in the busy manufacturing season. Payments on the basis of daily tasks rather than on the basis of time were another mode of generating profit from labor. Planters hiked tasks as a strategy of disciplining coolies.[227] The working day was further prolonged through strategies of utilizing maximum hours of sunlight for work. As the sun rose earlier in the northeast of the Indian subcontinent, the plantation clock was advanced by an hour. Plantations kept to a time different from not only the rest of India but also the rest of Assam. "Everyday life and work on the plantations was scheduled on such 'garden time'" and was in vogue in Assam right until the 1980s.[228]

The elaborate processes of tea cultivation, outlined earlier, not only produced ecologies of the same but also played a role in the rationale for residential compulsion of labor.[229] The disciplining of the plant, plantation, and labor went hand in hand. Tea continues to be planted in divisions or sections such that they flush in an orderly manner where the labor force can work its way through a plantation and then return where they started to pick the next flush. Sections are serialized and the number of workers needed to pluck each section optimized. Lines of tea plants, "as far as practicable," have to "run with geometrical regularity" so that it is easier, not just to pluck leaf but to measure the amount of work done. The spacing of bushes too follows the logic of optimized yield.[230] The layout of plantations is thus panoptic: they work to discipline the worker's body, homogenize plants, and maximize profits. These result in simplified ecologies where plants coordinate with replicas and the time of the market,[231] but not in a way that is apolitical and given. Simplified ecologies are the products of a quest to produce cheap natures through an exploitation of living labor on plantations, a process that has morphed but continues in its racialized, postcolonial form until the present day.[232]

Plantation logics of homogeneity, predictability, calculability, and control also extended to the practice of forestry (figure 1.6). The core of imperial forestry, in Assam and other parts of South Asia, was to convert forests into revenue-generating assemblages. Although only sections of forest tracts reserved by the Forest Department were transformed into plantations containing uniform stands of valuable timber, the latter were significant sources of revenue, particularly because the margins derived from natural forests with heterogeneous stands of trees were considered too low. As Arun Agrawal shows, timber plantations in South Asia were inspired by models of an "ideal forest." In such a model, only annual increments would be extracted such that the yield of timber was sustained over time. Although no actual forest mapped onto an ideal, the underlying rationale played an important role in how forests were managed.[233]

Homogeneity was an important feature of working forests into timber plantations, achieved through felling and improvement. The former included clearing and weeding forests to remove inferior trees and replacing them with more valuable ones. Trees of lesser commercial value were felled and sold to nearby sawmills, while large investments were made to grow teak imported from Burma, as well as *Cinchona* and rubber. Tropical forests were also far more heterogeneous than European ones where much of forestry science had initially developed. In order to bring forests into the realm of control and calculability, statistical techniques and mathematical relations pertaining to forest and timber growth were applied. Many of these techniques were imported from Europe, and in order to apply them, forests had to be simplified. An avalanche of statistics also became available through annual reports published by various forest departments, which were then utilized for the project of improvement.[234] Forestry thus resulted in a simultaneous cheapening and simplification of nature, creating assets for future investments and killing off beings not recognized as such,[235] a process that proceeded through mass enclosure of the commons and forcing the peasantry to work under coercive conditions.

The creation of simplified ecologies often leads to virulence, challenging and disrupting a plantation from within. Assam's plantations have been continual witnesses to pest outbreaks, largely of local insect fauna that become virulent due to conducive conditions set up by monocultures. Such insects, writes Arnab Dey in an eloquent analysis of the history of pests in Assam's tea plantations, "gnawed away at profits, ideas of scientific control, and expert proclamations of agrarian improvement."[236] An exponential increase in blights, particularly those created by the tea mosquito bug (*Helopeltis theivora*) and the red spider mite (*Oligonychus coffeae*), challenged colonial authority. Virulence was endemic, in that such bugs were not agents that had arrived from afar, but emerged from within a plantation, as its diagrammatic logics rearranged bodies, distributed them homogeneously, and, in its quest to optimize production, simplified which beings interacted with one another. Pathogenicity and the production of cheap nature and cheap commodities were inexorably linked. The "very conditions necessary for successful tea harvests created the host environment" for pestilence.[237]

Simplified ecologies also create conditions of virulence for people. The historian Arupjyoti Saikia shows how plantations also aggravated the

1.6 Simplified ecologies: forestry plantation in Goalpara, Assam, c. 1917. Source: Troup, *The Work of the Forest Department in India.*

malaria situation in Assam, a state that has some of the highest rates of the disease in South Asia. Between 1877 and 1920, a tenth of all deaths of workers in tea plantations was from malaria. The large-scale felling of forests and their conversion into tea resulted in major changes in the hydrological structure of Assam. Soil porosity decreased, creating pools of stagnant water that furnished niches for the malaria-causing *Anopheles* mosquito to breed. Deep drains dug in tea plantations became further sources of slow-moving water conducive for *Anopheles*'s reproduction. Planters unknowingly contributed to the generation of a malarial environment. Workers' deaths were compounded by malnutrition. Most survived on rice provided by planters at a subsidized rate, and their low wages limited access to adequate protein.[238] These factors combined to make plantation labor susceptible to malaria, a situation that continues to haunt Assam's plantations today.

Purveyors of the plantation dealt with virulence in particular ways. The rise of imperial sciences such as entomology went hand in hand with the institution of a plantation landscape, whether in forestry or on tea plantations themselves.[239] Furthermore, virulence was not only a health concern that affected the productivity of labor, thus rendering plantations sites of biopolitics; it was deemed a disruption to economic production, both in terms of crop loss and the expenditure in labor required in weeding and pest control.[240] There is perhaps a colonial conceit—of quelling and dominating pests—underpinning the ways in which virulence is recognized and continuously rectified. Tea remains an intensively managed crop. Technical fixes and the use of pesticides to deal with virulence have only created problems, many of which did not exist before. The routine use of chemical pesticides, materials that might be seen as part of a Plantationocene's rather than an Anthropocene's ecology, has resulted in pest resurgence, secondary outbreaks, and even the development of resistance in many arthropods. This is not willful resistance, but the agentic outcome of such virulence is a barrier to endless accumulation. From nonprescribed use to substandard chemicals, a number of cultural and political economic factors have aggravated pathogenicity.[241]

Virulence generated in the landscape even spreads outward: the red spider mite described from Assam in the 1860s now affects plantations as far away as Uganda and Malawi.[242] Estimates suggest that 11 to 55 percent of annual yield can be lost due to pathogenicity emerging from a plantation's simplified ecosystem. Pesticide residue is an ever-present problem. In the early 2000s, the export of Assam tea was even stymied for exceeding prescribed residue levels.[243] Pesticides, as they leach from plantations, enter flowing water, permeate other beings, and precipitate in working bodies, leave their deep mark on plantation labor. The spate of elephant poisonings that took place in Sonitpur in 2001 using organophosphorus is most likely to have been sourced from their widespread use in tea plantations. Simplified ecologies of a Plantationocene thus enact a slow violence,[244] which seeps into the present and whose effects accumulate over generations, continually remaking virulent conditions and marking out the same vulnerable bodies time and time again.

Ongoing Condition

A plantation multiple enables grasping how colonial endeavor extended to a number of spheres and sought to bring them into the ambit of accumulation. The quest to produce cheap nature was inexorably linked to a racial and colonial economy that created a labor force that was cheap, plentiful, immobilized, and disciplined.[245] Similar logics permeated attempts to coerce the peasantry to work in forest villages, although it took on a very different shape and form. Plantations, as diagrams of power, proceed through specific spatial arrangements. They create enclosure and enclaved economies that are simultaneously tied to expanded infrastructures and a world ecology of capital.[246] Such spatial topologies, involving enclaves and expansion at the same time, enable situating a Plantationocene. Holding planet and plot in the same analytical plane reveals how transformations proceed in highly uneven and geographically differentiated ways, where they forge new ecologies and how they redistribute harms. This act of situation stands in contrast to certain strands of political ecology that espouse uniform global accounts of capitalism in the Anthropocene.[247]

A plantation multiple shows how colonialism and race lie at the center of planetary transformation. These are not just conditions of the past. As the historian Jayeeta Sharma argues, "the logic of the plantation production system remained intact," continuing "into the twenty-first century, in a not very different form from its colonial antecedents."[248] Plantations have a certain fixity to them, in that the transformations they bring about make it difficult for space to be repurposed.[249] In fact, many of the ecological consequences of colonial plantations are only becoming apparent now. The circulations historically set in motion by plantations are beginning to inflict a slow violence upon the landscape, aggravating the use of chemicals and pesticides that, as materials of a Plantationocene, come back to affect vulnerable laboring bodies. Studies indicate that as much as 45 percent of tea plantation workers in Assam suffer from waterborne diseases. Many report birth defects and other illnesses caused by pesticides.[250] For every kilogram of packaged Assam tea sold, less than 5 percent goes toward workers' salaries. Concentrated in the lowest-paid plucking roles and shouldering most of the unpaid domestic care work, women bear the heaviest burden of systemic inequality. A maximum of six hours of sleep is routine for thirteen hours of physical work. In 2017, Assam's tea estates recorded 363 maternal deaths per 100,000 live births, which is more than double the national average for India.[251]

A colonial economy continues on plantations, creating persistent underdevelopment and persistent poverty of minority lives.[252] Statutes of the Plantation Labour Act of 1951 are seldom fully implemented. Substantial parts of wages are paid in kind, and the cash component of tea workers' wages remains well below the minimum wage level of unskilled agricultural workers in the state. There is a growing tendency to employ temporary workers, often consisting of the *basti* or *faltu* reserve army, so that they are not eligible for the Plantation Labour Act–mandated benefits. Debt has become a consistent feature among tea workers, aggravated by the closure of plantations. Many, to avoid starvation, have resorted to menial jobs or to selling wood "stolen" from reserved forests.[253] This is a problem compounded by long histories of indenture and immobilization. Several thousands of tea worker families have no land or means of subsistence other than selling their labor power. As Tania Murray Li has argued, the violence of plantation infrastructures sometimes leaves the subordinated with "no 'outside' to turn to for recourse."[254]

In an analogous vein, colonial forestry and forest administration have important bearings on the lives of former plantation workers, the rural peasantry as well as other-than-human denizens of the landscape. Spatial binaries instituted by colonial power dictate how human-elephant relations unfold on the ground. The conversion of jungles into plantations, coupled with deforestation and the ruinous landscapes produced by nonnative flora, have meant that the animal's habitat has been depleted, giving rise to situations where elephants are increasingly taking to entering human habitation and raiding crop fields. It is historically myopic to see these alterations as mere biology, for the evidence that emergent behaviors are responses to human agency is increasingly clear.[255] I, however, do not term such fauna *anthropogenic*, for it elides the colonial political-economic pathways through which elephants' altered ecologies have emerged. Rather, such fauna are postcolonial. Recognizing them as such provides an antidote to the Anthropocene and its specifications of planetary change through the agency of a cumulative humankind. The latter is a falsification that erases colonial histories and dispossession in the present.

Assam's Plantationocene present is also marked by other postcolonial tensions. With almost all major tea companies headquartered in Calcutta, the erstwhile imperial capital, Assam continued to remain "a colonial hinterland."[256] Persistent underdevelopment has been aggravated by a "neocolonial power structure based in New Delhi," which not only adopted a paternalistic and neglectful attitude toward the region, but has played a role in continual extraction of oil and forest resources where benefits have been unevenly shared.[257] These have been sources of angst and gave rise to Assam's sustained right to self-determination movement in the late 1970s and secessionist militancy thereafter.[258] While tainted by chauvinism and degenerating into violence,[259] such movements cannot simply be dismissed. Rather, they become vital for understanding the condition one calls a Plantationocene, for the latter's oppressive forces do not work on plantation workers alone but affect a wider community and milieu.

This endeavor of situating and specifying ecologies of a Plantationocene, while working from the margins of South Asian postcolonial theory, has significant relevance for thinking about world ecologies elsewhere. Labor and other-than-human work, the spatial enclosures and connections brought about by plantation infrastructures, the circulations set in motion, and the simplified, pathogenic ecologies created by a plantation multiple are widespread features of our contemporary world. Plantations continue to expand with ever-greater voracity, whether in scaled-up meat production, monocrop agriculture, or the explosion of palm oil in many parts of the world.[260] Assam's tea plantations too have expanded, taking a different trajectory than those of the recent "mega-plantations" of Southeast Asia, albeit with the same logic of producing cheap commodities to whet planetary appetites. Of particular importance is the explosion of small-scale growers but also renewed forms of primitive accumulation through land grabs that underscore some of this growth. It is this ongoing condition that I elucidate in subsequent chapters of this book. In what follows, I examine the lives of both people and elephants in the aftermath of colonial plantation logics and amid ongoing postcolonial plunder. What kinds of life emerge amid a Plantationocene? In what ways do plantation logics continue to operate as durations, conditioning habitability and the ways in which people make do? What does it mean to situate one's inquiry not just in the Global South, but in the South within the South, and what consequences does such a grounding have for thinking about planetary environmental transformations? Such questions come into sharp relief when we turn to other-than-human life and infrastructure.

2

The Slow Violence of Infrastructure

"Elephants have a particular way of moving," says Santosh, a farmer from Sundarpur, a village in Assam's Golaghat district. "Their habits are peculiar, in that they move and forage at the same time, spending some time in one place then going to another. Elephants also take paths they are accustomed to, returning to the same place after a few weeks," Santosh explains, as he narrates how friction between people and elephants is on the rise in their village, following the construction of a large oil refinery in the wider landscape. "Earlier elephants would come through our village about once a month," Santosh recollects, "but ever since the Numaligarh Refinery was built, that too in a jungle that was an elephant haunt, their incursions into our crop fields became more frequent. Construction did not initially deter the elephants from moving through the refinery." He adds with a hesitant smile, "but then they built a massive wall to keep the animals out" (figure 2.1). "Nowadays they go toward Numaligarh, come against the wall, and return

2.1   Immobility: infrastructure and elephants' habitus. Photo: Samarjit Sharma.

immediately. As a result, elephants feeding on our crops has intensified. They don't even budge when you make noise. Only firecrackers or lighting fires is effective. What else will the animals do?" Santosh asks me. "There is hardly anything left for them to eat."

Situated at the edge of the Lower Doigurung Reserve Forest, Sundarpur is home to an Adivasi community that came to Assam to work on the plantations during the turn of the nineteenth century. Many had left the Bukhial and Letekujan tea estates generations ago, settling on the plantation's land grants or by reclaiming parts of the reserve forest. Sundarpur is a site where frictions between people and elephants have escalated, and these developments drew me to the village, for I wanted to learn how people dwelled alongside elephants within a wider plantation milieu. Santosh, with whom I spent long periods conversing, was an astute observer of how and why such frictions unfolded, just as he provided perceptive explanations of their spatially and temporally dispersed effects. At the heart of Santosh's account of elephants' encounter with a wall erected to keep the animals at bay, and the cascading effects it had on elephants' mobilities and people's lives, lies a thesis of immense significance: infrastructure and its role in conditioning Plantationocene life.

Infrastructures are systems of substrates and architectures of circulation undergirding modern societies, and their social, political, and economic life.¹ There is a large body of work on infrastructure, highlighting how infrastructures generate and sustain ambient environments, settle particular social orders, and regulate people's activities and economic practices.² Anthropologists have coined the term *infrastructural violence* to reveal how the life courses of infrastructures can be substantially deleterious, becoming channels for the exercise of power and causing "dramatic suffering."³ Walls create enclaves; fences exclude. They sediment unjust social relations, usually to the detriment of the marginalized.⁴

Yet much of this scholarship on infrastructure and infrastructural violence remains anthropocentric in its outlook. As such, it leaves one with an impoverished analytical repertoire for grasping the significance of Santosh's explanations of infrastructure, its ecological effects, and its consequent bearings on plantation workers' lives. To draw out the implications of animal-infrastructure enmeshments, their material and affective repercussions on everyday lives of the vulnerable and the dispossessed, one needs to work toward a wider ontology of infrastructure, an ontology that accounts for how infrastructures condition and constrain both human and other-than-human life.⁵ It means drawing on and expanding the notion of habitus,⁶ broadly understood as the melding of habit and habitat, to reveal how monumental interventions such as refineries and mundane structures such as walls modulate animals' mobilities. At the same time, a wider ontology must historicize infrastructure in order to understand the latter's material and affective journeys. In Assam's Plantationocene, struggles over resource extraction and resistance to enclave economies mark the politics of infrastructure.

The Numaligarh Oil Refinery that Santosh was referring to was the demand of a long agitation of the Assamese against the neocolonialism of the Indian state, an agitation that easily qualifies as one of the "greatest mass upheavals in the history of post-Independence India."⁷ When building of the refinery began in the midst of what was an elephant haunt, it set in motion cascading effects, conditioning the possibilities of life and the landscape's future habitability. These effects are slow, taking place over multiple durations, through dispersed spaces and heterogeneous bodies. In contrast to spectacular and speculative transformations associated with narratives of infrastructure in the Anthropocene,⁸ Santosh's account draws attention to infrastructural effects that are gradual, accretive, and often muted. I call this the slow violence of infrastructure, a violence that is a wearing out of the earth and a deterioration of people and elephants that becomes a very nearly defining condition of their being and historical experience. Slow violence, as Rob Nixon specifies, is the violence of "delayed destruction" that is attritional and often "not viewed as violence at all."[9] However, such violence is neither invisible nor out of sight, at least not to those who are exposed to its calamitous ramifications and harms. As Laurent Berlant puts it in her essay "Slow Death," such violence prospers "in temporal environments whose qualities and whose contours in time and space are often identified with the presentness of ordinariness itself."[10] The slow violence of infrastructure, as the violence of erosion and delayed destruction, is necropolitical, marking out particular bodies rather than humanity as a whole. It calls for situating the politics of the present as a Plantationocene rather than the Anthropocene, as infrastructural violence acts through particular ecologies and invariably works upon communities considered disposable,[11] resulting in a gradual degradation in their ability to reproduce predictable life.

Therefore, in this chapter, I read a Plantationocene through the politics of infrastructure and vice versa, taking cues from the experiences of people from the Adivasi community who, like Santosh, are exposed to the slow violence of infrastructure in a zone of ordinariness. I ask what might it mean to situate the material effects and affective journeys of infrastructures in wider struggles over habitability in a plantation milieu, rather than as outcomes of "Earth" being "stalked by Man."[12] To this end, this chapter first traces an affective politics of infrastructure and resource extraction that emerged in response to Assam's persistent underdevelopment. Treading already-established ground and drawing on the insights of a number of scholars,[13] I argue that infrastructure was a central pivot around which agitations against neocolonialism in Assam were couched. The chapter then examines the material and ecological effects of infrastructural expansion, particularly those put in place to undo a Plantationocene's discontents. To do so, I move from the spectacle of development and progress that has accompanied recent infrastructural projects in Assam to the hidden theater of resource extraction and its cascading repercussions on a landscape's sentient topography.[14] Many of these repercussions emerge from an informal idiom of infrastructural expansion that proceeds through purposeful inaction and an active disavowal of known and anticipated harms. Finally, the chapter turns to the slow violence infrastructures inflict, tracking the latter through situated accounts of elephants and people's lives. In conclusion, I discuss what a wider ontology and the concomitant politics of infrastructure offer up for understanding the contours of life in a Plantationocene.

Infrastructural Agitations

On the second of January 1990, the Indian prime minister V. P. Singh arrived in Numaligarh. The premiere's visit to what was then an obscure village on the outskirts of Golaghat's forests came as an overture to pacify over a decade of political agitation and turmoil in Assam. During his visit, Singh formally declared that Assam's fourth refinery would be built in Numaligarh and that the state's "reserves of gas and oil . . . would be used better for the development of the region."[15] With a capacity for refining three million metric tons of crude oil, the Numaligarh Refinery would, Singh claimed, "usher in a new era of rapid and sustained local resource-based industrialization."[16] A term of French origin, first used in relation to railway construction in the 1870s, *infrastructures* are material and affective vehicles heralding modernity and become synonymous with modernity itself.[17] In this sense, Singh's announcement that the Numaligarh Refinery would usher in growth in a state whose economy was ailing was in no way new. However, if one were to put his phrase "local resource-based industrialization" under careful scrutiny, a whole other story of infrastructure comes to the fore, a history of affective struggles against neocolonialism and a history of resource extraction in a Plantationocene milieu.

Marked by persistent underdevelopment, Assam's economic growth has been constrained since colonial times. The expansion of plantations, aided by concessions granted in the nineteenth and twentieth centuries, widened the gap between its commercial and subsistence sectors. Planters had vast tracts of land under their control, tax-free, while Assamese peasants paid land taxes to the colonial administration. In a manner typical of their racial and enclaved economies, plantations siphoned off and invested their surplus elsewhere. The *longue durée* of Assam's Plantationocene, discussed earlier, shows how the region's economy, particularly its agrarian sector, had become structurally constrained.[18] Even after Indian Independence, and the changing of plantations from British to Indian hands, the tea industry's role remained "predominantly colonial,[19] not even making marginal investments to develop economic infrastructure of the region. Enormous profits reaped from the plantations, several times more than the revenue receipts of the state,[20] contributed little in the form of taxation. Head offices of plantation companies remained in Calcutta, the erstwhile imperial metropole, while Assam got half the amount in taxes from tea of its neighboring state of West Bengal.[21]

Assam's Plantationocene present therefore makes one pause and query what constitutes the *post* in *postcolonial*. As Tilottoma Misra argues, Assam remained "a colonial hinterland" long after Indian Independence,[22] where past forms of exploitation had not simply withered away but were continually renewed. Rather than the *post* of *postcolonial* signifying a break from a colonial past and an undoing of colonialism's travails, the prefix is better understood as signaling a duration and political economy of continuity, although who personifies colonial and capitalist exploitation changes. Such continuity is particularly stark in the case of natural resource extraction in Assam, a sector in which "the Indian big bourgeoisie" had attained monopoly control by pumping in surplus capital.[23] Assam's postcolonial present in fact witnessed "the persistence, indeed aggravation of the colonial pattern of underdevelopment."[24]

Such patterns were even more glaring when it came to oil, another major resource of the province. Structures of exploiting petroleum, put in place during colonial rule, largely remained unaltered after Indian Independence.[25] Agitations against petro-colonialism in Assam have been affective as much as economic. Much of Assam's crude oil was being refined elsewhere in India, thus generating feelings of deep resentment among people of the state. Since the 1950s, Assam has seen a number of movements that sought to secure the rights to dictate how oil ought to be exploited and who should be employed in its petroleum sector. These agitations were interspersed with periodic appeasements by the center, but they remained largely tokenistic and in no way an attempt to salve what were deep-seated forms of petro-colonialism.[26] For instance, in 1962, the Indian government, shocked into action by protests, sanctioned a second refinery in Assam. It was small-scale infrastructure and perceived as a "toy refinery" by the people who remained aggrieved as the bulk of the state's crude was still transported hundreds of miles to Barauni in the state of Bihar. The discovery of new oil reserves in Assam in the late 1960s only added to the angst, giving rise to further protests. Then Prime Minister Indira Gandhi promised to set up yet another refinery in Assam in 1971, which began functioning three years later.[27] Grievances, however, continued to simmer, in part because the extractive petroleum industry never quite delivered. Oil therefore generated contradictory affects, evoking hope and anger, aspiration and discontent.

The agitations that ultimately led to the establishment of the Numaligarh Refinery took on the form of a mass movement in 1979. The All Assam Students' Union (AASU), a student body revived as a pan-Assam outfit in the early 1970s, spearheaded the Assam Movement, as the agitations are widely called.[28] Demands of the Assam Movement were political, economic, and cultural. Strongly majoritarian in its outlook, these included making Assamese the medium of higher education instruction, reserving 80 to 90 percent of jobs for youths from the state, sending back refugees of the 1971 Bangladesh War, and having greater say over the use of Assam's resources, particularly oil.[29] One can read the Assam Movement as an affective and reactionary backlash against plantation logics, particularly against the constraints such logics introduced into the state's agrarian and urban economy. As Udayon Misra shows, during the period leading up to the movement, Assam witnessed a paucity of productive capital. The state's growth rate was a paltry 0.4 percent compared to the all-India average of 1.43 percent. Unemployment rose at a phenomenal rate, with applicants on the live register of the Employment Exchange going up by as much as 270 percent. The job sector in the Assam state government remained virtually stagnant while the central government's attitude toward employing local candidates in its public sector undertakings was discriminatory.[30]

The Indian state's failure to provide for the people of Assam, while continually extracting the land's natural resources, generated an atmosphere of immense discontent by the late 1970s. Leaders of the Assam Movement channelized people's resentment to drum up an affective politics of resource use. They pointed out to the Indian government that even in matters of taxes on crude oil, Assam only got 54 rupees per metric ton while the central government accrued more than nineteen times that amount.[31] New Delhi's refusal to listen to the Assam government's pleas for revision of royalties on crude oil exacerbated a feeling "that the Centre was merely bent on exploiting the resources of the region without in the least being worried over Assam's ever-deteriorating economic situation."[32] "Tej Dim, Tel Nidiu," meaning "We will give blood, not oil," soon became one of the Assam Movement's most visceral slogans. Dulal Sarma, a firebrand agitator, even slashed his chest with a blade and wrote the slogan in letters of blood on a street wall in Guwahati, the state's major metropolis. This happened during an oil blockade staged by the agitators in 1980, which prevented the transport of oil from the city's refinery to other parts of India.[33]

The Assamese therefore experienced petro-colonialism as extractive theft without public and community benefit. As a result, the thesis of Assam remaining a colonial hinterland gained further ground as the Movement unfolded. Insurrectionary anger was stoked repeatedly by drawing comparisons between New Delhi's treatment of Assam and the ravages of West Pakistan in its east, or what is now Bangladesh.[34] However, the Assam Movement cannot be equated with an "environmentalism of the poor," as the latter implies grassroots action against forces perpetuating environmental harms.[35] As the public intellectual and scholar Hiren Gohain has long argued, the movement was a predominantly middle-class and upper-caste phenomenon where questions of the peasantry's access to land or the working conditions of plantation labor were not central concerns. Rather, when disaffected rural masses were mobilized, it was largely by sections of the urban Assamese elite "raising an alarm on the threat to Assamese identity by 'foreigners.'"[36] In fact, from the early days of the movement, chauvinism had taken on an organizational form. The "blind rage of people" against persistent underdevelopment was channeled to "foment a suffocating chauvinist and fascist atmosphere."[37] Dissenting voices, including those that drew attention to the tyranny a majoritarian program would unleash,[38] were intimidated and silenced.

Continual violence marked the agitations, violence that was episodic and structural, and violence that was accretive, slow. The central government, by framing the agitations as the "Assam problem," largely failed to introspect on neocolonialism. Neither was the center able to recognize ethnic and political fault lines that ran deep. In 1983, a decision by the center to hold a set of controversial elections as the agitations raged on resulted in a gruesome genocide. "More than three thousand people—mostly Muslims of Bengali descent—were killed" in a place called Nellie.[39] Skirmishes between agitators and the police, unleashed by the state, resulted in 855 youths losing their lives during the six years of the Assam Movement.[40] There was a normalization of violence, seeping into the fabric of everyday life and continuing to persist, at times as spectacular eruptions, at other times in slow, incremental ways.

To salve what it saw as "the Assam problem," the central government in New Delhi under the leadership of Rajiv Gandhi began making overtures for a solution. Informal talks with agitators in 1984 paved way for formal negotiations and the signing of the Assam Accord in 1985, a memorandum of settlement between the Government of India and leaders of the Assam Movement.[41] Besides promising to stop the influx of non-Indian citizens into the state, clauses of the Assam Accord included securitizing borders and providing "safeguards" to "preserve and promote" Assamese culture and heritage,[42] all of which were majoritarian, reflecting the interests of

Assam's upper class and castes. The Government of India also assured agitating publics that it was renewing its "commitment for the speedy all round economic development of Assam, so as to improve the standard of living of the people."[43] The development of infrastructure became synonymous with the amelioration of a violent condition and state of persistent underdevelopment, although, ironically, it was not against extraction per se. Rather, infrastructural promises were about reorienting who the beneficiaries of extraction should be. The accord promised to establish a fourth oil refinery, besides reopening paper and jute mills declared "sick" and setting up a premiere institute of technology in the state.[44]

First announced in 1989,[45] the Numaligarh Refinery is thus the product of a long violent and visceral agitation. Sometimes referred to as "the Assam Accord Refinery," it has been an affective vehicle for the state to deal with a region torn by ethnic friction and agitation. "Divide everything," V. P. Singh remarked in front of a 100,000-strong crowd in Guwahati when he came to formally declare the setting up of Numaligarh, "but do not divide people."[46] Two years later, when Prime Minister P. V. Narasimha Rao laid the foundation stone for the refinery, he remarked it was a step to "restore peace in the state" after years of turmoil, violence, and political upheaval.[47] Numaligarh was in some ways an effort to undo the predicaments of a Plantationocene, including constrained infrastructure and the travails of petro-colonialism. However, in its planning and implementation, the refinery set in motion other effects unanticipated in the project's inaugural assembly.

The choice of Numaligarh as the location for the promised refinery of the Assam Accord involved meeting a number of criteria. In October 1989, a site selection committee evaluated eight different localities before recommending Numaligarh.[48] In a personal conversation with the author, one member of the 1989 committee stated that the availability of a large tract of uninhabited land was the first consideration. Given that Assam is prone to periodic flooding, especially during the monsoon rains, refining plants had to be situated on elevated ground. Outside of forest reserves, there was limited availability of such tracts of land in Assam—a constraint that the extensive land grants given to tea plantations in the colonial era had put on the state and its scope for economic development. The availability of water, low seismic activity, and the proximity to big towns were other major considerations.

A river, the Dhansiri, flowed through Numaligarh. Besides being a source of water for the refinery, it was to become a major conduit for the transport of "over-dimensional and over-weight structures" that the plants required. Much of these came along the old economic corridors of the colonial plantations: from ports via Bangladesh and upstream by the Brahmaputra to a jetty "specially constructed at Numaligarh on the Dhansiri river."[49] Numaligarh also had better proximity to existing towns, many of which failed to grow as Assam's plantations realigned infrastructures to suit their colonial, enclave economy. It was hoped that new infrastructure for refining oil would reinvigorate such centers that had been left behind to stagnate.

Yet no installation of infrastructure is outside of a political and ecological milieu, and this is precisely why infrastructures have to be read in a political ecological vein. While welcomed by local communities, who hoped to benefit from refinery-related employment, the siting of the refinery in Numaligarh sparked concerns among environmentalists, primarily because of its proximity to Kaziranga National Park, a UNESCO World Heritage Site home to globally significant populations of the one-horned rhino. The Ministry of Environment and Forests (MoEF), which provided environmental clearance to the project in 1991, specified that the refinery's layout should be "as far as possible" from the eastern boundary of Kaziranga.[50] However, to pave the way for oil infrastructure, the MoEF waived a rule that prohibited industrial projects coming up within a distance of 25 kilometers from a national park.[51] There were certain inconsistencies in the application of site selection criteria as well. Numaligarh scored high in terms of its proximity to an "environmentally-sensitive area," a criterion against which all sites had been ranked, but one report stated its distance from Kaziranga was 40 kilometers, while a separate impact assessment gave figures ranging between 25 and 35 kilometers. "From a reading of the documents," critics argued, "it would appear that the choice of Numaligarh was predetermined and factors were tailored to ensure its selection as the site of the refinery."[52] Locational factors had in fact caused significant delay in the construction of the Assam Accord Refinery,[53] and the AASU leaders were increasing pressure for the clauses of the accord to be implemented. "Political compulsions" had forced the government "to push through with finalizing the site."[54] The central government in New Delhi wanted to cultivate an image of implementing the Assam Accord, while the Asom Gana Parishad government in the state sought to use the refinery in its election propaganda, given that its popularity had begun to decline after failing to meet many promises.

Effluents, rather than elephants, were the main point of environmental concern,[55] as pollution was the obvious perceived outcome of refining plants. The dispersed and dissipated violence of infrastructure, to which Santosh alluded in the opening vignette of this chapter, was either not anticipated or downplayed. In fact, matters of concern gravitated toward the visible and the spectacular. Kaziranga National Park was on the world map, and the start of a mega-infrastructure project in its vicinity caught the attention of the press and environmentalists as well as regulating agencies. The siting of the refinery near Kaziranga led an environmental group, called the Bombay Environmental Action Group, to protest and insist that the refinery should be relocated. However, "the advanced stage of the proposal" meant that the central government could not "reverse the order."[56] To stem further development, India's MoEF declared a radius of 15 kilometers around the refinery as a "No Development Zone," although this corrective measure to curb pollution and congestion came much later in 1996, when the project was well underway.[57]

There were ominous signs as construction in the 720-hectare site began in 1994. In May of that year, an elephant herd caused considerable damage around the refinery and in the wider landscape. Panka, where the refinery is located, was the worst affected. Residents lamented that "elephant depredation ha[d] become their biggest concern."[58] A couple of months later, the herd damaged the newly constructed wall of the refinery.[59] "When we first went to Numaligarh, it was a site without any settlements," says Monoranjan Thakur, a civil engineer who worked at the refinery in 1994–95 as it was being set up. "The landscape was undulating with several swamps and deep ravines." One of the early tasks of engineers was to level the landscape and prepare the ground for the later construction of refining plants. "At the time, there was a large banyan tree in the northeast corner of the site, and a herd of fifty to sixty elephants would regularly forage in that area," Thakur recounts. "A large, twelve-foot wall had been erected to demarcate the refinery's boundary, and the elephants would repeatedly break the wall near the tree. I would supervise building in the evening and return the next day, only to find the wall being broken again." Thakur tells me that this happened at least five or six times during the one and a half years he was there: "It had become a recurring problem. The animals seemed adamant to be near that particular tree and, according to people from the neighboring villages, it was a site where they gave birth to calves." There were concerted efforts to keep the animals out of the refinery during its initial days. "In the end we managed by building a much more solid wall. A police outpost was also established in the refinery site, and personnel would burst firecrackers to chase the elephants away whenever they came, which was periodic but regular," says Thakur.

Elephants, as ethologists have observed, are wary of new objects in their landscape. They often approach infrastructural elements with caution, at times with interest, and often demolish things or structures considered suspect.[60] It is plausible that infrastructural activity frightened elephants, given that older members of the herd had never in their lifetime witnessed construction activity on such a scale. At the same time, and as Assam's eminent forester and elephant expert Bhupendra Nath Talukdar observes, these structures were instrumental in "impeding the elephants' easy and traditional access to the Dhansiri River."[61] Instances of elephants repeatedly breaking walls are an indication of how the animals themselves challenge or resist infrastructural activity, a form of resistance that cannot be equated with human forms of organization and political activity, but which nonetheless poses a challenge to human intervention.

In effect, infrastructure, by disrupting elephant movement, began altering the sentient topography of the landscape, which, as we saw in the introduction, entails ways of sensing, knowing, and inhabiting landscape through proboscidean proclivities and their conjunctions with people's rhythms. This altered topography was in the form of a rise in friction between people and elephants. As archival records indicate, between 1989 and 1993, four people died because of encounters with elephants in the Golaghat district. In the subsequent three years, as construction of the refinery's 250-acre residential site or township was underway, the number of human mortalities shot up to thirty-two. Infrastructures disrupted elephant movement, forcing them to find sources of food in human settlements and agricultural fields. There was a sudden spike in houses damaged by elephants, increasing from thirty-seven reported incidents in 1995 to 132 in 1996.[62] These difficult encounters draw attention to a spatially and corporeally dissipated violence inflicted by infrastructure, one that disrupts the quotidian activity of world making. The refinery led to blockages and a gradual degradation of elephant habitat, while the animals' disrupted mobilities had cascading effects on people. Frictions eroded possibilities for reproducing predictable life, altering horizons and foreclosing particular futures.

The building and expansion of the refinery's infrastructure followed a pattern symptomatic of postcolonial planning and development, akin to what urban scholars have called informality from above.⁶³ Informality as an idiom of infrastructural expansion makes possible new frontiers of development but also creates conditions for slow violence to proliferate. The construction and expansion of the Numaligarh Refinery followed formal procedures but, at times, reversed the order of permission and implementation. Construction was often initiated and the process of obtaining clearances either done in parallel or after some time, thereby opening up space for negotiations or for a loosening of rules. For instance, the initial environmental clearance issued by the MoEF in 1991, prior to the construction of the refinery, stated that its proposed township had to be moved, given that it was "only 19.5 kms from the boundary of Kaziranga National Park."⁶⁴ In 1994, the refinery applied for an exemption and managed to obtain a no-objection certificate. The township therefore was built as initially planned and in the midst of an elephant haunt. Furthermore, the 1991 environmental clearance stated that a green belt with a minimum width of 500 meters should surround the refinery. The refinery, on the other hand, settled for 100 meters, arguing that "almost all the surrounding areas" had "tea gardens with shade trees" and, therefore, "a wide natural green belt already existed all around."⁶⁵ The incremental deviations from plan and the informal idiom of infrastructural expansion, which lies at the heart of India's formal development and planning, were thus crucial in giving postcolonial ecologies their shape.

"Although crop raiding by elephants had begun to intensify," Santosh recollects, "it was largely during the harvesting season." In 2004, however, there was a spate of elephant-related human deaths in the landscape surrounding Numaligarh, including Sundarpur where Santosh lived. "They began blasting in the hills," he explains, "and the elephants were scared. What's more, these hills to the west of the refinery were a major conduit for elephants to move between the Kaziranga reserve and the landscape around us. If Numaligarh had resulted in elephants spending more time in our crop fields, then blasting made matters even worse. The elephants began developing a habit of taking shelter in the Doigurung forest next to our village in the daytime and entering people's fields at night." Crop depredation and house damage became even more acute due to these disruptions. The blasting that Santosh was referring to was taking place in stone quarries that had been set up in the forest landscape, and, as it turns out, such quarries supplied building material for yet another infrastructural project struck on the anvil of the Assam Accord.

Excavating Infrastructure

Crusher dust floats through the air and then settles, coating rocks and plants, roads and people's faces. Some of it comes down streams flowing down to the plains of Golaghat from the Karbi Anglong Hills. As running water slows down, crusher dust begins to sediment. Waterways get blocked and, during the monsoon rains, the homes of tea plantation workers are flooded. Yet another layer of silt is deposited as the waters recede, coating verandahs and gardens with sand, ruining homesteads and crops. "This is the outcome of quarrying," says Kurmi, a tea plantation worker. "The extraction is relentless, with truck after truck of stone brought out of the hills every day," he adds angrily. "Yes, it generates employment but it also causes loss. My front garden has now risen by a good two feet, all because of the siltation caused by the stone quarries."

The quarries that disrupted elephants' mobilities, and which later began to choke waterways in the landscape, had come up to supply stone for the construction of a 4.9-kilometer road and railway bridge across the Brahmaputra River. Known as the Bogibeel Bridge, this was yet another infrastructural outcome of the Assam Accord, commissioned by the central government to promote the state's economic development.[66] The development of road and railway infrastructure in Assam was coded by plantation logics, in that they predominantly served interests of planters and bolstered plantations' economic zones, whether for the circulation of cheap commodities or to organize the indentured coolie trade.[67] Such infrastructures did not foster inclusive forms of connectivity. Rather, they reproduced the plantation's enclaved spatiality. Very little had changed in terms of Assam's road and railway infrastructure until as late as the turn of the millennium.[68] Together with having greater say over the exploitation of the state's oil resources, economic improvement through the development of transport infrastructure was one of the Assam Movement's demands.

The central government announced the Bogibeel Bridge in 1992 as a means to ameliorate people's faith in the government, which had been shaken with the slow implementation of the Assam Accord.[69] The project was couched as the government's "desire... to ensure rapid progress and prosperity of the State," a trope that continually recurs in the poetics and politics of infrastructure.[70] However, material extraction and the infliction of slow violence elsewhere accompanies the spectacle of infrastructure as a harbinger of modernity. In 2000, the Northeast Frontier Railway floated tenders for the supply of stone. These were for "man-size boulders" to be extracted from river and hill quarries in both the north and south banks of the Brahmaputra that the bridge was to connect. The supply period was initially three years, and each contract was to be for the sum of approximately 250–300 million rupees each.[71]

The Karbi Anglong Hills adjacent to Sundarpur and Numaligarh, where quarrying was taking place, contain granite from the Precambrian period.[72] Much of the harder, better-quality stone from river quarries had already been extracted, as leases were being granted in the area by the Forest Department since the 1960s, although such extraction was predominantly small scale and manual.[73] What remained was largely lower-quality granite that required excavation through open-pit mining. The stone contained large amounts of feldspar, a mineral that made the stone soft. However, it was easier to break into desired sizes and, as mining permits outlined, could be "used as road metal" and as "building materials."[74] Supplies for Bogibeel included stone for building the bridge, as well as for constructing numerous roads and creating embankments to close and divert the river channel. Contracts were given to larger businesses who used capital-intensive means of extraction, and increased demand meant that they initially used blasting devices. Criticism from local residents and pressure from environmental groups brought blasting to a stop,[75] although quarrying continued. This process generated depleted landscapes one could associate with a Plantationocene. It also entailed, one could contend, an undoing of geological time and its sediments by the time of capitalist extraction.

The monumentality of infrastructure and its spectacle of progress often masks the degradation that slow violence brings about. No matter what its purpose or form, infrastructures are undergirded by material exploitation that often cheapens nature and the conditions of life. Bridges and buildings, roads and refineries become vehicles of affect summoning progress and development, while the reproducibility of life is slowly eroded elsewhere. Infrastructures, as some contend, are things that enable the circulation of other things. They are matter that enables the circulation of matter.[76] Yet this thing-like quality can be called into question when one tracks materials back to the sites from where they are drawn. By undoing the fetishism of infrastructure, however temporarily, we begin to witness its accretive violence, whose witnesses and protagonists can be human as well as proboscidean.

By 2003, there were more than forty stone quarries in operation in the area,[77] many of which were inside what had been designated, by the government, as the Kaziranga-Karbi Anglong Elephant Reserve. All of these were supplying stone for the Bogibeel Bridge, on the back of clearances for open-pit mining granted by the MoEF.[78] If the bridge was opening up connectivity in one locale, it was creating blockages elsewhere, blockages that become visible when one is attentive to proboscidean bodies and their movements. A 2.5-kilometer stretch in the hills adjacent to Sundarpur had been dug and blasted, and the movements of the animals were "greatly disturbed." As a result, elephants stopped using a pathway they had forged over generations, and took to entering settlements and cultivation in search of shelter and food.[79]

The political economy of resource extraction too followed the idiom of informality, generating profit from a kind of temporality that constitutes Assam's Plantationocene. Mining does not simply follow the intensive time of speed typical of capitalist production but also draws from the extensive time of delays and deferrals.[80] These are durations that emerge from rules not being followed or deliberately not being implemented, whereby the time of extraction and the time of generating surplus value are stretched and prolonged. These are "time thefts" that happen through informality and deliberate inaction on the part of the State,[81] in spite of an awareness of infrastructure's ecological harms. Holding onto these insights, also perceptively made by Dolly Kikon in her landmark work on resource extraction in the region,[82] is critical for developing postcolonial understandings of infrastructure and for reworking infrastructures as political questions of a Plantationocene.

In 1996, before extraction had become full blown, the forest officer Bhupendra Nath Talukdar wrote to his department stating it must reconsider a proposal to set up a stone crusher industry in a place called Panbari promoted by a local businessperson belonging to the Marwari trader community. "Panbari," Talukdar wrote, was perhaps the only "open area in the region" without human settlement. It lay on a vital route of the "seasonal migration of elephants" from Kaziranga to the Karbi Anglong Hills, as well as to the wider landscape including Numaligarh and Sundarpur. The department must consider alternatives, Talukdar argued, for "a stone crushing industry" would generate "constant noise" and "associated pollution" that would harm the ecosystem "tremendously."[83] Permission to set up stone crusher units was granted in spite of the anticipated degradation of landscape and elephant habitat. Such suppression of warnings about ecological consequences is not incidental but endemic to postcolonial resource extraction, endemic because it is the very idiom through which material extraction and infrastructural expansion proceeds. A Plantationocene's political economies thus involve a disavowal of sustainable futures and their reorientation into the time of sustained exploitation.

The quarrying that happened in the Karbi Anglong Hills exemplifies how "cheap nature," that is, the generation of cheap commodities accompanied by a concomitant cheapening and degradation of nature,[84] is produced in the quest to revive the scale of profit. A crucial aspect to this is the realization of relative surplus value,[85] albeit not through technological innovation as Marx envisaged. Rather, relative surplus value accrues through deregulation and via informal concessions. Permits to set up quarries are largely obtained by Marwari traders. Merchants by profession, Marwaris came to Assam from the western Indian state of Rajasthan in the early nineteenth century with the advent of colonial rule. The community played a major role in Assam's transition from a nonmonetized to a market economy, acting as bankers and commercial agents to tea plantations.[86] A community controlling much of Assam's contemporary commerce, Marwaris owned the fixed capital for extraction. The latter included the stone crusher units for breaking boulders into smaller stones, trucks, and Poclain excavators or "Poklan machines" as they are locally called after the manufacturing company (figure 2.2). These infrastructures of extraction, particularly the passing of trucks through villages and tea estates, also contributed to the siltation in the landscape.

Land in which open-pit mining happens typically belongs to members of the indigenous Karbi community, who have long been denizens of the hills south of the Brahmaputra, rich in deposits of granite and other minerals. In the 1930s, the colonial government introduced a land tenure system that prevented non-Karbis from settling on their land. In post-Independence India, leases given by some communities, coupled with rampant resource extraction, gave rise to an usufructuary system where non-Karbis gained significant access to land in the region.[87] During the period of the Assam Movement, the Karbi community mobilized and made demands for a political unit separate from Assam. While they have been granted autonomy, the grip of extractivist capital on Karbi Anglong's resources continues unabated. "The Karbis usually get a pittance for providing land," Manoj, a resident earlier involved in quarrying, says as we walk along the edge of a quarry, our hands and faces covered with dust. "Many provide land because it lies fallow," Manoj adds, "and even a marginal sum received from the Marwari owners of the per-

2.2　Excavating stone: material for the expansion of infrastructure. Photo: Rohit Choudhury.

mit comes across as a large amount." In other instances, reports by inspecting teams found that land belonging to the Forest Department, which had been lying vacant, was usurped for mining.[88] Anonymous or *benami* transactions were rife, with permits typically held in the name of individuals from the Karbi community while stone was extracted by those who owned fixed capital.[89]

The production of cheap nature is further aided by drawing on the reserve army of ex–tea plantation workers. "Many of them being out of work means that they are willing to work when paid the minimum wage," says Manoj, "and work in the quarries does not even yield the marginal benefits that the plantations dole out." In fact, the deregulated milieu in which mining took place led a number of youths from the wider landscape to open their own quarries. These were small-scale endeavors that usually involved those owning minable land, operated by renting excavators and trucks from the wealthier Marwari enterprises. A bulk of their excavated stone was sold to the latter at prices considerably below the market rate. "The profit margins are slim," says Manoj, who had a small quarry. "We lack the capital to rent, let alone buy Poklan machines. Hence, borrowing Poklans from the Marwari businessmen and having the rent deducted when we sell them stone is the only option." For many of these youths, running a small business alongside a larger operation was a means of earning a basic livelihood, an act of simple reproduction that made them vulnerable to exploitation by those who owned the means of extraction.

This distinction between larger contractors and local youth in the extraction of stone is analogous to what the political economist Kalyan Sanyal, in his evocative account of postcolonial capitalism, calls the "accumulation economy" and the "need economy."[90] An accumulation economy is driven by the logic of expansion, where surplus value is plowed back for a further round of material extraction and accumulation. It involves capital-intensive means of production and the deployment of labor power, furnished in this instance by the reserve army of ex–tea plantation workers. A need economy, on the other hand, is about supporting a certain level of consumption. It is however different from a subsistence economy, for a need economy entails the generation of surplus value, although surplus is not for the purpose of accumulation but for obtaining money to purchase a consumption basket and to invest some of it in labor and, as exemplified by Manoj's enterprise, rent the means of production.[91] This distinction is crucial for understanding the political economy of a Plantationocene. There is no unitary circuit of capital in operation, for capitalist and noncapitalist modes of production coexist. On the other hand, the former parasitizes the latter, rendering the two circuits codependent. Noncapitalist processes and spaces outside the realm of extraction have to constantly be available to being folded inside. This doubleness of relation, at once divergent and codependent, lies at the heart of plantation logics and their forms of capitalist accumulation. Equally, the need economy becomes a realm of those who are castaways of a Plantationocene's uneven development. As Manoj ironically remarks, "What is the point in applying for government jobs if you don't have any contacts? I applied for a number of them, and the entire process was futile."

In a Plantationocene's accumulation economy, the process of extraction is not unregulated but deregulated. Mining permits obtained by the wealthier capital-intensive units typically contain a "production plan," which specifies the duration of a lease based on the mineral reserves present and the optimum level of mining. The production plan stipulates annual limits to the extraction of stone and the number of days for working a mine, which is usually the total quantity to be excavated divided evenly for the duration the contract is given. "For the comfort of the mine workers and for any other eventualities, 5 days no-mining days' cushions are considered every month."[92] "Such stipulations are usually not followed," says Manoj. "What the bigger players do is that they supply the entire amount they are contracted for the Bogibeel project in two years instead of three. Even if payments remain pending, they can recuperate the money afterwards. In the meantime, they get an extra year for mining, and as a result extraction becomes excessive."

Manoj's observations are an extension of what Marx called "'small thefts' of capital," where surplus value is generated through "additional time" gained by extending the working day or by robbing the worker of rest.[93] Here, there are "small thefts" from nature or, more appropriately, nature as mediated by the mining production plan. There is in fact a distinct micropolitics to this informal and deregulated accumulation economy. "You need to pay a royalty of 200 rupees to the Forest Department per cubic meter of stone extracted," says Manoj. He explains how the department means to keep tabs by issuing a TP or Transit Pass and a *challan* or royalty receipt every time a truck carrying stone leaves a quarry. "What happens instead is that the same TP and *challan* are used a number of times," Manoj tells me. "That way the account books show one thing while the amount of stone extracted is another." Micropolitical acts, fostered by a nexus between businesspersons and the Forest Department, therefore produce both an extensive duration of mining and extraction in excess of specified limits.

Such cheapening of nature, therefore, becomes synonymous with slow violence, degrading habitability and the conditions for sustaining life. Slow violence is a wearing away, in that it leads to the attrition of the subject, both human and other-than-human, and it is also a gradual accrual, manifesting through material excess as silt sediments in particular places, and disrupts specific ecologies. Purposeful inaction by the state amplifies both slow destruction and accretion. In 2003, the director of Kaziranga National Park noted in a letter to the head of Assam's Forest Department that "the impact of quarrying along hills" was becoming "quite visible." The degradation of hill slopes was aggravating erosion and inducing a slow change in the course of streams. "I am also not convinced," the director wrote, "about the clearance" granted to "some (if not all) of these quarries," for they "defeat the object of long term conservation of wildlife."[94] It remained unclear what action was initiated by the authorities, although in 2006 the same department floated tenders for opening up new mines in the area to supply 10,000 cubic meters of stone for the Bogibeel project.[95] Four years later, the accruing effects of quarrying were magnified. "Heavy siltation" was taking place in the agricultural fields around Panbari, another concerned forest officer wrote in 2007, as stone crusher plants ran "throughout the day round the year." It had resulted in a water shortage for the national park's herbivores, while people's fields had become "unsuitable for growing paddy crops." Local farmers, the official noted, were being driven "towards poverty." "For the greater interest" of wildlife and "the people of the neighbouring area," the crusher units needed to be stopped.[96] Park authorities referred the matter to the Karbi Anglong Forest Department,[97] although no direct action was taken.

Together with the subversion of regulations, deliberate inaction, and the suppression of known and anticipated ecological harms, extraction thrives upon the slowness of adjudication. In 2003, upon being asked by the Forest Department to furnish copies of quarrying approvals from the MoEF, mining operators took the matter to court. Litigation continued for eight years and, ultimately, the Guwahati High Court delivered a judgment making it mandatory to obtain MoEF permission prior to setting up any industrial unit within 25 kilometers of Kaziranga National Park.[98] The protracted process of adjudication, interspersed with delays and adjournments, enabled mining to carry on. For instance, the Northeast Frontier Railway released a fresh tender for stone in 2008,[99] and quarries adjacent to Kaziranga and Sundarpur continued supplying the Bogibeel project while the matter remained sub judice. Mining operators therefore exploited the slow time of adjudication that marks Assam's overburdened courts.

A similar temporality of excavation played out when the issue of quarrying was taken to the Supreme Court of India by Rohit Choudhury, an environmental activist from the Golaghat district. Choudhury, a member of the same community that owned many of the larger mining businesses, was concerned by the degradation to the wider ecosystem. He filed a public interest litigation in the National Green Tribunal, pleading that "unregulated quarrying and mining activities" ought to be stopped as they were threatening endangered wildlife in Kaziranga.[100] After submitting an information request to the MoEF, Choudhury found that there was no record of permits being granted to stone crusher units, many of which were in the No Development Zone declared by the MoEF in 1996 to rectify the harms of siting the Numaligarh Refinery in the wider landscape. Subsequent inquiry by the MoEF revealed twenty-six stone crusher units operating in the area, and an order to suspend permits had been sub judice before the Guwahati High Court.[101]

A year after Choudhury's appeal, a displeased Green Tribunal directed both the MoEF and the Assam state government to refrain from granting fresh approvals for quarrying until further notice. The legal body also directed the MoEF to take necessary action against unlicensed units.[102] In its verdict given in 2012, calling for the closure of stone quarries, the tribunal poignantly referred to the very conditions that enabled a slow, sedimentary violence to permeate and persist. "The Central Government and the State Government," the tribunal exclaimed, "maintained stony silence with regard to the implementation of notifications. . . . Non-implementation . . . speaks volumes with regard to their callousness and apathy in protection of ecology of Kaziranga National Park, which resulted in causing pollution thereby damaging the environment as well as ecology" of the landscape.[103]

In spite of the court dictate, there were further delays in implementing the closure of mines. The Forest Department in Kaziranga wrote to its counterparts in the Karbi Anglong Hills requesting stringent action.[104] No immediate measures, however, were taken, which enabled mining to continue, albeit intermittently and in a covert manner. Stones were transported from quarries to crusher units in the late evening or at night in order to avoid detection. Products would leave by trucks for delivery only at night. A government-led investigation team found quarry operators to be cognizant of inspection visits by senior forest officials. All activities at the quarrying site and stone crusher units would be temporarily suspended "until the departure of officials from the field."[105] According to a police report, a clandestine economy was at work. Mining operators were taking advantage of a Guwahati High Court judgment that had granted them marginal relief by allowing "already extracted stone" to be "removed from the site," using it as a pretext to transport freshly quarried stone.[106]

The violence of accretion was becoming even more evident in the landscape. Material effects of unrelenting extraction sedimented in many locales, including those of the Adivasi community who had little voice. "Our fields are covered in silt," says Kurmi. "The owners of the quarries kept digging it out of the streams with JCB excavators because people were angry, but it kept coming every year. Our paddy fields have so much debris that they have become higher ground. It is impossible to plow, and in the end we had to abandon cultivation altogether" (figure 2.3). With labor in the plantation where he worked increasingly becoming casual, Kurmi's family, like many others, faced a simple reproduction squeeze, a constraint in the ability to subsist and maintain everyday life. The accrual of violence stemming from resource extraction to build infrastructure aggravated this constraint, resulting in a slow wearing out of the community's life. "With little other choice, many of our family members began working as wage laborers in the quarries," he tells me. In fact, a report from the civil administration found that as much as 350 hectares of land in various villages in the wider landscape had become "unfit for agriculture" as "runoff water" containing "earth and stone from the mining sites" made its way into people's fields. "If the mining activities continue in the hills of Karbi Anglong at this rate," the inspecting civil administration officer remarked, "more paddy land . . . may be affected." Resentment among farmers of the affected villages toward quarries was rising and, as the administration noted, "untoward incidents have already taken place." Siltation from the quarries was creating significant tension, making the likelihood of a "flare up" imminent.[107]

Quarries continued to operate informally until 2018 as the Bogibeel Bridge project got drawn out. "Informal quarrying stopped the day the bridge was opened," says Manoj. This observation is a telling summary of the ways in which the state allows resource exploitation to take place through deregulation, inaction, and a suppression of knowledge of its consequences, whether ecological or social. At the same time, the state puts an end to such practices when materials are no longer needed for infrastructural expansion. A deregulated milieu actively enabled by the state opens up space for those who are part of the need economy to become involved in mining. This is in no way a democratization of extraction, for the owners of capital subject those like Manoj to exploitation. When mining activity was finally ended, the stone crusher enterprises had already made vast profits. It was wage labor from the Adivasi ex–tea plantation worker community and those involved in quarrying as a means of simple reproduction that were most affected. In a letter to the Kaziranga National Park authorities, the principal chief conservator of forests of Karbi Anglong made a perceptive remark. While conservation was of critical importance, the closure of quarries, he stated, had "created large scale resentment due to loss of employment to the people. . . . It is pretty bad," the conservator wrote, "to have [a] discontented community with no employment around protected areas, you would agree as a wildlife manager."[108] The closure of quarries created a set of "left-behinds"—those caught between a rock and a hard place, a ruined earth and a simple reproduction squeeze. The owners of fixed capital, on

2.3 The quarry and its sediments: a silted-up stream and paddy field where cultivation has been abandoned. Photo by the author.

the other hand, simply moved their machinery elsewhere, opening up new quarries and creating the grounds for yet another episode of slow violence.

Infrastructure and Habitus

"Elephants have become like cattle and goats," says Rabidas, a farmer from the Adivasi community who lives in a village near Sundarpur, alluding to their frequent visits and incursions into crop fields as infrastructure and mining blocked and altered the animals' movements. "Many people abandoned cultivation," he tells me, indicating how increased friction between people and elephants aggravated what was already a simple reproduction squeeze: "When we should be getting fifty *maunds* of rice from our fields, we end up getting ten *maunds*, as the elephants eat it all. People can barely cope, so what is the point in putting in all the effort? It might just be better working as day laborers in a quarry. What is the government going to do?" When I ask him about state intervention to ameliorate the problem, Rabidas responds, "The government has gone mad, and the elephants have gone mad. With crops being destroyed relentlessly, people too are going mad."

"Going mad" is a visceral exposition of a despoiled habitus. It reveals the degradation of elephants' habitat by infrastructural expansion just as it rallies attention to the animals' altered habits. "Going mad" is an allusion to the state's inability and failure to respond to the travails of people while it continues sanctioning a milieu of extraction and degradation. "Going mad" also refers to an attrition of the subject,[109] particularly of those from the Adivasi community and their struggle to reproduce everyday life. Crop raiding by elephants, as Rabidas's and Santosh's explanations indicate, should not be seen as a simple change in the animals' habits. Rather, it needs to be read as the product of the rapacity of capital and of the slow violence it inflicts upon a Plantationocene's landscape, its sentient beings. The concatenated effects of roads, walls, and quarries, as they modify habitat and modulate habits, point to a wider ontology of infrastructure, where the latter begins to undergird not just human but also other-than-human life.

One way of articulating such a wider ontology is to attend to the ways in which infrastructures become ecological keystones, as some biologists are beginning to argue.[110] Traditionally, the concept of keystone species denotes those organisms whose impact on an ecosystem is disproportionately large relative to their abundance. A term borrowed from architecture, a keystone is the wedge-shaped piece at the crown of an arch that locks other pieces in place. The ecological analogy is that certain species play a similar role in ecosystem function, maintaining the structure of a community and determining the composition and abundance of other species. Just as in the case of infrastructure, roles played by ecological keystones become evident in breakdown. Their removal leads to trophic cascades that can change the composition and function of an ecological community.[111] Infrastructures too might be seen to play a similar ecological role when roads carve up landscapes and become barriers to animal movement, affecting species dispersal and community composition. In a similar vein, by modulating the flow of water, dams can have disproportionately large effects on the structure and function of ecological communities. Remarkably durable, the relative permanence of infrastructures means that their ecological effects persist over time, modifying an animal's habitat and habit, and usually not in benign ways.

In Sundarpur, and the wider Golaghat landscape, infrastructure had the most visible bearings on the patterned movement of elephants. It resulted in animal immobility—periods of being stuck, with confined movement and reduced home ranges—as the refinery and stone quarries introduced blockages along their usual paths. "In around 2004, as quarrying began to increase, the herd of seventy to eighty elephants that move between Doigurung forest and Numaligarh started entering labor lines in and around tea plantations," says Santosh. "Breaking labor quarters in search of food became a habit." Studies by wildlife biologists also seem to indicate that during this period, the herd was largely confined to a matrix of villages and tea plantations between Sundarpur and Numaligarh rather than moving between Kaziranga and the Nambor forest as they did in the past.[112] "Blasting in the quarries no doubt scared the elephants," Santosh observes, "but disturbance was further increased by the hundreds of trucks that went in and out of the quarries carrying chips and metal for the Bogibeel Bridge each day." These blockages to elephants' mobilities are some of the quotidian, often hidden, impacts of infrastructure that happen elsewhere, which remain out of sight from the bridge where the drama of spectacular infrastructure plays out, promising new connections, speed, and access to frontiers. However, such effects are discernible to those who are affected, be it elephants or tea plantation workers, discernible in a zone amid the dust and silt of quarries' surrounds and in spaces of ordinariness. Immobilities, as sensed by elephants and those who live alongside them, provide vital counterpoints to specifications of animals' mobilities in the Anthropocene,[113] revealing important themes of stuckness and stasis that have long marked histories of a Plantationocene.

Erosive, keystone effects of infrastructures and the delayed degradation they brought about resulted in a new pattern of elephant movement. "Nowadays, the elephant herd takes to staying in the Doigurung jungle during the day," says Rabidas, "and then venture into people's fields at night." As we saw with the SP04 herd in Sonitpur, new habits are forged in relation to people's activities. "Elephants know that they cannot stay outside reserves during the daytime because of people," Rabidas tells me. "That is why they go back into the forest during the day." During the course of my fieldwork, we found that the herd often splintered, forming smaller family groups in the evening in order to raid crops (figure 2.4). This might be an adaptive strategy, given that the elephants are easily detected if they forage in large groups. As in Sonitpur's SP04 herd, the elephants in Golaghat too might be considered postcolonial fauna. "In the past, elephants were quite afraid of people, but this herd has become quite fearless and clever." Rabidas explains, "If they hear people at night, they wait very silently. The other day, they broke two houses in our village, and we didn't even know it had happened. Only later, when we heard the cracking sound of bamboo, did we realize that elephants had entered the village."

2.4 Infrastructures carve up landscapes: females, calves, and subadults crossing a highway near Sundarpur. Photo: Jyoti P. Das.

Some of the elephants' behavior, one could argue, is a response to an ecology forged by infrastructure. As sensate and sentient beings, the animals are witnesses to the modification and despoliation of their worlds. They apprehend the slow violence infrastructure inflicts and respond to it in proboscidean ways. "Sometimes this elephant herd tries to remain in tea plantations, where it is relatively quiet," says Santosh. "However, they are seldom left in peace. Plantation management is usually not happy with elephants being around, as it disrupts plucking, and the animals sometimes destroy the tea bushes." Forest Department personnel are called to chase the animals away. "What invariably happens is that the elephants are pushed back into the Doigurung reserve, and we in Sundarpur are among those most affected," Santosh tells me. His account of a despoiled habitus, affecting both people and elephants, reveals how slow violence can be "machinic," in that it has cascading effects cutting across human and other-than-human divides.[114] Infrastructures disrupt elephants' mobilities and alter the predictable pathways of the animals' own reproduction. Modified habits of elephants then impinge upon people's lives.

Although dispersed and diffused, such violence materializes somewhere, in particular places and in particular bodies. The bodies exposed to slow violence in the zone of ordinariness are often those who have the least voice and are least likely to attract inquiry into causes, effects, and potential redress. When they do, causes and effects are mobilized through the language of "human-wildlife conflict," a discursive practice that has come to the forefront of state and NGO-led conservation. Statistics pour in to reveal the magnitude of conflict: reports are replete with numbers of elephant and human deaths, houses damaged, and crops lost. The term *conflict*, which means to come together and to collide, gives equal agency to people and elephants, but elides structural dispossession that exposes both parties to harm, just as it evades, or rather annuls, historical conditions that render certain communities more vulnerable to its repercussions. Such annulment happens through practice, particularly in the ways in which the state and conservation NGOs seek to mitigate—an action that is implicit in the very metaphor of conflict. Interventions gravitate toward the visible and the symptomatic—minimizing crop loss and house damage, human and elephant mortality—while concealing what is a slow degradation of life.[115] In other words, the rhetoric of conflict belies a constitutive point—that slow violence or the structurally motivated attrition of subjects proceeds because of their membership in certain populations that have historically been marked out for wearing out.[116]

Conflict and its mitigation produce dramas that obscure a more fundamental aspect of conservation: that it is not just a biopolitics of managing, securing, and fostering life but also a form of necropolitics that proceeds through the disposability of certain human lives.[117] This becomes evident when we scrutinize the category of human deaths, listed as mere numbers in state and conservation reports.[118] A majority of these tragic incidents occur in the Adivasi community in Golaghat, but also many parts of Assam. The names of Dipak and Manika Paja, and Deepa and Shravan Tanti, all of whom passed away after fatal encounters with elephants in the landscape surrounding Sundarpur, are relegated to anonymity, rendered a nameless mass analogous to the colonial cancellation of people's names when they were brought to indenture on Assam's plantations.[119] The kinds of necropolitics witnessed here are not spectacular but operate in the realm of the ordinary, the quotidian, knowable only when we take the perspective of those exposed to slow violence's harms. Life becomes disposable through its gradual but sustained erosion, where the survival of certain people and communities is articulated as slow death.[120]

The violent ecological effects of mundane infrastructure, like the refinery wall Santosh drew my attention to, can themselves remain concealed from wider purview unless concerned publics are sparked into being. In 2011, the refinery erected the boundary wall 2.2 kilometers long and 12 feet high as part of its "township" or residential site expansion program. "Even though the township had come up and elephants' movements were blocked, they have continued venturing into the refinery area over the years," says Santosh. "Recently there was an incident when a female, which got separated from the herd, went into the main complex," he tells me, highlighting how elephant mobilities are never fully thwarted as the animals act against the grain of hostile designs. "There was mayhem, and the elephant panicked, damaging a number of motorbikes and cycles parked inside. The entire herd had tried to enter through the main gate that morning, but the security guards prevented them from doing so. This particular individual somehow got in." Such incidents lay at the heart of the refinery's decision to construct such a tall and sturdy wall, for it was seen as "essential for the safety of their residents."[121]

The refinery wall is an example of hostile infrastructure (figure 2.5). The peculiarity of such infrastructure is that it works in a dual register: excluding the targeted while remaining inconspicuous and benign to the nontargeted.[122] To the residents of the refinery and to sections of the wider public, the wall was an unobtrusive marker of the township's boundary. For elephants, on the other hand, the wall became an obstruction to their pathways of movement and to their pathways of reproducing life. It was a spate of elephant deaths, caused as result of elephant movement being disrupted by the wall, that brought the inconspicuous hostility of infrastructure into public purview. In 2015, a carcass of an elephant calf was found near the wall, triggering significant media attention.[123] When going up slopes, elephants prefer taking a gentle gradient rather than climbing steep hillsides. The construction of the wall forced the animals to find alternate routes that were not as safe. "The calf tumbled down the hillside and died due to hemorrhage," Kailash, a local resident, tells me. It soon came to public light that between 2011 and 2016, the wall resulted in the deaths of twelve elephants,[124] many of which happened as a result of elephants having to take alternate, less safe, routes while foraging. Furthermore, the hostile design of the wall also included concertina barbed wire coiled on top, a material developed to stop troops during World War I. "On a number of occasions elephants tried to pull it down with their trunks and got badly bruised," says Kailash.

Using images of the death of an elephant caused by hostile infrastructure, Choudhury filed a petition before the National Green Tribunal pleading that

2.5   Hostile infrastructure: partially demolished boundary wall with concertina barbed wire on top. Photo by the author.

the boundary wall should be demolished and that the refinery ought to pay compensation for the destruction of forest land. The wall for the extended residential site, Choudhury and his counsel argued, had come up in the No Development Zone and had been constructed without following due procedure.[125] As in earlier instances of construction preceding permission, the erection of the wall and the accompanying felling of trees resulted in a gradual erosion of environmental stipulations—a process that is inherent to slow violence. Initial permission granted to expand the refinery's township in the early 1990s specified that construction "should not involve any forest area" and should not come up on hill slopes.[126] However, according to the Forest Department, the refinery went against these clauses. Trees were felled on slopes "serving as an important elephant corridor" in 2008, and that too before a final approval was issued. Although an order to suspend activities was later issued, construction was already underway.[127]

In August 2016, the National Green Tribunal observed that the proposed township and its boundary wall had thwarted elephants' mobilities by coming "in the way of elephant corridors."[128] Dismissing the refinery's argument that the wall had been constructed to demarcate land rather than obstruct elephants,[129] the Green Tribunal ordered the structure to be demolished. The refinery was also asked to pay a compensation of two and a half million rupees to the Forest Department, besides undertaking "compensatory afforestation" of ten times the number of trees felled.[130] Importantly, the tribunal took note of the hostile design that underpinned what was seemingly mundane infrastructure. Its judgment can be read as an intervention in the material politics of design. "Fencing material," the tribunal stated, "is to be of certain specification . . . so that it does not cause life hazard to the elephants and this has to be strictly complied with."[131]

In compliance with the court order, and amid widespread media coverage, the refinery demolished parts of the wall. However, the media spectacle generated around demolishing hostile infrastructure masked the refinery's token gesture. It has now gone to Assam's Gauhati High Court asking for "clarity on the township extension."[132] By demolishing 289 meters of the wall, the refinery states that it has complied with the Green Tribunal order of freeing up elephant corridors. Furthermore, having returned one hectare of land it had encroached on to the district's civil administration, the refinery has pleaded for permission to "start construction of the quarters" on eight hectares of land.[133] In its application before Assam's premiere court, the refinery states that "the question of further demolition" of the wall "does not and cannot arise."[134] Having obtained a stay on the order, the matter is now sub judice in court, initiating what will perhaps be another long-drawn-out legal battle. "These are delaying tactics," says a local journalist, who believes that, inevitably, the wall will have to be taken down. However, such delays mean that the structure persists and, therefore, conditions that inflict slow violence continue.

The Slow Violence of Infrastructure

This ethnography of more-than-human encounters, spanning over a decade, tells a specific, but important, story of infrastructure. It reveals how in Assam's context, the politics of infrastructure is a response to the uneven development fostered by plantation logics. Plantations' transport corridors historically dictated the growth of the region's infrastructure, with the latter serving an enclave economy and generating planetary connections on one hand and creating stagnation, isolation, and stasis on the other. Resource extraction too followed colonial logics. Their legacies did not wither away with Indian Independence: petro-colonialism, coupled with the structural constraints plantations introduced, aggravated the pattern of colonial underdevelopment in Assam.[135] These histories therefore point to reading infrastructure as a key question of a Plantationocene and the fraught spatiality it produces,[136] rather than couching the politics of infrastructure in terms of the Anthropocene and its universalized accounts of human agency. At stake is not simply an escalation of scalar projects achieved through resource-technology complexes but also, as Barbora and Phukan argue, the perpetuation of obsolescence,[137] which brings a nonlinearity to infrastructure and condition futures as hazardous, where disasters lie waiting to detonate.

Infrastructure was an important dimension of the self-determination movement Assam witnessed from the late 1970s onward. The reading of the Assam Movement offered here, drawing liberally from the critical insights of those who have deeply engaged with the region,[138] reveals how agitators, to gain traction for their movement, stoked an affective politics of infrastructure and sought to reterritorialize resources against imperatives of the Indian big bourgeoisie and state. However, the Assam Movement, as an affective and political backlash against a Plantationocene's discontents, was majoritarian. Largely driven by urban elites, it was not an environmentalism of the poor. Rather, people were mobilized by generating hatred toward "foreigners" and "illegal immigrants."[139] While many in Assam experienced modernity as extractive theft, the agitations were not necessarily about ameliorating the plight of those confined to the need economy or those whose lives have been historically marked out for wearing out.

The emphasis of this account has been on the affective journeys and material effects of spectacular infrastructure sited in response to the Assam Movement. Understanding such effects and repercussions has entailed developing a wider ontology that takes infrastructures as constitutive of both human and other-than-human life. Infrastructures, by restructuring habitat and forging habits, become part of a creature's habitus. They inflict a slow violence upon the landscape, shoring up particular bodies and ecologies, and setting in motion a set of cascading actions and effects. Slow violence can be deemed machinic, for it cuts across ecologies of capital, environment, and mind,[140] reorienting the horizon of reproducing predictable life. Santosh's account of the landscape's ecology is an exemplary guide to the machinic nature of slow violence, for he draws attention to how other-than-human bodies sense and respond to infrastructure and the consequent repercussions they have on the Adivasi community's lives. In similar vein, moving from the spectacle of infrastructure to sites of material extraction that underpin all infrastructural expansion destabilizes the dominance of the latter as an analytical category and enables apprehending where slow violence manifests and which lives are exposed to its harms. A wider ontology thus reveals how the administration of life via infrastructure can be necropolitical, acting not on *anthropos* or humanity as a whole but on certain populations that shoulder the burden of history.

The temporality of slow violence is that of delayed degradation.[141] It manifests in accretive ways, in spaces of ordinariness and often months or years after infrastructures are installed. Its temporality is also one of "ongoingness,"[142] dispersed and measured out, but unrelenting in its effects. Conditions for the persistence of slow violence are fostered by the deliberate suppression of known and anticipated harms. This is witnessed in the ways in which planning regulations are loosened and concessions for mining are given, even though the state is aware of the repercussions they are likely to have. Enabling harms to proliferate, despite knowledge of repercussions and consequences, can be seen as a central dynamic of postcolonial landscapes and the ecologies of a Plantationocene.

Slow infrastructural violence and its temporalities are also related to economy. As the micropolitics of resource extraction reveals, the speedup of excavation and the degradation it fuels happen under circumstances that are deregulated rather than unregulated. The owners of capital also exploit the time of adjudication in order to continue mining. An informal idiom of infrastructural expansion, including a deregulated milieu and the disavowal of known and possible repercussions, as well as exploitation of the delays associated with adjudication, results in an undoing of geological time by the time of extraction and of postcolonial capital. Rock is broken down and hillsides are carved up to feed a Plantationocene's infrastructure. At the same time, subjective relations are made in and through geology.[143] By coding geology as road metal and construction material, a field of dispossession is auctioned, where violence becomes a defining feature of materially organizing extraction.

A wider ontology that takes infrastructure as part of a creature's habitus reveals how mines, refining plants, walls, and roads condition other-than-human mobilities. They result in a gradual grinding down of particular ways of being and doing. Infrastructures disrupt not only elephants' paths of movement but also the pathways through which the animals reproduce their everyday lives. In this sense, the effects of infrastructure on mobility are metabolic—an insight one can draw from Santosh when he equates elephants' movement with nourishment, as one of feeding and moving at the same time. It is these world-forming and metabolic dimensions of movements that hostile infrastructure such as walls wear out. Hostile infrastructures cloak slow violence, particularly to those who remain unaffected: walls appear as benign markers of boundaries while they exclude elephants and render them creatures without a *domus* or home. Slow violence often sediments elsewhere, not just in the site of infrastructural activity, whether in the form of silt from quarries or the cascading and dispersed effects of elephants' mobilities on the Adivasi community's lives.

There is a distinct necropolitics enacted in the slow violence of infrastructure, for it is not *anthropos* that becomes the target, but always particular bodies and ecologies. Time and again, slow violence marks out those whose historical experience has been one of attrition, who have experienced survival as slow death, whether in Assam's plantations or those exposed to infrastructure's toxicity elsewhere.[144] The couching of slow violence in terms of conflict, a discourse mobilized by conservation NGOs and the state, is often explicitly and intentionally a redefinitional tactic, a distorting gesture that renders long-running processes into an event. What such tactics mask are particular casualties and the wearing out of lives within zones of ordinariness, where necropolitics becomes endemic. Unlike epidemics, which are thrust upon people, endemics are permanent factors that sap a population's strength, constraining their ability to work and to live. Equally, by deflecting blame onto those, like Manoj, confined to the need economy, the drama of conflict sidelines persistent forces of underdevelopment.

It is only a color-blind account of infrastructure that pinpoints this condition as the Anthropocene. A Plantationocene, on the other hand, foregrounds the lives of the dispossessed and those relegated as disposable, lives that get muted and rendered invisible by universals. For many who inhabit such a condition and are exposed to slow violence, slow death, and slow extinction, agency is one of maintenance, not making. When Santosh asks, "What else will the elephants do?," it is a profound insight into a Plantationocene present. Here, agency is no longer an act of grandeur or full-on resistance but a response to a simple reproduction squeeze. It is an act where further attrition might be delayed or somehow kept at bay. It is a labor of the exhausted.

3

Material Politics

From the Politics of Matter to a Material Politics

Guarding crops from elephants at night is a routine activity in Sundarpur. Men stay up in shelters constructed in their fields every night for almost four months of the year, from the time of planting paddy until the harvesting of grain, to ensure that their crops are safe. One evening, while sitting in the *tongi* or crop-guarding shelter of Bogai, a farmer, we hear firecrackers in the distance. Elephants have entered the village, and it is only a matter of time before they will come our way. Bogai insists we take preemptive action. Flashlight in hand, I follow him down an undulating path with the intent of making noise to scare the elephant away. Moments later, the beam illuminates the body of an elephant making its way toward Bogai, fifteen feet ahead of me. "Come back," I yell, as Bogai stands his ground, facing an animal ready to charge. My fear of witnessing a man being trampled is stalled in the nick of time. A group of alert villagers on the elephants' heels throw burning torches at the bull, making him stop and slowly turn around. Bogai is safe. I am relieved. He returns mumbling that elephants do not scare him. Later that evening Budhu, another farmer who learns of the incident, asks me, "Didn't you know Bogai was inebriated?" Unknowingly, I put our lives at risk by confronting elephants in the dark, without torches or firecrackers and accompanied by a person under the influence of alcohol.

A few weeks later, I come across a poster on the wall of a villager's house. Printed and circulated by the conservation NGO World Wildlife Fund (WWF), it advises people to stop brewing alcohol at home. The poster depicts a man distilling *sulāi* or country spirits (figure 3.1). A large earthen pot, indicating fermenting molasses, stands on the side, beside which lies a jerrycan, a fuel container in which the intoxicant is stored and sometimes transported. The most startling element of the poster is the two elephants, with accentuated and anthropomorphized eyes, breaking through the walls of the home distillery and reaching out for the brew with their trunks. The caption in Assamese alerts people to the consequences of constructing distilleries at home: elephant incursions will be imminent. Upon asking the villager what he makes of the message, he remarks, "Elephants are drawn to alcohol. You saw Sutu's house that was damaged the other day. It happened because he was brewing *sulāi* at home. The elephants got scent of the brew and broke in."

These two events happened during the early part of my stay in Sundarpur, and, as in a lot of ethnographic work, they put at risk the discourses and analytics through which I sought to understand the landscape. Frictions between people and elephants, it appeared, were not solely the outcomes of deforestation or the degradation of habitat by infrastructure. There were other actors involved in the making of a Plantationocene's ecologies, its material and political life. How then might one read these enmeshments between people, elephants, and alcohol alongside the actions of the state and the plantation industry in the forging of habitable and hostile worlds? What happens to social and political outcomes when one accounts for a volatile material that acts through human and other-than-human bodies? And how should materials and material agency be situated in relation to a Plantationocene's colonial and postcolonial history?

There has been a surge in writing about materials in the social sciences, spurred by the advent of new materialism, which seeks to recuperate the agency of things and the actions of matter in shaping social practices and

3.1 Warning people against brewing alcohol at home. The caption in Assamese is a couplet: "Do not construct distilleries any and everywhere, or for elephant harassment do prepare." Photo by the author.

political outcomes.[1] New materialism considers agency to be the product of assemblages. It deploys the concept of "thing-power" to articulate how objects that are usually considered inanimate generate effects that are not simply material or mechanical but political as well.[2] New materialisms deviate from the older historical materialism in that they strive to take matter seriously, not just as the mere stuff of raw materials and commodities but also as a force that acts, influences, and modifies a state of affairs. This political agency of matter becomes a means to espouse new forms of collectives—a parliament of things—that can register dissent and affirm new ways of acting and intervening in the world.[3] New materialism and its associated neovitalist accounts of agency have inspired a body of innovative work in anthropology, geography, and the wider social sciences that takes as its point of departure the ways in which "worlds are formed through the constant interplay of life and matter."[4]

My invocation of material politics shares some of these concerns but also deviates from neovitalist accounts of agency. First, in lieu of a politics of matter, I espouse a material politics. The two might seem synonymous at the outset, but I want to draw attention to some crucial distinctions. The first entails a contrast between materials and matter. New materialist accounts of political matter and thing-power,[5] while relational, emphasize the properties of things. Properties are attributes or characteristics that reside within things. To analyze properties, they must be parsed, dissected, and measured. Materials, on the other hand, index qualities, which are continually generated and dissolved as materials flow through porous bodies and their surrounds.[6] To apprehend and understand qualities, one must follow materials, track how substances are produced, and evaluate how they act in specific situations and milieus. In other words, understanding materials requires an archival and ethnographic mode of inquiry, often missing in new materialist accounts of the vibrancy of matter.

Second, a material politics situates agency in historical terms. When and how materials act or influence sociopolitical outcomes are never outside histories of their production, circulation, and use. Specifying when a particular material emerges, under what conditions of production, is crucial to denaturalize materials, while retaining a sharp focus on how they act, beyond the ambit of human activity. An affiliated concern here is the generation of information about materials that is used to subject the latter to surveillance and regulation.[7] How materials garner agency is therefore contingent upon their actions within regulatory regimes and their historicity. Furthermore, to propose a material politics in lieu of a politics of matter is to open up questions of asymmetry. New materialism's enchantment with matter, as critics point out, veers toward an ontological monism that puts all actants on the same plane and credits each with an equal capacity to act.[8] A material politics, on the other hand, strives to attend to the ways in which materials affect bodies differentially, where the dynamics of gender, race, and class dictate vulnerability and exposure to material effects,[9] exemplified in the case of alcohol in a plantation milieu, historically, and in current times.[10] A material politics is thus different to neo-vitalist accounts privileging the anonymous force of matter or life structuring social, political, and economic relations, for it does not foreclose an analysis and critique of these relations.

Following on from the material effects and slow violence of infrastructure fleshed out in chapter 2, I now turn to the lives of people from Sundarpur's

Adivasi community to explore how habitability in a Plantationocene is forged. Focusing on the enmeshments between people, elephants, and alcohol, illustrated by the opening vignettes, I further develop understandings of material politics on a transformed planet. Moving away from new materialist accounts of political matter and its transhistorical tendencies, I situate material politics within colonial and postcolonial histories of generating materials and the political economies of fostering and regulating their use. As the chapter shows, such histories have bearings on the expression of material agency, which bodies they affect, and how. Furthermore, by attending to materials ethnographically and ethologically, I reveal how material agency can exceed human deliberation, although the political effects of an interplay between life and materials are situational, influenced by a Plantationocene's political and economic designs. A material politics therefore questions notions of anthropogenic nature and the Anthropocene, for the altered material life of the planet proceeds through particular pathways, creating specific vulnerabilities and particular affective ecologies of harms. In conclusion, I argue that a material politics opens up avenues for thinking critically about what constitutes habitability amid a transformed world.

Labors of the Exhausted

Bogai is a temporary or *faltu* day laborer in a tea plantation close to Sundarpur. His parents had left the plantations and settled on land adjacent to the Doigurung Reserve Forest in the early 1980s. However, like many other residents of Sundarpur, Bogai's family remain closely tied to plantation life, serving as a reserve army of labor. Bogai cultivates the few *bighas* of paddy land that he owns, and although this barely suffices to feed his family of four for the entire year, cultivation remains a substantial part of their slender income.[11] The cascading effects of infrastructure, disrupting elephants' movements and their pathways of reproducing life, mean that crop raiding by elephants in Sundarpur has intensified. To protect his livelihood, Bogai guards his fields from elephants every night, sitting up in his *tongi* or shelter with his neighbors Budhu and Mangla.

Crop guarding is a labor of endurance, and it is a labor that the exhausted take up, those for whom slow violence has been a defining condition of their historical experience, first planted in Assam to work under conditions of indenture, then relegated to a need economy and barred from knocking on capitalism's glittering doors. Sleep is erratic while guarding crops, as people have to be on constant vigil. Elephants are very silent animals—to the uninitiated, surprisingly so. They often go undetected at night, leaving behind uprooted stalks and trampled fields, to the dismay of farmers the next morning. Bogai and his neighbors get worried if elephants do not show up in the first hours after nightfall, for this usually means having to stay alert until the early hours of the morning. The labor of staying up at night is acutely felt the next day. Tiredness pervades our bodies as they yearn for sleep. My privileged position as an ethnographer means that I can rest during the afternoons, but Bogai has to do intense labor in a nearby tea plantation the next day. Like others who share his predicament of managing labor and household pressures, Bogai sometimes goes to a local distillery in the evening to grab "a quarter," a small bottle of *sulāi* or distilled country liquor. "It kills the tiredness," Bogai remarks. "I am able to cope with the fatigue. The stuff helps me stay up and face the elephants."

There are many reasons for the consumption of spirits. The fatigue caused by two full shifts of work is not the sole reason for alcohol consumption, but one among others in a cultural milieu and ecology of dwelling. Bogai and Mangla remark on how drinking *sulāi* in moderate amounts helps them to confront elephants at night: "Elephants are very quick when they move through paddy fields. They can move like a bullet. You need courage when face-to-face with such large, powerful creatures. Having a drink or two gives you that courage." The inhabitants of Sundarpur often get very close to the animals when warding them off from their fields. Armed only with firecrackers and burning torches, they drive the animals out and try to guide them into the nearby Doigurung reserve. Initially I thought these confrontations to be frivolous, but soon began to respect the risk villagers take to protect their livelihoods and lives.

The Adivasi community's perceptions of elephants were laden with ambiguity, not the neat, settled taxonomy of being a revered animal that conservation NGO discourse sometimes mobilized.[12] "Elephants are gods," says Mangla, during one of our many conversations in their *tongi*, referring to the Hindu deity Ganesh. Budhu interjects, "The elephant that was Ganesh used to be a god, but not these elephants. They are mere animals." I often heard villagers say, "Dinot hole Hāti, rāti hole Bābā," which meant "Elephants during the day, gods at night." This suggests how perceptions are not the outcomes of a bounded and autonomous subject. Rather, they are forged through dwelling alongside elephants, for the animals are less of a threat during the daytime, while encounters are laden with risk at night, and being reverent means acting with caution on people's part.

According to Bogai, Mangla, and Budhu, certain elephants were increasingly bold as they became habituated to people's presence. There was a particularly "notorious crop raider" that people had named Bolldejaar or "bulldozer" (figure 3.2). The name is reflective of what people believe elephants are—a locus of ongoing activity, encapsulated by what the animals do rather than a taxonomized marker of what they are. This emphasis on doing is one way to understand how people perceive elephants as agents with the capacity to act and to respond. "He has an enormous trunk and a solid body," says Budhu. "Bolldejaar comes straight for you . . . *khajkhajkhajkhaj*," adds Mangla, imitating a mechanical sound of a machine, "and we have to run." Crowds gather to see the animal when he passes through the village during the daytime, simultaneously evoking affects of awe, fear, and anger. "Bolldejaar's method of feeding on paddy is by scaring people first," Budhu tells me. "He charges at them and then grazes in our fields, unperturbed. If people shout from afar, he comes back to chase them again." The individual is so fearless that he will not budge when people try to scare him off with firecrackers or flaming torches. "There are some people who have harmed him in the past," Budhu adds, "and I have noticed him targeting particular villagers."

Encounters between elephants and people can even be fatal. Paddy fields are slippery and uneven, making it very difficult to run through them in the dark. Unlike Budhu, Mangla, and the other villagers of Sundarpur, my body is out of tune with the landscape. I run a short distance, slip, and fall. Budhu counterpoises my ineptitude with his competence: "You are from a place with electricity. We on the other hand have dealt with elephants for ages. We don't fall, even when it is dark and the ground is uneven." Yet larger amounts of alcohol can induce physiological effects, including exaggerated and overcompensated movements of the body, which alter this skillful corporeal attunement with the nocturnal landscape. By affecting the human body, alcohol can lead to impaired judgment, for in such instances judgment is a bodily craft enacted and performed through immersion in the landscape rather than a technology of practice dependent on vision. During the course of my fieldwork, a farmer under the influence of alcohol was unable to escape in time. A charging elephant fatally trampled him.

Just as one needs to see fatigue as one among other reasons for alcohol consumption, one needs to go beyond attributing causality to the immediate

3.2   Bolldejaar amid other elephants of the Sundarpur herd. The individual, second from right, was in *musth* at the time, a condition in which testosterone levels rise that results in highly aggressive behavior. Photo: Amarjit Lahkar.

material effects of alcohol. In Assam's plantations, the intake of alcohol is underscored by cultural practices and histories of indenture and work-time discipline,[13] as well as structural inequalities that keep people in a persistent state of underdevelopment. Throughout India, elephant-related human mortality is of the rural poor rather than the urban middle classes and elites. The impacts of fatal events run deep, inflicting ruination upon the ex–tea garden worker community who have limited land and support networks.

Kanu, a young man in his midtwenties whom I befriended in Sundarpur, lost both his father and brother-in-law to elephant-related incidents. His family's mud or *kucca* house was situated right beside a track that elephants created and used when entering the village. Only sixteen when an elephant trampled his father while guarding their fields, Kanu dropped out of school and took up work as a daily laborer in a nearby sand-collection depot. Not only was Kanu's education abruptly ended, but his future prospects for a better job were foreclosed. A couple of years before I met Kanu, his brother-in-law, drunk on country liquor, picked a quarrel with him over the purchase of kerosene. The man rushed off alone in the dark to buy kerosene from a store on the outskirts of the village. A little while later, news reached Kanu that he had a fatal encounter with elephants en route. The entire burden of looking after the family, including his widowed sister, now fell on Kanu. To repay debts incurred by his brother-in-law, Kanu sold two and a half *bighas* of land he had inherited from his father to a nearby tea plantation owner, who converted the land to tea.

Such events diminished the family's already-limited means of subsistence. At the same time, they contributed to the debt-driven selling of land that has continually marked the lives of many among the Adivasi community in Assam's plantations, aggravating the simple reproduction squeeze the family was undergoing. Kanu's mother narrates their predicament: "With my son-in-law and husband gone, Kanu has to work in the depot to keep us afloat. There is no one to cultivate the few *bighas* of land we have left." Sharecropping, she remarks, has become unfeasible, as there are no men left in the family to guard their fields. "Even if we give it out for sharecropping, Bābā comes and takes it all," she says. Her use of the reverential term *Bābā* for elephants is a sign of despair, just as it is an indication of respect rather than anger in the face of adversity. Nowhere in her language is the element of blame, and this is an important reason why elephants are able to persist in Assam's landscape in spite of the degradation of life encounters with the animals can generate.

Elephants are thus not mere presences in a Plantationocene landscape, but become part of the milieu in which people dwell. Crop guarding and the slow violence inflicted upon people influence the drinkscape or the wider landscape of alcohol consumption in Sundarpur, although other factors, including leisure, social rites, and ceremonies, are equally important. Recurrent elephant presence and crop raiding make this community of ex–tea plantation workers strive hard to protect what is their most important source of livelihood. Conducted for almost four months of the year, crop guarding involves continual risk taking and prolonged periods of poor sleep. The intensive physical labor that many workers perform the following day generates exhaustion and morbidity. It is within these highly uneven structural conditions that one needs to read the fatal agency of materials. Alcohol is affective, enabling people to brave elephants at night and to cope with bodily fatigue. At the same time, it furthers vulnerability and brings about a slow degradation in the ability to reproduce life. An ethnography of crop guarding therefore enables us to see how drinkscapes are not the outcome of actions by autonomous selves but constituted through a wider ecology of relations. At the same time, they are influenced by colonial history and postcolonial imperatives of generating and regulating materials.

Materials of a Plantationocene

The vignette of elephants breaking into a distillery in Sundarpur gives us a foretaste of another trajectory through which the material life unfolds: the actions of alcohol as it works through elephant bodies. Both the incident of house damage and the poster, startling as they are, provoke a shift from viewing alcohol as a coping mechanism to being an active agent that binds people and elephants in unforeseen, if not novel, ways. The event prompts one to go beyond humanist accounts and to attend to other pathways that forge a landscape and politics of inhabitation. Crucial in this regard are the affordances of alcohol, that is, the qualities of the material that render it apt for the purposes of a subject,[14] in this case the elephant, with its acute faculty of smell and particular proclivities of taste.

Sulāi, the most commonly consumed local spirit, is a clear, colorless alcohol brewed from molasses or, occasionally, rice.[15] Molasses, usually unrefined treacle obtained at low prices, is first fermented in a large vessel under anaerobic conditions. Distillation then commences by heating the molasses in a cylindrical vessel or pot over a fire. A rectified spirit that does not undergo multiple distillations, *sulāi* has a high content of alcohol, giving a person what Budhu calls a *jhatka*, an instant kick. The strong, pungent odor emanating from the distillation process is distinctive and carries a long way. The act of brewing for human consumption is potentially open to elephants as well, given the role olfaction and gustation play in their proboscidean lives. Elephants rely strongly on their sense of smell, particularly when foraging. The large cranial sinuses elephants develop upon maturity make them among the most macrosmatic mammals in the world. Their olfactory discrimination skills surpass those of people, and the animals discern differences between structurally similar odorants, a process learned quickly and retained through their long-term memory. Olfaction and taste are closely linked. Elephants have a sweet tooth and relish saccharides.[16] This makes fermenting molasses particularly attractive to them. Their strong, far-reaching odor affords easy detection through proboscidean sensibilities. The qualities of *sulāi*, sensed and realized through the olfactory and gustatory proclivities of elephants, render distilleries susceptible to

3.3 Trenches crisscross the village, dug to safeguard homes from elephant intrusion. Photo by the author.

elephant incursions. When coupled with a high capacity for social learning and a powerful ability to remember effects and sources of food, the raiding of distilleries could become part of the skills elephants acquire when inhabiting landscapes of a Plantationocene.

The local political economy of alcohol is intricately enmeshed with modes of dwelling alongside elephants. Budhu sells *sulāi* at home in order to beef up his family income, in part spurred by the fact that losing a substantial proportion of crops to elephants each year makes it difficult to make ends meet. The substance is bought in bulk from a distillery at the outskirts of the village, which he then sells in used commercial liquor bottles in measures of a "half" and a "quarter." As brewing without an excise permit is illegal, villagers are cautious about what they disclose and to whom they sell alcohol. Elephant are a concern, as events in which distilleries or unlicensed shops are broken into spark Excise Department raids. Budhu stores alcohol in a small room behind his house as a precaution, not just for alcohol to go undetected but for his family to be safe lest elephants break in. Many people in Sundarpur, including Kanu, Mangla, and Bogai, have dug trenches around the peripheries of their homes as a protection from elephants (figure 3.3). The distillery where Budhu purchases *sulāi* conducts the process of fermentation and distillation in a small *kucca* shed at the edge of their garden, a fair distance from the owner's house. "Brewing *sulāi* in the house is a recipe for trouble," the owner remarks. "Elephants get attracted to the scent and will break in."

The illicit status of *sulāi* stems from a colonial history of seeking to profit from alcohol manufacture and consumption. In the early days of colonial administration in Assam, an excise tax or *abkaree* on the sale of liquor brewed by indigenous communities was introduced. *Abkaree* was a means of generating revenue, although the colonial administration rationalized its introduction on the grounds of moral authority. Intoxication, the government claimed, "had become prevalent among many lower orders of people owing to the inconsiderable price at which it was sold."[17] The introduction of a tax would therefore curb consumption. The colonial government witnessed losses in revenue due to irregularities, which led to the passing of an act—Act XXI of 1856—making it obligatory for the police to carry out excise duties. In the 1870s, further rules to govern and profit from brewing were put in place. *Sulāi* or country spirits could only be manufactured by a licensed, private distillery. These had to operate within designated premises, supply no more than specified quantities of alcohol, and pay a duty before removing an article.[18]

The material itself was subjected to scrutiny and regulation. Prior to retail, a district-level excise establishment, headed by a *daroga* or police officer, tested the manufactured spirit with a hydrometer to ensure that the ethanol content did not exceed prescribed limits. Manufacture and retail were kept under constant surveillance. Daily accounts of quantities produced and sold were kept; stills had to be open at all times for inspection; and excise duties had to be paid without fail.[19] Contemporary patterns of state governance of spirit production and retail are a living inheritance of these earlier logics of rule. By regulating materials, the state becomes an important actor in this assemblage. The state also alters the ontology of materials in that *sulāi* gains the status of being licit or illicit, depending upon where it is manufactured and by whom. The brewing of spirits outside state purview renders it liable for seizure and prosecution of the distiller.

Tea plantation worker communities are, and have long been, the primary consumers of *sulāi* in Assam. Reported rates of alcoholism in the community are high, as are incidents of alcohol-related abuse and domestic violence.[20] Yet these conditions are neither ahistorical nor apolitical. The Santhal, Munda, and other Adivasi communities brought to indenture in Assam's plantations traditionally drank *handia* and *pachwai* or other indigenous rice beers, the brew being an integral part of their cultural life. Colonial accounts suggest that these communities initially preferred home-brewed beers to distilled spirits like *sulāi* and, still today, it is the former that is consumed during traditional ceremonies. In the 1870s, as plantations expanded, excise revenue from alcohol grew at an unprecedented rate. Yet the colonial administration consistently maintained that revenue from the sale of liquor was meager.[21] The relatively high consumption of *pachwai*, rather than government-controlled country spirits, was viewed as the major barrier in generating revenue. The colonial administration, however, was reluctant to make brewing rice beers illegal, as it was a customary practice among many tribal and indigenous communities of Assam. Doing so would create an unwanted and "vexatious" issue for the administration. Rather, what the colonial administration attempted to do was to make plantation workers switch from their preferred rice beer to country spirits or, more aptly, "from untaxed liquor to taxed liquor." This was partly achieved by opening "grog shops" near plantations and by banning the commercial sale of *pachwai*.[22]

The rapid expansion of plantations at the time also brought about changes in work regimes, making the labor process more intense, with harsher, longer contracts. This resulted in drink following the rhythms of work rather than those of tradition and culture. There was a shift in what one drank: people began to consume the readily available *sulāi* rather than traditional rice beers. There was also an alteration in when one drank: from rituals and ceremonies to the day off work.[23] Colonial capital, therefore, profited from tea workers not once but twice, first as living labor producing cheap commodities, then as vulnerable bodies that consumed cheapened commodities. In other words, there was a necropolitical economy that went hand in hand with the biopolitics of labor in Assam's plantations, one that sought to generate surplus value through the disposability and debasement of human life.[24] To allude to alcoholism outside of these histories is to disavow a necropolitics that is endemic, sapping a population's strength and constraining its ability to live.

A Plantationocene's necropolitics profiting from the debasement of Adivasi lives is not a thing of the past but continues to seep into the present. This becomes even more acute when one turns to numerous incidents of methyl alcohol poisoning that have marked Assam's plantations. Profiteers, to meet demand and generate even higher gains, sometimes use the cheaper but life-threatening methanol when preparing spirits. This is a contraband activity punishable by law, but its profit motive stems from a reasoning that takes plantation workers' lives as expendable. In 2019, 157 people, mainly from the Adivasi community, died of methyl alcohol poisoning in the Golaghat landscape where Sundarpur is situated.[25] A human tragedy, this painful event is but one of a spate of similar incidents that happened in Golaghat at the time. "While tea garden executives and state bureaucrats put down these frequent deaths to 'lack of awareness,'" writes the journalist Arunabh Saikia, "interviews with garden workers, activists and officials point towards a more systemic web of apathy coupled with administrative inertia and corruption."[26] The state Excise Department claimed that regulating the sale of methanol was not within its remit and stated that it could not regulate stills because it was understaffed. Others drew attention to the fact that in order to expedite the fermentation process, distillers introduced urea, a fertilizer readily available on plantations, and even batteries into *sulāi*. Plantation owners were symptomatically silent about the conditions of toil that rendered alcohol consumption endemic, deflecting the issue by asking whether Saikia had "seen the conditions in slums in Delhi and Mumbai."[27]

Sulāi, one could contend, is a material of a Plantationocene. Its proliferation is closely tied to a racial and colonial economy that aims to accrue surplus value through the expenditure of human life. *Sulāi*'s effects permeate beyond people's bodies to the wider ecology of a plantation landscape, although the material's agency is inexorably linked to the colonial and postcolonial regulation of alcohol. The rise of distilleries has altered the process of alcohol manufacture when compared to traditional, precolonial forms of brewing. Molasses are used instead of rice, and the quantity of alcohol brewed is far greater than that for home consumption. Elephants' proclivity for saccharides and the odor emanating from large-scale brewing makes distilleries far more detectable, and therefore susceptible, to elephant incursions. This situated agency of alcohol is expressed in a number of reports: they discuss how elephants are "attracted" by country liquor and are "drawn" in by its pungent smell.[28] That alcohol has agency in drawing and attracting elephants is finding further support from ecological studies in tea plantation landscapes. One such study in eastern Bengal, neighboring Assam, indicates that elephant incursions into villages are high when alcohol production is prevalent.[29] This suggests that incidents of elephants breaking into distilleries are not merely one-off events but a patterned activity that arises given elephants' abilities to learn, remember, and cultivate particular habits.

I did not encounter intoxicated elephants during the course of my fieldwork, although there were incidents where houses storing alcohol had been broken into. My informants mention what sometimes happens if elephants consume large quantities of fermented molasses. "They move a little oddly," says Bogai, "and on one occasion an elephant was sleeping in the middle of a field." Reports from elsewhere are more dramatic. They describe incidents of elephants falling "asleep hither and thither, throwing life completely haywire" and, after purported intoxication, running amok, damaging rows of houses, injuring or even killing people.[30] Budhu says that particular individuals develop proclivities for the brew: "Bolldejaar opportunistically breaks houses, but I have not observed him specifically target those that store *sulāi*. He primarily raids fields. However, another older animal that used to be around here a few years ago was particularly troublesome. A number of incidents involving him have made people wary about storing liquor." For that particular elephant, alcohol had become a *nisā*, an addiction. While not directly corroborated, news reports from the locality mention that a fifty-year-old elephant had become "an addict . . . and often strayed into human habitat, especially tea estate labour colonies, in search of liquor." The individual was later severely injured due to fighting with another elephant and had to be tranquilized for treatment by the Forest Department.[31]

Relations between elephants and alcohol are thus affective. They are also eventful, sparking situations that go beyond the expected run of play. Through the affective relations between alcohol and elephants, distilleries become sites of frictions, completely unanticipated in the latter's inaugural assembly. Public outcry ensues once house damage follows events of elephants breaking into distilleries. This in turn brings units, deemed illicit by the state, within the purview of the Excise Department, sparking raids and eviction drives.[32] At times, it is the intra-actions between elephants and alcohol, rather than a concerted effort to curtail bootlegging, that mobilizes the state into action. Yet it would be fallacious to posit the agency of an elephant-alcohol-distillery assemblage outside colonial and postcolonial histories. Affective relations between elephants and alcohol spark micropolitical events precisely because the production of *sulāi* is inexorably linked to the regulation of materials, just as it is steeped in a plantation economy of profiting from vulnerable Adivasi communities. To further elucidate a material politics of a Plantationocene, I now turn to the relations between elephants and alcohol, or the affective ecologies that exceed human designs.

Affective Ecologies

If elephants breaking into distilleries and houses with stored liquor is a consistently observed pattern in a plantation landscape,[33] how might one understand these forays from the elephants' perspective? This is a difficult proposition. Are elephant worlds ever knowable, given they are so different from ours? Is drinking not an anthropomorphic account of elephant behavior, couching their activities in human terms? My aim is not to provide a conclusive answer, but to stay with these difficulties and to see where they might lead us. Being attentive to elephant worlds, I argue, opens up other avenues for understanding a Plantationocene's material life.

Intoxication in elephants has been a matter that has generated sustained interest among ethologists and physiologists. Much of this stems from lore that African elephants travel long distances to feed on fallen marula fruit, and durian in the case of Asian elephants, drawn by their ethyl alcohol content.[34] Such a practice can become integral to the life histories of certain herds and individuals that not only gain a tacit knowledge of a landscape and its fruiting phenology, but acquire particular tastes and cultivate certain habits. In a different but somewhat analogous vein, elephants in Golaghat developed novel behaviors to seek out sugarcane, the plant from which molasses used in *sulāi* is prepared. Elephants in the Nambor forest, south of Sundarpur, had learned to stop trucks loaded with sugarcane and only let them pass once a toll consisting of sugarcane stalks was dished out.[35] The elephants had initially taken to feeding on sugarcane that had fallen from trucks, but over time became more bold, stopping vehicles to access cane.[36]

This phenomenon is worth mentioning briefly, as it is an exemplar of how postcolonial fauna arise in a Plantationocene. Based on oral histories, the naturalist Anwaruddin Choudhury suggests that elephants stopping vehicles for sugarcane came into vogue in the 1970s,[37] when cultivation of the plant shot up in Golaghat. Rich rural peasants had mobilized people to start growing sugarcane in the late 1960s, partly by reclaiming land that had been enclosed into forest reserves, as well as by forcibly "encroaching" on surplus, uncultivated land held by tea plantations.[38] As sugarcane production grew, sugar mills increased in the district and, with them, the frequency of vehicles transporting cane. The first observed incident of elephants stopping trucks goes back to March 1982, when a forest officer saw a herd of eighteen elephants pulling cane out of a lorry before retreating into the Nambor forest.[39] By 1990, the phenomenon became a tourist attraction, and numerous stalls selling bananas opened in the locality, further fueling the rise of this behavior in the population.[40]

Returning to the example of marula and elephants' proclivity for saccharides, there is video footage that shows the animals being inebriated after the consumption of fermenting fruit, although the edits add a layer of anthropomorphism by adding music to accentuate drunkenness.[41] Biologists have argued that the alcohol content produced through these other-than-human assemblages is not sufficient to lead to intoxication in a large-bodied animal like the elephant. That alcohol can be produced under anaerobic conditions within elephants' digestive systems is refuted by the relatively quick gut passage times of the animal. Tales of drunken elephants, certain biologists therefore argue, result "from humanizing elephant behaviour."[42] More recently, there have been criticisms of these interpretations for drawing conclusions by extrapolating from human physiology. Elephants in fact lack genes that accelerate ethanol metabolism and therefore could get inebriated with relatively low quantities of alcohol. The dismissal of inebriation in elephants, long observed by indigenous communities, as anthropomorphism is itself plagued by biologists "anthropomorphizing animal physiology."[43]

The bindings of elephants and alcohol in Assam, on the other hand, have a different affective ecology. *Sulāi* produced within the fraught economies of a Plantationocene has very different qualities than fermenting fruit in the wild. People control brewing and, therefore, generate highly anaerobic conditions. The alcohol content of fermenting molasses, prior to distillation into an even stronger colorless spirit, is far greater than what the animals would consume in the wild. What matters, therefore, are not the properties of a substance, but its qualities, that is, the attributes of materials as they flow between bodies and how they are produced in relation to surroundings. Qualities are sensed not only by people but through elephants' propensities as well. The animals like the taste of alcohol and, as the vignette of the animals stopping trucks to access sugarcane indicates, can adopt new habits to get preferred food.

My attempts to apprehend this metabolic and affective ecology take a different turn after coming across two experiments on the physiological effects of alcohol on captive elephants conducted by the ethologist Ronald Siegel and his colleagues.[44] Siegel's first experiment had to do with the gustatory proclivity of elephants. The question he posed is whether elephants will drink alcohol even if they are not hungry. Alcohol, in strengths varying from 0 to 50 percent ethanol solution, was provided to three Asian elephants raised in captivity. All three individuals preferred a solution of 7 percent, equivalent to the alcohol content of a strong ale. They refused to drink anything stronger than 10 percent ethyl alcohol solution. The animals appeared inebriated, and the behaviors they displayed hinged on the dramatic. They began growling, a vocalization associated with arousal, and flapped their ears more than usual in order to regulate body heat. The elephants responded poorly to the commands of their handler, and one individual even slipped and fell.[45] These physiological effects mirror media reports of wild elephants intoxicated after drinking *sulāi* or consuming fermented molasses.

Siegel's second experiment had to do with the conditions under which elephants might be drawn to alcohol. Do elephants, Siegel asked, seek intoxication under the stress of competition for food in the wild? To answer this question, Siegel and his colleagues looked at a herd of seven African elephants that ranged freely in a spacious California game park. The herd had close bonds and formed a tight-knit group where pushing, shoving, and aggressive vocalizations were almost nonexistent. Alcohol, provided to the elephants in drums at a designated place, generated affects that were a reversal of their normal behavior. Physical contact decreased, and the animals were unable to regroup. The dominant bull and cow displayed greater aggression toward other herd members as well as the observing ethologists. Submissive individuals became meek, avoiding physical encounters. Alcohol consumption in fact increased in those situations where Siegel and his colleagues, to create a proxy for environmental stress, confined the elephants to a smaller, one-hectare area of the park they shared with other animals. Intake of alcohol returned to normal levels once the elephants' range was enlarged to its earlier size and animals like rhinos that they found bothersome moved out. Continuous exposure to alcohol was avoided, lest it would create dependency. However, months later when a construction crew was working in the park, the elephants congregated in the same area where alcohol was once available. Although undertaken in captivity, which produces its own set of stresses, Siegel's experiments unsettle deterministic explanations of elephants' alcohol-seeking behavior. His contention is that in the game park, elephants seem to seek periodic intoxication in order to reduce discomfort. "In the wild, stressed from poaching and deforestation, perhaps they accept intoxication for the same reason."[46]

It is difficult to prove from my ethnographic observations whether elephants enter the villages of tea worker communities solely in search of alcohol or whether finding liquor is the incidental outcome of breaking into houses for food. Similarly, Siegel's experiments are the products of situated practices; concentrating animals in a game park is very different to the fissured milieus elephants inhabit in Asia and Africa. The purpose here is not to pinpoint alcohol as the sole agent drawing elephants into settlements or to extrapolate from a situated experiment. Rather, it is to open up thinking about the potentialities of alcohol and to draw attention to fraught modes of living in a postcolonial milieu. The elephants in Sundarpur are under considerable stress. They too are subject to the slow violence of a Plantationocene, fleshed out in chapter 2 and encapsulated by Rabidas's evocative statement that elephants have "gone mad." Besides the despoiled habitus brought about by the installation of infrastructure and by mining, frictions between people and elephants happen on a quotidian basis. During the time of my continuous stay in Sundarpur, there were 179 incidents of crop and house damage by elephants in the vicinity.[47] The Forest Department, which regularly intervenes to drive animals out of people's fields and into the Doigurung reserve, describes the situation as a "land war" where "even bullets" fail "to deter . . . elephants [from] destroying houses, crops and killing people in search of food."[48]

In this landscape, duress is affective, permeating and materializing in elephants' bodies and ethologies. The animals are nervous when they enter villages, maintaining a compact grouping to keep calves secure. The herd of seventy to eighty animals often fragments into smaller groups when confronted by farmers at night. Regrouping proves difficult, sometimes occurring days later. This is particularly stressful for an animal that forms closely knit bonds and has a herd structure based on kinship. It is not unusual for us to hear elephants rumbling and trumpeting at night, trying to make contact with one another as family groups become dispersed. Furthermore, many of the animals in the herd appear emaciated, suggesting a corporealization of stress. Subadults in the herd, having grown up in this riven milieu, are bold, unafraid to charge people.

Bolldejaar, the *mukhna* that had gained a reputation for attacking people when provoked, bore bodily scars of retributive action by people. Budhu's descriptions of how Bolldejaar charged, sometimes targeting particular villagers, could typify what ethologists call "retaliatory cunning," that is, calculated and directed attacks on people who have harmed him in the past.[49] In contrast, elephants can also deliberately avoid hurting people. As the ethologist Cynthia Moss describes in the context of a herd of African elephants she was studying for years, the elephants "went out of their way to avoid hurting a person" even when they had "every opportunity to injure or kill" people, and even when "they had every provocation."[50] Furthermore, elephants read human bodies and their affects. "Nowadays, Bolldejaar only leaves when the Forest Department personnel come with their firearms," Budhu tells me, "making the activity of guarding our crops doubly difficult." His statement indicates that Bolldejaar might be distinguishing between villagers and Forest Department personnel, which is highly plausible given studies on African elephants suggesting that the animals distinguish between ethnic communities based on their garment color.[51] The lifeworlds of elephants thus enable us to grasp how a Plantationocene is an affective condition, mediated by materials and moods of both its human and other-than-human denizens.

This condition prompts one to speculate: to ask whether there is a quest for intoxication in elephants and what staying with this thought might mean. Just as one cannot pinpoint alcohol as the sole cause for breaking into distilleries, one cannot rule out the possibility that intoxication is one among other reasons elephants do so. Evoking Frantz Fanon, certain ethologists describe the situation of "the native elephant" as "a nervous condition."[52] We might therefore ask whether the Sundarpur elephants, whose life histories are littered with violent interactions with people, an extractive economy, and the state, seek alcohol as a sedative. One cannot provide a definite answer, but it is a productive speculation. What is clear is that a Plantationocene present gives rise to affects that generate stress and duress, for both elephants and people. These are affects that work through the temporality of delayed degradation. They shore up bodies historically marked out for wearing out, percolating through and sedimenting in them. Alcohol may be an ameliorative, but it also may be a source of proboscidean joy, reflected in Budhu's comment that one animal had become "an addict." Here, there are divergences of other-than-human worlds from those that are human, suggesting that necropolitics is not a totality, and that lives— whether those of people or animals—are not singularly those of abjection.

Material Politics in a Plantationocene

Bindings between people, elephants, and alcohol reveal the material life of a Plantationocene. It is one where Adivasi communities, long immiserated by plantation logics, struggle to make do amid a simple reproduction squeeze and exposed to the cascading repercussions infrastructures have on the landscape's sentient topography. A Plantationocene's material life is also one where elephants' habitus is altered by extractive economies, a situation with which they cope and respond by inventing their own affects. *Sulāi*, as a material of a Plantationocene, percolates through both human and other-than-human bodies, not in a passive manner but as an agent drawing people, elephants, and the state together in ways exceeding human designs. Its volatile choreography troubles routine explanations of who acts in a Plantationocene present and what aggravates its persisting asymmetries.

Affective compositions between different bodies as they respond to slow violence point to a "material politics" of a Plantationocene rather than the politics of matter in the Anthropocene.[53] The analysis here provides correctives to some of the issues with neovitalist accounts of agency,[54] particularly the latter's transhistorical accounts of materials, its tendencies to gravitate toward an ontological monism at the expense of situated knowledges, and often being light on ethnography, thus not fully attentive to the thickness of situations that produce material effects and the situated knowledges that ventriloquize them. This account's departure from new materialism starts with its emphasis on the qualities of materials rather than the properties of matter. An ethnographic account of the Sundarpur landscape reveals how the qualities of *sulāi* do not reside within things but are continually produced as alcohol differently affects the bodies of plantation labor, the wider Adivasi community, and those of proboscideans. *Sulāi* can invoke affects of courage, just as it generates highly gendered conditions of harm. Qualities of materials are therefore social: they are never cleaved from the incessant traffic of life as beings and entities come into composition, work upon one another, and disentangle. An endeavor to understand qualities is therefore ethnographic and nomadic. In contrast, to attribute qualities to properties is to cleave materials from the history and social situations of their production, generation, and use.

Attention to the material life of a Plantationocene allows us to think critically about the political agency of materials. *Sulāi*, I have argued, is a material of a Plantationocene. Histories of its production reveal how certain materials were generated to profit from uprooted and planted bodies. Coercive and intensified conditions of work and the colonial administration's greed for revenue altered traditional drinkscapes, inducing a shift from preferences for home-brewed beers to commercial country spirits. Alcohol consumption unfolded along the axis of work and leisure rather than being grounded in ceremonies and traditional rites. In the present-day Sundarpur landscape, alcohol consumption is also an activity of the exhausted, of those bodies whose historical experience has been one of unrelenting exposure to slow violence. Paddy cultivation becomes a much more intense, prolonged, but also uncertain activity. Here alcohol consumption is calibrated with the rhythms of added labor that the exhausted perform. These histories and situations strike at the heart of the ontological monism that flattens differences between bodies, disavowing how materials act differentially, and mark out and unevenly expose certain communities to harm. A material politics thus fosters a critique of uneven political, economic, and social relations rather than forecloses them.

The colonial regulation of materials in legal and statutory terms, and the postcolonial inheritance of these logics, alters the ontological status of alcohol as a material. Alcohol becomes either licit or illicit, depending on whether one has the necessary excise permits to produce *sulāi* or not. Elephant incursions into distilleries and homes retailing spirits become political matters in part because of this illicit status. The state, as a body regulating alcohol, intervenes in order to curb bootlegging. At the same time, the commercialization of alcohol and its mass production for a plantation workforce underpins the detectability of the material by elephants. It is therefore apolitical and ahistorical to attribute the rise of materials like *sulāi*, and the affective ecologies it spawns, to a blanket, undifferentiated agency of *anthropos* or to an independent force of matter. The spirit proliferates as plantation logics of profiting from immobilized workers take hold. The expression of material agency is therefore never outside a colonial, necropolitical economy,[55] one that is not a feature of the past but is continually renewed in a Plantationocene present, profiting from a debasement of Adivasi lives. However, one cannot cast such lives as simply those of abjection. Alcohol consumption can be a line of flight, one of entering other terrains, however momentary or passing its ameliorative potential might be. In a similar vein, it is important to bear in mind that elephants drinking alcohol can be a source of proboscidean joy, a reflection of their own ways of being and doing in a Plantationocene present.

This is not to say that the force and affects generated by materials do not matter. They do, but what is important is the ways in which a micropolitics of materials dovetails with a macropolitics of dispossessing people. Micropercepts of alcohol, such as the strong, pungent odor of *sulāi* and its detectability by a highly macrosmatic creature like the elephant are crucial to understanding how frictions between people, elephants, and the state are generated. At the same time, the proboscidean desire for the sedative affects of alcohol is one, speculative, means of understanding how the animals might themselves respond to the slow violence that despoils their habitus. These micropolitical dimensions of a Plantationocene encapsulate relations between materials and other-than-humans in excess of human assembly. They are too easily evacuated from much political ecological and multispecies analysis, although such micropercepts are crucial to understanding who or what forges social outcomes and political agency. Yet they must be read in light of the immense burdens dwelling alongside elephants poses for the rural poor. As witnessed in the predicaments of Kanu and his family, day-to-day life is ruptured by elephant presence, while the effects of fatal encounters run deep, bringing ruination to those adversely affected.

An affective ecology of a Plantationocene, in contrast to the grand narratives of the Anthropocene, also allows us to apprehend what a riven milieu might be like for elephants themselves, with and in excess of the grain of human designs. Elephants show an acute awareness of their surroundings, corporealizing stress and responding to slow violence in their own proboscidean ways. They are, I argue, observant participants of the world, and of landscapes marked by the slow degradation of habitat and habitability. The behaviors exhibited by animals such as Bolldejaar are but one example. The ways in which the *mukhna* retaliates when villagers try to drive him out of paddy fields, but leaves in haste when Forest Department personnel carrying firearms arrive, shows how proboscidean bodies learn and respond to a milieu marked by relentless friction. Like Sonitpur's SP04 herd, the animals in Sundarpur too are postcolonial fauna. They are elephants of a Plantationocene.

A material politics therefore provides further inroads into apprehending the ecologies of a Plantationocene. It draws attention to persistent inequalities and states of underdevelopment that mark a Plantationocene's present. It also reveals an ongoing necropolitics, endemic to this present, that continually debases human life, albeit not in a totalizing manner. Within this milieu, intoxication is not a solution, but a means of making life endurable. Yet it is amid such exhaustion and evisceration that both elephants and people make worlds and invent lines of escape. A material politics reveals how both attempt to salve the effects of slow violence and carve out possibilities of habitation against the grain of depletion.

4

Accumulation by Plantation

Plots of tea were cropping up everywhere in Sundarpur. Home gardens were cleared, drains dug, and saplings planted. Even small plots of paddy land were fenced, left to lie fallow for a while, before being converted into tea. "People are planting tea, selling their land, and again planting tea," says Santosh, who had started a small plot of his own. "Paddy cultivation is on the decline. Now our family still cultivates rice, and a bunch of others as well, but not like before. Most people are now trying to grow tea. Tea cultivation began when the ULFA arose," he adds, referring to a secessionist militancy group that emerged in the wake of the Assam Movement in the 1980s, which once held significant sway in social and political matters of the state.

Assam was in the midst of a small tea grower revolution: the cultivation of tea by the peasantry at smaller scales than that of colonial estate plantations (figure 4.1). The rapid rise of small tea estates was preceded by rampant deforestation in the wider landscape surrounding Sundarpur in the 1990s, soon followed by the virulent spread of *Mikania*, a nonnative climbing vine. "Now where will the elephants feed?" Santosh asks a second time, first when referring to the travails of infrastructure, then in light of the changes in the landscape's vegetal ecology. Already intense frictions between people and elephants were further aggravated by such changes, intensifying the animals' dependence on paddy. The growth of small tea estates in part proceeded through violent land grabs that dispossessed the Adivasi community even further.

Plants, and their relations with people and other denizens of a landscape, provide a different opening for understanding how worlds are forged in a Plantationocene. They are an inherent part of the simplified ecologies that mark plantations, notorious for their cultivation of a dearth of biological difference irrespective of their scale and size.[1] The work performed by plants, coupled with the sanction of forced and coerced labor, is a crucial aspect of the production of a Plantationocene's cheap commodities, one that proceeds by keeping people fixed or "planted" in a locale while erasing their own senses of place.[2] This process is complemented by the biotic circulations that plantations set in motion, notably those of nonnative plants like *Mikania*, which exceed the enclaves of plantations and forge ruinous ecologies in a plantation's outside. Plants become mediators of elephants' geographies; what they afford or furnish for human subjects has ramifications for animal life often in excess of human desire and assembly.

Plants are beginning to garner significant attention in the social sciences, particularly with the interdisciplinary fascination with questions of nature and society invigorated by scholarship on the Anthropocene. Scholars draw attention to the ways in which plants lie at the heart of signature challenges of the Anthropocene, including questions of food security, invasive species, and biodiversity conservation.[3] Steeped in a posthumanist anthropology, others even propose "Planthropos" rather than *anthropos* as a guiding figure for crafting forms of livability on an altered planet, where plants and humans might form a collective being—a holobiont—that attests the interdependency of plants and people.[4] Inspired by neovitalist accounts of nonhuman agency, scholars foreground the vegetal agency of plants and the bearings they have on the social and spatial organization of human activity over varying durations and scales.[5] Vegetal economies—the ways in which "plantiness" or the vegetal properties of plants and economic practices intersect—are beginning to open up productive avenues for thinking about the role of plants in forging the ambit of accumulation,[6] capitalist or

4.1   A typical small tea garden in Golaghat. Erstwhile home gardens are rapidly being replaced by tea. Photo by the author.

otherwise. Of particular importance is the concept of "vegetal work" and the ways in which plants enliven economic and social possibilities.[7] Others foreground vegetal politics, documenting "collaborative and conflictual relations between humans, plants and others," and even deploy ways of plant being as a model for political action.[8] Collaborative relations with plants, as Dolly Kikon and Dixita Deka show, can entail forms of adaptability and curiosity on the part of people, often against the grain of large-scale development models.[9] Plants, in turn, mediate encounters, staging relations between denizens of landscape.[10]

In this chapter, I wish to draw these burgeoning fields of vegetal geography and plant anthropology into closer conversation with critical scholarship on the Plantationocene.[11] A Plantationocene is a condition where both people and plants bring one another into being, albeit in ways that can be highly exploitative.[12] Plantations bind plants and people in projects of coercive cobecoming. They are sites where relations between people and plants are staged in ways that are instrumental, extractive, and generally violent. A Plantationocene is also a condition where plants become hypermobile, moved around the world unintentionally or by a plantation regime that aims to deploy life to not just govern but generate value from life.[13] There is a distinct vegetal ecology to the expansion of tea in the Sundarpur landscape, one that intersects with violent land grabs, deforestation, and the encroachment of forest and revenue land in the aftermath of political and secessionist violence that marked Assam in the 1980s and early 1990s. I refer to this process as accumulation by plantation. It is a form of accumulation by dispossession or the generation of capital through extralegal and extraeconomic means, often involving expulsions, displacement, and the stripping of public assets,[14] but also underscored by a range of other forces and ecological conditions that foster the expansion of plantations.

In the sections that follow, I first attend to questions of vegetal agency. Tracking the political ecologies forged by *Mikania*, a climbing vine put into circulation by plantations, I argue that vegetal agency is expressed under certain historical circumstances. Specific conditions lead to *Mikania* exceeding a plantation's order and colonizing its outside: stymying relations that do not form part of a plantation's interiority and resulting in a depletion of the landscape's livability. The chapter then turns to vegetal economies, focusing on the rise of the small tea estate sector. It shows how vegetal attributes of the tea plant and violent histories of deforestation and dispossession intersect in transforming the Sundarpur landscape into a Plantationocene. The third section of the chapter presents an expansive vegetal politics. Chiming with the recent work of Elizabeth Oriel and colleagues,[15] it examines the ways in which plants mediate relations between people and elephants, and how elephants are enrolled into the dynamics of converting land to tea. These strands are tied together to read a Plantationocene through vegetal life, while bringing the latter into dialogue with a critical political economy in order to flesh out the dynamics of accumulation by plantation.

Vegetal Agency

"Mekanic Lota clamps down on everything," says Budhu, pointing to sheets of *Mikania micrantha* that cloak the Lower Doigurung Reserve Forest bordering Sundarpur (figure 4.2). "All other vegetation is completely suppressed with no chance of coming up," he tells me, as we stare at the verdant climber that has virtually taken over what remains of the forest. "It was not that excessive before, but since the mid-1990s, as trees were felled, the forest has been literally covered by *Mekanic.*" The presence of the vine has had effects on simple reproduction for the Adivasi community. "If felling of trees reduced firewood, the spread of *Mekanic* means we do not even

4.2 Vegetal agency: on the far bank, *Mikania* cloaks the undergrowth of the Lower Doigurung Reserve Forest. Photo by the author.

get that," says Budhu. "What's more, even the paths for entering the forest have been blocked. You have to hack your way through all this vegetation to get anywhere, and this makes the entire exercise of finding firewood completely futile." The required effort has also made walking through the forest a risk-laden activity. "You cannot see if there are elephants," he says, explaining how the animals' forage too has been diminished, for "*Mekanic* barely lets any other plants grow."

As outlined in chapter 1, plantation logics lie at the heart of *Mikania*'s circulation and spread. The plant was introduced as a cover crop for tea and was naturalized in Assam by the early twentieth century. It was becoming visible in the Assam plains in the 1930s although the plant's distribution was relatively local. It was a geological event—the 1950 Assam earthquake—with its upheaval of the region's topography and subsequent periodic flooding of the Brahmaputra valley that led the plant to proliferate "in an alarming fashion." Forests relatively clear of the plant in the early 1950s were, by 1958, being "virtually smothered" by *Mikania*.[16] By the 1970s, it had expanded into many parts of the state, giving its forests the appearance of "ruins."[17] The vegetal geographies created by *Mikania*, one could argue, are those that become endemic to a Plantationocene, in that they emerge from within a plantation mode of production. Plantations' monoculture and simplified ecologies, where replicas coordinate with the time of the market,

ACCUMULATION BY PLANTATION   125

are marked by the quest to use life to accumulate capital from life. From cover crops like *Mikania* to nitrogen fixers for enriching soil, shade trees that modulate atmospheres to runners for hedges sealing colonial enclaves from their surroundings, plantations set a host of nonnative plants in motion. At the heart of such an endeavor is to tap into vegetal work, that is, the metabolic, reproductive, and ecological propensities of plants utilized within a given economic formation,[18] for purposes of generating further profit from other vegetal life.

The expression of *Mikania*'s virulent agency, which happened long after the formal end of colonial rule, is inexorably linked to the wider ecology of plantations. It is a form of vegetal agency that operates over a number of scales and durations. The vine is propagated by runners rather than seeds, forming a thick mat of vegetation wherever sunlight is available in the dense forests of Assam. Although *Mikania* does not have clinging roots or thorns, it spreads with the aid of offshoots, forming "loops alternating from opposite directions to embrace tall trees to climb up" or spreads "from one bush to another in search of light."[19] The creeper in fact multiplies when it encounters plantations. "In the exploited forests where silvicultural tending operations have been carried out," the forester A. K. Choudhury writes, "this climber tends to be ruthless." A similar pattern was observed in commercial forest plantations where valuable timber was grown "by clearfelling high forests."[20] As a cover crop introduced by tea plantations, *Mikania* came back to bite. By the mid-1960s, it began "steadily invading many of the tea areas" of Assam, particularly those adjacent to forests, smothering "the tops of tea bushes with a mat of vegetation" and putting many plantations out of production.[21]

Efforts to eradicate *Mikania* have been unsuccessful, as most wars against plants that become invasive tend to be. Tea plantations, however, are able to control the vine, a practice that comes with considerable costs. Initial work conducted at the Tea Research Association's Tocklai Experimental Station found that spraying an herbicide named 2,4-D was relatively successful. However, extensive use of the chemical resulted in the proliferation of *Polygonum*, another weed that was beginning to present an even "greater problem."[22] The use of 2,4-D also resulted in an increase in plantation area under chemical weed control,[23] raising costs as well as impacting the quality of tea. Furthermore, chemical removal is difficult, especially when the plant rises above the plucking surface of tea. The common practice nowadays is manual removal. This comes with significant costs and requirement for labor power, especially at a time when the demand for labor to carry out other activities such as plucking is high.[24]

There is a distinct political ecology to the spread of *Mikania* in the Doigurung forest, one tied to a rampant deforestation of the landscape, especially that which happened in the aftermath of Assam's political agitations in the 1970s and '80s. Parts of the Lower Doigurung Reserve Forest had been clearcut and settled by landless peasants mobilized by leftist political parties, as well as by members of the Adivasi community who left the plantations in the late 1950s. The Forest Department, however, evicted many people who were deemed "encroachers."[25] In the 1980s, there was a wave of deforestation, happening in the midst of violent border disputes between Assam and the adjacent Indian state of Nagaland. The Forest Department lost control over large tracts of forests, and clandestine felling of trees soon commenced. Several reserves became "forests in name only."[26] Figures suggest that between 1974 and 1991, forest cover declined by 12 percent in the Lower Doigurung Reserve while that of the district of Golaghat was reduced by a staggering 84 percent.[27]

A second wave of deforestation took place in the 1990s and was a fallout of the violent backlash against colonial underdevelopment that the state witnessed with the Assam Movement. This was when, according to Budhu and other residents of Sundarpur, *Mikania* multiplied extensively in the Doigurung reserve. By the time the Assam Accord was signed in 1985, people's confidence in the central Indian government was waning. A vacuum created in the political scene was soon "filled in by forces which propagated separation from India through armed struggle."[28] The United Liberation Front of Assam (ULFA), a militant organization, surfaced as a major force in the state,[29] in part fueled by the disillusionment with the six-year agitation led by Assam's student body. Most of ULFA's cadres were drawn from the student movement, amid a climate where avenues of employment were increasingly "managed by corrupt politicians, officials and their brokers," and most youths lacked "even the small capital" needed to start businesses involving petty commodity production.[30] By highlighting deep-seated grievances and focusing on the neocolonialism of the Indian state, the militant outfit won for itself a wide support base that even included sections of the Adivasi community.[31] Thus ULFA was able to tap into the sentiments of a public for whom the Indian state appeared to be an instrument of repression and exploitation, and whose expectations from the agitations remained unfulfilled. This militant phenomenon, as Hiren Gohain observes, was "the product of the total alienation of frustrated Assamese youths from the Indian state."[32]

The outfit took a chauvinistic and violent turn.[33] The gunning down of non-Assamese businessmen who failed to meet the organization's demands, the targeting of politicians belonging mainly to the Congress (I) party, and, later, the discovery of mass graves in the organization's camps "sent shock waves throughout the state and ultimately contributed to the collapse of many a popular myth about the organization."[34] When ULFA began targeting the state's influential tea lobby, Indian security forces were brought in to crush the insurgency. Operation Bajrang—one of the Indian military's largest peacetime operations—was launched in 1990, followed by Operation Rhino. These counterinsurgency operations resulted in the busting of several militant camps, the killing of scores of cadres, and the arrests of hundreds. The Indian army's successes were, however, neutralized by the excesses it committed against Assam's civilian population, some of which involved extralegal and extraconstitutional means.[35]

To deal with this violent milieu, the Assam government, under the leadership of then Chief Minister Hiteswar Saikia, launched a "100 Per Cent Special Margin Money Scheme" to "rehabilitate" surrendered militants.[36] Worried that many youths would return to militancy if they failed to find avenues for employment, the government granted surrendered ULFA cadres, widely referred to as SULFA in Assam, a range of formal and informal concessions. Surrendered cadres were allowed to retain their weapons, and many continued what they were doing before. Extortion became rampant, and, by the late 1990s, SULFA ran syndicates controlling business activities in the state. Many landed government contracts, and some even entered the real estate business. Between 1992 and 1997, 3,439 cadres were "rehabilitated" under the Margin Money Scheme but at a significant economic and social cost to the state and public.[37] State agencies also used some of the SULFA to try and "solve" the militancy "problem," encouraging them to gun down their former comrades.[38]

The SULFA also muscled into the timber trade, amassing huge fortunes through illegal felling. In October 1994, a newspaper report stated that SULFA had lit "a pyre of destruction" in Golaghat's forests. Camps were set up in protected reserves to fell trees, and logs were floated down rivers, with the state's Forest Department either "turning a blind eye" or "becoming complicit" in what was organized deforestation.³⁹ It was perhaps not a coincidence that Chief Minister Saikia held the additional portfolio of Assam's minister of forests at the time. Estimates from the time suggest that fourteen to fifteen truckloads, carrying two hundred cubic feet of timber each, left Golaghat's forests every day. Public roads through the forests were closed to prevent logging from being detected. Sections of civil society expressed dissatisfaction, but many were afraid to raise their voice.⁴⁰ People's fear was not unfounded. Taufil Ahmed, an ordinary citizen from the town of Nagaon, was murdered by SULFA for protesting against deforestation.⁴¹

A violent situation that enabled deforestation to proceed generated the grounds for the virulent spread of *Mikania*. Such deforestation is a form of extralegal accumulation,⁴² what one could call an accumulation by deforestation that involves the raiding of state resources and public assets. A figure from 1995 suggests that over the years, SULFA felled trees worth 2.5 billion rupees, equivalent to a staggering US$72.46 million at the time.⁴³ The nature of the concessions was such that, according to the Forest Department, the police failed to nab a single offender.⁴⁴ Indicative measures suggest that between 1991 and 1995, Assam lost 567 square kilometers of forests to felling.⁴⁵ By 2004, forest cover in Golaghat's protected reserves decreased by 40 percent when compared to what remained in 1991.⁴⁶ Felling resulted in the creation of openings and scrub jungle in what had been closed-canopy forests, rendering the landscape ripe for the multiplication of *Mikania*. "Mekanic Lota was present in the Doigurung reserve but not as much as it is now," recalls Santosh, confirming what Budhu and other farmers had observed. "The cutting of trees exposed almost the entire forest to sunlight. Furthermore, all that was left were shrubs and small trees, which Mekanic could easily clamp down on."

Mikania is not a passive actor but generates its own "vegetal places" in the landscape.⁴⁷ As Santosh tells me, "Mekanic takes over a place." Such places are not benign. They have effects on the lives of people and contribute to the simple reproduction squeeze the Adivasi community is faced with. When Budhu and I try to walk or, rather, hack our way through the *Mikania*-clad Doigurung forest, our bodies are tired. A sticky substance coats our clothes, and the odor of the vine borders on the nauseating. Moving through the forest becomes an arduous task, not just for us but also for the cattle that are an integral part of the lives of Budhu, Santosh, and other farmers in Sundarpur. "There is no way our cattle can graze here," says Budhu, as we labor to move through the landscape. "The vegetation is so dense that they simply refuse to come here. You only think of this place from a human viewpoint," he tells me, "but if you look at it from the perspective of cattle, it is risky. Not only are they unable move through Mekanic, our cows cannot see predators when the vegetation covers the landscape."

In fact, the only trails that Budhu and I are able to walk along after a while are those created by elephants. "They are large, and they muscle their way through," Budhu tells me as we walk along *dandis* or tracks created by the animals. Elephants do not feed on *Mikania*, and its multiplication has diminished forage for the animals as well. "Elephants' dependence on our fields has increased," says Budhu, reflecting on how the vine inflicts another form of slow violence upon the landscape. The animals rest and remain in the Doigurung forest in the daytime, and the vegetal places created by *Mikania* mean that disturbance is relatively less. Elephants, one could argue, craft worlds within these vegetal places, in excess of human agency. The forest becomes a place to be other-than-human within a Plantationocene, albeit being worlds that result in a gradual attrition of proboscidean lives.

Mikania thus emerges from within plantations and the circulations they set in motion. Its vegetal agency, expressed due to particular historical and material conditions, becomes evident long after the formal end of colonial rule. It is a kind of ruination of the landscape, an uneven temporal sedimentation of a Plantationocene's violent histories. Ruins, as Ann Laura Stoler argues, are not leftovers or relics. Rather, they are "what people are *left with*":[48] a degraded landscape where simple reproduction becomes an arduous task and where possibilities for growing livable worlds are constrained. To ruin is to destroy particular forms of agency. Here, a particular form of vegetal agency makes worlds unlivable and unbreathable, not necessarily for everyone, but for the Adivasi community who are subject to relentless violence and, as we shall see, further dispossession.

Vegetal Economies

"A group of surrendered militants from Golaghat came and set up camp in our house in the 1990s, around 1994–1995," says Santosh, "staying for many weeks at a time, looking for land and negotiating with people to start their plantations." Santosh is referring to yet another fallout of the violence that emerged after the Indian state sought to quell secessionist militancy: a series of extralegal land grabs for the purpose of growing tea.

"They took away a lot of our land, at a throwaway price," he tells me with remorse. "My father was reluctant to sell his land, but they would threaten us with their pistols." Santosh, who was in high school at the time, could do very little: "I was very young, and my father was often drunk. They would coax and intimidate him at the same time. Being the eldest son in the family, I tried to intervene. Whenever I did so, they would beat me up." Frustrated, Santosh dropped out of school and joined a company doing contract work in the Numaligarh Refinery. It was his attempt to escape from a violent atmosphere at home created by the SULFA cadres in their quest to grow tea.

A major change taking place in Golaghat and the Sundarpur landscape was the rapid rise of small tea gardens—tea grown by peasants in their smallholdings[49]—whose explosion coincided with the political turmoil of the late 1980s and early 1990s. While Assamese peasants cultivated tea in the colonial period, its extent was marginal.[50] When estate plantations came under Indian ownership after Independence, they encouraged Assamese peasants to start small estates, and in the latter half of the 1970s a group of well-to-do peasants from Golaghat took up tea cultivation on their homesteads.[51] In 1978, the district's peasants voted Soneswar Bora, a socialist leader, into the Assam legislative assembly. Bora was given the portfolio of agriculture and cooperatives minister in the Janata government, and the popular story narrated by the region's small growers is that he encouraged youths to take up planting tea in their smallholdings.[52]

The impetus for what has come to be known as the "small growers revolution" came in the late 1980s when the Indian tea industry was undergoing a crisis, with a significant decline in production.[53] Prices soared, and the government curtailed exports to prevent an increase in the cost of tea in the domestic market. The age of tea bushes was a major contributing factor to underproduction. In 1987, 44 percent of the bushes in Assam's plantations were over fifty years old and had passed the age of optimum economic productivity.[54] The Tea Board of India's efforts to mobilize plantations to substitute new plants for older bushes were largely unsuccessful.[55] Pathogenic conditions of a Plantationocene, particularly the increased use of fertilizers and pesticides, also contributed to a fall in international demand for Assam tea.[56] Under India's Eight Five Year Plan (1992–97), the board began encouraging unemployed youths and landed peasants to start small tea estates, an effort targeted at increasing production as well as improving the quality of tea.[57]

Among early farmers to grow tea in Golaghat was Gangadhar Saikia (1934–2015), a schoolteacher by profession who was also active in the Assam agitations. Saikia, according to accounts of Golaghat's small growers, played a pivotal role in the spread of tea. Between 1965 and 1971, he had mobilized peasants to "encroach" upon surplus, uncultivated land belonging to tea plantations in order to grow sugarcane. A legal suit ensued, and Saikia, in 1977, was successful in "seizing 857 *bighas* of land."[58] By the late 1970s, Saikia had taken to planting tea, and, under his leadership, a district-level small tea growers association was formed in 1985. This later morphed into the All Assam Small Tea Growers' Association in 1987, and, through support from the Tea Board of India and expertise from the Assam Agricultural University, the organization played a key role in the small grower sector's expansion.[59] According to one estimate, Assam had twenty-one registered small tea estates in 1987. In 1991, there were 237 small growers in Golaghat alone. This figure rose to 837 in 1994, and by 1999, there were 2,148 registered small tea growers in the district, whose estates covered an area of 7,342 hectares.[60]

As outlined in chapter 1, the political economy of plantations is caught up with the vegetal work carried out by plants,[61] underscored by the sanction of forced or underpaid labor. Vegetal work entails processes of growth, including the reproductive, metabolic, and photosynthetic processes of plants, brought into the ambit of economic activity. Vegetal work becomes intrinsic to the process of valorization in a plantation, while benefits to the plant's own ways of being or other forms of cobecoming with people are lacking or subsidiary. In contrast to political economic analyses derived from a factory-based model of commodity production, where commodities are deemed to be made, the quintessential cheap commodity of a Plantationocene is grown.[62] Plantations set up conditions for plants to take on particular forms and dispositions through the simultaneous and often violent exploitation of labor power and unpaid work. The time of vegetal life is reoriented into the time of production and, together with the labor of the Adivasi community, vegetal work forms part of the dead labor embodied in a plantation's commodities. Vegetal work, however, is not a physiocratic allusion to living biology being the source of all wealth. Rather, as a concept, vegetal work is a material abstraction, where abstract, temporal imperatives of accumulation are operationalized at the level of the vegetative body.[63]

The transformation of Golaghat's landscape into a Plantationocene thus entails both the cheap work of the tea plant and the cheapened labor of Adivasi workers, a cheapening evident in both colonial plantations and the postcolonial small tea estate sector.[64] In fact, the latter has been able to flourish in part because of the reserve army of Adivasi workers, who form an essential part of the small tea estates' workforce. Facing a simple reproduction squeeze, such estates are often the only avenue for wage labor for many people in Sundarpur. For instance, Bogai, who cultivated paddy in his modest landholdings, also worked part time in a neighboring small tea estate, planting saplings, digging drains, and spraying pesticides. His wife Dipa performed the demanding labor of plucking tea leaves in the same tea estates, although she was paid a lower wage. Gendered wage discrimination runs rife in Assam's plantations. Women being paid lower wages than men and more frequently hired as temporary workers is commonplace.[65] Women also bear the heaviest burdens of systemic inequality. "I have to wake up at four o'clock in the morning, clean the house and cook, see the children off to school, and then go to the *bagaan* to start work," says Dipa, referring to the plantation where she worked, "and in the evening, after work, it is the same routine all over again." Recent reports indicate that women on Assam's plantations do thirteen hours of physical labor, coupled with up to six additional hours of domestic work. Children often pick up the task of social reproduction, especially looking after infants if their mothers work regularly, perpetuating a vicious cycle of undereducation and exploitation.[66]

Small tea estates in Sundarpur and elsewhere in Assam are a scaling down of the plantation model, a shrinking rather than an expansion of a project,[67] but they do not necessarily lead to a dismantling of plantation logics. Rather, in this form of scaling down, coercive internal relationships of a plantation remain, as do the forms of routine violence that characterize plantation zones.[68] Although Adivasi workers are not always "planted" in small tea estates, the lack of an outside to turn to for recourse means that many remain dependent on the sector, one whose expansion has been fueled by the violent aftermath of secessionist militancy and the deforestation that followed it. As Santosh's account narrated above indicates, SULFA too began investing in the small tea sector. They were in part aided by Chief Minister Hiteswar Saikia's Margin Money Scheme, which promoted "mini tea gardening" as an avenue for self-employment of the surrendered cadres.[69] In Saikia's own words, encouraging surrendered militants to start "pursuing their livelihood through tea" was one means for facilitating their "return to the mainstream."[70] In 1992, Saikia mooted a scheme to refinance small growers across Assam and asked estate plantations to provide support so that people did not "find any problem in marketing their products."[71]

Concessions that the state had given to SULFA, and the state agencies' use of surrendered militants in counterinsurgency measures,[72] rendered the atmosphere ripe for violent land acquisition. Santosh's family lost considerable amounts of land, as did others from the Adivasi community in Sundarpur. Land grabs are an exemplary form of accumulation by dispossession,[73] and some of the capital for starting plantations—certain SULFA-owned estates were as large as a thousand *bighas* with permanently settled labor—came from money cadres had extorted prior to surrendering. As Sanjoy Hazarika's work on insurgency in the region reveals, in the early 1990s, ULFA made monetary demands on tea companies, including approximately US$700,000 from Unilever-owned estates, fixed at a rate of two rupees per kilogram of tea produced on their plantations. Other companies such as Lipton and Brooke Bond "were told to cough up five per cent of their net profits."[74] Many cadres had "forgotten" to deposit huge sums of extorted plantation capital with their linkmen when leaving the outfit.[75] "One of the militants came overground with huge stacks of cash," says Budhu. "The Doigurung forest used to be their camp . . . and some of us were entrusted with safekeeping the money at gunpoint." The cadre later plowed back this extorted plantation capital into business ventures, including the acquisition of land to grow tea. Through extortion and the unaccounted economy, plantation capital thus flowed back for the further expansion of tea.

The histories of a Plantationocene have significant bearings on the dynamics of land acquisition. A key feature here is the pressure on land that colonial plantations and forestry have exerted in Assam. Planters remained in possession of significant tracts of land, a lot of which remained fallow until the second half of the twentieth century. After Indian Independence, the state introduced a ceiling on landholdings, whereupon surplus land was to be taken over by the civil administration with the wider aim of redistributing it to the landless. The process of acquisition has, however, been incomplete. The Assam government has periodically implemented the Ceiling Act, but as records indicate, plantations still hold on to more than 17,000 *bighas* of "ceiling surplus" land in Assam.[76] For instance, Bukhial Tea Estate, for which villagers of Sundarpur were a reserve army, has delayed handing over close to 7,900 *bighas* of ceiling surplus land.[77] Although richer peasants had managed to take control of ceiling surplus land, tea labor and student unions argue that "eighty percent of tea and ex-tea labourers in Assam don't have their own land."[78] Not redistributing surplus means that many from the Adivasi community have to "live in tea estates forever,"[79] working as *faltu* labor with marginal or no welfare benefits, and serving as a reserve army, if that. Those in Sundarpur had reclaimed forest land. The village was established by opening up parts of the Lower Doigurung Reserve Forest in 1980 when erstwhile plantation workers were unable to find cultivable land near the plantations in which they resided.[80] Most individuals from the Adivasi community remained smallholders, although certain individuals came into possession of larger tracts. It is primarily such categories of land that have been at the heart of SULFA's land acquisition, proceeding through the plowing back of extorted capital and through violent means.

Plantations also have an overwhelming material fixity to them, remaining from one generation to the next, where people's agency to alter their character in a fundamental way is severely constrained.[81] There is a vegetal dimension to this fixity. A tea plant continues to yield until it is at least fifty years old, if not longer, and bushes are replaced when productivity declines. This is a much longer turnover time than the three-year turnover of crops like sugarcane, once cultivated extensively in Golaghat. Some of the small tea estates have taken over Forest Department land, and larger plantations' expansion into forest reserves is a recurrent process in the landscape.[82] The durability of tea allows estate owners to keep possession of disputed land in ways that other, perennial crops might not. As one of the small growers of Golaghat writes, one of the aims of "the movement of mini tea garden" was to "cover ... vacant land on the borders of our state with a permanent crop," both as a means of solving unemployment and to "block" immigrants from "from occupying vacant land."[83] Vegetal time thus underscores the political economy of land acquisition in that it has material bearings on the processes of expanding tea and taking possession of land. At the same time, the occupation of deforested land is seen as a deterrent for so-called Bangladeshi immigrants, a sentiment that harks back to the chauvinism of the Assam Movement.

Deforestation in the aftermath of secessionist militancy and the encroachment of forest land by small tea growers also overlap, revealing how the conversion of a landscape into a Plantationocene operates through a number of intersecting forces and across different scales. The planting of tea in forest land requires trees to be felled, and much of this was already achieved through the actions of SULFA in the early 1990s. All prospective growers needed to do was to clear the undergrowth. The Assam Small Tea Grower's Association has consistently pushed the government to allocate forest land for cultivating tea, arguing that deforested tracts are no longer "beneficial to the Forest Department."[84] The dynamics through which small tea estate expansion has happened are reflected in the fact that 60 percent of Assam's small growers do not have *pattas* or land settlement documents.[85] The Small Tea Grower's Association has made incessant demands on the state to regularize their landholdings, a demand that the government has promised to meet.[86]

The phenomenon of small tea gardens and their expansion is a reverse déjà vu: an entry into a condition that appears novel but whose drama of enclosure, expulsion, and accumulation has played out before. Extralegal deforestation, violent land grabs, and the rush to acquire ceiling surplus land, all for purposes of planting tea, is in a sense the repetition of "a late nineteenth-century drama," whereby "prospective Assamese tea planters" officially "known as 'small farmers'" have become part of a new affluent rural populace.[87] The beneficiaries of the small tea garden revolution are primarily rural elites from upper castes or from communities that wield political power, including local landowners, contractors, surrendered militia, and politicians.[88] As Arupjyoti Saikia perceptively remarks, the expansion of the small tea estate sector reflects "the most fundamental continuity between the colonial and postcolonial state,"[89] a continuity that fosters the expansion of a Plantationocene. Yet, beyond actions of the state, there is a whole other ecology to landscape transformation.

Vegetal Politics

A JCB excavator scoops up soil from the edge of the Doigurung forest. The undergrowth is being cleared to pave the way for the machine. Dust flies up in the air and then settles down, only to rise up again. The trench, about six or seven feet deep and five feet wide, starts to demarcate a boundary between the forest reserve and a tea plantation (figure 4.3). "It is deep enough to prevent elephants from crossing," says Budhu, who accompanies me to the site. "The plantation management is digging the trench to prevent elephants from coming into their estate, as the animals sometimes damage bushes and put a halt to plucking," he explains, then drawing my attention to a subtle process of land reclamation. "You can see how close they are getting to the forest. Even a few extra feet makes a huge amount of difference. And once tea is planted it becomes easy for the estate to claim that strip of land."

4.3 Newly dug trench between tea estate and Lower Doigurung Reserve Forest. Photo by the author.

There are certain gaps in the trench. "These have been left strategically," he claims, narrating how they will channel the movement of elephants. "The animals will now be forced to move through particular paths when they come out of the forest. Have you noticed where the gaps are?" Budhu asks as we walk along the trench's length. He then describes how the gaps lie in places where there are people's homesteads and small settlements in between plantations, often on elevated ground conducive to growing tea. "Leaving these gaps means that elephants will now start to move through those settlements," says Budhu. "Over time people will have no option but to move out. It's a slow process of making people shift so that the plantation can expand."

As outlined in previous chapters, the installation of hostile infrastructure and mining has given rise to a riven landscape for elephants. Coupled with deforestation, the virulent spread of *Mikania*, and the conversion of the landscape to tea, the animals' dependence on crops has increased immensely. As Budhu explains, the altered ecology of elephants, particularly their patterned movement of staying in the Doigurung forest during the daytime and raiding crops or breaking into settlements at night, is now being channeled to generate further dispossession. Encounters and frictions between people and elephants happen along particular tracks and pathways rather than across uniform space. By tacitly intervening in the landscape,

4.4   Paddy field next to a hamlet remaining amid a tea plantation, trampled by elephants. Photo by the author.

plantation management is intensifying frictions along certain routes. Besides the newly dug trench, the plantation has also installed electric fences along the borders of the Doigurung forest. "These fences have also stalled elephant movement into the plantation and deflected their pathways toward people's homesteads," says Budhu, pointing to a strip of paddy that has been completely trampled by the herd (figure 4.4). "Earlier the elephants would pass through the plantations," he says, "but with the electric fence, they can only move through places where there are gaps." The compromise of people's safety, Budhu explains, would lead them to sell their land and look to set up homesteads elsewhere. In other words, elephants were being enrolled into the dynamic of land acquisition.

"This is where my earlier home was," says Budhu, pointing to what looks like a nondescript spot amid the tea plantation, now covered with orderly bushes. Budhu had been "asked" to sell his land and relocate, a euphemism for a coercive land grab. Gradually, signs of past settlement begin to appear through a closer reading of the plantation landscape: the *Albizia* shade trees that grid and intersperse the tea are only about ten years old, while an occasional mango and bael or *Aegle* that dots the view is much older. Not conventionally used as shade trees for tea, the latter are remaining testimonies of what was once the Adivasi community's land and homesteads (figure 4.5). "Many people relocated from the edge of the reserve as the elephant

4.5 Erstwhile Adivasi homestead, now taken over by tea plantations. Note the young age of shade trees and remnant nonshade trees in the background. Photo by the author.

problem got aggravated, particularly those who were staying in isolated hamlets, as it was not safe anymore," Budhu tells me. "They sold their land to the owner of the tea estate. One can hardly expect any other buyers here."

Elephant movement had bearings on where people lived. During the course of my fieldwork, Somra, another farmer who also worked as *faltu* labor in a small tea estate, moved his dwellings closer to those of other villagers. "My house, although situated in the village, was a bit isolated," says Somra, explaining his reasons for moving. "It was not safe for my family, especially if I have to be out in the *tongi*, guarding crops at night." While Somra did not sell his land, vulnerability to elephant incursions played a role in the acquisition of land for the plantation of tea, vulnerability that has been aggravated by deforestation and the expansion of plantations. Dwelling alongside elephants has costs that run far deeper than encounters with elephants and their immediate aftermath.[90] It can aggravate preexisting poverty, as we saw in the instance of Kanu and his family in chapter 3. To repay debts inherited from his father, who passed away following an encounter with elephants, Kanu sold two *bighas* of land to one of the plantation owners. The remainder of the money was used to dig a trench around their home, a measure to reduce the risk of elephant incursions, as the family's dwellings were right beside a *dandi* or elephant track. With no other men left in the family, paddy cultivation, especially the risk-laden activity of guarding crops, had become difficult.

There is a distinct vegetal ecology to tea plantations, especially when viewed from the standpoint of elephants. Being megaherbivores that consume up to 2 percent of their four-ton body weight each day,[91] elephants' lifeworlds are mediated by plants. Plant-herbivore relations reveal how the former are not simply mute and passive. Rather, plants are active agents that catalyze larger ecological relations.[92] They afford or furnish particular worlds for elephants,[93] sensed and apprehended according to the latter's own propensities and proclivities. Plants influence elephants' movements, dwelling, and encounters with people. The rapid spread of tea, therefore, is not just an alteration of a landscape into monoculture. It entails an alteration of the landscape's vegetal geographies in ways that have significant bearings on other-than-human life.

Tea is not a plant upon which elephants forage; therefore, the plant does not afford nutrition to proboscidean bodies. Besides incidental damage to bushes, plantations are relatively immune from elephant incursions. In the past, significant tracts of Golaghat's forests reclaimed by Assamese peasants remained uncultivated due to a paucity of wage labor. Such land remained in the form of "home gardens" harboring a heterogeneous array of plants upon which elephants could graze.[94] The rapid conversion of these lands into tea generated a landscape whose vegetal ecology was hostile to elephants. The animals' dependence on rice paddy increased, as the paddy is analogous to wild grasses elephants feed on, but with a much higher nutrient content. Although bull elephants are known to opportunistically raid paddy fields,[95] an altered vegetal landscape means that female-led herds also do so with regularity in places like Sundarpur.

A vegetal politics becomes evident when plant-herbivore relations are foregrounded.[96] Continuous raiding of fields by elephants has further sparked farmers to cultivate tea, given that the damage suffered is much less, and it does not require the additional labor of guarding crops. Santosh and some others in Sundarpur who still owned land too began growing tea in their plots, a pattern that is becoming increasingly discernible across the village and wider landscape. "It is mainly because of the elephants," says Santosh. "How many trenches can you keep digging?" he asks. Santosh had converted some of his erstwhile paddy land to tea, cordoning off the area with a bamboo fence, adding earth to raise the ground, and digging drains to ensure soil is not waterlogged (figure 4.6). Although there has been an ongoing crisis in the small tea estate sector, particularly due to a fall in prices and, therefore, the rate of profit, it has not stopped the proliferation of tea. "People are planting tea seedlings, selling land, and then again others are planting tea," says Santosh, pointing to the speed at which change is happening. "Paddy has almost disappeared." In 2013, Golaghat had 11,286 small tea growers registered with the Tea Board of India,[97] having grown to almost six times the number at the turn of the millennium. In 2019, this number had increased to a little over 13,000, covering an area of 13,900 hectares.[98] A number of intersecting forces contribute to the continual planting of tea. For some it is aspiration: to start ventures that they hope will provide some returns, often coupled with endeavors of seizing land, a process termed *māti dakhal* in Assamese, usually carried out by rural elites who wield political clout, but not always so. For others, especially the Adivasi, planting tea is an act of emulation, of finding some kind of opening even though those openings might not lead anywhere. The viability of such an enterprise sometimes becomes a moot point, although the fixity of plantations makes small estates obdurate, giving them an enduring form. The expansion of tea has had significant bearings on elephants' lifeworlds. "Now where will the elephants feed?" asks Santosh, who shows an acute awareness of this fraught vegetal ecology and its political ramifications.

"Tea will yield benefits in the future, for my children," Santosh tells me, a statement reflective of the aspirations and dreams behind growing tea. The small plots that he and others in Sundarpur cultivate primarily involve labor from within the family or neighbors who work on the basis of daily wages. Santosh's statement rings of hope amid immiseration, although the small tea estate revolution has primarily benefited wealthier sections of the rural Assamese peasantry. Irrespective of scale and size, plantations foster inequality. Small growers like Santosh are green leaf producers who lack capital for making processed tea. To sell their produce, most depend on estate plantations, and more recently "bought leaf factories" for manufacturing tea owned by richer sections of Assamese society. Prices have to be negotiated constantly. In Sundarpur, small growers sell their leaf to a large SULFA-owned plantation that, like other estates, uses various means to keep the price of green leaf low. As sociologists Chandan Sharma and Prarthana Barua show, the expansion of this sector has been aligned with plantation logics: the tea industry reaps benefits of a supply of fresh tea leaves without making new investments and "by passing the risk of crop failure or market downfall on to the small growers."[99]

4.6   Santosh's paddy field now planted with tea. Photo by the author.

Accumulation by Plantation

A reading of the landscape's vegetal ecology vis-à-vis plantation logics brings a whole new dimension into understanding how Plantationocene worlds are made, unmade, and remade. It reveals how planetary transformations entail the generation of simplified ecologies where the plantation becomes an engine of landscape change, from its creation of monoculture through the exploitation of labor to the circulation of nonnative plants. Not only does such a reading foreground the agency of plants and the ways in which the vegetal underscores economies and politics of planetary change, but it brings a much more critical outlook into posthumanist readings of a Plantationocene.[100] As situated histories of the landscape reveal, plantation logics and their racial-colonial economies do not wither away.[101] Despite a reaction to the persistent underdevelopment plantations spawn, they continue to operate as durations, usually by morphing into new means of oppression.

Situating a Plantationocene in Assam opens up a number of vistas on planetary change. It shows how, in a South Asian context, the role of the state can be neocolonial and how secessionist militancy is intrinsically caught up in questions of extractivism and resource use.[102] The ULFA phenomenon, as Hiren Gohain argues, is the product of "the total alienation of frustrated Assamese youths from the Indian state."[103] Although "one cannot dismiss the entire enterprise as criminal and fraudulent," its idealism "emerged out of a background of political immaturity, anarchic worship of violence as the only solution, adventurist tendencies and depletion of human sympathy largely related to the fortunes of the Assamese people in historical circumstances not entirely of their own making and choice."[104] The aftermath of attempts to quell militancy was a violent one. Not only did it permeate conditions for slow violence, evident in chapter 2 on infrastructure, but it accentuated the uneven development that marks and reproduces a Plantationocene. This is evident in the extralegal concessions given to SULFA but also in the Assam government's push to plant tea as a means of undoing persistent underdevelopment, a push that in fact marks a "fundamental continuity between the colonial and postcolonial state."[105] The ecological ramification of this violent condition is that it leads to a subordination of space, people, and diversity to plantations.

Events in Sundarpur gesture toward a more expansive, ecological reading of the dynamic of accumulation by dispossession: the forcible displacement of populations from land, the privatization and enclosure of the commons, land grabs, and asset restructuring, which ultimately give rise to rightless communities and wage labor.[106] Accumulation by dispossession points to primitive accumulation being an ongoing and continuous aspect rather than an originary feature of capitalism, as Marx's use of the German word *ursprüngliche* denotes.[107] One might call this process an "accumulation by plantation," the grounds for which are created by stripping public assets through informal concessions and extralegal means, witnessed in the instance of deforestation, as well as the violent dispossession of people through land grabs, notably those belonging to the Adivasi community. There is further encroachment of forest and revenue land through the planting of tea, resulting in a concomitant enclosure of a working commons or spaces that enable certain forms of simple reproduction. Accumulation by plantation creates a certain amount of proletarianization,[108] in that those who are part of the subsistence sector of the rural economy increasingly have to gravitate toward wage labor and work on plantations or small tea estates for marginal wages and long hours.

Attending to questions of vegetal agency enables understanding some of the broader conditions that aggravate dispossession. Plants like *Mikania*, for instance, did not simply appear. They were brought to Assam to aid in the production of cheap nature. This is not only an instance of using life to govern life,[109] but also one of the use of life to accumulate capital from life.

Such forms of accumulation, typical of a Plantationocene and its simplified ecologies, are rambunctious. *Mikania* exceeds the order of plantations and comes back to disrupt processes of accumulation from within. The ruinous effects of the vine manifest long after the formal end of colonial rule. A more critical reading of biotic circulations seen to characterize the Anthropocene foregrounds how colonial legacies operate as durations, bursting through at particular moments and disrupting settled orders of life.[110] The expression of vegetal agency is dictated by historical circumstances, albeit those of contingency rather than necessity, and not solely through a plant's vegetative properties or "thing-power," as neovitalist notions of agency would like to suggest.[111] As in a material politics as opposed to a politics of matter, vegetal agency has to do with qualities. The latter form under certain situations and circumstances, exemplified by the conditions that made *Mikania* virulent. Plantation regimes in the form of colonial forestry played a vital role, as did the violent forms of accumulation that spurred deforestation in Golaghat and across much of Assam's landscape.

Mikania's agency reverses the usual order of plants being subordinate to people and the vegetal places it forges are not benign. Plants in this sense are world makers,[112] although those put into circulation by plantations can become coercive, not by their own doing but through the grounds and conditions that plantation logics create. The vine seals spatial access to forests for people and cattle, stymying simple reproduction and bringing about a slow degradation of elephant habitat. Here, vegetal beings mobilized by plantations colonize a plantation's outside: they leak from a plantation's order, take over spaces beyond its enclaves, disrupt relations to nature and land not crafted by a plantation's coercive organization of labor, and engulf ways of being and doing that do not form part of a plantation's interiority. Elephants are able to forge worlds amid the ruination brought about by *Mikania*, not by eating the plant, but by dwelling in the vegetal places it creates. Such places offer habitability to a creature, albeit a depleted one.

Accumulation by plantation proceeds through a range of extralegal means. The deforestation that happened through informal concessions given to surrendered militants had multiple effects. It was a form of accumulation that opened up forests for the expansion of tea, depleted habitat for elephants, aided the proliferation of nonnative plants, and increased frictions between elephants and people. Vegetal qualities of the tea plant underscore the establishment of small tea estates on deforested land. The long turnover time of a tea bush and its durability give plantations and plots of tea a material fixity, where the ability to alter their character is severely constrained.[113] This enables small growers and plantations to make claims on forest and revenue land. Plantations skew and arrest rather than attest the "involutionary interdependency" or mutual cobecomings of plants and people.[114] By subordinating the quality of life to a quantity of life,[115] accumulation by plantation curtails commitments to earthly survival. Such processes of accumulation are driven by a history of contingency rather than a history of necessity or probability. As David Harvey argues, accumulation by dispossession is "inchoate, fragmentary, and contingent. . . . Destruction of habitat here, privatization of services there, expulsions from land somewhere else . . . creates its own dynamic" of generating surplus value.[116] The same contingency is witnessed in the instance of accumulation by plantation, which emerges as a result of deforestation, the virulent spread of nonnative plants, land grabs, and the enrollment of elephants to further expand tea.

The creation of value in a vegetal economy, particularly that exemplified by the plantation, proceeds through a planting of human labor: rendering people immobile so that they can work year-round and in keeping with the continuity of the production process that tea cultivation demands.[117] Immobilization was a key feature of colonial plantations and their aim to ensure that labor was cheap, plentiful, and easily disciplined.[118] The sessile nature of plants and their processes of growth have bearings on the organization of the labor process. The vegetal thus brings new directions to the specification of bioeconomies centered on exploiting other-than-human life.[119] Labor is not always planted on small tea estates, but a number of factors ensure that people are relatively immobile. Land grabs and plantations holding on to ceiling surplus land are factors which, as plantation labor and students' unions argue, mean that the Adivasi community have to live on plantations or are dependent on them forever.[120] The ruination of commons and the slow violence inflicted upon particular bodies through a colonization of plantations' outside mean that wage labor, involving low wages, a gender pay gap, and long hours of work, remains the only option for many. Immobilization is thus the logic of the plantation. It is also a logic of contemporary carceral capitalism witnessed in many parts of the world that seeks to accrue profit from the disposability of human life.[121]

An expanded, ecological reading of dispossession through the dynamic of accumulation by plantation shows that the latter involves a distinct vegetal politics, that is, the tacit politics of planting particular crops and orienting the agency of vegetal bodies that emerges from such practices. Not only does it mean working with the affordances plants generate for people,[122] but it also involves channeling the affordances plants have for other-than-human bodies. Tea is a plant that does not furnish palatability for elephants. Plantations, therefore, are relatively immune from elephant incursions and crop depredation, making tea a convenient crop to grow in friction-ridden landscapes. The expansion of tea further reduces forage for elephants and increases their dependence on crops. The vicious cycle set in motion, encapsulated by Santosh's remark that people are planting tea, selling land, and planting tea again, becomes a crucial motor for accumulation by plantation. This reproduces conditions of a Plantationocene and makes the labor of designing plantscapes otherwise doubly difficult. As an ethnography of elephant movement in Sundarpur reveals, the animal can in fact get enrolled in processes of landscape transformation. It is an uncanny repetition, albeit through difference, of a long history of using elephants to create Plantationocene worlds.[123]

The scalar complexity of a Plantationocene becomes evident when plant and planet, plantation and plot are held in the same analytical plane. The expansion of vegetal economies in the form of the small grower's "revolution" is an undoing of plantations' scale, but it does not alter the internal, coercive dynamics of plantations. Rather, small estates exemplify how a Plantationocene proliferates through a concatenated web of relations and in fractal, accretive ways. As Bengt Karlsson argues, small tea estates are emerging resource frontiers, caught in a dynamic tension between capitalist desire and ethnic closure.[124] Perhaps a "Planthroposcene" where other becomings between people and plants might get enacted is desirable and, in some ways, is being operationalized by indigenous communities growing certain crops in the region.[125] This however, is not the case with tea. Changing the terms of encounter with the latter means addressing a whole suite of other relations that go beyond the immediacy of staging other relations with plants. The floral and faunal arrangements that a Plantationocene generates, the persistent underdevelopment and dispossession that plantations spawn, and the violence that continually marks this condition are not easy to wish away. Salving this condition requires other kinds of designs and cartographies. These are beginning to take shape, albeit in a new form of coercion. This is the diagram of connectivity.

5

The Diagram of Connectivity

On a cold November morning in 2010, a group of fifty-odd farmers assembles in a paddy field outside Kaziranga National Park in Golaghat, where a public meeting is underway. The paddy is ripe, ready for harvesting, but the mood of the gathering is tense. Midway through the meeting, the farmers rise and start shouting slogans: "Inqhilab Zindabad! Land grabbing will not be allowed! Stop the NGO from touting land! Inqhilab Zindabad!" The protest is against having to give up their paddy fields in order to pave the way for an elephant corridor (figure 5.1). During the past year, a succession of government notices had arrived in the village, asking farmers to hand over their land at a predetermined compensatory price. A series of negotiations over land transfer had ensued, involving landholders, civil authorities, the Forest Department, and wildlife conservation NGOs. The government and NGO are trying to convince the farmers that channeling the movement of elephants through the designated corridor would result in a reduction in

5.1 Connectivity conservation: elephant corridor in Panbari outside Kaziranga National Park, September 2013. Photo: Arnaud Brohe.

crop raiding and help secure a long-term future for the animal. The farmers are less certain of this linear logic, emphasizing the unruliness of elephant behavior. "Are your elephants so polite," asks Jatin, "that they will use no other path besides the corridor?"

Corridors for wildlife exemplify a new model of conservation: that of connectivity. In Assam's Plantationocene, corridors have come to be seen as a panacea for undoing the effects of habitat fragmentation that have resulted from deforestation, mining, planting tea, and the siting of infrastructure. There is a distinct political ecology to the fragmentation of elephant habitat, brought about through various forces, including an affective and political backlash against the persistent underdevelopment plantations and neocolonialism have spawned. The rise of connectivity conservation results in the emergence of new force fields of power, a shift from the colonial diagram of enclosure to the postcolonial diagram of connectivity. This informal dimension induces a shift in emphasis from protected areas of the forest reserve, which are about creating inviolate spaces and a binary between forest and cultivation, to linkages that enable flows. Corridors are a response to the ecologies of a Plantationocene and are a new strategy for governing land. While enclosure emphasizes populations and entails molds or containers in which life is managed, connectivity is about steering mobility and managing life through modulations.[1] Connectivity conservation is increasingly being scripted through the spatial idiom of infrastructure. If protected areas are static, about preserving natures of the past, then connectivity is about the expansion of conservation and an attempt to govern the future.

This chapter looks at the politics of connectivity conservation, situating this politics within the wider dynamics of a Plantationocene and its fraught political economy. There has been a recent surge in writing on animals' mobilities, examining how other-than-human worlds are forged through movement, the implications these have for understanding spatial practices, and the ways in which such movements are governed.[2] Of particular importance is the relations between other-than-human mobility and infrastructure, including the ways in which infrastructures hasten the circulation of other-than-humans, forging new, "cosmopolitan" biotic assemblages, the building of infrastructures to foster animal movement, and the "cosmopolitics" of encounters between animals and transport systems.[3] The interest in specifying other-than-human mobilities has been invigorated through attempts to specify ecologies of the Anthropocene.[4] For instance, roadkill is seen as "a key figure" of this epoch, driven by "the total human effect on life and ecologies" via petro-capitalism and the expansion of infrastructure.[5]

In a somewhat different vein, others look at the politics of connectivity, notably corridors and the ways in which they are becoming "the most visible expression of the new landscape conservation boom."[6] Wildlife corridors are new strategies of transterritorial conservation, involving new alliances between the state, conservation NGOs, and private capital, that aim to govern landscapes from afar.[7] Deploying a science and technology studies lens, corridors are understood as "boundary objects" that have plural meanings in different meanings in different social worlds but with a structure common enough to make them recognizable across these worlds.[8] The politics of connectivity is articulated through contestations of the corridor concept and the hegemony of science in dictating connectivity on the ground.[9]

My intervention is somewhat different than these accounts. I argue that connectivity is a diagram of power: a luminous arrangement that connects, distributes, and modulates resources and bodies. It works through the discursive, including epistemologies and principles of reserve design, and the nondiscursive, in the form of practices of intervening in the lived worlds of animal movement. Going beyond the concept of a boundary object, which emphasizes how a thing or discursive object knits different epistemic bodies together,[10] a diagram is a map of power. The diagram of connectivity morphs from the older diagram of enclosure as one set of logics are superimposed upon another and new force fields of power are drawn. Furthermore, I relate connectivity conservation to the travails of a Plantationocene, where habitat fragmentation and disruptions to animal mobilities follow very specific historical pathways, rather than viewing connectivity as that which emerges from global narratives that Anthropocenic ecologies spark.[11] Furthermore, I argue that there are particular epistemologies to connectivity, and the postcolonial world is crucial to how these are operationalized. Contexts such as Assam are not mere receptacles for ideas imported from outside, but constitute the very grounds where connectivity is practiced and tried out.[12]

The sections that follow first turn to the histories of connectivity conservation, paying close attention to the science of reserve design from which corridors draw their epistemic roots. I show how reserve design principles are diagrammatic strategies in themselves, setting up new interventions between the formed and the unformed. Asian elephants have played a crucial role in this regard. They were enrolled to render habitat fragmentation visible, and the creature's inhabitation of the world on a dispersed and distributed scale were vital in the transition from conservation's emphasis on enclosure to that of connectivity. Second, I look at the politics of connectivity in relation to a Plantationocene present. Drawing on how a conservation dilemma in Kaziranga unfolded over a decade after initial protests against corridors took place in 2010, I reveal how connectivity is inexorably linked to land political economy as well as differing interpretations of other-than-human mobility that, as Sanjoy Barbora argues, also operate at the "interstices of class, culture and commerce."[13] Third, the chapter examines how, with the rise of connectivity, conservation is increasingly becoming infrastructural. Infrastructure, I contend, is posited as a technology of governance that operates by targeting flows. Through this infrastructural idiom, connectivity conservation becomes increasingly intertwined with postcolonial capitalism. It further relegates people to a need economy,[14] where already existing constraints on simple reproduction in a Plantationocene are aggravated further. The diagram of connectivity, I argue, enables us to interrogate emerging modes of control through conservation amid a Plantationocene.

The Rise of Connectivity Conservation

The science of connectivity conservation is crucial to understanding how elephants become vectors for governing large tracts of land. Between 1977 and 1984, following observations from professional foresters that elephant migration routes had been disrupted,[15] and that populations of the creature were under serious threat, conservation biologists initiated a series of surveys to determine the status of Asian elephant populations. Under the auspices of the International Union for the Conservation of Nature's (IUCN's) Asian Elephant Specialist Group, formed in the late 1970s, there were attempts to map the extant distribution of elephants in various parts of its known range. These surveys and their attendant cartographies of elephant distribution rendered population declines visible. Ranges had contracted sharply and, importantly, had become fragmented. If Asian elephants were to be preserved, conservationists argued, then "serious policy and management decisions" were imminent, for at stake was not just conserving a species but its habitat, comprising "rich tropical forests with all their biotic wealth."[16]

These concerns were raised at a time when the growing insularity of forest reserves was becoming a matter of global conservation concern.[17] Arguing that science should not play second fiddle to politics in controversies regarding land use and wildlife preservation, ecologists were keen to develop principles of reserve design that could offer policy guidance.[18] The epistemic basis for these principles was drawn from the equilibrium theory of island biogeography, proposed by Robert H. MacArthur and Edward O. Wilson, two Harvard ecologists, in 1967, which saw species diversity as a dynamic equilibrium between the extinction and immigration of species on a given island.[19] This disarmingly simple idea was key to the design of nature reserves, given that many ecologists contended that protected areas were "destined to become an island in a sea of habitats modified by man."[20]

By the mid-1970s, American conservation biologists were laying out a number of geometric rules to develop guidance on which designs of reserves were better and worse. A key proponent of these rules was the biogeographer

Jared Diamond, better known for his environmental determinism,[21] who argued that species diversity and survivability in a forest reserve ultimately boiled down to its area. "In practice," Diamond admitted, "the area available for reserves must represent a compromise between competing social and political interests."[22] However, the recommendations that followed were simplistic, less Manichean, and were diagrammatic representations par excellence (figure 5.2). First, larger reserves were deemed better than smaller ones. Second, if area had to be broken down into several smaller reserves, these should be equidistant from one another rather than being grouped. Third, Diamond argued that strips of protected habitat should connect forest reserves such that they could serve as corridors and "dramatically increase dispersal rates over what would otherwise be negligible values."[23] Reserve shape also mattered. Round shapes were preferred over elongated ones or those with more edges, as these were likely to increase dispersal outside protected areas and create island-like effects.

The science underpinning reserve design was by no means settled. A debate, known as the SLOSS or "single large or several small" reserves debate, soon unfolded.[24] Diamond's schema came under criticism from other conservation biologists who argued that the equilibrium theory of island biogeography had not yet been validated and, in certain instances, a small set of reserves might contain more species than a single large one. Furthermore, the ability to disperse was a species-specific trait, making generalized prescriptions problematic.[25] In his typical antipolitical style and summoning the undifferentiated agency of *anthropos*, Diamond responded that the wider debate on conservation was becoming pro-development, even when evidence showed that "human destruction of habitats" was accelerating. Not favoring large reserves, Diamond argued, would lead developers to state that larger protected areas were not needed at all.[26]

Simplified geometric rules of design attracted significant attention. In 1980, the World Conservation Strategy reproduced Diamond's principles, stating that "generally, a large reserve is better than a small one."[27] An international document of immense influence, the World Conservation Strategy was drafted by the IUCN and had buy-in from several government and nongovernmental agencies, including the United Nations Environment Programme and the World Wildlife Fund (WWF). The strategy laid down principles of sustainable development, later popularized by the Bruntland Report of 1987, explicitly arguing that development could be a means of achieving conservation rather than being an impediment to it.[28] However,

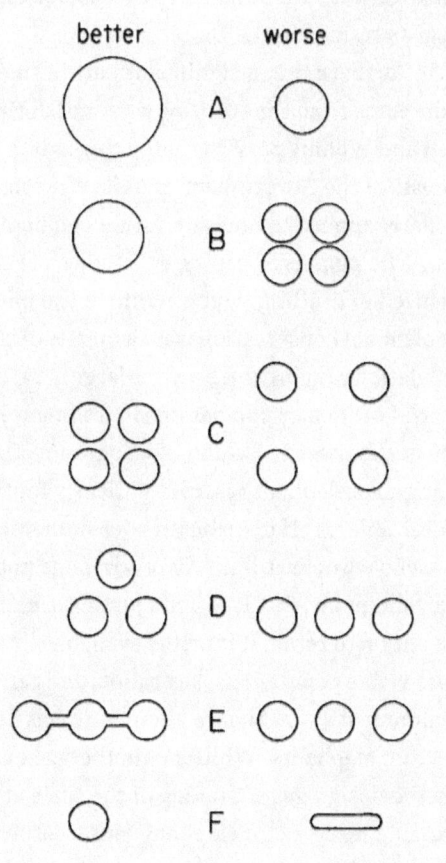

5.2   Diagramming conservation: geometric principles of reserve design derived from island biogeographic theory. Schemas on the left are better while those on the right are worse. Source: Diamond, "The Island Dilemma."

by uncritically reproducing Diamond's schema and by ignoring caveats to the principles of reserve design, the World Conservation Strategy conveyed the impression that "scientists knew with certainty that certain designs would result in lower extinction rates than other designs."[29]

Principles of reserve design had a significant influence on conservation biology in India. At the time, there were a number of collaborations between nongovernmental Indian and US ecologists. Many Indian conservation biologists trained in the United States or worked under those who had done so.[30] Furthermore, a significant part of the funding for wildlife ecology in India came from the IUCN, WWF, and, during the mid-1980s, from the US Fish and Wildlife Service routed through the Ministry of Environment and Forests of the Government of India.[31] Reserve design principles were particularly applied to envision future elephant landscapes. As Raman Sukumar, who pioneered ecological studies of Asian elephants and was closely involved in drafting policy, wrote in the mid-1980s, designing landscapes for elephant conservation was "a matter of either having one large elephant population ranging freely over a large area, or allow[ing] it to break up into a series of smaller populations in fragmented patches."[32] A direct application of the theory of island biogeography, the verdict was in favor of large, contiguous elephant reserves. "Clearly for the elephant a single large area is desirable.... If distributed over numerous smaller habitats the species as a whole would still survive even if one population becomes extinct. This is a valid point. But it is not a justification for fragmenting a large area if the option to retain it intact is available."[33] Calculations factoring in minimum viable populations, sex ratios, and carrying capacity suggested that a minimum of 4,400 square kilometers was needed to conserve a population of 2,200 elephants. While a hypothetical example, applying the science of reserve design gave "an idea of the scale at which one should think when planning reserves for elephant conservation."[34]

By the late 1980s, it was beginning to dawn upon conservation biologists and professional foresters that deforestation and habitat fragmentation were the most serious threats to the survival of elephants. "Future land-use planning," Sukumar argued in his influential monograph on the ecology and management of elephants, "should aim at preserving habitat contiguity." For this, corridors that supported "the free movement of elephants" were necessary.[35] Other ecologists too were beginning to point to the effects of habitat fragmentation on large mammals.[36] However, corridors were not yet the panacea they were to later become. The emphasis lay on creating new management units that would allow for conserving an entire elephant range. Extant models of conservation, including the "core-buffer concept" promoted by Project Tiger, India's flagship conservation program and perhaps the most famous international environmental initiative of the early 1970s, was seen as "virtually useless" when it came to reserve design for elephants.[37] What was needed were elephant reserves that

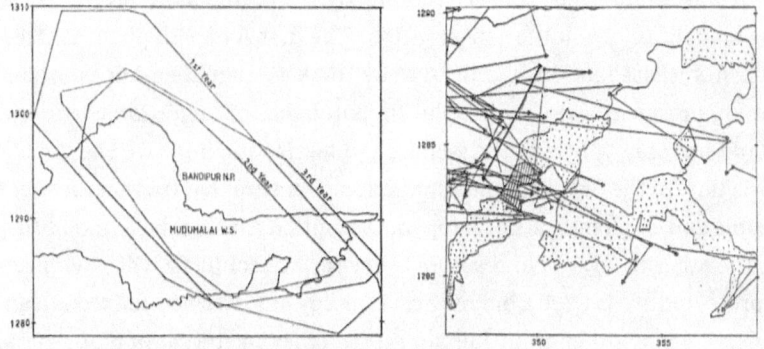

5.3   Rendering mobility visible: polygons depicting elephant home ranges through time. Home ranges are generated by joining the outermost points of recorded elephant movement. Source: Baskaran and Desai, "Ranging Behaviour of the Asian Elephant."

would account for "the range-utilization strategy" of the animal, some of which could not be "insulated from disturbance by man [sic]" but would nonetheless have "the principle of total protection" applied to "crucial habitat pockets."[38]

Soon thereafter, Project Elephant, an initiative modeled along the lines of Project Tiger, was launched in 1991–92 under India's eighth Five Year Plan.[39] A major aim of the initiative was "to conserve and protect, and where necessary, to open up, existing traditional corridors linking the parts of the habitat being used by elephants."[40] Elephants were in fact enrolled as actors to render habitat fragmentation and connectivity visible. As large-bodied mammals, elephants were able to carry the relatively heavy transmitters used at the time and were deployed to reveal how animals utilized landscapes. Studies of radio-collared elephants from south India conducted by the ecologist Ajay Desai and his colleagues from the Bombay Natural History Society fleshed out elephant ranging patterns and grounded the relatively abstract concept of corridors within landscapes (figure 5.3). These studies showed that elephant home ranges were much larger than previously assumed, thus leading to new definitions of the minimum area required for an elephant herd or clan. Furthermore, elephants were found to show "strong fidelity to the routes used during their seasonal movement,"[41] giving credence to corridors as concrete, material entities.

It was around this time that connectivity became more prominent in the biopolitics of wildlife conservation. The first Asian Elephant Conservation Action Plan, drafted in 1990 by IUCN's Asian Elephant Specialist Group, presciently states that the "maintenance of migration corridors" would not only "prevent the isolation of herds, and improve the genetic variability of the overall population" but also ensure that frictions between people and elephants do not happen. Disruptions of elephants' mobilities, on the other hand, would result in "very serious conflicts" with people.[42] If protected areas were a biopolitical strategy of fostering life through enclosure, where other-than-human life becomes the target of biopower at the level of populations,[43] then corridors came to be seen as promoting population viability through the steering of pathways. The Elephant Specialist Group explicitly began to argue for forms of land-use planning that would recognize "established migration routes" and "protect them from incompatible forms of development and settlement."[44] Here, strategies for landscape-scale governance were geared toward channeling mobility rather than the old model of containment.

Connectivity came full steam in the early 2000s, when the Wildlife Trust of India (WTI), a conservation NGO that has long invested in elephant conservation, began a country-wide exercise of mapping elephant corridors. Concerned by the rampant loss of elephant habitat, WTI took up the challenge to "pragmatically ... minimize the effects of habitat degradation and fragmentation" by identifying corridors and finding means to secure them for future conservation.[45] The trust's first step was to "ground truth" each corridor in India listed by Project Elephant by geolocating their boundaries and determining extant land-use patterns as well as identifying threats and potential conservation interventions. At the time, there was significant difference among experts as to what constituted an elephant corridor. The WTI held in-depth discussions with Forest Department officials, field staff, and local NGOs when mapping corridors across the country.[46] These acts were crucial in building legitimacy and some sort of consensus on what would count as a corridor.

This exercise was crucial in rendering corridors into ecological facts—entities with certainty and a known function—for which a number of translations from field to paper needed to take place. The trust used a fact sheet that gave corridors a name, based on the existing forest reserves that the linear segments connected. Names brought corridors into existence, rendering them legible and projecting a particular function onto them. Naming was crucial to standardize corridors and to rationalize their function, that is, the forests a conduit was seen to connect.[47] Alternate and existing names were also included in the WTI's report. Their inclusion was crucial for the process of standardization to take place, a process that also rendered corridors into protolegal conduits toward which future action could be directed.

The designation of strips of land as corridors was accompanied by a number of metrics that rendered them targets of governance. Crucial in this regard was the criterion of ecological priority, that is, the ranking of corridors on a scale of urgency and significance. Priority was derived from the frequency and regularity of elephant movement and the size of the elephant population in the forest reserves being connected, as well as the area of habitat a linkage would secure. Furthermore, the presence of linear transport infrastructures such as roads or railway lines passing through the corridor were incorporated into the metric.[48] There were disagreements among ecologists and professional foresters as to what constituted priority for conservation action. Rendering priority a measurable criterion and scoring corridors along a spectrum of high, medium, and low priority were vital in terms of arriving at some sort of an agreement on where action should be directed.[49]

A further criterion devised by the trust was the "conservation feasibility" of each corridor. Feasibility was graded "completely independent of ecological priority" and accounted for factors such as land ownership and the number of settlements in an identified linkage, as well as "the political and on ground feasibility of securing the corridor."[50] Assigning feasibility enabled directing conservation actions and funding toward specific landscapes. With buy-in from major players in wildlife conservation, including various state Forest Departments, ecologists conducting long-term research on elephants, and other conservation organizations including the WWF,[51] the trust's report garnered not only momentum but significant epistemic authority. A third of the eighty-eight corridors identified in the report were deemed to be of high ecological priority, of which the Panbari corridor in Kaziranga was one. The major barrier to securing corridors was the presence of people's settlements,[52] and, given that Panbari was free of dwellings, it scored high in terms of conservation actions. However, the omission of local stakeholders and, therefore, vernacular interpretations of elephant movement from the exercise came back to bite.

The Politics of Connectivity

"As far as the elephant is concerned, the problem is not about the fact that there are too few elephants. The problem is there is too little space," says the director of WTI. "Linkages, corridors [are] the most critical thing you can do for elephants today." He reflects on how poaching was seen as the major problem in the 1990s. Now on the decline, "habitat has again come back as the thing that haunts us. In a land with [a] billion people, even if I want to leave something for my son, what will you leave?" he asks me. "The first thing you think of leaving for the next generation is land. So if you want to leave something for wildlife in this country, it has to be land. And what is the land that we should prioritize? Simply that bit of land that connects two protected areas." Corridors, he argues, need to be secured, some, not all, through the purchase of land. Those in Kaziranga, particularly the one in Panbari, is a high priority.

The Panbari corridor mapped by the WTI is part of what has been a long-term vision to foster connectivity in the wider landscape. Since the late 1960s, Assam's Forest Department has voiced the need to bring the Karbi Anglong hills to the south of Kaziranga into the fold of protection.[53] In 1972, Paramananda Lahan, a forest official who pioneered modern-day wildlife management in Assam, wrote that Kaziranga's elephant population did not remain static throughout the year. Rather, elephants periodically moved to the Karbi Anglong hills, using two major routes, one of which was Panbari. "Such migration of elephants," Lahan and his colleague R. N. Sonowal observed, "have been greatly reduced during the recent years due to opening up of the valley lands and the lower hills for cultivation." Depredation by elephants along the foothills was rising and, when driven away, the animals retreated into the sanctuary. A "gradual decrease of habitat in the hills" not only was "widening the gap between the sanctuary and the nearby hills" but would "in time force the elephants of the sanctuary to remain within it."[54] Lahan's remark was prescient, in that over time the population of resident elephants in Kaziranga has increased.

That elephant movement through Panbari should not be disrupted was a concern the Assam Forest Department continued to raise. The site, as M. K. Sinha, a forest official posted in Kaziranga between 1979 and 1980, argued, had to be maintained as "a clear space for elephant migration."[55] Shortly thereafter, in 1985, when Lahan was in charge of managing Kaziranga, certain additions to the national park's area were officially proposed. This was a vision of ensuring habitat connectivity, initiated at a time when pressures on land were comparatively low. An area of 69.76 hectares in Panbari was earmarked as a "proposed third addition" to Kaziranga National Park.[56] This attempt to delineate and secure corridors was, in many ways, ahead of its time, given that connectivity conservation garnered saliency in India almost a decade later.

Under the Indian Wildlife (Protection) Act of 1972, the state government could extend boundaries of protected areas provided there were valid ecological reasons. The district's civil administration was directed to inquire into the rights of people and to provide compensation prior to handing the land over to park authorities,[57] upon which cultivation and grazing rights would be extinguished. In June 1985, the state appointed the Upper Assam commissioner to initiate the process of land acquisition. According to the commissioner's report, people's claims on land were not specific, and their objections to land acquisition were "general in nature."[58] In spite of an initiation of the process, the land for the proposed addition remained unreleased for several years. The Forest Department argued that local politicians stalled the process of land acquisition in order "to cultivate a vote-bank."[59] In effect, this created an impasse. People living around Panbari continued cultivating the paddy in the proposed addition, albeit in a continuous state of uncertainty where future rights to the land remained unclear.

The quest to acquire the corridor received renewed attention between 2008 and 2011 when the WTI, following its nationwide mapping of elephant corridors, put forward a proposal of compensation for landholders. This included alternate homestead land, houses with sanitation, and electricity as well as replacements for cultivation that amounted to 1.3 acres of land per family.[60] Some of the funding for the trust's initiative came from the International Fund for Animal Welfare (IFAW), a US-based animal welfare and wildlife conservation organization. For both the WTI and IFAW, the Asian elephant is a "flagship species," a species that is deployed to raise funds for conservation. "What makes elephants so effective" for fundraising, the WTI's director tells me, "is that they have forward-facing eyes." Visual materials crafted by both organizations orchestrate affects to highlight the creature's plight, particularly the effects of habitat fragmentation, and to evoke empathy among Western publics and international donors.[61]

There is a distinct politics to the mobilization of the elephant's appeal. The latter might be seen as a form of "nonhuman charisma," although such charisma does not operate as a counterforce to more mundane and bureaucratic forms of conservation practice, as seminal evocations of the concept propose.[62] Rather, affective encounters with elephants rest on micropolitical manipulations: presenting the animal with a face, accentuating the creature's friendliness and social bonds, and the threats that the creature faces.[63] The orchestration of affects is both actual and virtual, including haptic encounters with the creature in captivity or through anthropomorphized replicas, and the presentation of images and videos on screens, usually accompanied by conservation messaging.[64] The charismatic affects of elephants are vital to fundraising, and they are put to the services of a spectacular form of conservation that is increasingly intertwined with capitalism.[65]

The appeal to the elephants' charisma for purposes of securing corridors becomes fetishistic, in that it sometimes masks or omits undesirable encounters with the creature just as it fails to grasp the unruliness of the animal and the relations people have with elephants on the ground. Efforts to acquire land met with considerable resistance from people living in and around Panbari. There were a number of protests against land acquisition in 2010 and 2011. During one such protest, a landholder in Panbari pointed out that there were "several other corridors" in the Kaziranga landscape. "Why are you not doing anything about other corridors?" he asked a WTI representative. "There are so many hotels and resorts coming up in paddy fields surrounding the national park. One of them has even erected a high wall, completely barricading elephant movement. Instead of grabbing people's land in Panbari, why are you not stopping these other corridors from becoming defunct?" The representative responded by stating those were "movement tracks, not corridors," pointing to a definition that was given in the report the trust had produced: "a corridor is a linear landscape element where the immigration rate to the target patch is increased over what it would be if the linear patch was not present."[66] Failing to translate in the heated moment, the landholder retorted by saying that *dandis* or tracks used by elephants constituted their pathways of moving from one place to another. Such tracks, the landholder contended, were corridors that the trust should focus on. In effect, the failure to integrate vernacular understandings of elephant movement into landscape planning meant that the very term *corridor* had come under scrutiny and became a point of contention.

In fact, some residents of the area also sought to question the corridor concept by arguing that elephant movement was being deliberately funneled through their land. "The Forest Department and NGOs have erected an electric fence all along the national park boundary," says Jatin, a resident of the locality, "in order to help people protect their fields from crop raiding by animals. However, they have left a gap in the designated corridor." The effect is reminiscent of channeling elephant movement in order to displace people and grow tea. "This is a policy of the NGO and Forest Department," says Jatin. "They want to make sure that the elephants only move through here, so that crop depredation increases in our fields, and we inevitably have to sell our land for the corridor project."

There were other factors contributing to people's reticence in accepting the compensation package offered by the state and the conservation NGO. The market value of land increased almost exponentially since 2005, as Kaziranga became a site for speculative investments with a boom in the tourism industry. "The news is that the compensation package is twenty thousand rupees per *bigha* of land," Manoj, who was a resident in the area, told me in 2010. "For a farmer who owns twenty-five *bighas*, that amounts to a lot of money," he explained. "However, news has spread that the NGO is willing to give more, even thirty thousand for a *bigha*. As the value of land has risen, people feel they are likely to get much more." Some of the land around the corridor was also subject to speculative investment. Rural elites had purchased, in other instances captured, plots of land from their erstwhile Adivasi owners, with the hope that they would get bigger returns in the future with Kaziranga's tourism boom. The politics of connectivity is thus inexorably enmeshed with the political economy of land, sometimes glossed over by more-than-human accounts of connectivity. Amid this milieu of speculative investments and expectations of higher compensatory payments, people believed that the conservation NGO was involved in land deals.

Farmers from the locality resorted to a number of strategies to hold on to their land when the Forest Department had served notices for corridor acquisition. "In 2007, cultivation had declined in this area. This was in part because of the silt from the stone quarries," Manoj told me. "Our local MLA then intervened and warned people to not leave their fields fallow, otherwise authorities would find it easier to seize them."[67] Soon thereafter, full-fledged cultivation began," said Manoj. People, mainly from the Adivasi community, were also settled in parts of the corridor bordering the national park. Landowners, particularly those who lived far from the corridors, gave their land for sharecropping, hoping that the presence of people's dwellings would validate their claims to land ownership. In 2010, activists from the Krishak

5.4   Intensive spaces: the Panbari Elephant Corridor. People harvesting paddy, November 2010. Photo by the author.

Mukti Sangram Samiti (KMSS), a peasant-based political organization, joined forces with local residents, encouraging them to hold on to their land. Few people came forward to accept the offered compensation, and in 2009–10 WTI was only able to secure 4.4 out of the of 69.76 hectares that constituted the corridor and proposed addition.[68]

In contrast to the state-NGO model of elephant corridors being inviolate spaces, certain landholders proposed alternatives. "Why can't we have an arrangement where people cultivate land and elephants can pass through as well?" one individual remarked when there were heated discussions with civil authorities and the WTI. "This would be a unique example for conservation worldwide" (figure 5.4). Authorities did not pay heed, given that inviolate areas have deep roots in state-led conservation. Yet the suggestion is a possible alternative to the model of enclosure. "People who cultivate crops in Panbari are in fact guardians of wildlife," the individual went on to add. "They create safe passages for elephants and ensure that no one harms the animals. Rather than throwing these people out, what the Forest Department and NGO need to do is give them a stipend."

Two overlapping forms of spatiality emerge here. The first entails space that is extensive: spaces demarcated by boundaries and limited by edges, which are additive in nature.[69] Corridors become extensive spaces when steeped in the state model of enclosure. They are additive, in that corridors become links between two protected areas and work to increase the measure of contiguous habitat. Here, the lines forged by animal movement become subordinated to the point.[70] What matters is not a world of movement, but the end points or habitats that corridors link. In contrast, the spatiality that the farmer in Panbari drew attention to is an intensive space: spaces forged along lines of movement that cannot be cleaved from the phenomena forming them,[71] in this instance elephants' mobilities and their relations with people. Residing within phenomena, intensive spaces are polyvalent and non-Euclidean. They cannot be striated, cut up, or divided without producing a qualitative difference. The Panbari elephant corridor remained such an intensive space as a legal battle between resident farmers and the Forest Department ensued.

Litigation and Loss

As contestations over the corridor unfolded, residents of Kaziranga, with support from the KMSS, filed a petition before the Guwahati High Court in 2013, asking for planned evictions to be stopped. The petitioners stated that the Forest Department and civil authorities were intent on "removing" them from their land by claiming they were "encroachers."[72] Those living in Panbari claimed that the land they were cultivating or residing on was ancestral. "Our community lived in Kaziranga even before it was declared a forest reserve in 1908," one petitioner told me in 2014. "This is evidenced by the fact that many of the place names inside the reserve even today have Karbi names, which is the language that we speak. We moved to Panbari at around the time of Indian Independence, when the village we now reside in was established." Many petitioners showed existing land deeds, some of which were granted in 1962.[73]

"Evictions," the petitioners stated, "would be an unjust deprivation of constitutionally mandated rights."[74] They requested the court to establish a "high-powered Committee" to inquire into the nature and extent of the rights of valid land deed holders and to ensure that valid claimants were not evicted without a due process of law. In response, and as per court order, the Forest Department submitted a four-hundred-page "vision document" on the future of Kaziranga National Park. The Panbari corridor, the document stated, was notified in 1985 as part of the Third Addition to Kaziranga

National Park. Acts of cultivating land or setting up dwellings in the corridor fell "in the category of encroachments" and were therefore in need of eviction.[75] The counsel for the respondents further argued that there were "improprieties and illegalities" in the process of granting land deeds and that the government was encouraging encroachment.[76] Securing the Panbari corridor, the Forest Department noted, was vital. Kaziranga was a fragile ecosystem and given that Panbari was "the last corridor on the eastern side" of the national park that provided "safe passage to wild animals," the conduit needed to be free of human interference.[77]

The petitioners responded by stating that they were "willing to cooperate in every manner" to ensure conservation in the wider landscape, but challenged the idea that "the fragility" of Kaziranga's ecosystem was "due to the presence of the people that legally inhabit the area."[78] Habitat fragmentation, the petitioners argued, was "an overstated fact." In lieu of creating inviolate spaces, what was needed was a conservation model that would integrate people and provide them with "incentives and livelihoods."[79] Their rejoinder, in fact, pointed to some of the undesirable outcomes of connectivity. It was a widespread public opinion, the respondents argued, that animals moving into the Karbi Anglong hills were unsafe. "More often than not," animals that ventured into the hills did not return due to a "lack of any sort of protection" beyond the boundaries of Kaziranga National Park.[80] The support of local residents, therefore, was vital for wildlife conservation, a value that park authorities have recognized since the 1960s.[81]

The high court verdict, however, went against the petitioners. There were a number of anomalies in the paperwork presented. For instance, several landholders were, after investigation by civil and revenue authorities, deemed "non occupants" of the plots they laid claim to.[82] This was largely the product of speculative investments in land by certain rural elites who were not inhabitants of the locality. Settling sharecroppers on the corridors did not help people's cause. Images from Google Earth presented by the Forest Department showed no dwellings in May 2010, while those from January 2014 revealed that houses had been built,[83] feeding into the narrative of deliberate encroachment that the respondents put forward. The judgment stated that residents were aware of the process of acquisition set in motion since 1985, and that "only formal issuance of final notification" of the Third Addition was waiting.[84] These were not grounds for people to "overstay." Under provisions of the Land Acquisition Act, land could be acquired by the state and compensation followed later. To this end, the court's verdict was to take "expeditious steps" to evict unlawful inhabitants and adequately compensate those who were bona fide landholders.[85]

Further legal directives for securing corridors came from the National Green Tribunal. As witnessed in chapter 2, in 2016 the tribunal had ordered the Numaligarh Refinery to demolish the boundary wall that blocked elephant movement. Noting that "elephant corridors" were vital "for migration and regeneration of their species," the tribunal's directive for freeing up elephant movement extended to the wider Kaziranga landscape, as it formed part of a No Development Zone declared around Numaligarh in 1996.[86] Complaints regarding rampant mining in Kaziranga's surrounds, filed by the environmental activist Rohit Choudhury in 2018, led to the setting up of a Supreme Court–appointed "Centrally Empowered Committee" to investigate impacts on wildlife corridors. The committee further highlighted the importance of securing animal corridors between Kaziranga and the Karbi Anglong hills.[87]

Such developments have in fact led to an expansion of connectivity conservation. Following orders from the Supreme Court, the Assam government set up a committee for delineating corridors in the Kaziranga landscape in 2019.[88] Here, the principles of reserve design come back full circle. The committee's report reproduces the theory of island biogeography when outlining the need for establishing connectivity. "At equilibrium," the report states, "the frequencies of local extinctions and colonization are in balance at a landscape level. . . . The absence of connectivity," on the other hand, "disturbs the equilibrium" by restricting dispersal, resulting in local extinctions of species.[89] The committee identified nine corridors, six of which are additions to those mapped by the WTI. Boundaries of the newly defined corridors, such as that in Panbari, exceed the area of the Third Addition notified in 1985.[90]

"The acquisition of land is a process of slow expansion," says Kartik, who lives in Panbari. "If you look at the new corridor map, it is even more worrying because claims are now being made on a much larger tract of land." Some people even contend that conservation NGOs that aided the Forest Department's exercise of mapping new corridors released captive elephants to establish animal use of conduits. "They set up camera traps and tried to push captive elephants into the area," Kartik tells me. "However, people from our village recognized these animals and chased them away. Complaints were also made to the Forest Department." Although I was unable to verify this claim, it is a poignant reflection of people's resistance to the idea of inviolate corridors and the means through which they are constituted.

Part of this expansion is enabled through categories of corridors introduced by the new delineations. The first of these entails "structural corridors," defined as strips of forest areas that connect fragmented blocks of landscape. Such corridors, the committee recommended, need to be inviolate, that is, "made free of all human induced disturbance."[91] Structural corridors are extensive spaces. They are mapped, notified, and then acquired through a range of means that include statutes, interventions by the state-capital nexus, and legal directives. The second category involves what is defined as "functional corridors" or land "where there is recorded movement of species."[92] Functional corridors are viewed to become important when structural corridors are disturbed and, therefore, need to be brought under regulation with restrictions imposed on land-use change.[93] Functional corridors are intensive spaces, forged by animal movement and not necessarily tethered to a structural linkage like a forest strip. The Forest Department's aim of securing functional corridors is to territorialize them: render paddy fields inviolate spaces. There is, however, a risk of losing such function, if land-use patterns—especially that of cultivation which draws elephants—are altered. In the meantime, and before intensive space is rendered extensive space, the state seeks to maintain a status quo: imposing restrictions on land-use change so that there is no other loss of function. In Assam's Plantationocene, this exercise of managing intensities is now becoming infrastructural.

Scripting Conservation through Infrastructure

Conservation and infrastructure get increasingly intertwined in the paradigm of connectivity. Infrastructures are typically seen as antithetical to conservation in the model of enclosure and its quest to generate inviolate areas. Infrastructures generate ecological effects, disrupting elephant movement, causing alterations in the animals' home ranges and habits, and inflicting a slow violence on the creature's material lives. Connectivity conservation, in this regard, is a response to the disruptive effects of infrastructure. As elephant conservationists have begun to argue, it is crucial to find a balance between the retention of elephant habitats and "transport systems needed for the movement of goods and people."[94] A more recent development of the last decade has been to design infrastructures that foster and modulate elephant mobilities. These are what one might call "reconciliation infrastructures,"[95] that is, roads, bridges, and other built elements designed to accommodate and facilitate animal movement while going ahead with transport development projects. In such instances, infrastructures are not antithetical to conservation. Rather, they are poised to become technologies of governance with distinct power functions. Reconciliation infrastructures distribute bodies across space, not so much through containment or molds, but through a "canalization" of bodies and the modulation of their flows.[96] They become biopolitical apparatuses of governing life by acting upon other-than-human mobilities.

Transport infrastructure had become a pivotal issue when protests against corridors were taking place. In the mid-2000s, the Union Ministry for Transport embarked on a project to convert the two-lane National Highway 37, parts of which run along the southern fringe of Kaziranga, into a four-lane road. Objections from the Forest Department as well as pressure from various environmental NGOs, who argued that the highway expansion would further disrupt connectivity between Kaziranga and the Karbi Anglong hills, led to a reconsideration of the initiative. Conservation organizations claimed that the only viable alternative was to divert the proposed four-lane highway to the northern bank of the Brahmaputra River.[97] In November 2007, then Assam Chief Minister Tarun Gogoi met with the union transport and highway minister, requesting the four-lane to be diverted,[98] possibly on recommendation from the Forest Department and conservation NGOs. The following August, work on highway expansion was halted. Pressure from the UNESCO World Heritage Committee, who saw the project as "a potential threat to the integrity" of the park, also played a role. The Forest Department suggested creating a new bridge on the Brahmaputra River in order to enable the bypass.[99] By November 2008, the central government formally announced an alternate alignment of the four-lane highway that was to avoid the national park.[100] The following year, a new bridge over the Brahmaputra was sanctioned,[101] an intervention, as we have witnessed earlier, replete with its own slow violence of extraction and degradation.

Members of local communities living in Kaziranga's periphery opposed the proposal to divert the four-lane highway and formed a Demand Committee to orchestrate their response. "This road," a pamphlet produced by the committee states, "brings the light of civilization to the entire area." The highway was a means through which "unemployed local youths" found "self employment by means of small tourism industries and businesses."[102] The wording used is poignant. That the road brings "the light of civilization" is an expression of possibilities of progress and development that infrastructures have long been associated with.[103]

Transport infrastructures in Assam have far broader historical entanglements and political potency than suggested by the immediacy of the protests against connectivity conservation. As argued earlier, plantation logics had curtailed the development of Assam's transport infrastructure. Roads and railway lines largely served plantations' economic zones, resulting in the stagnation of old towns and trading centers.[104] National Highway 37 was overlaid on the colonial Assam Trunk Road, whose construction began in a full-fledged manner in 1866. The imperial British administration wanted a conduit that was a "metalled and embanked highway ... aligned in a manner that should render it possible at any time to convert it into a railway." Prohibitive costs prevented its expansion into a railway line, which, in hindsight, was a fortunate event given that it would have further fragmented the Kaziranga landscape. The colonial administration instead settled for a "permanent alignment, but made of the smallest section that would suit the traffic."[105] With the aggravation of the pattern of colonial underdevelopment in Assam after Indian Independence, there was little expansion of the state's road transport infrastructure. National Highway 37 remained a major conduit, especially for interstate travel, connecting oil- and tea-bearing regions as well as important towns the railways had bypassed.[106] Infrastructure had become one of the Assam Movement's key demands in the 1980s. Investments by the central government in Assam's transport network are therefore seen as much more than simply laying roads. They carry an affective charge and are viewed as a balm for decades of persistent underdevelopment.

"If the four-lane goes along the north bank of the Brahmaputra, traffic will completely stop plying through this stretch. There will be darkness in Kaziranga," Bipin, a member of the Demand Committee, told me in 2009. "What is more, the road will become a haven for dacoits. Robbery will increase, and no one will want to travel along this stretch." The metaphors of light and darkness are expressions of the affective charge infrastructures carry. A detour of the highway, the committee argued, would not only jeopardize livelihoods but also "ruin a long awaited dream of creating a world famed tourist city in the region."[107] The committee submitted a memorandum to the union minister for road transport, demanding the detour be canceled and the highway constructed along its original alignment.[108]

Mobility, whether of people, automobiles, goods, or animals, thus becomes a central point of contention in the paradigm of connectivity conservation. At stake here is a politics of movement that unfolds over a highly asymmetrical terrain rather than over a flat, pluralist world of connectivity. For many residents of Kaziranga, the government's rigid stance was viewed as one that was going to "deprive people of fundamental rights."[109] As with the promotion of wildlife corridors, residents saw the detour of the four-lane highway as a top-down, externally driven exercise that was "one-sided and anti-people."[110] Long-standing grievances regarding neocolonialism were rekindled, directed toward what people saw as a state-NGO nexus. Concerned authorities and "so-called NGOs" were hatching a "conspiracy" to "eject the local inhabitants" of Kaziranga's periphery.[111] "In the name of being animal lovers, conservation NGOs are using Kaziranga for *their* livelihoods and personal gains," Bipin told me, "ignoring the human aspect" of conservation. In a letter to the Forest Department, a member of the Demand Committee stated that "the time is not far when the department will be administered by such NGOs—sitting in AC [air-conditioned] room from abroad and outside the state."[112]

A major point of concern was the collisions between animals and speeding vehicles on the national highway. Wildlife biologists and NGOs believed that "conservation should take priority over development." Expanding the highway would "not just increase the width of asphalt to be crossed by animals, but also encourage vehicles to move fast." Existing statistics on roadkill had to be taken seriously before "any plan of widening the highway is embraced."[113] In contrast, the development committee argued that the statistics cited were "only partially correct" and did not present the entire picture. "The death of animals due to road accidents are [*sic*] quite negligible" when compared to "deaths due to poaching, floods and other reason."[114] To drive home their point, the committee produced a pamphlet contrasting the number of rhinos killed by poachers in the national park versus those killed due to road accidents. The latter column showed zero deaths over a period of twenty-eight years while those that were poached totaled a staggering 595. "There is not a single instance" of "rhinos and elephants" being hit by "vehicular traffic," the committee's pamphlet states.[115] The "ill intention of masterminds to create . . . an under developed area" by diverting the four-lane would, on the other hand, result in "a paradise for poachers."[116] While Forest Department statistics revealed that smaller animals and reptiles too were victims of road collisions, the Demand Committee drew attention to wildlife management practices that they saw as far more detrimental. The annual burning of Kaziranga's grasslands to prevent their succession into woodland was called out for "killing snakes, turtles and other alike reptiles."[117]

Furthermore, there was a widespread sentiment that imperatives of realizing connectivity in a top-down fashion would erode the support local communities extended for conservation, a sentiment that continues today. People living around Kaziranga "are not enemies" of wildlife "but unrecognized forest guards of the park," wrote a Demand Committee member. Villagers in the park's periphery "give shelter" to animals as they move to higher grounds during monsoon floods. They work "hand in hand" with Forest Department authorities to "keep vigilance over the affected animals so that they do not fall prey in the hands of poachers."[118] Keeping people on board, it was argued, was essential for the "effective security of wildlife."[119]

What people demanded was the construction of a four-lane highway using "modern technology" and implemented in a "scientific way" so that it would not harm animals while simultaneously allowing traffic to flow.[120] They could include elevated stretches with an adequate number of flyovers and tunnels that could act as "checks" for animal movement and enable elephants and other wildlife to cross the highway. A lack of desire to apply such technology on the government's part, the Demand Committee had earlier argued, "cannot be the sole reason of diversion of the Four lane High Way as proposed."[121] Conservation NGOs were partially open to this suggestion, being cited in the news stating, "we are open to consider a proposal where technology and investment could be brought in to ensure that highway improvement could be carried out while protecting the movement of wildlife."[122]

Reconciliation Infrastructures

While the detour is now well under way, the last decade has also witnessed another mode of connectivity conservation, one that is increasingly scripted through the spatial idiom of infrastructure. Over the years, the Forest Department's tune on transport infrastructure has changed. In a vision document for the Kaziranga landscape, written in 2014, park authorities state that it is "an irony that NH37 is doomed to die due to a historical mistake and wildlife activism over-zeal which misunderstands 'development' and conservation paradigm."[123] A state like Assam, the document observes, "has a very poor network of highways," although underdevelopment is attributed to terrain rather than colonial legacies underpinning the creation of transport infrastructures. "Building more highways with ultra modern technologies which are eco-friendly, green and least damaging to the forests and wildlife, is in the interests of the State, for its future economic growth and prosperity." Instead of depending on a single "life-line," what was needed were additional highways, both to the north and the south of the existing one, which could include building an "elevated expressway" that would take mobilities of both wildlife and people into consideration.[124]

The idea of a flyover was not entirely new. In 2003, park authorities submitted a proposal to create a flyover or tunnel below the national highway.[125] The plan fell by the wayside but was revived in 2012 when Kaziranga was in the spotlight for rampant rhino poaching. A team from India's National Tiger Conservation Authority visited the landscape and submitted a proposal to embark on such a project.[126] Later that year, the union minister of environment and forests, on a visit to Kaziranga, said that flyover construction would be taken seriously.[127] Legal interventions also played a role. Disruption of elephant corridors was a key element to the public interest litigation filed against mining and the Numaligarh Refinery and, during one of the hearings, the National Green Tribunal judge stated, "First of all this road should not have been there. It was the duty of the state to build a road which does not touch the ground. You could have made a flyover."[128] In response to the tribunal's query on animal-vehicle collisions, the Assam State Government proposed creating "animal underpasses, ecoducts/animal overpass and overpass/flyover in four potential animal corridors" as a long-term measure and to make the particular stretch of the highway "wildlife-friendly."[129] In 2016, tenders for the design of an elevated four-lane highway were floated.[130] Contracts for the elevated sections, costing a staggering 26.25 billion rupees (approximately US$353.5 million), were awarded to two engineering companies in 2019, one of which had even been blacklisted by the government in 2017.[131]

Underpasses created for wildlife are an example of reconciliation infrastructure: roads, bridges, buildings, and conduits designed in ways that accommodate other-than-human life.[132] A field of "reconciliation ecology" underpins such interventions.[133] In contrast to "reservation ecology," or conservation in protected areas steeped in the model of enclosure, reconciliation ecology is about conservation amid human enterprise. In a similar vein, reconciliation infrastructures involve an active design of infrastructural environments in order to foster other-than-human life. Such infrastructures incorporate ecology into architectural assembly and, in effect, are an imperative to modulate the habitus of a creature. Their design takes the corporeal and ethological dispositions of animals into consideration, generating affordances that might be realized by other-than-humans.[134]

At the same time, reconciliation infrastructures can be read as technologies of environmental governance. They are attempts to engineer animal worlds and to regulate animal mobilities in ways that conservation desires. There in fact are attempts to mainstream reconciliation infrastructures by various epistemic bodies. For instance, the Wildlife Institute of India, a leading government-funded ecological research body, advocates ensuring that infrastructural development has "clear biodiversity goals." This includes rendering infrastructures "'animal friendly' by providing pathways for movement of species" and to "mitigate any negative impacts on sensitive habitats."[135] Two "measurable outcome" structures designed for animals ought to highlight the scripting of conservation through an infrastructural idiom. The first entails preventing the decline in wildlife populations in the long term, that is, ensuring population viability. The second involves reducing infrastructure-induced mortality of animals. More significantly, such "green infrastructures" are seen to offer a "blueprint for 'smart conservation'" that is "proactive," protecting or restoring "natural corridors and networks" and "harmonizing," promoting both conservation and development.[136] In a similar vein, the Asian Elephant Specialist Group advocates better design in order to meet conservation challenges in a world of infrastructural explosion. They recommend developing a consistent nomenclature for elephant passages in order to intervene more effectively. The group also calls for developing structural design guidelines so that animals' mobilities can be integrated into infrastructure project planning. These are to be coupled with economic cost-benefit analyses of deploying mitigation measures versus not intervening and keeping elephant habitats intact.[137]

The design of the proposed flyover in Kaziranga follows guidelines drawn up by the Wildlife Institute of India, a key consultant for the project. Given that elephants are one of the main animals such infrastructural interventions target, the elevated linear infrastructure will be constructed in a way that accommodates the creature's bodily propensities and mobilities (figure 5.5).

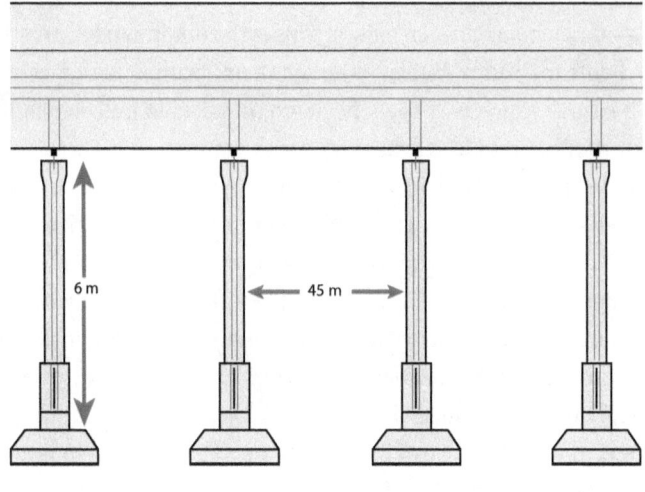

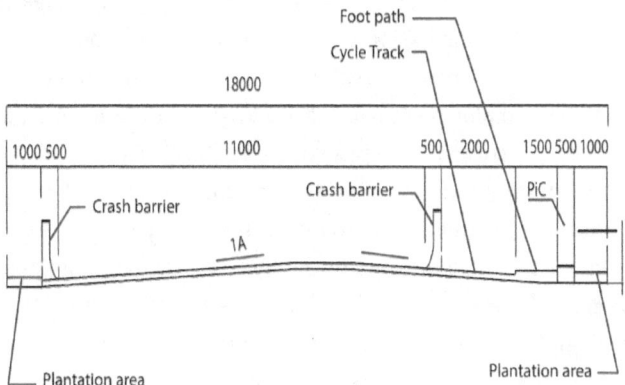

TYPICAL CROSS SECTION OF FLYOVER

5.5 Reconciliation infrastructures: (*top*) span arrangement of flyovers with spacing of pillars such that an elephant can pass; (*bottom*) cross-section of flyover with plantations as noise barriers and cycle track for people. Redrawn from designs presented during public consultation, September 5, 2021.

The vertical height of the proposed underpass is 6 meters, and there is a 45-meter span between pillars. This is the minimum height stipulated by the Wildlife Institute of India, although their documents suggest that a height of "8–10m," which is "thrice the height of an adult bull elephant," is desirable in order to provide safe passage for the animals.[138] These elevated sections of the National Highway cover a stretch of 54 kilometers, with flyovers in three segments of 18, 11.5, and 4.9 kilometers respectively.[139]

Reconciliation infrastructures typically aim to work with rather than against the habitus of a creature. They are concerned with not only mobility but the sensory dispositions of animals as well. For instance, the flyovers in Kaziranga are to have noise barriers on both sides (figure 5.5), given that elephants rely on auditory signals, and vehicular traffic noise acts as a major deterrent in their use of infrastructure. This extends to visual cues as well. According to engineers of the PWD, "the height of noise barriers will be such that the glare of vehicles will not fall on the animal movement tracks." The flyovers will use prefabricated structures along their sides to reduce disturbance.[140] Reconciliation infrastructures simultaneously regulate human subjects. "The speed of vehicles will be regulated and there will be a complete ban on blowing horns," PWD engineers state. "Adequate signages to create awareness will be placed at specific locations."[141]

Visibility for animals is a further consideration of reconciliation infrastructures. Animals tend to avoid narrow passages, as there are dangers from predators. The piers of the flyovers "will be vegetated with creepers to minimize the tunnel effect," state PWD engineers.[142] Prescriptions from ecologists include maintaining visibility for animals along roads and retaining a verge so that animals do not have to confront a highway immediately when coming out of a forest.[143] All of these interventions are increasing the "permeability" of transport infrastructure and, therefore, modulating animal mobilities.[144]

Each of the proposed interventions are site-specific. During a visit in 2014 to review the Government of Assam's proposal for creating flyovers, a team from the Wildlife Institute of India recommended realigning the highway near a locality called Deosur Hill so that the area could serve as high ground for wildlife during peak floods. Flyovers were not a viable option, as this would reduce the area available for animals. Officials of the PWD have offered "a solution" by suggesting an animal "overpass" so that the entire hill can be used as high ground. "This is a very active corridor," an engineer said during a consultation with the public in 2021, "and the topography does not allow an underpass to [be] built." The suggested animal overpass will involve tunnels for vehicles. The latter are to be constructed from precast reinforced cement concrete segments in order to minimize disturbance during on-site construction. "The road tunnel will be ventilated naturally," the engineer added, "so no power sources that could create sound pollution are involved." The tunnel will also involve barriers to prevent the entry of animals, particularly rhinos and elephants.

Only time will tell whether reconciliation infrastructures are actually able to manipulate the habitus of a creature. While the Wildlife Institute of India maintains that overpasses should only be a last resort for crossings involving elephants,[145] other conservation biologists working in the landscape contend that the design needs to be reconsidered. "A tunnel is better than the flyover at places like Haldibari and Panbari," states Firoz Ahmed, a conservationist from the environmental NGO Aaranyak. "It has less sound impact on the surface. The entire surface land is available for wildlife to use as refuge and habitats. Flyovers cause immense sound effects underneath that may disturb animals."[146]

Reconciliation infrastructures seek to intervene in intensive spaces, that is, spaces forged by movement. Their aim is to remove the barrier effect created by the highway. Farmers in Panbari draw attention to the nature of such intensive spaces. In contrast to linear conceptions of corridors where other-than-human mobility is conceived as two-way traffic, sometimes indicated by bidirectional arrows on maps, people point to the nonlinearity of elephant movement. "Elephants move through the designated corridor area," Manoj and Kartik tell me, "but their paths take different trajectories." "Their movements are more like interlacing trails," Kartik adds, as he draws various paths over a map of the newly designated corridor (figure 5.6). Each of these trails is a vector: they have direction, purpose, and intent. "Much of the movement is dictated by the lay of the land," says Manoj. "Elephants will not climb up steep gradients, and thus there are very specific points at which they cross the highway and move through the landscape in Panbari. These depend on the slope, sometimes more than the presence of forest cover."

Farmers allude to the tracks of animal lifeworlds, which are alive and sentient, as opposed to the extensive space of the state and conservation NGOs, where the corridor becomes a connector and is subordinate to the predetermined points or forest reserves they link. Intensive spaces are inexorably linked to cultivation. "There are a few elephants here," says Manoj, "and quite often it is the same individuals that move through.

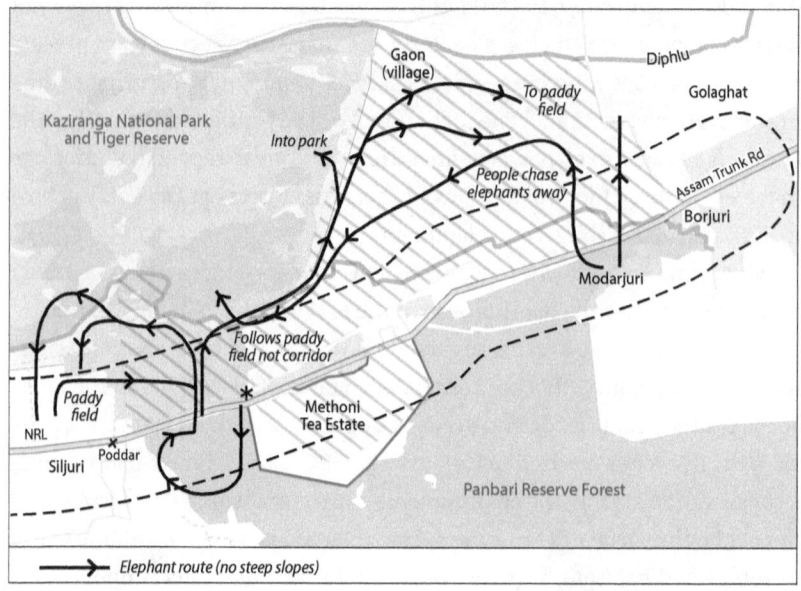

5.6 Interlacing trails: a storied cartography of elephant movement. Solid black lines are elephant tracks outlined by farmers in Panbari, drawn over a map of the corridor (indicated by shaded lines) delineated by the Forest Department. Redrawn from author's notes, 2021.

Paddy cultivation plays a very important role in their movement. If you stop cultivation, I can assure you that elephant movement through this area will decrease." Countermapping the corridor as an intensive space is, in many ways, a challenge to notions of inviolate space that proponents of connectivity conservation desire. "Many of the elephants in this landscape move along paddy fields at the time of cultivation," says Manoj, as he tracks lines of elephant movement over the area designated as a "functional corridor" by the Forest Department (figure 5.6). "Elephants' movements are determined by smell," Kartik tells me, drawing out an olfactory geography of animal mobility and the ways in which intensive spaces come into being in excess of vision. "They can smell paddy from miles away, perhaps even when they are behind one or two hills." "In fact we cannot even plant the Johā variety of rice," says Manoj, referring to a fragrant cultivar that is popular among people. "Elephants will come crashing through, so intense is its smell for the animals."

"It is possible that elephants will start to use the underpasses," Manoj replies when I ask him about the efficacy of reconciliation infrastructures. "They are really clever animals and learn very quickly. However, it is not a simple question of elephant movement being dictated by the flow of traffic. Rather, paddy cultivation also matters." Both Manoj and Kartik argue that their practices of cultivation are important for elephant movement. "It is not just the case of there being a forest strip present. That idea of a corridor is like those in offices," Manoj adds. Farmers in Panbari tell me that there is little room for counterarguments in the debate around connectivity. The consultations never question what constitutes connectivity, but are focused on whether people are agreeable to a proposed solution or not. In effect, by speaking for the elephant and silencing other cartographies of elephant movement, the diagram of connectivity becomes a new mode of control in a Plantationocene.

What social and gendered impacts reconciliation infrastructures have will only be discernible later, once they are installed and running. During a public consultation held by Forest Department authorities and the PWD in 2021, certain people argued that the flyovers will bypass their settlements, causing them to stagnate. "I have a shop by the roadside," remarks a resident of Kaziranga, "and the construction of these flyovers will mean that I will go out of business, for passing vehicles will no longer stop. This is not just a predicament for me, but for several people in places where flyovers are going to come up." State authorities have largely seen such activities along the National Highway as a hindrance to connectivity, contributing to the barrier effect of infrastructure. As the vision document for the Kaziranga landscape states, the highway has "become a zone of mushrooming developmental activities such as hotels, *dhabas*, shops and commercial space" rendering "several identified corridors for animal movement . . . dysfunctional."[147] The proposed elevated infrastructures do have a bicycle track that, the Forest Department argues, will enable people to commute. Yet it remains to be seen to what extent such infrastructures will become hostile the other way round: facilitating animal mobilities while thwarting those of people. As the resident remarks, "many of the older women here do not even know how to ride a bicycle. It is going to be particularly difficult for them to commute."

Reconciliation infrastructures appear to be a win-win strategy,[148] fostering both conservation and vehicular mobility. However, such infrastructures also run the risk of becoming engineering fixes to what is a wider sociopolitical issue and where there are other, intensive cartographies of elephant movement. As the Forest Department's vision document presciently notes, building flyovers will only help animals cross a busy highway, not necessarily foster connectivity in the wider landscape in the face of urban sprawl.[149] To this one might add that they may not ameliorate concerns regarding development voiced by people who protest against the diversion of infrastructures. Reconciliation infrastructures are far from benign. While they are a techno-managerial intervention in a conservation problem, they encourage greater automobility rather than curbing it. As a consequence, petro-capitalism continues unabated.[150] In this mode, connectivity conservation becomes the flipside of a capitalist form of conservation that expands while relegating people to a need economy.

Retrofitting Connectivity

Reconciliation infrastructures in and of themselves do not enable landscape-scale connectivity. "Most of the corridors are blocked," the Forest Department vision for the Kaziranga landscape notes, and what is needed for connectivity in the long term is "corridor retrofitting." Retrofitting involves actions whereby "all obstacles" are cleared, "if necessary by removing existing construction, buying of land, including tea garden lands at market prices," and by "relocating buildings."[151] Visions for retrofitting include delineating a 1.5-kilometer buffer around corridors on both sides. If more than 50 percent of a village falls within this buffer, then the entire village "would be required to be included in the corridor."[152]

A more grand proposal for restoring connectivity is to convert some of the large tea plantations surrounding Kaziranga into "wilderness" by purchasing them at market rates.[153] This proposal, however, is not a vision of altering a Plantationocene. Rather, the proposal is one where the old nineteenth-century tug-of-war between the Forest Department and the plantation industry plays out anew.[154] "It cannot be denied," the Forest Department argues, "that most of these tea gardens were once upon a time virgin forests." Even though certain plantations were set up before Kaziranga was declared a reserved forest in 1908, in the "wake of threats of climate change . . . migration of species, inundation of land . . . there is an urgent need to completely rethink . . . how to reclaim these areas back into the fold of forestry and wildlife as a future shield of protection."[155] Furthermore, the wildlife of Kaziranga "need more land to survive" and the conversion of tea plantations into wilderness is one means through which such expansion might be achieved.[156]

Here, connectivity conservation entails an attempt to undo the material fixity of plantations, a project that requires significant capital. According to the Forest Department, costs of purchasing the ten or so plantations around Kaziranga would amount to 4 to 5 billion rupees (US$53–66 million), inclusive of a "rehabilitation package" for workers. The suggestion comes on the back of land acquired by the department in 2010, when it purchased 29 hectares of tea plantation land at a cost of 15 million rupees (US$2.01 million). Converting tea into habitat for wildlife is viewed as a means for "resolving the conservation versus development paradigm." "Additional land" will become available for conservation, and therefore development pressures on wildlife will ease.[157]

If the diagram of enclosure involved colonial attempts to create environmental subjects who would become accomplices in the generation of revenue from forestry,[158] then the diagram of connectivity entails creating new entrepreneurial subjects. The vision of uprooting plantations goes hand in hand with visions to enroll the Adivasi community in an "experiment within the Kaziranga landscape" where people might have a "better socioeconomic model to follow in lieu of what the community has been used to for almost a century."[159] This includes "special rehabilitation" and "alternate livelihood packages," and plans for the "uplift of the tea garden communities through well orchestrated green growth and low carbon strategies." Citing studies which suggest that "enterprising" members of the Adivasi generate additional avenues of income when compared to their peers, the vision includes "a complete and wholesome skilling" of workers, including women and youth. This biopolitical project extends to improving health parameters of women and "100% education for all" such that workers in the Kaziranga landscape earn equal or better wages than the national average.[160]

However, there lies the risk of generating yet another surplus population that has few means of simple reproduction and is confined to becoming part of a need economy. Most people from the Adivasi community have limited land of their own, if any. The removal of plantations could create a population of landless workers for whom transiting to other livelihoods will be far from simple. There is a high likelihood that they will become yet another group of castaways that are mere spectators to the drama of connectivity conservation. One need not go far to find actually existing examples of what happens when plantations are uprooted. In Assam, certain plantations have been abandoned by their owners after they were declared "sick," a condition akin to bankruptcy. This includes the Bogidhola Tea Estate, not very far from Sundarpur. Abandonment does not necessarily give rise to new states of nature, celebrated in accounts of feral biologies of the Anthropocene,[161] but aggravates the plight of the Adivasi community and, as Sarah Besky has shown, plantation workers more broadly.[162] Many people, left to their own devices, have taken to stealing firewood from forest reserves to make ends meet, a preoccupation typical of a need economy that puts people in extremely vulnerable situations. Some now work as temporary labor in neighboring small tea estates, with not even the slender benefits people got under the Plantation Labour Act (1951). Others commute long distances to neighboring towns in search of daily work, which comes at an enormous social cost, especially for women.[163]

In effect, retrofitting is a technopolitical fix. Expanded land for conservation, while important, does not mean that the dilemmas of urbanization and development are automatically resolved. Besides the danger of creating surplus populations, it can intensify the highly deregulated form of urbanization and development that marks Indian planning. Management of the wider Kaziranga landscape, according to the Forest Department, is to follow strategies of zonation drawn from a master plan.[164] As decades of research on planning in India reveal, it often results in informality from above, where elites who wield power bend rules and acquire land and assets against the grain of play.[165] Urban sprawl in the Kaziranga landscape, lamented by conservationists, includes significant speculative real estate investments. In recent years, a number of buildings have come up in the corridors delineated by the state, without due permission and, in some cases, well after the Supreme Court ruling against new construction in such spaces.[166] Directives to demolish "illegal" buildings are kept at bay by tacit negotiations and delays,[167] and when demolishing does take place, it is directed at certain constituencies who either lack clout or fail to comply with political power.

Informality from above generates further asymmetries and dispossesses the rural poor. "The price of land has become so steep in this area that it is now virtually impossible for local people to buy land," Kartik tells me. In a welcome move, the Forest Department, through the constitution of a Kaziranga Landscape Authority, has sought to protect the interests of local communities by proposing to place a restriction on outsiders buying land.[168] Yet spectacular megafauna and a boom in tourism have driven up land market prices. The introduction of more regulations, particularly around banning a change in land-use patterns, when coupled with an informal idiom of urbanization and development, means that those who wield capital and power can continue to engage in transactions. "There are a number of bigwigs who are building lodges in paddy fields and restaurants in elephant corridors," says Kartik, "and this is ironic when we have to pave the way for corridors." In a state where colonial forces, particularly tea plantations, have historically locked up large tracts of land and introduced severe constraints for the expansion of the rural agrarian sector,[169] deregulation and speculative investment by urban elites aggravate the problem of land scarcity. Their effects are likely to be felt even more acutely in years to come.

Conservation in a Plantationocene

Connectivity is a new diagram of control and power in a Plantationocene. It emerges from various genealogies including the science of reserve design, responses to fragmentation of elephant habitat triggered by deforestation, and the conversion of the landscape to tea, themselves outcomes of violent, extralegal accumulation, as well as new intersections between conservation and capitalism through the spatial idiom of infrastructure. This diagram of power is marked by a shift from enclosure to connectivity, as well as a move from governing extensive spaces to intervening in spaces of intensity. If enclosure involved protection and conservation for pattern or the composition of biodiversity, the diagram of connectivity entails conservation by process, particularly of regulating mobility. The biopolitical target of conservation becomes flows rather than contained populations.[170]

Corridors are seen by the state and conservation NGOs as a panacea for undoing the fraught effects of a Plantationocene. The epistemology of reserve design, from which the idea of connectivity emerges, mobilizes an abstract geometry of shapes and connectors that are inherently diagrammatic. They visualize landscapes in highly simplified terms that enable theory to travel and retain coherence across worlds. Diagrams also work to actualize worlds: they provide guidelines on what models of landscape conservation are desirable and should be put into practice. Circles, connectors, and polygons are thus not merely representative schemas but describe the pragmatics of landscape. The diagram of connectivity, however, is not a homogeneous or universal entity, simply overlaid upon worlds.[171] Rather, its potency is derived from situated practices, whether these are the mapping of elephant corridors or the visualization of the lived worlds of elephants by tracking their mobilities. Practices of mapping elephant movement, in part enabled by the affordances of the proboscidean body and its ability to carry the bulky transmitters of the early 1990s, grounded habitat fragmentation and rendered visible the need for connectivity. There is thus a distinct postcolonial history to the actualization of reserve design principles, one deeply enmeshed with the emergence of a Plantationocene.

One might decompose this further by attending to the practices of diagramming Plantationocene landscapes and the political consequences of such abstractions. In its avatar as an extensive space, constituted by limits and boundaries, the corridor is a "connector," a line that is subordinated to the point.[172] Here, the tracks of elephants that constitute their inhabitation or wayfaring in the world become subservient to end points or the forest reserves that corridors connect. Formal definitions of elephant corridors as linear landscape elements that affect rates of immigration draw upon, and influence, this diagrammatic logic.[173] As connectors, corridors become strategies of biopolitical intervention, aimed at governing other-than-human populations by creating a network of protected areas and enhancing animal mobility through this network. The same logic pervades the drawing of polygons depicting elephant home ranges (figure 5.3). The area of such a range is a product of joining the outermost points of an animal's movement through a landscape. As such, it is the superimposition of Euclidean geometry upon the world and works to visualize which spaces need to be brought into the fold of protection and conservation.

In contrast, vernacular accounts of elephants' mobilities draw attention to the spaces of intensity forged by the animals' movements and their relation to the vegetal geography of a landscape. Here, the tracks of elephant movement are alive and world forming. They are also storied, intimately enmeshed with what particular animals do, how they are drawn to cultivation, and the ways in which elephants respond to the actions of people with whom they cohabit (figure 5.6). In state and conservation NGO models of connectivity, corridors need to be inviolate spaces, and they ought to be secured as such. In a vernacular appreciation, connectivity is not outside of the phenomena forming elephant movement. These contrasting understandings of elephant corridors, coupled with having to give up land for connectivity, result in frictions between local communities and the state–conservation NGO nexus. The latter often defines what constitutes a conservation problem and captures in advance what the solutions are. Although there are periodic consultations with communities, these have to do with whether a predetermined solution is acceptable and not with what constitutes a corridor or connectivity. As a consequence, corridors do not fully translate into the worlds of farmers, and they can get reinterpreted as coercive, externally imposed entities, even though the latter might not always be corridor proponents' intended aims.

At the same time, the politics of connectivity cannot be read outside of the political economy of rural urbanization and land. Fragmentation, as a condition of elephant landscapes, is an outcome of extralegal accumulation, whether to do with informal concessions for cutting down forests or speculative investments in land and fixed assets by those who wield power. The latter was in fact one reason for local communities losing the court case they filed, for the proceedings revealed anomalies in land ownership that did not fit the narrative of belonging that the petitioners sought to convey. The enactment of connectivity in a highly deregulated, rather than unregulated, milieu means that the rural poor face a further squeeze in simple reproduction. Legal statutes constrain what they are able to do with their land and what they are not, while elites are able to muscle their way into acquiring land and building assets.

The diagram of connectivity is increasingly scripted through the spatial idiom of infrastructure. Here, infrastructures are not antithetical to conservation, as implied in the model of the forest reserve, but become a technology of governance that aims to regulate mobility. This infrastructural turn can be equated with environmentality or a mode of biopower that acts upon circulations and modulates flows,[174] although there is a distinct set of situated actions at work in this postcolonial context, which is not a mere receptacle for ideas but the very grounds where environmentality is practiced and perfected. Reconciliation infrastructures such as flyovers and underpasses seek to undo some of the slow violence of hostile artifacts in the wider landscape that impact elephants and people alike. At the same time, and in their current guise, reconciliation infrastructures are also sites where engineering consultancies, corporations, real estate interest, environmental NGOs, and the state come together and align. Here, connectivity becomes the flipside to a capitalist form of conservation, where automobility and petro-capitalism continue with business as usual. Reconciliation infrastructures run the risk of becoming engineering fixes, for they do not intervene to thwart forces of capitalist accumulation that generate fragmentation in the first place.

Neither do reconciliation infrastructures intervene in social relations that plant the rural poor in a need economy.

Connectivity conservation might be viewed as a new form of territorial expansion, one that is not antithetical to plantation logics but commensurate with them. Landscape-scale connectivity is a counterforce to the expansion of tea plantations that has been a feature of Assam's Plantationocene since colonial times and which has been renewed with the small tea estate revolution of the 1990s and early 2000s. The need for corridors and connectivity enables another facet of a Plantationocene—enclosure through conservation—to hold sway. Future landscape visions of undoing plantations and converting them to wilderness to foster connectivity run the risk of producing a new set of castaways and left-behinds. Here, people can be rendered placeless while simultaneously planted and kept in place. Rather than seeking to create new entrepreneurial subjects out of the plantation workforce, better implementation of actually existing labor laws might do more to ameliorate the plight of people.

More creative solutions to undoing the harms of fraught Plantationocene ecologies are warranted. The need to regulate urban sprawl and to protect local communities from speculative investment in land are some of this conservation model's proposed suggestions and certainly have heuristic value. However, the creation of connectivity by reproducing coercive models of conservation, including the creation of inviolate corridors, needs serious rethinking. Alternative, more democratic visions of spaces outside protected areas ought to be scripted. These should incorporate civic senses of place rather than gesture to them in tokenistic ways. Vernacular notions of connectivity that derive from intensive spaces forged by both wildlife and the practices of people are critical to a more inclusive vision. Altering intensities can in fact become counterproductive for conservation, as would alienating people, although the latter is well underway.

6

Decolonial Cartographies

During the course of my fieldwork in Sundarpur, Budhu asked me a profound question. It is one that resonates even today. We were sitting up in their *tongi* one evening, keeping vigil and talking about our usual topics of village life: whether the season's harvest would be successful, how many liters of kerosene would the district administration give, what amount might be pilfered and what amount distributed, and, of course, whether elephants would come to the fields that evening. Budhu stoked the fire that kept us warm on a cold November night, then turned away from the smoke that had begun to drift into his face. "You have seen elephants move through the fields, raid crops at night, and then return to the reserve during the daytime," he said, "and at other times elephants go towards Numaligarh and even the Kaziranga reserve." I nodded, acknowledging Budhu's observations. "Tell me one thing," he continued. "How do elephants know where to go and what to do? Can you explain how elephants make choices about their movements and decide where they should be on a particular day?"

I paused and shook my head, hoping Budhu would provide an explanation. He gave me a wry smile. "Elephants have a guardian, a *devatā* or spirit that we call Dāngariyā. It guides elephants through the landscape, acting as a scout to see if there is any danger, whether it is safe to venture, where to graze and where to drink water," said Budhu. "Dāngariyā is responsible for elephants' decisions. It is with its help that elephants are able to move effectively across such a large area and inhabit the wide-ranging landscape in which they dwell."

Budhu's explanation of how elephants negotiate landscapes, one corroborated by several others in Sundarpur and in the wider region, is a very different opening for understanding how Plantationocene worlds are dwelled in and inhabited. It could not stand in greater contrast to ecological explanations of elephant movement. The latter, some of which are rooted in models of neoclassical economics, are the basis for explaining the size and extent of elephants' home ranges and therefore the area an individual elephant or population needs. The ecological sciences, as we have seen, also underpin connectivity conservation. Networks of forest reserves connected by corridors become the dominant mode of designing and arranging landscapes for elephants and, as we saw in earlier chapters, are steeped in particular geometries of power.

In contrast, a cartography where animals are guided by spirits brings a different kind of landscape to the fore. My use of the term *cartography* here is broader than simply discussing the practices of mapping. By cartography, I am referring to processes of mapping into life and to the different ways in which life is spatially, culturally, and economically arranged. A cartography that is not bound by perimeters but unfolds along tracks and trails of movement, I argue, is also a deep-seated resistance to plantation logics and colonial enclosure. It indexes arrangements that are akin to what Katherine McKittrick, in reference to a very different context, evocatively calls "demonic grounds": senses of place that refuse "comfortable belonging" and the alteration of place by the dispossessed "albeit on different terms than we may be familiar with."[1] Budhu's reference to Dāngariyā allows us to engage with a narrative that locates and draws on Adivasi knowledge and to make visible other lives even though they may be uprooted and planted, worked upon by diagrams of power and relegated to the confines of a need economy. In other words, this is a landscape produced by the interplay between domination and dispossession on the one hand, and Adivasi worlds on the other.

It is these other cartographies that I wish to draw out in this brief chapter. The endeavor here is not to discover lost senses of place. Rather, I want to direct attention to other ways in which landscape, dwelling, and ecology give Adivasi lives meaning amid the slow violence of a Plantationocene. Such an endeavor means going beyond work in multispecies scholarship and political ecology, which overturn Western, Cartesian dualisms of Nature and Society, but do not always sufficiently engage with non-Eurocentric ontologies and ways of knowing.[2] Other-than-humans of very specific kinds are brought to the fore in such work: there is little room for spirits or supernatural entities that, in the Western tradition, straddle an uneasy location between being and nonbeing. The worldviews of my Adivasi informants and their situated knowledges, on the other hand, raise a raft of other questions and explanations of how to inhabit and negotiate landscapes in spite of coercive designs. To evoke another cartography, one starting from a different worldview than that of Western thought, I argue, is not about resorting to "ontological idealism," as some critics maintain.[3] Such criticism stems from a concern that the question of capital is the only one worthy of real analytical concern, for capitalism destroys other worldviews, making them powerless or redundant in the contemporary world. In many ways, this is misplaced critique. Not only does it fail to recognize the ontological violence Eurocentric epistemologies authorize; such critique ends up reproducing this violence. The notion of redundancy is a cover-up for a failure—and often lack of ability, ethnographic or otherwise—to venture into demonic grounds.

A decolonial cartography, therefore, ought to expose how colonialism and capitalism are ontological projects that impose their own version of the real while violently erasing other ways of apprehending and inhabiting the world. At the same time, such a cartography needs to write politics into ontology and keep epistemology in clear focus. One way of doing so is to retrieve other ways of enacting place: those emerging from transversal exchanges, cultural sharings, new ways of dwelling even though a population's strength might be sapped from within. Another crucial avenue for a decolonial cartography is to account for other knowledges—a situated epistemology that enables questioning dominant ways of knowing and pervasive claims to mastery. These enactments brim with potentials for other political projects and modes of living in a Plantationocene. A decolonial cartography has a number of resonances, from McKittrick's demonic grounds to AbdouMaliq Simone's concept of "unsubsumable fragments,"[4] arrangements of living that are never swallowed by colonialism and capitalism in spite of unrelenting immiseration and the creation of a populace who have to do without. Such a cartography also echoes Sylvia Wynter's articulation of the "plot"—a space of creativity that a plantation superstructure hides but does not fully erase, a space that offers up avenues for resistance to the overriding plantation economy.[5]

In fact, a cartography emerging through the actions of spirits, elephants, and people can be seen as a plot forged in and through movement: the outcomes of interlacing trails of human and other-than-human life, where loci of creativity and resistance are place binding rather than place bound. Adivasi worldviews, as I shall later show, also mean rethinking what an animal is. Unlike taxonomized knowledge emanating from the colonial project, where beings are pinned onto a hierarchical grid and their attributes derived from that grid, an Adivasi ontology of an animal is to take them to be doings: beings that are a signature of activity, enmeshed in the ongoing movement and traffic of life.[6] This opens up different ways of knowing and understanding the diversity of life and provides a vital counterpoint to classificatory knowledges of the state and capital, which institutionalize the rejection of difference and inform plantation logics of creating ecologies of the same. In this sense, plots, demonic grounds, and unsubsumable fragments have an epistemological dimension and enable formulating a critique of coercive economic and political projects.

In what follows, drawing from insights of my Adivasi interlocutors, I provide an outline of a decolonial cartography. This outline is not intended as a prescription for another world to come, but is an endeavor of unsettling the colonial underpinnings of a Plantationocene. Neither is this outline an attempt to speak on behalf of the destitute and the downtrodden. It is an experiment in writing with the thoughts of one's interlocutors, drawing from their gestures to alternate ways of knowing and therefore inhabiting or imagining worlds, acts that are not quietist but which have their own political potential. My request is that this chapter be read in the context of those that precede it, rather than as a stand-alone, decontextualized argument, for many of the political, economic, and social relations that it challenges can only be understood if a reader is familiar with how plantation logics have been instituted and how they operate across different fields. The chapter first turns to the Adivasi community's accounts of spirits and the kinds of cartographies they draw in their wake. Second, the chapter attends to other ontologies of what an animal is. An Adivasi worldview, where an animal is not a bounded entity but a locus in the ongoing movement of the world, opens up further avenues for inhabiting landscape against—and along—the grain of colonial and postcolonial dictates. Thus, and third, the chapter elucidates what a cartography forged by tracks and trails—rather than connectors and perimeters—might look like. In conclusion, the chapter argues that a critical engagement with other senses of place, animal, and dwelling, and different ways of knowing, narrating, and naming, signals ways for resisting plantation logics. Such forms of resistance might be covert rather than confrontational, but they are in no way cleaved from a politics of inhabitation against the tide of oppression and immiseration. What emerges is not a ready-made platform or manifesto for political action but an attention to ways of knowing and being that have the potential to alter existing order. Equally, foregrounding other ways of being is an acknowledgment—not of the marginal or the unacknowledged—but of creative and world-making activities, for it is the way in which those who have to do without render a Plantationocene more livable.

Spirits

"Two days ago a few of us were guarding crops in our *tongi*, and we heard elephants crossing the Doigurung River," says Dingla, a farmer from the Adivasi community in Sundarpur. "It was around nine o'clock at night." Dingla and the others with him pointed flashlights toward the river: "We could not see anything. And then we heard a high-pitched sound barely audible to the ear." The farmers turned on their lights again. All they could see was running water. "There were no silhouettes of animals crossing. We then heard the noise of plantain being torn," Dingla tells me. Those at Dingla's *tongi* lit a fire and moved toward the source of the sound. "They kept going round in circles, searching for elephants, but there were no signs of the animals. A couple of people even lost their way in the dark. There were no elephants at all," says Dingla. "It was Dāngariyā."

Losing one's way in the dark while following sounds of elephants that are not there is akin to being unmapped: an entry into another terrain from within the fissures of a Plantationocene. Dingla, Budhu, and others maintained that disorientations were the work of Dāngariyā and meant that elephants were going to come at some point. "If you hear a sound by the river or in the fields that seems like elephants, but do not see any animals, then you know for certain that elephants are going to arrive," adds Sutu, another farmer who guarded crops with Dingla. "Something crosses the field or water—is it an elephant, you ask? You turn on flashlights and see nothing. After a while, elephants will surely come." Dāngariyā made such sounds, Dingla and Sutu explained, while guiding elephants across the landscape, for they were also the animals' guardians. "From what our forefathers, who cleared the forest reserve and settled here, told us, Dāngariyā is a *devatā*, a spirit who is Mahādev or Shiva's cowherd," says Dingla.[7] "Dāngariyā therefore is the *mālik* of elephants," their owner or guardian. "Just as we keep a cowherd to look after our cattle and buffalo, Mahādev keeps Dāngariyā," Dingla explains. "Dāngariyā guides elephants where to feed, where to graze, which path to take, and what route to avoid."

That spirits are the guardians or owners of elephants rather than the government marks subtle and deep-seated forms of resistance to state claims over the animal, a claim that has a distinct colonial history going back to the Elephant Preservation Act of the late nineteenth century. "All of the animals and wildlife that inhabit reserves—Dāngariyā is their deity," Dingla explains, further indicating how the diagram of enclosure is contested, albeit subtly. Sutu elaborates this claim further: "Just as we keep cattle and are their owners, and just as we rear cows, buffalo, goats, pigeons, and ducks, in return for which we need to feed and look after them, protect them, in a similar vein god has delegated responsibilities of looking after elephants to Dāngariyā. Which way one should go on a particular day, where and in what direction, those decisions that an elephant has to make all depend on Dāngariyā."

The villagers further add that Dāngariyā empowers elephants to become discerning. "Whenever the Forest Department comes in their vehicles to chase elephants away, they never meet the animals," Dingla tells me. While an ethological explanation of such behavior would be that the elephants have learned to recognize the sound of the department's Jeep—which they probably discern from a distance, given the animals' auditory prowess—in the Adivasi worldview it is Dāngariyā prompting elephants, telling them what to do and how to respond. Both views take elephants as knowledgeable beings, except that in the former skills are conferred through genetic or cultural transmission, while in the latter becoming skilled is an environmental process, learned through negotiations and during the course of an individual or herd's history, while being honed by spirits.

An Adivasi view of how cartographies are forged through the actions of elephants, people, and spirits stands in contrast to Western models of elephant foraging that inform connectivity conservation. A dominant model in this regard is optimal foraging theory. Rooted in neoclassical economics, this model argues that animals adopt foraging strategies that provide the most benefit for the lowest cost, such that net energy gained is maximized. The time elephants spend in one patch before moving to another is taken to be based on rational choice, the basis for which is ultimately coded in an animal's genes. In this view, as the anthropologist Tim Ingold shows, "the rationality of the optimal forager" is "installed at the very heart of nature."[8] The time an animal spends in a patch of forest or field depends on the availability of food, and movement is couched as a trade-off between utilizing what is left in a patch and what might be available elsewhere at any given moment in time. This reduction of movement to neoclassical economic models leaves little room for skills that are generated during the course of an individual or herd's life. "Foraging," as Ingold argues, is not about algorithms and optimal choices, but a process of learning or "novices' practical involvement with the constituents of their environment—under the guidance of more experienced mentors—in the conduct of their everyday tasks."[9] An Adivasi ontology of elephant movement is not dissimilar: Dāngariyā is an experienced mentor from whom elephants learn how to go about their quotidian tasks.

"Dāngariyā cannot be seen. There is no image or iconography," Sutu tells me when I ask whether they have ever observed elephants being guided through the landscape. "Dāngariyā is like the wind," Dingla adds. "One cannot see it but only witness its effects." The analogy is important, for the wind blows and therefore exists. It cannot be perceived unless acting upon another body, whether the drifting of clouds in the sky or the rustle of leaves on a tree. The wind can be a trace on the ground or a thread in the sky.[10] In a similar vein, Dāngariyā's effects are noticed or heard. They leave traces as they create openings for elephants in a landscape, just as the threads of the wind bind the landscape and its human and other-than-human inhabitants into an intricate mesh.

For both villagers in Sundarpur and those who cultivated paddy in the elephant corridor in Panbari, appeasing Dāngariyā is important for staying out of the way of harm. "We keep paying obeisance to Dāngariyā," says Dingla. "That is why our home has been safe." He then goes on to tell me how the misfortune that fell upon Kanu's family—narrated in chapter 4—

was because of their *ahankār* or arrogance. "They would say, 'We are not afraid of elephants. We will kill them,'" Dingla recounts. "Can people really kill elephants?" Sutu joins in, referring not so much to the legal statutes that protect the animal as to the moral and ethical impossibility of doing so: "Bad luck came upon Kanu's family because they did not pay heed to Dāngariyā." When I ask Dingla and Sutu whether Dāngariyā could be controlled or tamed, they shake their heads. "People will die if they even try doing so," Sutu replies. "Even if a *bej* or shaman tries to tame Dāngariyā, he will be killed. Elephants will kill them."

To ensure that they had a good harvest and were not affected by elephants raiding crops, Dingla and the other villagers would do an annual ceremony for Dāngariyā. This included sacrificing a duck and praying to Lord Shiva, as he, according to Sutu, was "ultimately the guardian of all *devatās*." The ceremony would be held after completing a successful harvest, usually in April. The community in Panbari too performed the same ritual in their paddy fields after harvesting rice. "Initially people make a wish that their crops should remain safe and that no untoward incident involving elephants happens during the course of cultivation," says Kartik from Panbari, "and later as an act of gratitude a *puja* is held in the fields."

This account of how spirits mediate relations between elephants and their surroundings is an entry into demonic grounds. It opens up another way of mapping into a Plantationocene landscape, a cartography that marks forms of resistance to the violence colonial epistemologies authorize. While colonial powers uprooted communities and planted them in Assam, subjecting them to work and time discipline, converting some to Christianity, other ontologies and situated forms of knowing are never entirely erased. When Dingla states that the *mālik* of all elephants is Dāngariyā, it is a refutation of the state's claim over wildlife. Such claims are of course never binary or oppositional. At times, for many of my interlocutors, the elephant becomes "the government's animal on our fields" when issues of damage and compensation arise. It is precisely this uneasy relation between being biopolitical subjects and lives otherwise that marks a Plantationocene present, a relation that unfolds in a terrain forged between the "inhabitability of the normal" and the spaces of living in which other subjectivities are enacted.[11]

In a similar vein, Nicolas Lainé's rich ethnographic work on elephant capture in eastern Assam shows how other ontologies become ways of subverting state ownership of elephants. The Khamti, among whom Lainé worked, worship a spirit called Chao Pling Chang who was seen to live inside the forest and take care of wild elephants. Every elephant capture operation begins with an offering to this spirit, one that takes the form of a ritual exchange.[12] The Khamti also establish a similar ritual exchange with another spirit called Hodon-Modon, from whom the *phandi* or elephant catcher makes a request for an animal from the forest. Lainé goes on to show that such spirits are linked to defined territories over which they exercise control, including the beings that dwell within them.[13] Here, the colonial imperative of owning elephants and claiming them to be resources or forest produce is undermined, albeit not in a confrontational manner.

A cartography that Dāngariyā draws by herding elephants is not one of enclosure and enclaves, where life is disciplined, reduced to sameness, and calibrated with the time of the market. It is one encompassing a lifeworld that is nonbinary and rooted in codes of reciprocity and exchange. Such a lifeworld includes beings that do not neatly fall within Western classifications of what constitute life. In an Adivasi ontology, Dāngariyā is a being. In the Western scheme of things, Dāngariyā is an apparition, straddling an uneasy place between being and nonbeing. Here, Adivasi ways of knowing—their epistemologies—foster an analysis and possible transformations of power relations. If reciprocity involves not just relations between people and elephants, but those between elephants and Dāngariyā, and between people and spirits, then the biopolitical project of governing people and their relations with nature, whether through diagrams of enclosure or connectivity, faces a serious challenge, for such a project—steeped in the Western idea of life or *bios*—has little means to enter into such demonic realms.

It is in this vein that decolonial cartographies are "unsubsumable fragments."[14] That Dāngariyā cannot be controlled or tamed is a further indication of how resistance works. Elephants' mobilities, by their association with spirits, cannot be channeled or tempered in ways that the state desires, irrespective of how landscapes are enclosed or corridors drawn. The inhabitability of the normal is thus alterable, albeit by those who have to constantly do without, who have been subjected to historical dispossession and relentless contemporary exploitation. Decolonial cartographies are not about reifying marginality: they point to other forms of life and ways of living amid a Plantationocene and its coercive designs.

Animals

"Another name for the elephant is *matanga*," a farmer in Golaghat once told me. The name is evocative, for it translates to "leaves muddy tracks as it goes." If the word *elephant*, originating in the Greek *elephas*, meaning both ivory and elephant, refers to a bounded entity, *matanga* indexes a happening, a movement, a mood. In this worldview, elephants are what they do: they are a signature of activity, whether it involves leaving tracks while being guided by Dāngariyā through a landscape, opening up new pathways, or creating rhizomatic connections between places. Here, the elephant is not a noun but a verb.[15]

If we were to take this perspective seriously, then it becomes apparent that an animal and its tracks are inseparable. An elephant or "leaves muddy tracks as it goes," then, is not so much a bounded entity interacting with other, preformed beings in the world as a locus in an emerging set of trails. Each of these paths are laid down as the animal encounters people and other beings, and journeys from place to place. At the same time, tracks or trails are references to history: of particular actions and events, both past and present, known to both people and elephants. To think of the elephant as a thoroughfare, then, is another avenue for espousing a decolonial cartography. Just as relations between elephants and spirits open up other grounds, alternatives to taxonomized being provide insights into a possible "interhuman and environmental project through which 'new forms of life' can be conceptualized."[16]

It is perhaps trite to repeat that taxonomized understandings of the diversity of life have been crucial to the projects of colonialism and race, proceeding through hierarchical codes that have long organized populations and the planet. Yet this view is deep seated in the very meaning of *species*, a category through which many conservation imperatives and even some strands of multispecies ethnography proceed. To characterize beings as species means slotting each individual into a place or class with a taxonomic hierarchy, one that progresses upward to categories of wider generality. This progression tends toward a higher term each category imitates by "graduated resemblance."[17] The project of classification enacts an inversion: taxonomy vertically integrates diversity into a system of classification based on series, archetypes, and models, where nature is "out there," divided in advance into things in themselves.[18] Classification, by constructing a yardstick through which specimens from diverse localities are juxtaposed and compared, becomes crucial to rendering animals and their populations amenable to biopolitical governance.

What a taxonomic worldview erases are the relations of an animal with its surrounds and the situated knowledges through which those relations are summoned, just as it edits out wider histories in which beings are enmeshed. Adivasi ontology that sees an elephant as "leaves muddy tracks as it goes" is about resisting classificatory knowledge. Instead, it posits a different way of knowing where the animal is one locus in a world of movement and becoming,[19] inseparable from the relations that have brought it there. Such an ontology of an animal, elicited through situated knowledges, provides a counterpoint to the colonial project, and from which certain state and NGO-led conservation imperatives derive, for elephants are "identified not by fixed attributes but by their paths of movement in an unfolding field of relations."[20] To leave muddy tracks is to story the world: it is a reference to encounters, occurrences, and the ways in which lives—whether of people or elephants—get bound up in the other's story. It is in these bindings that forms of knowledge, whether human or other-than-human, are generated, and it is through tracks that alternate cartographies of a Plantationocene might be forged.

There is purchase to be drawn from an Adivasi ontology of an animal, particularly for conservation. Here, we might contrast the vocabulary of human-elephant conflict, operationalized by the state and certain conservation NGOs, with how elephants are understood by the Adivasi community and others living alongside elephants in Assam. Conflict creates its own field of visibility, a luminous environment that renders people, wildlife, and land object-targets of, and in need of, governance. This perspective reorients the world into one in need of constant intervention, whether through mitigation and resolution or capture and control. Conflict, as I have argued in chapter 3, not only belies the structurally motivated attrition of particular subjects but fixes sentient relations between people, elephants, and a landscape as a problem in need of particular intervention. The resonance, and even import, of the term *conflict*, from peacekeeping discourse, implies that resolution and mitigation are the only ways of living alongside. Popular discourse even likens the situation to a war, a battle for which international cooperation, knowledge, and funding are needed.[21]

In contrast, the Adivasi view of elephants as a signature of activity reveals how frictions are only one dimension of dwelling alongside. "Elephants come" and "elephants pass through" are frequently descriptions of the animals' activities, not because people are unaware of elephants' behaviors, but because the animal is understood as a locus in a matrix of trails. In a similar vein, when referring to frictions, people state that elephants "came and fed on paddy," or "broke into a house" or people's *tongis*. Each of these are references to a storied rather than species world. The term *conflict*, translated as *xanghāt* in Assamese, is virtually absent from people's vocabulary (although it forms part of the idiom of local newspapers), for dwelling alongside elephants is about reciprocity, accommodation, and respect, whether that involves being mindful of elephants or the actions of Dāngariyā. A storied rather than a disembodied and coded account of dwelling alongside is political. It does away with militarized discourse and practice, as well as the coercive designs they bring with them, to actualize other modes of living alongside. In fact, in an Adivasi worldview knowledgeability is multiplied. People are not the only ones with situated knowledge; elephants possess knowledge too. Storying then becomes a form of creative work that intervenes in the "commonsense teleology" of violence. It invokes a decolonial poetics through which other futures become imaginable.[22]

It is people's generosity that enables elephants to persist, in spite of an intensification of frictions, large-scale deforestation, the slow violence of infrastructure, and the unending quest to transform landscape into plantations. Just as acknowledging the power of Dāngariyā is a resistance to colonial enclosure of resources, to see the animal as a thoroughfare is to resist projects of territorial control or to impose another territoriality: that stemming from the actions of people and a range of beings that inhabit and make worlds. Such action does not repeat in a chronometric way. As a consequence, everyday life is turned into that which is "nearly impossible to police."[23] No doubt, encounters with elephants can be far from benign, and have always been so, but the importance of people's affective generosity as the cornerstone of conservation cannot simply be sidelined. Situated conservation practitioners, whether belonging to the state or wildlife NGOs, recognize its importance, although it is often lost in their quest to create environmental citizens and entrepreneurial subjects. To further explore the consequences of this ontology of an animal, we need to turn to cartographies forged by tracks.

Tracks

"The trails of elephant movement are called *dandis*," says Budhu, "and they are formed as elephants come and go. The landscape is opened up by such movement, and very soon they become established tracks." For the Adivasi community in Sundarpur, like some of the villagers in Panbari, *dandis* or tracks delineate a cartography of dwelling. Such tracks enable people to tell which directions elephants will come from and where they will go, and guide people into reserves when collecting firewood or moving through *Mikania*-clad vegetation. More importantly, people see elephants' tracks as alive. "*Dandis* keep opening up. As elephants move, and people follow, *dandis* become broader. People and animals then begin to follow *dandis* as they proliferate, go here and there," Budhu explains, therefore "opening up the forest even more."

These facets of a *dandi* or track are very different than the colonial project of forest enclosure and enclaved plantations. As one has seen throughout this book, the demarcation and expansion of state and capital territory in a Plantationocene follow a cartography of points, perimeters, and connectors. In the colonial and postcolonial projects of creating wildlife reserves, there is a separation of the "in here" of society from the "out there" of nature,[24] a binary violently put in place in the nineteenth century as the Forest Department and plantation industry began competing for Assam's natural resources and land. The cartographic practice of enclosure is steeped in the trace of the perimeter: a line returns to its point of origin and is closed upon itself. By doing so, a perimeter seals the world into containers in which people are planted and rooted in place. Wildlife populations are confined to limits within which they must be conserved. The result is a neat delineation of an inside and outside—binaries that need to be maintained, surveilled, and policed such that inviolate areas are kept in place for wildlife. Perimeters invert the act of dwelling or inhabitation into that of occupation.[25] Here, people and elephants take up position in a ready-made world or a world laid out for them in advance according to colonial order.

The same logic operates with points and connectors. Points fix individuals to Cartesian coordinates and render them apt for control and calculation. Every datum or point is a thing that is given: a fact about where something is, but not what it is or what it can do.[26] Points are discrete and fixed. They are static and homogenize the flow of life. While recording and plotting points—witnessed in a number of conservation practices, from mapping elephant home ranges to demarcating the boundaries of corridors—the inscriptive trace is broken down into a series of punctuations. A form of mapping by taking oneself out of the world, trails of movement are erased, and such cartographies not only become a view from nowhere but entirely edit out the social relations that underpin mapping. This punctual logic is reproduced in the diagram of connectivity: the connector is a linear element that joins the dots between two or more pregiven points. A corridor, therefore, is a joint that welds two points—usually forest reserves—mapped in advance. These are not necessarily lines of animal movement or tracks of inhabitation, for the line "remains totally subordinated to the point."[27]

Tracks, on the other hand, are open to the world. *Dandis* give rise to spaces that are intensive, which, as we saw in Manoj and Kartik's account of elephant movement through the Panbari corridor, are formed by phenomena constituting them, whether involving actions of elephants or those of people. Tracks, like points that float or become unbound, unmap colonial cartographies. They give rise to other grounds that escape postcolonial territorializations. While the state and conservation NGOs are very aware of the nomadic qualities of elephants, their response is to create a network of reserves connected by corridors. The state model follows lines of closure where the only way of preserving life is to seal it within perimeters. Corridors become conduits that link two or more bounded spaces; they are linkages for extending enclosed habitat. A decolonial cartography stemming from tracks, on the other hand, is a starting point for an alternate landscape imaginary, one where conservation might happen through the shared fabrication of space.

Elephant *dandis*, as material tracks, are generative. Not only have elephant tracks played a role in how people in Assam negotiate landscapes, but, as Paul Keil has also shown, they were infrastructure for the state.[28] The colonial administration utilized the paths created by elephants through Assam's jungles to open up new frontiers for exploitation. The memoirs of John Rowntree, a British forest officer posted in Assam, vividly describe how this unfolded. Given the task of "improving" an existing forest track and turning it into "an extraction road," Rowntree was apprehensive of his limited knowledge of surveying. "I need not have worried," Rowntree writes, "because the elephants had done the surveying for us—that is, the wild elephants." "The Assam forests," he further elaborates, "are honeycombed with *dandies* [sic], that is, elephant tracks, beaten hard by the feet of generations of elephants. . . . Elephants have an eye, or nose, which is far more effective than a theodolite in wooded country, and an unerring instinct for choosing the most suitable alignment. All one had to do to make a road, was to widen an existing *dandi*, altering their alignment slightly where the elephants had been content to walk through a swamp instead of around it."[29] Assam's veteran forest officer Bhupendra Nath Talukdar, who extensively surveyed forest reserves in western Assam during the early 1980s, recounted a similar story of how tracks subtend engineering works carried out by the state. "Elephants," Talukdar told me while walking through the Nameri forest in Sonitpur, "make the perfect gradient of a road, after which people follow and ultimately the Public Works Department."

This infrastructuring activity of elephants was vital for colonial resource extraction, further revealing how the animal was integral to the opening up of frontiers. Although now on the decline, such infrastructuring acts point to ways in which tracks are generative, alive, and world forming. "Trails have memories for elephants," says Budhu, an observation that further highlights how the Adivasi community's situated knowledges cede to other-than-humans as knowledgeable, just as it foregrounds how more-than-human sentience goes into the making of other cartographies. Recent ecological studies are in fact beginning to indicate how sensory cues along well-beaten tracks become sources of information about other individuals.[30] Elephants deposit dung and urine when they move along *dandis*, which allow others to gauge the age and maturity of individuals they are likely to encounter in the landscape. Tracks thus act as a "public information resource," assisting navigating elephants to negotiate unfamiliar environments.[31] *Dandis* become particularly important in the periphery of an individual's range, including, for instance, agricultural fields and settlements, for they enable individuals to acquire memories and actively learn routes.

Tracks are akin to a plot,[32] albeit one forged through movement, both human and other-than-human. Plots, as Wynter and McKittrick argue, are sites where "secretive histories" of the plantation can be found. They entail creative spaces to challenge plantation order and to resist the overriding system of the plantation economy. Like the plot, tracks illustrate another cartography developed within a context of dispossession and dehumanization, one that forges a politics of living and dwelling impossible under a coercive plantation regime. These include emerging stories and narratives, cultural and ecological practices that materialize connections between Adivasi life and the land, and fostering other ways of dwelling that challenge slow and systemic violence. Tracks, and the cartographies they summon, thus provide a theoretical scaffolding for imagining a Plantationocene landscape otherwise. They are cartographies constituted through the incessant traffic of life, which deterritorialize enclaves of the plantation and the enclosure of forest reserves. The spatiality of interlacing tracks, whether those of people, elephants, or other denizens of a landscape, are those that plantation logics cannot entirely subsume. In being unsubsumable, tracks provide a vital counterpoint to the reproduction of plantation logics that otherwise seem "as though [they are] natural, inevitable, and a normal way of life."[33] It is precisely in this vein that decolonial cartographies are political. Tracks open up means for other forms of being and flourishing without further denigrating those who have to do without, and reveal how such a condition is not totally abject but has its share of creativity that can take on forms of resistance.

A further way to imagine the wider importance of this cartography is the affective generosity of people discussed above. Another pertains to how elephants' own movement is generative of livability. Studies in other landscapes show how elephant footprints, which quickly fill up with water, have crucial ecological roles. They serve as microhabitats for several invertebrates including beetles, mayflies, and dragonflies.[34] Elephant tracks thus become other passages for life, enabling pool-dwelling invertebrates to cross parched landscapes and built-up or agrarian environments. The history of these tracks also matters: older footprints tend to have higher amounts of organic matter and therefore harbor greater diversity.[35] Ecological work also indicates how elephant tracks serve as predator-free breeding grounds for frogs, where footprints filled with water become oviposition sites as well as nursery habitat for tadpoles.[36] Water-filled elephant tracks can function as stepping stones in dry landscapes, generating their own forms of connectivity and aiding the dispersal of life.

Tracks therefore are a cartography of enmeshment. An enmeshed generation of place, in contrast to an embodied one, is about how places are forged through the intersections of movement of a heterogeneous array of beings, whose lives are never cleaved from one another, whether these include people, spirits, elephants, or other forms of life. Unlike the enclosure and container, tracks have neither an inside nor outside, only directions, velocity, and traffic. In this sense, they signal a mode of inhabitation that resists evictions and expulsions. Tracks are associations that are not binary but rooted in codes of reciprocity, although the forms of exchange across human and other-than-human divides are neither smooth nor settled. Like the plot, tracks are a means of reading history against the plantation.[37] They generate another spatiality of dwelling alongside that refuses plantation logic, its quest toward monoculture and reduction of everything to the same. More importantly, tracks are avenues for creativity where new forms of life take shape. They are other kinds of infrastructure that do not submit to the plantation but enable more humanly workable, and alterable, practices of living.

Livable Worlds

Demonic grounds, unsubsumable fragments, decolonial cartographies—these are all references to spaces of elsewhere, to other modes of being that persist "in spite of. . . ." In spite of being uprooted, planted, and rendered "ungeographic," in spite of unrelenting dispossession meted out by colonial and capitalist forces, and in spite of being relegated to a need economy as processes of accumulation are renewed. Alterity is that which has to be fought for. It is a struggle or resistance, not always as direct confrontation but as that which operates beneath the zones of detectability and, therefore, always in articulation with the dominant order of a Plantationocene. As seen throughout this book, the dominant order of organizing Plantationocene landscapes entails diagrams of enclosure and those of connectivity. Habitability is carved out amid this dominant order and its attendant slow violence, the necropolitical profiteering from life considered disposable, and amid violent regimes of generating surplus value through extralegal means. Decolonial cartographies thus become a refusal of the violence immanent to a plantation milieu. What is vital to note, however, is that such avenues for working out life anew are never entirely rendered redundant by capital's ravages. Those having to do without express agency, and while it might be one of maintenance rather than making, demonic grounds, unsubsumable fragments, or decolonial cartographies index pathways of creativity for leading lives otherwise.

One therefore cannot focus on the economic alone as the basis for charting decolonial cartographies, for analyses and calls for action steeped in the economic often hold on to one set of processes and treat them as general, while blotting out others. Here, binaries between the social and the natural, which some proponents of the Capitalocene wish to maintain, also have limited purchase. Sociality cannot be understood solely through a Western lens, for there are other ways of enacting sociality, including through relations with heterogeneous kin. Here, Adivasi ontologies, their situated and distributed ways of knowing and the politics they summon become crucial. They provide a critical counterpoint to plantation logics, particularly the latter's imperative of reducing life to sameness, where landscapes are populated by vegetal beings that interact with replicas, where valueless trees are removed to create homogeneous and commercially viable forests, and where the lives of people are violently rendered synonymous with the production of cheap commodities. Yet we see how there is a resistance on people's part to being reduced to sameness, a resistance that is simultaneously social, spatial, epistemological, and ontological. This resistance emerges by creating diversity, not necessarily in a liberal sense of the term, but as an endeavor that is relational, involving reciprocity between a multitude of beings, some of which are not allowed into the category of life in the Western tradition. Neither is such diversity a taxonomic index that has been closely bound up with plantation logics and their racialized hierarchies. Here diversity might be understood as a generation of difference, a creative act unfolding by entering demonic grounds.

Furthermore, the political importance of a decolonial cartography is that it strikes at the heart of the diagrams of enclosure and connectivity. The spatial politics of the colonial plantation entailed confining people to its enclave such that labor was cheap, plentiful, and easily disciplined.[38] That of forest reserves involved enclosure and the institution of a binary between reserve and agricultural land or settlement. Their cartographies are inverted in that inhabitation is turned into an act of occupation, and the traffic of life is contained by perimeters and boundaries. In contrast, a spatiality of tracks has neither inside nor outside. They are vectors and rhythms that deterritorialize the forest enclosure, the enclaved plantation, and its economies of scale. Tracks are "lines of flight,"[39] loci of political resistance that are diagonal rather than confrontational. This does not mean other forms of resistance to the state and to capital never take hold. Peasant-based movements have sought to wrest control over forest land in the region,[40] the agitations that took place in the Panbari elephant corridor being an example. The latter, however, have failed and, instead, a network of corridors and zones has taken hold. These are attempts to reterritorialize the nomadic qualities of elephants and to impose particular regulations on how intensive spaces should be managed. Imperatives of landscape-scale conservation are no doubt important, but they entrench and deepen inequalities when mobilized in authoritarian ways. The importance of the Panbari agitations is that the ability to resist always remains latent, and people's allusions to a cartography unfolding along tracks point to possibilities for realizing worlds otherwise, in spite of reterritorializations and losses in their wake.

These forms of resistance reflect the creative agency of those who have to do without, for people are not entirely defeated by capital or a Plantationocene's travails. Considering spirits as owners of animal life, foregrounding a topography of landscape unfolding along tracks, and invoking other ontologies of animals are indicative of how lives are never fully subsumed. The actions of Dāngariyā, as it guides elephants through forests and people's settlements, is an index of an elsewhere and of proboscidean places amid a Plantationocene, just as it is an instance of the enactment of another epistemology, which enables making other ontological claims that can dispute a quest for mastery. A decolonial cartography would entail working from these forms of alterity to build broader alliances with other social and political projects, although giving such alliances a majoritarian form will not always yield results. As AbdouMaliq Simone argues, "surges of political affect do not always take on the recognizable vernaculars of autonomy, resistance, and freedom," and yet "rhythms of endurance," as we have witnessed in a number of instances so far, prove "more nuanced . . . more adept at working their way" in creating livable worlds.[41] Transversal connections that are forged amid dispossession and that derive from unsubsumable fragments are potentials: they might help actualize other, more livable, worlds even though not all potentials have equal power to become actual.

Decolonial cartographies need not be antithetical to conservation practice. Rather, they create avenues for reorienting what conservation could be. If colonial and postcolonial ravages have created a violent world for people, they have done so for elephants as well, witnessed in instances of hunting and the alteration of the animals' lifeworlds, the accretive and attritional effects of infrastructure, and the impacts of accumulation by plantation spawned in the wake of deforestation and secessionist militancy. The Adivasi community and others who dwell alongside elephants attest to their sentience and apprehension of a riven landscape. At the same time, an Adivasi ontology points to elephants' knowledgeability and their capacity to modify a state of affairs. This is precisely what is at stake when farmers ask NGOs whether elephants are polite, for they know too well that animals do not confirm to neoclassical economic models and act as rational agents.[42] Spaces for elephants ought not to be hylomorphically imposed but need to be arrangements that take elephants as loci in a matrix of trails where more creative and less coercive forms of conservation might happen. These of course might not materialize: contemporary forms of power are in fact becoming non-hylomorphic. Nonetheless, decolonial cartographies can unsettle the notion of authority. They invoke ways of redistributing knowledge and, importantly, expertise,[43] where there can be conversations across epistemologies and where statist or capitalist imperatives do not capture solutions in advance. Conservation, by acting across an array of concerns, whether these have to do with work, labor, or simple reproduction, could become a practice that intervenes to undo the harms of a Plantationocene rather than aggravating them. What we can learn from Adivasi practices of world making is the importance of reciprocity and generosity rather than techno-managerial intervention and spatial fixes.

Decolonial cartographies call for exercising caution with regards to the totalizing claims of the Anthropocene or, for that matter, an all-pervasive account of a Plantationocene. They show the significance of places on the planet that are grounds of alterity and through which other forms of livability are forged. Decolonial cartographies are skeptical of grand claims, whether analytical or political. Their significance is drawn from the thickness of experience and from the vantage point of those who matter, and who know better about what might be altered and what cannot. Such cartographies are not the panacea that the state and conservation NGOs aspire to through solutions such as corridors, as though they will somehow undo harms and create a frictionless landscape. Neither can decolonial cartographies be scaled up or down, for they refuse the scalar relations of the plantation. It is in such refusal that decolonial cartographies can become antidotes to oppressive orders of thought and habit, offering another set of visions for politics to be written back into the landscape. They are generative of other ways of imagining and making worlds amid a Plantationocene.

Conclusion
A Reverse Déjà Vu

I began writing this book in Assam in the midst of a lockdown introduced to curtail the effects of a disastrous second wave of COVID-19 infections that had ravaged India. The peak in cases was delayed in Assam, taking place after the Delta variant of the virus had run rampant in most parts of the country. The failure of the Indian state in providing care and the breakdown of health infrastructure generated waves of panic. There was nothing purely biological about a delayed peak of infections in Assam: it was a reflection of the state of mobility in the region, long conditioned by its colonial history and postcolonial infrastructure. By June 2021, as one lockdown followed another, the rural landscape around Kaziranga began to look desolate. Village shops and grocery stores were closed. There were no gatherings in the *charialis* and *chowks*. Those who earned a living by selling labor power were confined to their homes. Others involved in small acts

C.1   Plantation labor lines, May 2021. Sign preventing outsiders from entry. Photo by the author.

of making do were struggling to get by. Farmers tended their fields, hoping for a good monsoon that was never to come.

Tea plantations, however, were allowed to remain open. Plantation management made their own arrangements for workers, on the back of promises to subject the workforce to periodic testing for COVID-19 and the situation of quarantine facilities. June is when the prized second flush of Assam tea is produced, and without labor, plantations would not be able to reap their enormous profits. The almost weekly flushing of tea leaves creates a demand for a continuous supply of labor, and a failure to pluck at the right time can result in the entire year's crop being destroyed.[1] Signs sprang up in some plantations, stating that no outsiders were allowed to enter labor lines (figure C.1), an indication of how the Adivasi workforce was separated from their surroundings so that production could carry on, irrespective of the risks it posed for the worker community. When outbreaks of COVID-19 happened on the plantations, sections of labor dwellings were cordoned off and declared "containment zones" (figure C.2). These were enclaves within enclaves, doubly cut off from the outside world.

Concessions granted to plantations amid a serious pandemic index the clout that the industry wields. As the pandemic raged, the Assam government offered a three-year tax holiday to the industry,[2] seen by many as a tactic deployed by the newly reelected Bharatiya Janata Party to appease

C.2 Containment zone, an enclave within an enclave, May 2021. Photo by the author.

plantation owners and management and, therefore, consolidate its vote bank among the Adivasi workforce. Doing little to ameliorate the plight of workers, on whom only 5 percent of the entire turnover of plantations is spent,[3] such concessions in fact mark a continuity between the colonial and postcolonial state.

Amid this seemingly novel situation, the slow expansion of plantations continued. In Golaghat, the Rangajan Tea Estate had encroached into a three-hundred-acre area of the Nambor Wildlife Sanctuary. The conversion of forest land into tea initially began by clearing *Mikania* and other jungle, and cultivating small patches of ginger. This gradual incursion was scaled up in the midst of the lockdown. Trees were felled, soil leveled, and an enormous expanse created to plant tea seedlings. Drains were dug to keep elephants out, further disrupting the animals' mobilities and aggravating frictions between people and elephants in the landscape. A colonial drama of plantations vying for forest land and the postcolonial impetus of gradually enlarging the plantation frontier was playing out once more.

While tinged with novelty, only an ahistorical view can take these happenings to be without precedent. Like a lot of writing on the Anthropocene, these events evoke feelings of a reverse déjà vu. I use this particular expression, taken from Eduardo Viveiros de Castro,[4] to denote the appearance of encountering something for the first time while actually having experienced it before. Coercive forces repeat themselves and, throughout this book, we have witnessed the forced mobility and simultaneous planting of labor in a plantation's enclave, the extralegal conversion of forests to tea, concessions granted to plantations, and the concomitant depletion of elephant habitat happening time and again. This repetition of course takes the form of difference, in that it is difference that is repeated when forces realign and rearrange to map out other cartographies of power.

Invoking a reverse déjà vu allows us to see the interdisciplinary fascination with the Anthropocene, its grand narratives of awakening and arousal, in a different light. In a rush to specify novelty, there has been a tendency in certain strands of the social sciences and environmental humanities to couch planetary transformations in ahistorical terms. While nature/society binaries are dismantled, a dismantling sometimes attributed to the Anthropocene itself, for the latter is seen to require new modes of inquiry, the colonial project that instated such binaries in the first place gets occluded. Similarly, new materialist invocations of nonhuman agency often overlook the historical contexts through which agency is expressed. Materials are produced under particular circumstances, and there are specific pathways through which they are governed. Furthermore, a material politics rests close to the bio- and necropolitics of administering life. Challenges to livability that the Anthropocene is seen to pose do not confront an undifferentiated humanity in equal and uniform ways. Who is affected and how depends on which side of the ethnic, caste, and color line people end up on.[5]

Addressing planetary transformations critically, and in ways that go beyond the divisions of nature/society, history/biology, means grounding such transformations and being wary of an anesthetized politics that sidesteps the forces of colonialism and the ravages of race. This book's grounding of a Plantationocene proceeded by holding the planet and places on the planet in the same analytical plane,[6] thus shunning totalizing accounts of a Plantationocene's scale, speed, and complexity. Neither is this grounding an effort to produce yet another story of an underdeveloped region or to conduct ethnography in the margins of South Asia. Rather, it is an attempt to foreground the significance of places and what it means to think from them. In this sense, grounding a Plantationocene can be read as a challenge to the "geo-government of scientists" and the "White Geology" of the Anthropocene.[7] The latter attribute planetary transformation to socially indifferent causal factors such as the human footprint on the planet, and they claim to know what is best for those they relegate to being the uninformed.

Grounding a Plantationocene avoids the pitfalls of easy stories. They shore up difficult doings.

Conceptually, and analytically, this specification of plantation worlds has meant working between the intersections and tensions between political economy and posthumanist and postcolonial thought. It has involved querying the economic in political economy, for a planetary condition driven by the quest to produce cheap labor, nature, and commodities, as well as the desire to consume them, results in a direct exploitation of the work of nature.[8] Rather than seeing the economic as being embedded in an ecological base, this argument takes economy and ecology as constituted by one another from the very outset. To argue that the collapse of these distinctions is the product of the Anthropocene or a Plantationocene is equally misleading and would be another instance of a reverse déjà vu. It is neoclassical economics, and certain forms of economism in political ecology/economy that have kept them apart, while elevating economy as though it is the only matter of real concern, operating along a singular logic, independent of historical pathways, situated practices, and cultural difference.

To strike at the heart of totalizing narratives of the Anthropocene is also to provide a grounding to some of the extant alternatives to the Anthropocene concept. For instance, perceptive and important specifications of the Capitalocene as a world ecology are worked differently when moving between planet and plot.[9] Specific pathways of the inequalities that underpin, and arise from, environmental transformations come into sharp relief, as do the highly differentiated ways in which bodies and lives are dispossessed. Equally, circuits of postcolonial capital are brought into relief, showing how capitalist relations are variegated processes.[10] Grounding a Plantationocene allows us to understand how people are relegated to a need economy and how distinct communities are marked out for wearing out, historically and in the present.

Much of this has proceeded through what I have called a "more-than-human ethnography." It is sympathetic to, but diverges from, the more familiar multispecies label on three significant grounds.[11] First, the subject of ethnographic inquiry here is transversal, attentive to the living and material world, and to forces and relations that cut across heterogeneous bodies, communities, infrastructures, and modes of living. Second, and relatedly, such an ethnographic endeavor is skeptical of a taxonomized understanding of life as well as the notion of species being it invokes.[12] A pitfall of the latter is that it implies that relations between other-than-humans are confined within groups of the same kind. When people describe an elephant as that which "leaves muddy tracks as it goes," it is a reference to a rhizomatic sociality, of life that unfolds along a matrix of interlacing tracks and trails constituted by a suite of different beings. Such tracks also draw attention to a force field of power within which lives, whether those of people or elephants, are led. Third, a more-than-human ethnography shifts the emphasis from discourse to practice. It pushes ethnographic endeavor further by taking other-than-human life as observant participants of the same world that people inhabit. Elephants, as we have seen, sense events, happenings, and affects. And just as people have relations with elephants, so too do elephants have relations with people, although it is only the latter that writes up these relations in the form of an ethnography.

A more-than-human ethnography, attentive to a plantation multiple and the operation of plantation logics, brings to the fore a number of themes that are of wider salience for specifying and conceptualizing a Plantationocene. The first pertains to evoking postcolonial fauna: fauna that has been altered by a suite of forces, including colonial hunting and the upheaval of landscape, the generation of monoculture, and simplified ecologies, as well as the unending frictions and violence that continue in a Plantationocene's present.[13] "Postcolonial" is a contrast to the label *anthropogenic*, rife in accounts of the Anthropocene, for the latter suppresses a range of differentiated forces that lead to alterations in animals' lifeworlds. Postcolonial fauna index not just effects but a suite of extractive and exploitative practices that generate those effects. It also signals a distinct politics of dwelling alongside in ways that the anthropogenic or the Anthropocenic does not, for power-laden relations involving a host of actors and institutions come into the fray. Postcolonial fauna, however, are not just "out there" in the sites ravaged by colonialism. As I have argued elsewhere, ecologies of the former imperial metropole can also be postcolonial,[14] and thus, the term marks out other ways of understanding planetarity beyond a specific place or region.

Second, planetary transformations are situated within a wider ontology and history of work and labor. The conversion of Assam's landscape into plantations was struck on the anvil of indentured labor. The alteration of its jungles into forest monoculture was partially achieved by keeping sections of the peasantry rooted in place through coercive forest laws. Labor is crucial to understanding how plantation worlds, and a Plantationocene, emerges, for it belies abandoning critical perspectives in favor of the actions of an undifferentiated humanity.[15] As a condition, a Plantationocene's temporality is not originary or episodic but one of ongoingness, expanding in the present in slow, accretive ways. The conversion of rural landscapes into a patchwork of small tea gardens is a case in point. While small gardens undo a plantation's scale, internal relations and the coercive arrangements endemic to plantations do not change. They give rise to a new rural plantocracy while conditions of precarity for the Adivasi workforce are not necessarily ameliorated. Small tea growers make demands so that they do not need to meet stipulations of the Plantation Labour Act, while estate plantations, to remain competitive in international markets, resort to all sorts of means to keep labor costs minimal.[16] Rather than a patchy Anthropocene, one might contend that there is a patchy Plantationocene at work.

A more expanded understanding of work, however, is needed to forge a political ecology of a Plantationocene. Plants, one could argue, are simultaneously fixed and variable capital for plantations,[17] for the vegetal work they perform is crucial to the production of a cheap commodity. Simplified ecologies work by disciplining the vegetal body and its metabolic rhythms, all of which are mobilized to maximize yield. Tea bushes are pruned and maintained at a height that maps onto that of a working woman's body. Vegetal work also has bearings on human labor. The ways in which the tea bushes sprout new leaves creates a demand for a continuous supply of labor and, therefore, fuels processes of immobilization.[18] Capital thus acts on plants at the level of the vegetative body, and does so through a simultaneous racial and colonial disciplining of labor. A wider ontology of work is thus about conjugated disciplining and exploitation of both human and other-than-human life. It is also about attending to the ways in which plantations become sites of social reproduction and therefore of a particular kind of biopolitics: those who live and work on estate plantations perform what has been called "generational servitude,"[19] tied to particular estates with few other pathways of employment. The reserve army of *faltu* labor, on which this ethnography is focused, also often remains tied to plantations, as dispossession, whether through violent land grabs, usury, or new conservation practices, runs rife. Many face a simple reproduction squeeze, with no avenues to even sell their labor power and, often, with no outside to turn to for recourse.

Third, plantation worlds, and a Plantationocene, are violent conditions, sapping a population's strength from within. The setting up of enclaves and the enclosure of forest commons, the instillation of a binary between society and nature, all proceeded through significant violence, acting upon human and other-than-human bodies alike. Development took place along plantation corridors and in tune with the pathways of colonial enterprise. The backlash to underdevelopment witnessed in postcolonial Assam, taking the form of a mass agitation and, later, full-blown secessionist militancy, created an equally violent world. If one well-documented dimension is the violence within the social sphere that agitations and militancy spawned,[20] another is the ecological violence that happened in their aftermath. Mass deforestation and land grabs occurred through informal concessions granted by the state sought to pacify surrendered militants, of which further dispossession of the Adivasi community and the depletion of elephant habitat are evident outcomes.

A Plantationocene's violence, however, is not only spectacular. It can be accretive, as witnessed in the slow violence of infrastructure set up to pacify agitations against the Indian state. Postcolonial infrastructures have had cascading effects, affecting elephants and, consequently, the livelihoods and well-being of communities in the wider landscape. The slow violence of infrastructure operates as a duration and is often out of sight, albeit not to those exposed to its harms. It is a violence that results in the relentless generation of uninhabitable ecologies, for people, elephants, and other denizens of a landscape.[21] Both slow and spectacular violence are an integral part of what I have called accumulation by plantation, a form of accumulation by dispossession that is contingent, which works at the intersections of a suite of extralegal and economic processes and ecological events, and which contributes to the ongoing expansion of a Plantationocene. Such forms of accumulation entail a doubleness of relation, where that which exists outside the realm of capital has to be available for capture, to be folded inside the valorization process. One witnesses this not only in the expansion of tea but also in extractive industries such as mining, whose legacies hark back to colonial times and which spur new forms of dispossession and harm in a postcolonial present.

Fourth, a Plantationocene is forged through diverse kinds of movement, human and other-than-human, which might be characterized as hypermobility and stagnation at the same time. Plantations uprooted people and planted them in place, generating a population that had to do without, whether that included ties to the land, forms of ownership, or a good life. A racial hierarchy of mobility that characterized plantations now manifests more globally, where contemporary movement is about speed and velocity for some, and barriers, policing, and incarceration for others.[22] In fact, the plantation logics and racialized capitalism that underpin planetary mobilities call for a critical rethink of Anthropocenic inflections of movement, including those associated with labor, infrastructure, ecology, and politics. In Assam, the relegation of people to a need economy, especially those among the Adivasi community who form part of plantations' reserve army, is now creating what is beginning to look like a floating population, where some leave for other parts of India in search of wage labor, only to return as wages barely allow for simple reproduction, while others are rooted in place but with no opportunities for exit.[23] Such floating populations should not be read as parochial phenomena: they are integral to the function of capitalism in South Asia, and similar dynamics are at work across many parts of the world.

A Plantationocene's simplified and cosmopolitan ecologies are simultaneously generated by forms of other-than-human movement. Infrastructures set up along plantations' economic corridors, from railway lines connecting frontiers to ports to the ships that transport cheap commodities the world over, have all contributed to the unintentional circulation of animals and plants. Others such as *Mikania*, or a range of shade trees, were brought to bolster plantations' productivity, an instance of deploying life to foster further accumulation from life. Such plants can exceed a plantation's order, inflicting ruin upon a landscape and disrupting processes of accumulation from within, sometimes years after they are brought into a plantation milieu. The spread of *Mikania* is exemplary of how ruination, and its destruction of certain kinds of agency,[24] operates as a duration in a Plantationocene. The vine's spread, aided by a geological event, shows how shifts in the earth's strata work in conjunction with a plantation multiple, including the opening up of dense jungles by commercial forestry, to generate uninhabitable ecologies. The latter are a postcolonial rather than a "feral" condition,[25] for they cannot be read outside of the legacies of colonialism, which continue to reside within a landscape, bursting through at particular moments of time to inflict ruin and corrode livability long after the end of formal colonial rule.

The exploitation of precarious, often migrant, labor, the quest to reap profit through monoculture, the generation of simplified ecologies where beings relate to replicas, are aspects of Assam's Plantationocene that one witnesses in many contemporary contexts beyond the plantation and its surroundings. These plantation logics permeate factory farming and greenhouses in the Global North, where migrant labor works to produce the cheap commodity, and where there is striving to produce ecologies of the same.[26] Distinct forms of virulence emerge in such spaces, whether they have to do with factory farms or urban contact zones,[27] showing how the endemics that emerge as a result of plantation logics are not solely about outbreaks in the postcolony. One might further think of the relevance of the argument made here through the production of space in border zones. The externalization of borders in many parts of the world not only has created a racialized hierarchy of mobility but has given rise to forms of racialized capitalism that profit from vulnerable migrant lives, particularly through incarceration and informalized detention.[28] A close look at the plantation logics underpinning contemporary capitalism in the Global North thus gives credence to a wider reach of a Plantationocene.

Fifth, tracking a Plantationocene historically, politically, and ecologically allows us to see how its force fields of power morph. The shift from the diagram of enclosure to one of connectivity happens as a response to processes that are internal to a Plantationocene, including, among others, the carving up of habitat by postcolonial infrastructure, forms of accumulation by deforestation, and extractive mining in a highly deregulated mode. As alignments between forces change, power relations are rearranged, and new cartographies of power are drawn. Connectivity conservation now is increasingly being scripted through the spatial and material idiom of infrastructure, not just in Assam but throughout many parts of the world.[29] Infrastructures herald a shift in conservation targeting containers or molds to movements and modulations. In this sense, reconciliation infrastructures, which aim to accommodate and modulate animal mobilities, are becoming biopolitical technologies for administrating other-than-human life, although the extent to which they can regulate and govern animals' mobilities remains to be seen. Reconciliation infrastructures thus run the risk of becoming a technical fix, one that brings conservation into even greater proximity with capitalism, allowing carboniferous expansion to continue unabated.

Yet there is a nonlinearity to infrastructure in a Plantationocene. Just as more railways and roads, bridges and tunnels are being built, there is a simultaneous de-presencing of certain infrastructures. With conservation directives, quarries and mines are shut down, capital is moved elsewhere, and machinery is left to rust, leaving behind communities caught between a ruined earth and its excesses that clog up waterways and spill into fields. New proposals to retrofit corridors strive to bring plantations back into the fold of forestry, a vision of rewilding that challenges the obdurate, material fixity of plantations.[30] Such proposals go hand in hand with expulsions, dressed up in the promise to create entrepreneurial subjects out of the Adivasi community. As such, this marks a shift from the old regime of colonial governmentality where people were to be made into "accomplices" and serve as labor for forest enterprise.[31] If actualized, such transitions will by no means be simple for, as the extant abandonment of plantations and the closure of quarries show us,[32] overhauling processes without consideration of wider structural inequalities and limitations create yet another group of castaways who become mere spectators to the drama of capitalist accumulation.

Last, it would, however, be simplistic to denote a Plantationocene as a totalizing condition, one that subsumes and engulfs everything in its wake. Even those who are relegated to having to do without find alternate grammars of expression and create "demonic grounds" that have the potential to alter the status quo.[33] A cartography of tracks and trails, forged by other kinds of doings, and which issues along human and elephant pathways, strikes at plantation logics. To summon a world mediated by spirits can serve to deterritorialize state ownership of what it views as natural resources. A different ontology of animals goes beyond racialized hierarchies on which contemporary bio- and necropolitics thrive. These are all small mutinies that happen in the everyday, which make life endurable and even create avenues for realizing worlds otherwise.

Such ways of inhabiting and dwelling become possible when we return to a Plantationocene—rather than the Anthropocene—as a threshold but also as a condition and subject of historical and ethnographic critique. Through people's relations with elephants, we witness how there are attempts to forge common worlds, worlds that are not carved up by immiserating forces or which forge mutual grounds in spite of such forces, although these worlds also diverge and do not always come together in ways people or the state might desire. The diagrams of enclosure are unbound through improvisation, through subtle acts of resistance, and through speculative practices operating under the threshold of detectability. Such practices recognize difference and alterity. They do not draw from the vocabulary of Anthropocene discourse, which tells us there is a redefinition of what it now means to be human on Earth. This figure is one who is, unwittingly, a geological agent, an agent whose activities produce wildlife in the Anthropocene and at the same time is an environmental citizen, governed by reflexivity and plugged into ecosystem services.[34] In contrast, those who make worlds amid a Plantationocene have often been denied even entry to that very category of "the human,"[35] rendering the neoliberal project suspect from the very outset.

Recognizing their actions has meant starting elsewhere. There is a fashionable tendency in certain forms of political ecology and armchair economics to disavow other ontologies, on the grounds that they are unable to withstand the ravages of capitalism and are therefore impotent for bringing about desirable change. Worse still, such views rob those who have to do without of any agency, even if that agency might be, at times, one of maintenance rather than one of making. Elite obsessions with particular solutions exemplify a singularity of vision that usually leads to an unwillingness to engage other modes of thought and practice. While the means through which people render a Plantationocene habitable can often seem to look like simply standing by as witnesses to conditions and events, this is because improvisatory practices have none of the grand enunciations of the Anthropocene, nor do they posture toward starting some kind of conservation revolution.[36] There indeed are protests, agitations, and more overt forms of resistance, like those of the Panbari farmers, even though these do not always alter the larger structures against the poor or change the way in which territorial control over landscape is largely devoted to ensuring the inadequacy of collective action. Yet such protests must be at the center of one's consciousness, to further the potential for agitations and change, to act like a latent force, a duration immanent to a Plantationocene.

What a political project for a Plantationocene might look like, and how its cartographies might be decolonized, cannot be a set of prescriptions. What it should not do is start from a grand awareness that fails to see injustice from the point of view of those who are afflicted by the travails of a Plantationocene. Whether other cartographies of dwelling can be actualized or not, the possibility of another politics of inhabitation remains immanent in people's endurance and the collectives they form, however loosely defined, which are porous in terms of what bodies or nonbodies constitute their associations. A decolonial cartography involves a refusal to be incorporated into particular orders of power, just as it entails sidestepping processes that would otherwise subsume the little that people are left with. These are avenues of unbinding from a Plantationocene's diagrams, from which new affective climates and ecologies of belonging have the possibility to emerge. Even though it might be unreasonable to expect a politics of sustained antagonism, it is worth keeping in mind that a Plantationocene is replete with leaks.

GLOSSARY

abkaree Excise tax, introduced during colonial rule.

Adivasi Communities of different ethnic origin who migrated to Assam to work in tea plantations. Also known as Sah Janagusthi or Tea Tribes.

Bābā A reverential term for elephants, but can also refer to Lord *Shiva*.

bagaan Plantation.

bāri Homesteads and vegetable gardens. Also refers to a category of land over which peasants possessed hereditary rights in precolonial Assam.

basti Hamlet or settlement.

begār A practice of offering labor power to the colonial Forest Department, particularly by groups of peasants settled in forest villages in Reserved Forests in the early part of the twentieth century.

bej Shaman or healer.

bigha A commonly used unit of land measurement in Assam, covering an area of 1,337 square meters.

challan Royalty receipt.

chariali Crossroad, often involving small markets and centers of social activity.

chowk Corner; usually refers to a locality in a town or city.

coolie (pejorative) Plantation laborer in Assam. More widely used for migrant workers mobilized from India and China to work on Dutch and British capitalist plantations.

dandi A track made by animal movement.

Dāngariyā A spirit or deity.

daroga Police officer.

devatā Divinity.

dhaba Roadside restaurant, often situated along a highway and serving as a stop for trucks.

faltu A term invented in the 1930s that denotes labor from the Adivasi community that left colonial plantations generations ago, many of whom are part of the reserve army of tea estates. Nowadays also refers to plantation workers who are not on permanent contracts. In Assamese and Hindi, *faltu* means *redundant*, but has pejorative connotations of being useless.

handia or *pachwai* Indigenous rice beer brewed by various communities in Assam.

jhatka A shock or jolt.

Karbi Indigenous community primarily residing in the hills south of the Brahmaputra.

kheddah Stockade for the capture of elephants.

kucca Raw. In this instance, refers to dwellings that are not made of concrete.

labor line Housing for workers residing within plantations, typically consisting of rows of quarters on either side of a road.

mahal Lease. Also refers to a parcel of land leased to extract a specific resource.

mahout Elephant handler.

mālik Owner or guardian.

Marwari Community from the western Indian state of Rajasthan, some of whom came to Assam in the early nineteenth century with the advent of colonial rule, acting as bankers and commercial agents to tea plantations. They play a crucial role in Assam's contemporary commerce.

matanga Term for elephant, which translates to "leaves muddy tracks as it goes."

māti dakhal Seizure of land.

maund A measure of weight, equivalent to 40 kilograms.

mukhna Tuskless bull elephant.

musth A condition in bull Asian elephants when testosterone levels rise and which results in highly aggressive behavior.

nisā Addiction. Also refers to a state of inebriation.

patta Land settlement document.

phatak Prison.

Poclain/Poklan Excavators used in construction and mining. The term comes from the French manufacturing company.

poong Salt lick.

puja Prayer or religious ritual.

reserved forest Forests accorded protection, many of whose origins date back to colonial rule.

Sadani/Sadri/Assam Sadri A link language spoken by various communities in the tea belt in Assam. Lexical items and sentences have influences of Assamese, Bengali, and Hindi.

shikari Hunter or sportsman.

sulāi Distilled alcohol usually made out of molasses; referred to as *country spirits* and *country liquor* in the state Department of Excise terminology.

tea garden Tea plantation. The term *garden* is a translation of the Assamese *bāri*. In precolonial Assam, peasants possessed hereditary rights only over homestead and garden lands. Early colonial planters thus used the term *garden* to denote privately owned estate plantations.

thikadar Contractor of foreman.

tongi Crop-guarding shelter, usually built in paddy fields.

xanghāt Conflict.

NOTES

Introduction

Part of this introduction was earlier published as Maan Barua, "Bio-geography: Landscape, Dwelling, and the Political Ecology of Human-Elephant Relations," *Environment and Planning D: Society and Space* 32 (5): 915–34. Copyright © [2014] (SAGE Publishing). https://doi.org/10.1068/d4213.

1. Also see Münster, "Lantana Invades Teak Plantations and Turns Elephants Violent."
2. Haraway, "Anthropocene, Capitalocene," 48; Aikens et al., "South to the Plantationocene"; Wolford, "The Plantationocene"; Davis et al., "Anthropocene, Capitalocene."
3. Mann, *Progress Report of Forest Administration in the Province of Assam for the Year 1874–75*; Handique, *British Forest Policy in Assam*.
4. Gustav Mann, cited in Saikia, *Forests and Ecological History of Assam*, 54.
5. Saikia, *Forests and Ecological History of Assam*.
6. Deleuze, *Foucault*.
7. Campbell, "Notes on the Mode of Capture."
8. "Elephant Hunting in Assam," 1.
9. Hunter, *A Statistical Account of Assam*.
10. "Elephant Hunting in Assam," 1.
11. *Annual Report on the Administration of Land Revenue*.
12. Elephant Preservation Act, 1879.

13   Nongbri, "Elephant Hunting in Late 19th Century Northeast India."

14   See Ingold, *Being Alive*.

15   Saikia, *Jungles, Reserves, Wildlife*.

16   Deleuze, *Foucault*, 44.

17   Sukumar, *The Asian Elephant*.

18   Sukumar, "Ecology of the Asian Elephant in Southern India."

19   "The Deputy Commissioner of Durrang . . ."; "Damages by Rogue Elephants"; "A Rogue Elephant."

20   "A Wild Elephant," 5.

21   "Wild Elephants in Assam."

22   Milroy, *Progress Report of Forest Administration in the Province of Assam for the Year 1934–35*, 22.

23   Milroy, *Progress Report of Forest Administration in the Province of Assam for the Year 1935–36*, 16.

24   Bates et al., "Elephants Classify Human Ethnic Groups."

25   Nicholls, *Assam Shikari*, 76–77.

26   Nicholls, *Assam Shikari*, 102.

27   Srinivasaiah et al., "All-Male Groups in Asian Elephants."

28   Srinivasaiah et al., "All-Male Groups in Asian Elephants."

29   Nicholls, *Assam Shikari*, 13.

30   Behal, *One Hundred Years of Servitude*.

31   Allen, *Assam District Gazetteers*.

32   Allen, *Assam District Gazetteers*, 137.

33   At this juncture, it might be helpful to clarify the use of the terms *nonhuman*, *other-than-human*, *posthuman*, and *more-than-human* that populate this text. *Nonhuman* is usually deployed to refer to a range of bodies—whether plants, animals, or spirits—that are not human. However, the prefix *non* represents a lack, an inadequacy that comes with not being human. Following Mathilda Rosengren, I prefer using the term *other-than-human*, for *other* indexes different capabilities and differentiated capacities (Rosengren, "Wastelands of Difference?"). *More-than-human*, on the other hand, is about temporalities, spaces, and processes in excess of the human or that do not always have the human at the center of their assembly. While the term *posthuman* seems analogous, *more-than-human* conjures a different kind of historicity. It does not come after the human, as

34 Paramasivan, *Progress Report of Forest Administration in the State of Assam for the Year 1950–51*.

35 Payne, *Silent Thunder*.

36 O'Connell-Rodwell, "Keeping an 'Ear' to the Ground."

37 For a helpful distinction between living with and living alongside, see Latimer, "Being Alongside."

38 Behal, *One Hundred Years of Servitude*; Guha, *Planter Raj to Swaraj*.

39 Kalam et al., "Lethal Fence Electrocution."

40 Gureja et al., *Ganesha to Bin Laden*, viii.

41 Sukumar, *The Living Elephants*; Moss, *Elephant Memories*.

42 McComb et al., "Leadership in Elephants."

43 Gureja et al., *Ganesha to Bin Laden*.

44 I develop the term *plantation multiple* by drawing from Annemarie Mol's articulation of "the body multiple," which refers to the plural ways a body is articulated by different practices, but in a manner that is not fragmented into being many (Mol, *The Body Multiple*). On plantation logics, see McKittrick, "Plantation Futures."

45 See Wolford, "The Plantationocene"; Gandy, "An Arkansas Parable for the Anthropocene"; Davis et al., "Anthropocene, Capitalocene, . . . Plantationocene?"

46 Cf. Kirksey and Helmreich, "The Emergence of Multispecies Ethnography." On "more-than-human ethnography," see Barua, *Lively Cities*.

47 Nixon, *Slow Violence and the Environmentalism of the Poor*.

48 Coole and Frost, "Introducing the New Materialisms"; Bennett, *Vibrant Matter*.

49 Ingold, *Being Alive*.

1. Plantationocene

1 Saikia, *Forests and Ecological History of Assam*.

2 Saikia, "Mosquitoes, Malaria, and Malnutrition"; Behal, *One Hundred Years of Servitude*; Guha, *Planter Raj to Swaraj*.

3   Sukumar, *The Asian Elephant*.

4   Thrift and Dewsbury, "Dead Geographies"; Spencer and Whatmore, "Bio-geographies."

5   Crutzen, "Geology of Mankind"; Kolbert, *The Sixth Extinction*; Chandler, *Ontopolitics in the Anthropocene*; Mansfield, "A New Biopolitics of Environmental Health."

6   This was a phrase I encountered in a dismissive response to questions of postcolonial experience raised at a workshop on the Anthropocene at a British university. This was during the early days of social science and humanities engagement with the Anthropocene. The phrase has stuck with me ever since and continues to be a source of unease.

7   De Castro, *Cannibal Metaphysics*, 103.

8   Whatmore, "Where Natural and Social Science Meet?"

9   For example, Chakrabarty, "The Climate of History."

10 Yusoff, *A Billion Black Anthropocenes*.

11 Moore, "The Capitalocene, Part II," 1.

12 Davis et al., "Anthropocene, Capitalocene, . . . Plantationocene?"

13 Lewis and Maslin, "Defining the Anthropocene"; Crutzen, "Geology of Mankind."

14 Hecht, "Interscalar Vehicles," 113.

15 Moore, "The Capitalocene, Part I," 606.

16 Hecht, "Interscalar Vehicles," 114.

17 Moore, "The Capitalocene, Part I"; Malm and Hornborg, "The Geology of Mankind?"

18 Moore, "The Capitalocene, Part I."

19 Marx and Engels, *Manifesto of the Communist Party*, 47.

20 Marx, *Capital*, vol. 3, 23.

21 Moore, *Capitalism in the Web of Life*; Moore, "The Capitalocene, Part I."

22 Vergès, "Racial Capitalocene," 73.

23 Wolford, "The Plantationocene"; Mintz, *Sweetness and Power*.

24 Rodney, "Plantation Society in Guyana," 646. This crucial insight of Rodney's has been extensively developed in Assam's context by Rana P. Behal. See Behal, *One Hundred Years of Servitude*.

25 Rajan, *Modernizing Nature*.

26 Haraway, "Anthropocene, Capitalocene, Plantationocene, Chthulucene," 162.

27 Wolford, "The Plantationocene," 1.
28 Ishikawa, "Into a New Epoch."
29 Haraway et al., "Anthropologists Are Talking"; Davis et al., "Anthropocene, Capitalocene, ... Plantationocene?"; Aikens et al., "South to the Plantationocene"; Murphy and Schroering, "Refiguring the Plantationocene"; Jegathesan, "Black Feminist Plots."
30 Davis et al., "Anthropocene, Capitalocene, ... Plantationocene?," 1–3.
31 McKittrick, "Plantation Futures," 4.
32 Wynter, "1492."
33 Gandy, "An Arkansas Parable for the Anthropocene," 7.
34 Lewis and Maslin, "Defining the Anthropocene."
35 Gandy, "An Arkansas Parable for the Anthropocene," 8.
36 McKittrick, "Plantation Futures," 4; Li, "After the Land Grab."
37 Saikia, *Forests and Ecological History of Assam*; Handique, *British Forest Policy in Assam*.
38 Deleuze, *Foucault*.
39 McKittrick, "Plantation Futures," 11.
40 See Deleuze, *Foucault*.
41 McKittrick, "Plantation Futures," 9.
42 Davis et al., "Anthropocene, Capitalocene, ... Plantationocene?," 5.
43 Guha, *Planter Raj to Swaraj*; Gohain, *Assam*; Behal, *One Hundred Years of Servitude*.
44 Behal, *One Hundred Years of Servitude*, 4.
45 Chakrabarty, *Habitations of Modernity*; Chakrabarty, *Provincializing Europe*.
46 See, for instance, the exemplary scholarship of Udayon Misra: Misra, *The Periphery Strikes Back*.
47 Kikon, *Living with Oil and Coal*, 10.
48 Sharma, *Empire's Garden*; Verma, *Coolies of Capitalism*; Misra, "Assam Tea."
49 Dey, *Tea Environments and Plantation Culture*; Borkotoky, "Brewing Trouble or Transforming Nature?"
50 Gohain, *Assam*; Misra, *The Periphery Strikes Back*; Ambagudia and Xaxa, *Handbook of Tribal Politics in India*; Xaxa, *State, Society, and Tribes*.

51 Besky, *The Darjeeling Distinction*; Chatterjee, *A Time for Tea*; Jegathesan, *Tea and Solidarity*.

52 Saikia, *Forests and Ecological History of Assam*; Saikia, *Jungles, Reserves, Wildlife*; Handique, *British Forest Policy in Assam*.

53 Guha, *The Unquiet Woods*; Gadgil and Guha, *Ecology and Equity*; Rangarajan, *Fencing the Forest*; Rangarajan, *India's Wildlife History*.

54 Pachuau and van Schendel, *Entangled Lives*; Nag, *Pied Pipers in North-East India*.

55 Talukdar, *Elephants in Assam*; Talukdar, *Hasti Katha*.

56 Barbora and Phukan, "Mines, Plantations, and Militarisation"; Kikon and Barbora, "The Rehabilitation Zone"; Dutta, "A Phenomenological Exploration."

57 Saikia and Gogoi, "Bhupen Hazarika Setu and the Politics of Infrastructure"; Ziipao, *Infrastructure of Injustice*.

58 Büscher, "The Nonhuman Turn."

59 Hecht, "Interscalar Vehicles"; Chao, "Children of the Palms."

60 Hecht, "Interscalar Vehicles," 111.

61 Haraway, "Anthropocene, Capitalocene, Plantationocene, Chthulucene"; Tsing, "Earth Stalked by Man"; Tsing, "Holocene Resurgence against Anthropocene Plantation"; Ishikawa, "Into a New Epoch."

62 Münster, "Forest Atmospheres"; Lainé, *Living and Working with Giants*.

63 Clifford, *Returns*.

64 Cf. Li, "After the Land Grab." This definition of *plantation multiple* is drawn from Annemarie Mol's vital formulation of the "body multiple"; see Mol, *The Body Multiple*.

65 See Barbora and Phukan, "Mines, Plantations, and Militarisation."

66 Moore, "The Capitalocene, Part II," 1.

67 Moore, "The Capitalocene, Part II"; Barua, "Animal Work"; Haraway et al., "Anthropologists Are Talking," 556.

68 McKittrick, "On Plantations, Prisons, and a Black Sense of Place," 948.

69 Behal, *One Hundred Years of Servitude*; Sharma, "'Lazy' Natives, Coolie Labour, and the Assam Tea Industry."

70 Guha, *Planter Raj to Swaraj*.

71 Behal, *One Hundred Years of Servitude*, 1–2. *Coolie* is a term widely used for "migrant labourers who had been mobilized from India and China to

work on Dutch and British capitalist plantations in their overseas colonies, including Assam in India, during the nineteenth and twentieth centuries" (Behal, *One Hundred Years of Servitude*, 2).

72 Guha, "Colonisation of Assam: Second Phase."
73 Guha, "Colonisation of Assam: Years of Transitional Crisis."
74 Guha, "Colonisation of Assam: Second Phase."
75 Guha, "Colonisation of Assam: Second Phase."
76 Behal, *One Hundred Years of Servitude*, 3.
77 Behal, *One Hundred Years of Servitude*.
78 Guha, *Planter Raj to Swaraj*, 45.
79 Behal, *One Hundred Years of Servitude*, 111.
80 Behal, *One Hundred Years of Servitude*, 4.
81 Behal, *One Hundred Years of Servitude*, 94.
82 Dey, *Tea Environments and Plantation Culture*.
83 Saikia, *Forests and Ecological History of Assam*.
84 Saikia, *Forests and Ecological History of Assam*.
85 Saikia, "Forest Land and Peasant Struggles in Assam."
86 Palmer, "Putting Forests to Work?"; Ernwein, "Bringing Urban Parks to Life."
87 It might be helpful to clarify Marx's use of the terms *work* and *labor* here. In German, the word *arbeit* refers to both work and labor. Marx saw *work* as entailing a qualitative activity that creates use values, while *labor* is that which creates value and counts quantitatively. See Ollman, *Alienation*.
88 Palmer, "Putting Forests to Work?"
89 Ernwein, "Bringing Urban Parks to Life."
90 Behal, *One Hundred Years of Servitude*, 62.
91 Behal, *One Hundred Years of Servitude*.
92 Ingold and Hallam, "Making and Growing," 5.
93 Foucault, *The History of Sexuality*.
94 Behal, *One Hundred Years of Servitude*.
95 Porcher, "Animal Work"; Coulter, *Animals, Work and the Promise*.
96 Lewis, "Elephants at Work," 545.
97 Ramsden, *Assam Planter*.
98 Ramsden, *Assam Planter*.

99 Money, *The Cultivation and Manufacture of Tea.*

100 "A Visit to Kuch Behar."

101 Antrobus, *A History of the Assam Company*, 350.

102 Hollinsworth, "Assam," 104.

103 Barker, *A Tea Planter's Life in Assam.*

104 Antrobus, *A History of the Jorehaut Tea Company.*

105 Antrobus, *A History of the Assam Company*, 351.

106 Antrobus, *A History of the Jorehaut Tea Company.*

107 Antrobus, *A History of the Assam Company.*

108 Münster, "Forest Atmospheres."

109 Lewis, "Elephants at Work."

110 Lewis, "Elephants at Work," 555.

111 Mann, *Progress Report of Forest Administration in the Province of Assam for the Year 1876–77*, 37.

112 Mann, *Progress Report of Forest Administration in the Province of Assam for the Year 1876–77*, 33.

113 Lainé, *Living and Working with Giants.*

114 Mann, *Progress Report of Forest Administration in the Province of Assam for the Year 1876–77*, 33.

115 Lewis, "Elephants at Work," 557.

116 Mann, *Progress Report of Forest Administration in the Province of Assam for the Year 1876–77*, 37.

117 Antrobus, *A History of the Jorehaut Tea Company*, 212; Ramsden, *Assam Planter*, 81.

118 Ramsden, *Assam Planter*, 81.

119 Antrobus, *A History of the Jorehaut Tea Company*, 212.

120 Antrobus, *A History of the Jorehaut Tea Company.*

121 Guha, *Planter Raj to Swaraj.*

122 Birney, *The Story of the Assam Railways and Trading Company*, 46.

123 Lewis, "Elephants at Work," 560.

124 Elephant Preservation Act, 1879.

125 Antrobus, *A History of the Assam Company*, 351.

126 Sivasundaram, "Trading Knowledge"; Saha, "Colonizing Elephants." Such knowledge existed both in terms of practice and in written form. There

are, for instance, a number of Assamese manuscripts from the eighteenth century concerned with the capture and training of elephants. The most well known of these is the *Hastividyârnava* of Sukumar Barkaith (1734), a text arising from a matrix of observation and precedent knowledge of elephant management, circulating in the form of manuscripts across South Asia (Barua, "Some Thoughts on the *Hastividyârnava*"). Contents of the *Hastividyârnava* include themes such as the value of elephants for the state, taxonomies of elephants and their suitability for various kinds of work, ailments in elephants, and prescriptions for their cure (Barkaith, "Hastividyârnava").

127 Sukumar, *The Asian Elephant*.
128 See Münster, "Working for the Forest"; Lainé, "Conduct and Collaboration"; Lainé, *Living and Working with Giants*.
129 Lainé, *Living and Working with Giants*.
130 Verma, *Coolies of Capitalism*, 20–21.
131 Collins, *Report on the Caoutchouc of Commerce*; Mann, *Progress Report of Forest Administration in the Province of Assam for the Year 1874–75*.
132 Guha, "Colonisation of Assam: Years of Transitional Crisis," 139.
133 Guha, "Colonisation of Assam: Years of Transitional Crisis."
134 Handique, "Colonial Wasteland Grants."
135 Guha, "Colonisation of Assam: Second Phase."
136 Borkotoky, "Brewing Trouble or Transforming Nature?"; Behal, *One Hundred Years of Servitude*.
137 Behal, *One Hundred Years of Servitude*, 42–44. Early colonial planters first used the term *garden* to denote privately owned plantations. It is a translation of the Assamese *bāri*, a category of land for homesteads and vegetable gardens over which peasants possessed hereditary rights in precolonial Assam (Sharma, *Empire's Garden*).
138 Marx, *Capital*, vol. 3, 573.
139 Behal, *One Hundred Years of Servitude*.
140 Guha, *Planter Raj to Swaraj*, 15.
141 Borkotoky, "Brewing Trouble or Transforming Nature?"
142 Borkotoky, "Brewing Trouble or Transforming Nature?"
143 Gohain, "Once More on the Assam Movement," 58.
144 McKittrick, "On Plantations, Prisons, and a Black Sense of Place."
145 Saikia, *Forests and Ecological History of Assam*.

146 Railways were also major consumers of forest products, notably through their demand for wood used to make railway sleepers, the history of which is well documented in South Asia (see Gadgil and Guha, *This Fissured Land*).

147 Guha, *Planter Raj to Swaraj*, 36.

148 "Derailed by Elephants," 7.

149 "Wild Elephants on Lines," 8.

150 Sarma, Easa, and Menon, *Deadly Tracks*.

151 Thomas, "186 Elephants Killed on Railway Tracks."

152 Sarma, Easa, and Menon, *Deadly Tracks*.

153 Ahmed, Saikia, and Robeson, "Tracks of Death."

154 Saikia, "Coal in Colonial Assam."

155 Saikia, *Forests and Ecological History of Assam*.

156 Saikia, "Coal in Colonial Assam."

157 Saikia, "Coal in Colonial Assam."

158 Saikia, "Imperialism, Geology and Petroleum."

159 Saikia, "Imperialism, Geology and Petroleum."

160 Saikia, *Forests and Ecological History of Assam*.

161 Saikia, "Imperialism, Geology and Petroleum," 55; Baruah, "The Refinery Movement in Assam."

162 Saikia, *Forests and Ecological History of Assam*.

163 Barbora and Phukan, "Mines, Plantations, and Militarisation."

164 Behal, *One Hundred Years of Servitude*; Guha, *Planter Raj to Swaraj*.

165 Dasgupta, "Plantation Economy and Land Tenure System."

166 Borkotoky, "Brewing Trouble or Transforming Nature?"

167 Saikia, *Forests and Ecological History of Assam*; Handique, *British Forest Policy in Assam*.

168 Dey, *Tea Environments and Plantation Culture*.

169 Borkotoky, "Brewing Trouble or Transforming Nature?"

170 Saikia, *Forests and Ecological History of Assam*, 87.

171 Dey, *Tea Environments and Plantation Culture*, 134.

172 McKittrick, "On Plantations, Prisons, and a Black Sense of Place," 948.

173 Behal, *One Hundred Years of Servitude*, 253. On Adivasis, also see Xaxa, *State, Society, and Tribes*.

174 Saikia, "Tense and Aspect in Assam Sadri."
175 Tanti, *Post-colonial Poems*, 107.
176 Wynter, *Black Metamorphosis*, 1.
177 McKittrick, "On Plantations, Prisons, and a Black Sense of Place."
178 Cf. McKittrick, "On Plantations, Prisons, and a Black Sense of Place."
179 Behal, *One Hundred Years of Servitude*.
180 Besky, *Darjeeling Distinction*.
181 Behal, *One Hundred Years of Servitude*.
182 McKittrick, *Demonic Grounds*, 78.
183 McKittrick, "On Plantations, Prisons, and a Black Sense of Place," 950.
184 Cf. Davis et al., "Anthropocene, Capitalocene, . . . Plantationocene?"; Jegathesan, "Black Feminist Plots."
185 Wolford, "The Plantationocene," 4.
186 McKittrick, "Plantation Futures," 4.
187 Ishikawa, "Into a New Epoch," 593.
188 McKittrick, "On Plantations, Prisons, and a Black Sense of Place," 949.
189 Behal and Mohapatra, "'Tea and Money versus Human Life.'"
190 Behal, *One Hundred Years of Servitude*, 44–45.
191 McKittrick, "Plantation Futures."
192 Also see Crosby, *The Columbian Exchange*.
193 Mann, *The Tea Soils of Assam*.
194 Dutta, *Shade Trees, Green Crop and Cover Crop Plants*. One could extend the geographer Jamie Lorimer's argument on the deployment of life to govern life in this vein; see Lorimer, *The Probiotic Planet*.
195 Kumpf, "The Organic Monocrop."
196 Davis et al., "Don't Judge Species on Their Origins."
197 "The Drainage Problem"; Saikia, *The Unquiet River*.
198 Biswas, "Some Foreign Weeds."
199 Barua, "Infrastructure and Non-human Life"; also see Münster, "Lantana Invades Teak Plantations."
200 Bor, "A Sketch of the Vegetation," 217.
201 Choudhury, "Controversial *Mikania* (Climber)," 178.
202 Stoler, "Imperial Debris," 194.

203   Prasad and Williams, *Extent and Distribution of Some Invasive Plant Species*.
204   Choudhury, "Controversial *Mikania* (Climber)," 179.
205   Brühl, "Recent Plant Immigrants." The essay was couched in a language typical of its time. However, the overlaps between citizenship law and imperial botany run deep. Efforts to map plants based on their origins began in the 1830s, when John Henslow, a Cambridge botanist and tutor of Charles Darwin, used symbols to mark introduced species in his inventories of British flora. Subsequent accounts imported terms such as *native*, *denizen*, and *alien* from English common law to define what constituted native biota (for a rich account of this history of biotic nativism, see Chew and Hamilton, "The Rise and Fall of Biotic Nativeness."
206   Bamber, "The Cultivation of *Passiflora fœtida*," 145.
207   Biswas, "Some Foreign Weeds," 425.
208   Choudhury, "Controversial *Mikania* (Climber)," 179.
209   Shaw, "The Story of *Cuscuta*," 95.
210   Choudhury, "Controversial *Mikania* (Climber)," 179.
211   Choudhury, "Controversial *Mikania* (Climber)."
212   Tea Research Association, *Tea Encyclopedia Serials*, 1.
213   Puzari et al., "Distribution of Mikania," 72, 76.
214   Prasad and Williams, *Extent and Distribution of Some Invasive Plant Species*.
215   Thekaekara, "Living with Elephants."
216   Vattakkavan et al., *Silent Stranglers*.
217   Dutta, *Shade Trees, Green Crop and Cover Crop Plants*, 114.
218   Stoler, "Imperial Debris"; Berlant, "Slow Death."
219   Münster, "Lantana Invades Teak Plantations."
220   Hecht, "Interscalar Vehicles."
221   Wolford, "The Plantationocene," 7; Stoler, *Capitalism and Confrontation*.
222   McKittrick, "On Plantations, Prisons, and a Black Sense of Place," 949.
223   Foucault, *The History of Sexuality*.
224   Federici, *Caliban and the Witch*.
225   Behal, *One Hundred Years of Servitude*, 258.
226   Thompson, "Time, Work-Discipline, and Industrial Capitalism."

227 Verma, *Coolies of Capitalism*.

228 Behal, *One Hundred Years of Servitude*, 258.

229 One should note, however, that plantations are not always strictly monocultural. Shade trees, runners, and cover crops are important constituents of a plantation, including tea. In this sense, the term *simplified ecologies* is perhaps a more apt descriptor of plantations. Also see Besky, "Monoculture."

230 Money, *The Cultivation and Manufacture of Tea*, 43.

231 Tsing, "A Threat to Holocene Resurgence."

232 Misra, "Assam Tea."

233 Agrawal, *Environmentality*.

234 Agrawal, *Environmentality*.

235 Tsing, "A Threat to Holocene Resurgence."

236 Dey, *Tea Environments and Plantation Culture*, 78.

237 Dey, *Tea Environments and Plantation Culture*, 80–81.

238 Saikia, "Mosquitoes, Malaria, and Malnutrition."

239 For an extensive and brilliant history, see Deb Roy, *Malarial Subjects*.

240 Bhattacharya, *Contagion and Enclaves*; Dey, *Tea Environments and Plantation Culture*; Borkotoky, "Brewing Trouble or Transforming Nature?"

241 Dey, *Tea Environments and Plantation Culture*.

242 Hazarika, Bhuyan, and Hazarika, "Insect Pests of Tea."

243 Gurusubramanian et al., "Pesticide Usage Pattern in Tea Ecosystem."

244 Berlant, "Slow Death"; Nixon, *Slow Violence and the Environmentalism of the Poor*.

245 Behal, *One Hundred Years of Servitude*.

246 Moore, *Capitalism in the Web of Life*.

247 Cf. Büscher, "The Nonhuman Turn."

248 Sharma, "British Science, Chinese Skill and Assam Tea," 454.

249 Li, "After the Land Grab."

250 Oxfam, *Addressing the Human Cost of Assam Tea*.

251 Oxfam, *Addressing the Human Cost of Assam Tea*.

252 Misra, "Assam Tea."

253 Oxfam, *Addressing the Human Cost of Assam Tea*.

254 Li, "After the Land Grab," 332.

255 E.g., Büscher, "The Nonhuman Turn"; Srinivasaiah et al., "All-Male Groups in Asian Elephants."

256 Misra, "Assam."

257 Dey, *Tea Environments and Plantation Culture*, 200; Misra, "Assam"; Misra, *The Periphery Strikes Back*.

258 Misra, *The Periphery Strikes Back*.

259 For a lucid analysis, see Gohain, "Extremist Challenge and Indian State"; Gohain, "Chronicles of Violence and Terror."

260 Stuesse, *Scratching Out a Living*; Kenney-Lazar and Ishikawa, "Megaplantations in Southeast Asia"; Chao, "Children of the Palms"; Li, "After the Land Grab."

2. The Slow Violence of Infrastructure

1 Larkin, "The Politics and Poetics of Infrastructure"; Appel, Anand, and Gupta, *The Promise of Infrastructure*; Graham and Marvin, *Splintering Urbanism*.

2 Anand, *Hydraulic City*; von Schnitzler, "Infrastructure, Apartheid Technopolitics, and Temporalities of 'Transition'"; Simone, "People as Infrastructure."

3 Rodgers and O'Neill, "Infrastructural Violence," 402.

4 Appel, "Walls and White Elephants."

5 Barua, "Infrastructure and Non-human Life."

6 Bourdieu, *Outline of a Theory of Practice*.

7 Misra, *The Periphery Strikes Back*, 134.

8 Haraway, *Staying with the Trouble*; Wakefield, "Infrastructures of Liberal Life"; Hetherington, *Infrastructure, Environment and Life in the Anthropocene*.

9 Nixon, *Slow Violence and the Environmentalism of the Poor*, 2.

10 Berlant, "Slow Death," 759.

11 Ziipao, "Infrastructure."

12 Tsing, "Earth Stalked by Man," 2.

13 Misra, "Assam"; Misra, *The Periphery Strikes Back*; Gohain, *Assam*; Baruah, "The Refinery Movement in Assam."

14   For a poignant reflection on recent infrastructural projects, see Saikia and Gogoi, "Bhupen Hazarika Setu and the Politics of Infrastructure." Several scholars have critically engaged with resource extraction in the region (see Ziipao, *Infrastructure of Injustice*; Kikon, *Living with Oil and Coal*). Mayuri Gogoi, in particular, provides insights on this particular landscape, which have enriched my account (see Gogoi, "Kaziranga under Threat").

15   "VP Announces Assam Package," 1.

16   "Assam Poised for Industrial Growth," 15.

17   Gandy, *The Fabric of Space*.

18   Guha, *Planter Raj to Swaraj*; Sharma, *Empire's Garden*; Dasgupta, "Plantation Economy and Land Tenure System"; Gohain, "Once More on the Assam Movement."

19   Misra, *The Periphery Strikes Back*, 136.

20   Misra, "Assam."

21   Misra, *The Periphery Strikes Back*.

22   Misra, "Assam."

23   Misra, "Assam," 1357.

24   Gohain, "Extremist Challenge and Indian State." Here, underdevelopment should be equated with a paucity of development. Rather, as Walter Rodney argued long ago, underdevelopment "expresses a particular relationship of exploitation" where societies are deprived "of the benefit of their natural resources and labour" (Rodney, *How Europe Underdeveloped Africa*, 40).

25   Saikia, "Imperialism, Geology and Petroleum"; Barbora and Phukan, "Mines, Plantations, and Militarisation."

26   Baruah, "The Refinery Movement in Assam."

27   Barooah Pisharoty, *Assam*.

28   There is a rich body of work on the historical, social, and political-economic dimensions of the Assam Movement. See Barooah Pisharoty, *Assam*; Misra, *The Periphery Strikes Back*; Baruah, *India against Itself*; Gohain, *Assam*.

29   Barooah Pisharoty, *Assam*.

30   Misra, *The Periphery Strikes Back*, 134.

31   Misra, "Assam"; Misra, *The Periphery Strikes Back*.

32   Misra, *The Periphery Strikes Back*, 137.

33   "Memorial Etched in Martyr's Blood."

34   Misra, *The Periphery Strikes Back*.

35. Cf. Guha and Martinez-Alier, *Varieties of Environmentalism*.
36. Gohain, "Chronicles of Violence and Terror," 1012.
37. Gohain, "Chronicles of Violence and Terror," 1013–14.
38. Gohain, *Assam*; Gohain, "Once More on the Assam Movement."
39. Baruah, *India against Itself*, 132.
40. Barooah Pisharoty, *Assam*.
41. Barooah Pisharoty, *Assam*.
42. Government of India, *Accord between AASU, AAGSP and the Central Government*.
43. Government of India, *Accord between AASU, AAGSP and the Central Government*, 2.
44. Government of India, *Accord between AASU, AAGSP and the Central Government*.
45. Barooah Pisharoty, *Assam*.
46. "VP Announces Assam Package," 1.
47. "PM Approves of Saikia's Moves," 9.
48. Sharma, "Politics Threatens Assam's Rhinos."
49. Barua, *The Saga of Assam Oil*, 143.
50. Numaligarh Refinery Limited, *Submission of Half Yearly Compliance Report*.
51. Rai, "Refinery a Threat to Rhinos."
52. Sharma, "Politics Threatens Assam's Rhinos," 12.
53. Barua, *The Saga of Assam Oil*.
54. Sharma, "Politics Threatens Assam's Rhinos," 12.
55. "Assam Refinery May Hit Ecology," 20.
56. Gogoi, "Kaziranga under Threat," 2617.
57. Ministry of Environment and Forests, "Ministry of Environment and Forests Notification"; Gogoi, "Kaziranga under Threat."
58. "Bonoriya Hatir Upodrow'ot Raij Atankita."
59. "Depredations by Wild Elephants."
60. Moss, *Elephant Memories*.
61. Talukdar, *Elephants in Assam*, 47.
62. Talukdar, *Hasti Katha*; Talukdar, *Multi-dimensional Mitigation Initiatives*.
63. Roy, "Urban Informality."

64 Numaligarh Refinery Limited, *Submission of Half Yearly Compliance Report*.

65 Numaligarh Refinery Limited, *Submission of Half Yearly Compliance Report*.

66 Parikh, *Assam State Development Report*; Government of Assam, "Major Projects and Activities under Assam Accord."

67 Guha, *Planter Raj to Swaraj*.

68 Parikh, *Assam State Development Report*.

69 Government of Assam, "Problems Could Be Solved through Goodwill."

70 Government of Assam, "Problems Could Be Solved through Goodwill," 49; Larkin, "The Politics and Poetics of Infrastructure"; Saikia and Gogoi, "Bhupen Hazarika Setu and the Politics of Infrastructure."

71 Chief Engineer (Construction), "Northeast Frontier Railway (Construction Organisation) Notice."

72 Majumdar, "Need to Intensify Base Metal Exploration."

73 Government of Assam, "The Assam Gazette: 17 June 1964"; Gogoi, "Kaziranga under Threat."

74 Ministry of Environment, Forest and Climate Change, *Brief Summary of the Project*. I am grateful to Professor Pranav Jyoti Deka for these insights into the region's geology.

75 Gogoi, "Kaziranga under Threat."

76 Larkin, "The Politics and Poetics of Infrastructure."

77 Director, Kaziranga National Park, "Opening of New Stone Quarries."

78 "Elephant Corridors under Human Pressure."

79 "Wild Elephants Wreak Havoc in Golaghat Villages."

80 Marx, *Capital*, vol. 2.

81 Marx, *Capital*, vol. 1.

82 Kikon, *Living with Oil and Coal*.

83 Forest Range Officer, "Enquiry on an Installation of Stone Crushing Industry."

84 Patel and Moore, *A History of the World in Seven Cheap Things*.

85 Marx, *Capital*, vol. 1.

86 Baruah, *India against Itself*.

87 Athparia, "Karbi Folklore and Identity."

88 Singh, Barman, and Talukdar, *Report on Site Inspection*.
89 Officer-in-Charge, Rongmongwe Police Station, "Illegal Extraction/Excessive Extraction."
90 Sanyal, *Rethinking Capitalist Development*, 212.
91 Sanyal, *Rethinking Capitalist Development*.
92 Ministry of Environment, Forest and Climate Change, *Borjuri P.P. Land Area Mine Plan*, 20.
93 Marx, *Capital*, vol. 1, 352.
94 Director, Kaziranga National Park, "Opening of New Stone Quarries."
95 "Concern over Move to Open Quarry."
96 Forest Range Officer, "Siltation of Moridifaloo River."
97 Director, Kaziranga National Park, "Siltation of Mori Diffalo River."
98 "Renewing Licenses to Make a Killing?"
99 Chief Engineer (Construction), "Northeast Frontier Railway (Construction Organisation) Tender Notice."
100 National Green Tribunal, *Rohit Choudhary vs Union of India and Ors (7 September, 2012)*.
101 National Green Tribunal, *Rohit Choudhary vs Union of India and Ors (7 September, 2012)*.
102 "Inspect Industries around Kaziranga, MoEF told."
103 National Green Tribunal, *Rohit Choudhary vs Union of India and Ors (7 September, 2012)*.
104 Divisional Forest Officer, "Geleki Stone Quarry-Closure."
105 Somashekar, *Report on Rampant Mining*, 7.
106 Officer-in-Charge, Rongmongwe Police Station, "Illegal Extraction/Excessive Extraction."
107 Circle Officer, "Submission of Report on Damage of Paddy Land."
108 Principal Chief Conservator of Forests, "Gorh Ne Geleki?????"
109 Cf. Berlant, "Slow Death."
110 Johnson et al., "Growth-Including Infrastructure."
111 Caro, *Conservation by Proxy*.
112 Talukdar, "Quarrying Blocks Elephant Corridor."
113 Hodgetts and Lorimer, "Animals' Mobilities."
114 Guattari, *The Three Ecologies*.

115 Barua, Bhagwat, and Jadhav, "The Hidden Dimensions of Human-Wildlife Conflict"; Ogra, "Human-Wildlife Conflict and Gender."

116 Berlant, "Slow Death."

117 Biermann and Mansfield, "Biodiversity, Purity, and Death"; Mbembe, *Necropolitics*.

118 Bist, "Elephant Conservation in India."

119 "Pachyderms Kill 2 More"; "Elephants Kill One More"; "One Killed in Elephant Attack"; Behal, *One Hundred Years of Servitude*.

120 Berlant, "Slow Death."

121 National Green Tribunal, *Rohit Choudhary vs Union of India and Ors (24 August 2016)*.

122 Rosenberger, *Callous Objects*.

123 "Traditional Elephant Habitat Affected."

124 "(Reopens LGD26)."

125 National Green Tribunal, *Rohit Choudhary vs Union of India and Ors (24 August 2016)*.

126 Secretary (Environment and Forests), "Letter from Secretary (Ministry of Environment and Forests) to Secretary (Ministry of Petroleum and Natural Gas)."

127 Conservator of Forests, Eastern Assam Circle, "Construction of Boundary Wall."

128 National Green Tribunal, *Rohit Choudhary vs Union of India and Ors (24 August 2016)*, 19.

129 "Litterateur on Hunger Strike."

130 National Green Tribunal, *Rohit Choudhary vs Union of India and Ors (24 August 2016)*, 21.

131 National Green Tribunal, *Rohit Choudhary vs Union of India and Ors (24 August 2016)*, 12.

132 Numaligarh Refinery Limited, *Additional Details Sought by Member Secretary*, 69.

133 Gauhati High Court, *Numaligarh Refinery Ltd vs Union of India and 7 Ors*; Numaligarh Refinery Limited, *Additional Details Sought by Member Secretary*, 69.

134 Numaligarh Refinery Limited, *Numaligarh Refinery Ltd vs Union of India and 7 Ors*, 3.

135   Gohain, "Extremist Challenge and Indian State."
136   McKittrick, "Plantation Futures."
137   Barbora and Phukan, "Mines, Plantations, and Militarisation."
138   Misra, "Assam"; Misra, *The Periphery Strikes Back*; Gohain, *Assam*.
139   Gohain, "Once More on the Assam Movement."
140   Guattari, "On Machines."
141   Nixon, *Slow Violence and the Environmentalism of the Poor*.
142   Berlant, "Slow Death."
143   Yusoff, *A Billion Black Anthropocenes*; Kikon, *Living with Oil and Coal*.
144   Berlant, "Slow Death"; Murphy, "Alterlife and Decolonial Chemical Relations"; McKittrick, "On Plantations, Prisons, and a Black Sense of Place."

3. Material Politics

Parts of this chapter were earlier published as Maan Barua, "Volatile Ecologies: Towards a Material Politics of Human-Animal Relations," *Environment and Planning A* 46 (6): 1462–78. Copyright © [2014] (SAGE Publishing). https://doi.org/10.1068/a46138.

1   Bennett, *Vibrant Matter*; Coole and Frost, "Introducing the New Materialisms."
2   Bennett, *Vibrant Matter*.
3   Bennett, *Vibrant Matter*.
4   Greenhough, "Vitalist Geographies," 51.
5   Bennett, *Vibrant Matter*.
6   Ingold, "Materials against Materiality."
7   Barry, *Material Politics*; Lemke, "New Materialisms."
8   Bennett, *The Enchantment of Modern Life*; Klinke, "Vitalist Temptations."
9   Lemke, "An Alternative Model of Politics?"; Gandy and Jasper, "Geography, Materialism, and the Neo-vitalist Turn."
10 Verma, "For the Drink of the Nation"; Chatterjee, "An Empire of Drink."
11 A unit of land measurement in Assam, a *bigha* equals 1,337 square meters.
12 Barua, "Between Gods and Demons."
13 Verma, "For the Drink of the Nation."

14   Gibson, *The Ecological Approach to Visual Perception*.

15   *Sulāi*, also called *gelā* in colloquial Assamese, is referred to as "country spirits" and "country liquor" in Department of Excise terminology. It is a distilled spirit that differs from other regional rice beers like *handia*, *pachwai*, and *lāopani*, home-brewed by various communities largely for self-consumption. I am grateful to the late Kamini Prasad Barua for his insights into Assam's local spirits.

16   Rasmussen, "Chemical, Tactile, and Taste Sensory Systems"; Rizvanovic, Amundin, and Laska, "Olfactory Discrimination Ability of Asian Elephants"; Arvidsson, Amundin, and Laska, "Successful Acquisition of an Olfactory Discrimination Test."

17   Goswami, *Aspects of Revenue Administration*, 84.

18   Goswami, *Aspects of Revenue Administration*.

19   Goswami, *Aspects of Revenue Administration*.

20   Saha, Bhue, and Singha, *Decent Work for Tea Plantation Workers*; Saikia, *Stories behind a Hot Cup of Assam Tea*.

21   Verma, "For the Drink of the Nation."

22   Verma, "For the Drink of the Nation," 97–98.

23   Verma, "For the Drink of the Nation."

24   Mbembe, *Necropolitics*.

25   Karmakar, "Assam's Tea Country."

26   Saikia, "Will Assam Government's Ban on Using Molasses."

27   Saikia, "Will Assam Government's Ban on Using Molasses."

28   "Man-Elephant Conflict Turns Grim"; Sen, "Drink Drives Elephant to Kill."

29   Naha et al., "Elephants in the Neighborhood."

30   "Elephants on Drunken Rampage Kill Three People"; "Illicit Liquor Attracting Wild Elephants"; "Elephant Kills 5, Locals Live in Terror."

31   "Hurt Elephant Falls Prey to Its Own Herd."

32   "Herd Kills Labourer"; "Illicit Liquor Attracting Wild Elephants."

33   Naha et al., "Elephants in the Neighborhood."

34   Fowler, "Toxicology."

35   Choudhury, *A Naturalist in Karbi Anglong*.

36   Rai, "Picknicking Dangerously with Assam Tuskers."

37   Choudhury, *A Naturalist in Karbi Anglong*.

38 Saikia, "State, Peasants and Land Reclamation"; Baruah, "Father of Small Tea Grower Revolution."

39 Choudhury, *A Naturalist in Karbi Anglong*.

40 Choudhury, *A Naturalist in Karbi Anglong*; Rai, "Picknicking Dangerously with Assam Tuskers."

41 "Drunk Animals—Marula Fruit Party!!"; Bruinenberg, "Elephant Party in Addo-Park South Africa."

42 Morris, Humphreys, and Reynolds, "Myth, Marula, and Elephant."

43 Janiak et al., "Genetic Evidence of Widespread Variation." I am grateful to Thibault De Meyer for drawing my attention to this work.

44 Siegel and Brodie, "Alcohol Self-Administration by Elephants"; Siegel, *Intoxication*.

45 Siegel and Brodie, "Alcohol Self-Administration by Elephants."

46 Siegel, *Intoxication*, 134.

47 Das, Lahkar, and Talukdar, "Increasing Trend of Human Elephant Conflict."

48 "Numaligarh Gears Up for Land War."

49 Bradshaw, *Elephants on the Edge*.

50 Moss, *Elephant Memories*, 186.

51 Bates et al., "Elephants Classify Human Ethnic Groups."

52 Bradshaw, *Elephants on the Edge*, 69.

53 Barry, *Material Politics*.

54 Coole and Frost, "Introducing the New Materialisms"; Bennett, *Vibrant Matter*.

55 Mbembe, *Necropolitics*.

4. Accumulation by Plantation

1 Besky, "Monoculture."

2 McKittrick, "On Plantations, Prisons, and a Black Sense of Place."

3 Head and Atchison, "Cultural Ecology."

4 Myers, "From the Anthropocene to the Planthroposcene."

5 Bennett, *Vibrant Matter*; Fleming, "Toward Vegetal Political Ecology"; Elton, "Growing Methods."

6 Ernwein, Ginn, and Palmer, *The Work That Plants Do*.

7   Palmer, "Putting Forests to Work?"; Ernwein, "Bringing Urban Parks to Life"; Nally and Kearns, "Vegetative States."
8   Head et al., "Vegetal Politics," 861; Marder, "Resist Like a Plant!"
9   Kikon and Deka, "Strawberry Farms."
10 Oriel, Jayantha, and Dissanayaka, "Plants Are Worldmakers."
11 Davis et al., "Anthropocene, Capitalocene, . . . Plantationocene?"
12 Nally and Kearns, "Vegetative States."
13 Cf. Lorimer, *The Probiotic Planet*.
14 Harvey, *The New Imperialism*.
15 Oriel, Jayantha, and Dissanayaka, "Plants Are Worldmakers."
16 Shaw, "The Story of *Cuscuta*," 95.
17 Choudhury, "Controversial *Mikania* (Climber)," 178.
18 Ernwein, Ginn, and Palmer, *The Work That Plants Do*.
19 Choudhury, "Controversial *Mikania* (Climber)," 179.
20 Choudhury, "Controversial *Mikania* (Climber)," 179.
21 Tea Research Association, *Tea Encyclopedia Serials*, 1.
22 Tea Research Association, *Annual Scientific Report (1st April 1973 to 31st March 1974)*, 11.
23 Tea Research Association, *Annual Scientific Report (1st April 1977 to 31st March 1978)*, 16.
24 Puzari et al., "Distribution of Mikania."
25 Assam Legislative Assembly, *Assam Legislative Assembly Debates*.
26 Sonwalkar, "Boundary Row Denudes Assam Forest," 8.
27 Calculated from Sarma et al., "A Geo-spatial Assessment of Habitat Loss."
28 Misra, *The Periphery Strikes Back*, 145.
29 The organization became active in 1983. For a discussion of timelines of when the outfit was formed, see Barooah Pisharoty, *Assam*.
30 Gohain, "Extremist Challenge and Indian State," 2068.
31 Misra, "No Tears for the Liberators."
32 Gohain, "Extremist Challenge and Indian State," 2068.
33 Gohain, "Chronicles of Violence and Terror."
34 Misra, *The Periphery Strikes Back*, 149.
35 Gohain, "Chronicles of Violence and Terror"; Misra, *The Periphery Strikes Back*.

36 Sahni and Routray, "SULFA."
37 Sahni and Routray, "SULFA."
38 Misra, *The Periphery Strikes Back*.
39 Gogoi, "Axomor Bonanchal SULFA'k Eri Diya Hol Neki?," author's translation.
40 Kurmi, "Sorang Byaboxayir Douratmyot Tengani Bonanchal Nihshwexor Pathat."
41 "Abadh Bonanchal Dhangxat Badha Diya Babei Hatya Kora Hol Taufil'ok."
42 Harvey, *The New Imperialism*.
43 "Govt. Move Emphasises Threat."
44 "Forest Department Incurs Loss."
45 These figures are from the Forest Survey of India. Although exact numbers can be debatable, they provide an indicative figure. See Forest Survey of India, *The State of Forest Report 1993*, 13; and Forest Survey of India, *The State of Forest Report 1995*.
46 Calculated from Sarma et al., "A Geo-spatial Assessment of Habitat Loss."
47 Ernwein, Ginn, and Palmer, *The Work That Plants Do*.
48 Stoler, "'The Rot Remains,'" 9.
49 In Assam, the terms *tea garden* and *tea estate* are used interchangeably, and a specific history underpins this transposition. In precolonial Assam, peasants possessed hereditary rights only over homestead and garden land, known as *bāri* in Assamese. The term *garden* is a translation of *bāri* and was used by early colonial planters to denote privately owned estate plantations. For a discussion, see Sharma, *Empire's Garden*.
50 Sharma, *Empire's Garden*.
51 Sharma and Barua, "Small Tea Plantation and Its Impact."
52 Saikia, "Gongadhar Saikia." News reports from the time seem to indicate that there were government initiatives as well. See "Assam's Scheme to Aid Poor Farmers."
53 Sharma and Barua, "Small Tea Plantation and Its Impact."
54 Bhowmik, "Small Growers to Prop Up Large Plantations."
55 Bhowmik, "Small Growers to Prop Up Large Plantations."
56 Sharma and Barua, "Small Tea Plantation and Its Impact."
57 Bhowmik, "Small Growers to Prop Up Large Plantations."
58 Baruah, "Father of Small Tea Grower Revolution," 130.

59   D. Gogoi, "Ek Byatikrami Pratibha."

60   See Chakraborty, "Agriculture in Assam." There is considerable variation in data on small tea growers in Assam, as not all growers are registered with the Tea Board of India. The figures used here are meant to indicate trends rather than pinpoint exact numbers.

61   Ernwein, Ginn, and Palmer, *The Work That Plants Do*; Palmer, "Putting Forests to Work?"

62   Cf. Ingold and Hallam, "Making and Growing."

63   Cf. Cooper and Waldby, *Clinical Labor*.

64   Surveys in Assam's plantations reveal that the cash component of Assam tea workers' wages is well below the minimum wage of unskilled agricultural workers in the state (Oxfam, *Addressing the Human Cost*). Wage deductions are rife and extremely high compared to wages earned, affecting income disproportionately. As many workers remain on the same pay grade for fifteen to twenty years, they are unable to cope with inflation. Furthermore, although there is meant to be no wage discrimination across gender, women are often placed on lower wages than male workers in plantations (Saha, Bhue, and Singha, *Decent Work for Tea Plantation Workers*). All of these reflect strategies of cheapening labor.

65   Saha, Bhue, and Singha, *Decent Work for Tea Plantation Workers*.

66   Saha, Bhue, and Singha, *Decent Work for Tea Plantation Workers*; Oxfam, *Addressing the Human Cost*.

67   Tsing, *The Mushroom at the End of the World*.

68   Li, "After the Land Grab."

69   Rajya Sabha, "Scheme of Margin Money to Surrendered Militants."

70   Saikia, "Corruption Main Issue," 13.

71   Government of Assam, "Small Tea Growers to Be Promoted," 40.

72   Misra, *The Periphery Strikes Back*.

73   Harvey, *The New Imperialism*.

74   Hazarika, *Strangers of the Mist*, 197.

75   Gohain, "Extremist Challenge and Indian State," 2067.

76   "State Tea Estates Possess 17,919 Bighas."

77   Government of Assam, *Tea Garden Land Ceiling Cases Pending at District Level*.

78   "State Tea Estates Possess 17,919 Bighas."

79 "State Tea Estates Possess 17,919 Bighas."

80 Forest Department figures suggest that 83 percent of the 1,03,795 hectare reserve has been "encroached" upon ("Golaghat Villagers Move CM").

81 Li, "After the Land Grab."

82 "Alleged Encroachment in Nambor Reserve Forest."

83 Baruah, "A Tribute to Late Gangadhar Saikia," 46.

84 Ghosh, "Small Tea Gardens."

85 Seetharaman and Singh, "Assam Government's Move to Regularise Landholdings."

86 Government of Assam, *Handbook of Government Circulars*, 47–48.

87 Saikia, "State, Peasants and Land Reclamation," 111.

88 Sharma and Barua, "Small Tea Plantation and Its Impact," 145.

89 Saikia, "State, Peasants and Land Reclamation," 111.

90 Jadhav and Barua, "The Elephant Vanishes"; Jadhav et al., "Ecologies of Suffering."

91 Sukumar, *The Living Elephants*.

92 Myers, "From the Anthropocene to the Planthroposcene."

93 Gibson, *The Ecological Approach to Visual Perception*; Nally and Kearns, "Vegetative States."

94 Saikia, "State, Peasants and Land Reclamation."

95 Sukumar, *The Living Elephants*.

96 Oriel, Jayantha, and Dissanayaka, "Plants Are Worldmakers."

97 Das, "The Small Tea Growers of Assam."

98 Government of Assam, *Statistical Hand Book Assam 2019*.

99 Sharma and Barua, "Small Tea Plantation and Its Impact," 144.

100 Haraway, "Anthropocene, Capitalocene, Plantationocene, Chthulucene"; Haraway et al., "Anthropologists Are Talking." For a critical reading, see Davis et al., "Anthropocene, Capitalocene, . . . Plantationocene?"

101 McKittrick, "On Plantations, Prisons, and a Black Sense of Place."

102 Misra, *The Periphery Strikes Back*.

103 Gohain, "Extremist Challenge and Indian State," 2068.

104 Gohain, "Chronicles of Violence and Terror," 1018.

105 Saikia, "State, Peasants and Land Reclamation," 111.

106 Harvey, *The New Imperialism*.

107 Cf. Marx, *Capital*, vol. 1. For a discussion of the term, see Morris, "Ursprüngliche Akkumulation."

108 Cf. Marx, *Capital*, vol. 1.

109 Lorimer, *The Probiotic Planet*.

110 On biotic circulations of the Anthropocene, see Tsing, *The Mushroom at the End of the World*.

111 Bennett, *Vibrant Matter*.

112 Myers, "From the Anthropocene to the Planthroposcene."

113 Li, "After the Land Grab."

114 Myers, "From the Anthropocene to the Planthroposcene."

115 Besky, "Monoculture."

116 Harvey, *The New Imperialism*, 174.

117 Behal, *One Hundred Years of Servitude*. For a lively argument on plant time, see Brice, "Attending to Grape Vines."

118 Rodney, "Plantation Society in Guyana"; Behal, *One Hundred Years of Servitude*.

119 Barua, "Animating Capital."

120 "State Tea Estates Possess 17,919 Bighas."

121 Achtnich, "Accumulation by Immobilization."

122 Nally and Kearns, "Vegetative States."

123 Cf. Ursula Münster, "Forest Atmospheres"; Lainé, *Living and Working with Giants*.

124 Karlsson, "Resource Frontier."

125 Myers, "From the Anthropocene to the Planthroposcene"; Kikon and Deka, "Strawberry Farms."

5. The Diagram of Connectivity

Parts of this chapter were earlier published as Maan Barua, "Circulating Elephants: Unpacking the Geographies of a Cosmopolitan Animal," *Transactions of the Institute of British Geographers* 39 (4): 559–73. Copyright © [2013] (John Wiley and Sons). https://doi.org/10.1111/tran.12047.

1 Deleuze, "Postscript on the Societies of Control."

2   Hodgetts and Lorimer, "Animals' Mobilities"; Colombino and Palladino, "In the Blink of an Eye"; Bull, *Animal Movements, Moving Animals*.

3   Barua, "Infrastructure and Non-human Life"; Parks, "Mediating Animal-Infrastructure Relations"; Metzger, "The Moose Are Protesting."

4   Hodgetts and Lorimer, "Animals' Mobilities."

5   Fishel, "Of Other Movements," 352.

6   Goldman, "Constructing Connectivity," 335.

7   Barua, "Circulating Elephants."

8   Star and Griesemer, "Institutional Ecology, 'Translation,' and Boundary Objects."

9   Goldman, "Constructing Connectivity"; Green and Sandbrook, "Beyond Connectivity."

10 Star and Griesemer, "Institutional Ecology, 'Translation,' and Boundary Objects."

11 Fishel, "Of Other Movements."

12 For a compelling history of telemetry and tracking wildlife in a North American context, see Benson, *Wired Wilderness*. However, this work is not concerned with corridors per se.

13 Barbora, "Riding the Rhino," 1145.

14 Cf. Sanyal, *Rethinking Capitalist Development*.

15 Stracey, "Planning for a 'Project Elephant'?"

16 Lahiri-Choudhury, "Conservation of the Asian Elephant," 22.

17 Shafer, *Nature Reserves*.

18 Kingsland, "Creating a Science of Nature Reserve Design."

19 MacArthur and Wilson, *The Theory of Island Biogeography*.

20 Wilson and Willis, "Applied Biogeography," 525.

21 Correia, "F**k Jared Diamond."

22 Diamond, "The Island Dilemma," 144.

23 Diamond, "The Island Dilemma," 144.

24 For an in-depth account of the SLOSS debate and the science of reserve design, see Kingsland, "Creating a Science of Nature Reserve Design."

25 Simberloff and Abele, "Island Biogeography Theory and Conservation Practice."

26 Diamond et al., "Island Biogeography and Conservation," 1028–29.

27 IUCN, *World Conservation Strategy*.
28 Adams, *Against Extinction*.
29 Kingsland, "Creating a Science of Nature Reserve Design," 62.
30 Lewis, *Inventing Global Ecology*.
31 Lahiri-Choudhury, "Conservation of the Asian Elephant"; Sukumar, "The Elephant Populations of India."
32 Sukumar, "The Elephant Populations of India," 66.
33 Sukumar, "The Elephant Populations of India," 66–67.
34 Sukumar, "The Elephant Populations of India," 66.
35 Sukumar, *The Asian Elephant*, 206.
36 Johnsingh, Prasad, and Goyal, "Conservation Status of the Chila-Motichur Corridor."
37 Lahiri-Choudhury, "Saving Elephants for Posterity," 18.
38 Lahiri-Choudhury, "Saving Elephants for Posterity," 18–19.
39 The need for such an initiative had been voiced by professional foresters as early as 1977 (see Stracey, "Planning for a 'Project Elephant'?").
40 Ministry of Environment and Forests, *Project Elephant (Gajatme)*, 32.
41 Baskaran and Desai, "Ranging Behaviour of the Asian Elephant," 47.
42 Santiapillai and Jackson, *The Asian Elephant*, 2.
43 Foucault, *The History of Sexuality*; Biermann and Mansfield, "Biodiversity, Purity, and Death."
44 Santiapillai, "The Asian Elephant Conservation," 32.
45 Menon et al., *Right of Passage*, 11.
46 Tiwari and Easa, "Documenting Corridors," 35.
47 Tiwari and Easa, "Documenting Corridors," 36.
48 Tiwari and Easa, "Documenting Corridors."
49 Tiwari and Easa, "Documenting Corridors."
50 Tiwari and Easa, "Documenting Corridors," 36.
51 Menon et al., *Right of Passage*.
52 Menon et al., *Right of Passage*.
53 Barua and Das, *Kaziranga*.
54 Lahan and Sonowal, "Kaziranga Wild Life Sanctuary, Assam," 271.
55 Sinha, "Elephant Migration in Kaziranga," 18.

56 Government of Assam, "The Assam Gazette (Extraordinary) Notification."
57 Government of Assam, "The Assam Gazette (Extraordinary) Notification."
58 Director, Kaziranga National Park, "Information Regarding the Incident."
59 "Kaziranga Extension Plan."
60 "'Relocating Villages to Secure Jumbo Corridors.'"
61 Barua, "Circulating Elephants."
62 Lorimer, "Non-human Charisma."
63 Barua, "Lively Commodities and Encounter Value."
64 Barua, "Circulating Elephants."
65 Brockington, Duffy, and Igoe, *Nature Unbound*; Barua, "Affective Economies, Pandas."
66 Menon et al., *Right of Passage*, 26.
67 MLA: Member of the Legislative Assembly.
68 Menon et al., *Right of Passage*, 2nd ed.
69 Deleuze and Guattari, *A Thousand Plateaus*.
70 Deleuze and Guattari, *On the Line*.
71 Deleuze and Guattari, *A Thousand Plateaus*.
72 Gauhati High Court, *Sri Sunil Das and 7 Ors*.
73 Gauhati High Court, *Sri Sunil Das and 7 Ors*.
74 Gauhati High Court, *Sri Sunil Das and 7 Ors*, 14.
75 Yadava, *Detailed Report on Issues*, 164.
76 Cited in Gauhati High Court, *PIL (Suo Motu) 66/2012*, 14.
77 Yadava, *Detailed Report on Issues*, 55.
78 Gauhati High Court, *In the Matter of W.P (C) No. 4860/2013*, 8.
79 Gauhati High Court, *In the Matter of W.P (C) No. 4860/2013*, 9.
80 Gauhati High Court, *In the Matter of W.P (C) No. 4860/2013*, 9.
81 Barua and Das, *Kaziranga*.
82 Gauhati High Court, *PIL (Suo Motu) 66/2012*.
83 Gauhati High Court, *PIL (Suo Motu) 66/2012*.
84 Gauhati High Court, *PIL (Suo Motu) 66/2012*, 30.
85 Gauhati High Court, *PIL (Suo Motu) 66/2012*, 36–37.
86 National Green Tribunal, *Rohit Choudhary vs Union of India and Ors (24 August 2016)*, 19.

87 Somashekar, *Report on Rampant Mining*.
88 Government of Assam, *Report on Delineation*.
89 Government of Assam, *Report on Delineation*, 5.
90 Government of Assam, *Report on Delineation*.
91 Government of Assam, *Report on Delineation*, 6–7.
92 Population ecologists view structural corridors as a "spatial contagion of habitat," while functional connectivity is about actual dispersal. In practice, therefore, structural corridors are not necessarily synonymous with function or use (see Crooks and Sanjayan, *Connectivity Conservation*).
93 Government of Assam, *Report on Delineation*, 6–7.
94 Ament et al., *Protecting Asian Elephants*.
95 Barua, "Infrastructure and Non-human Life."
96 Foucault, *Power*, 361.
97 "NH Upgrade through Kaziranga Opposed."
98 "Gogoi Meets Baalu."
99 "Reprieve for Kaziranga."
100 "Centre Modifies Kaziranga Highway Bypass."
101 "New Bridge over Brahmaputra Sanctioned."
102 Conversion of NH-37 to 4 Lane Road Demand Committee, *Save Kaziranga National Park*, 1.
103 Gandy, *The Fabric of Space*; Harvey and Knox, *Roads*.
104 Guha, *Planter Raj to Swaraj*.
105 Hunter, *A Statistical Account of Assam*, 55–56.
106 Medhi, *Transport System and Economic Development*.
107 *Save Kaziranga National Park*, 2.
108 "Kaziranga Bypass Plan Opposed."
109 *Save Kaziranga National Park*, 1.
110 "Kaziranga Bypass Plan Opposed."
111 *Save Kaziranga National Park*, 2.
112 Cited in Yadava, *Detailed Report on Issues*, 400.
113 "'Conservation Should Take Priority over Development.'"
114 *Save Kaziranga National Park*, 1.
115 *Save Kaziranga National Park*, 1.

116 Cited in Yadava, *Detailed Report on Issues*, 401–2.
117 *Save Kaziranga National Park*, 1.
118 Cited in Yadava, *Detailed Report on Issues*, 399.
119 Cited in Yadava, *Detailed Report on Issues*, 401.
120 Yadava, *Detailed Report on Issues*, 361–64.
121 *Save Kaziranga National Park*, 2.
122 "'Conservation Should Take Priority over Development.'"
123 Yadava, *Detailed Report on Issues*, 53.
124 Yadava, *Detailed Report on Issues*, 52–53.
125 "Flyover to Ensure Rhino's Safety."
126 "Gogoi to Visit Kaziranga Today."
127 "Rs 1cr Upgrade Pill for Kaziranga."
128 "Green-Kaziranga 2 Last."
129 "State Govt Proposes Wildlife-Friendly Steps."
130 "Dispur Mulling Wildlife-Friendly Highway."
131 Chakravartty, "Controversial Kaziranga Elevated Road Project"; "Assam Awards Rs 2,625-Cr Flyover Contract."
132 Barua, "Infrastructure and Non-human Life."
133 Rosenzweig, *Win-Win Ecology*.
134 Metzger, "The Moose Are Protesting."
135 Wildlife Institute of India, *Eco-friendly Measures*, 5.
136 Wildlife Institute of India, *Eco-friendly Measures*, 6–7.
137 Ament et al., *Protecting Asian Elephants*.
138 Wildlife Institute of India, *Eco-friendly Measures*, 80.
139 Chakravartty, "Controversial Kaziranga Elevated Road Project."
140 "Dispur Mulling Wildlife-Friendly Highway."
141 "Dispur Mulling Wildlife-Friendly Highway."
142 "Dispur Mulling Wildlife-Friendly Highway."
143 Wildlife Institute of India, *Eco-friendly Measures*.
144 Wildlife Institute of India, *Eco-friendly Measures*, 59.
145 Wildlife Institute of India, *Eco-friendly Measures*, 80.
146 Cited in Zaman, "Villagers against KNP Flyover Project."
147 Yadava, *Detailed Report on Issues*, 55.

148 Rosenzweig, *Win-Win Ecology*.

149 Yadava, *Detailed Report on Issues*.

150 White, "Road Ecology."

151 Yadava, *Detailed Report on Issues*, 52.

152 Yadava, *Detailed Report on Issues*, 161.

153 Yadava, *Detailed Report on Issues*.

154 Dey, *Tea Environments and Plantation Culture*.

155 Yadava, *Detailed Report on Issues*, 193.

156 Yadava, *Detailed Report on Issues*.

157 Yadava, *Detailed Report on Issues*, 193.

158 Agrawal, *Environmentality*.

159 Yadava, *Detailed Report on Issues*, 193.

160 Yadava, *Detailed Report on Issues*, 197.

161 Tsing, "Holocene Resurgence against Anthropocene Plantation."

162 For a fuller account of "sick" plantations and the perils of designating these as feral, see Besky, "Exhaustion and Endurance in Sick Landscapes."

163 Saha, Bhue, and Singha, *Decent Work for Tea Plantation Workers*.

164 Yadava, *Detailed Report on Issues*.

165 Roy, "Why India Cannot Plan."

166 Supreme Court of India, *T.N. Godavarman vs. Union of India*.

167 "Kaziranga'or Animal Corridor'ot Nixedhagya Jari Kori Bandha Korile Xokolu Nirman Karjya."

168 Yadava, *Detailed Report on Issues*.

169 Dasgupta, "Plantation Economy and Land Tenure System."

170 This move is commensurate with the current biopolitical movement that is increasingly gravitating toward a carceral regulation of flows, witnessed more broadly in the instrumentalization of mobility, the creation of volatility, and various modes of profiting from circulation and unsettlement (Achtnich, "Accumulation by Immobilization"; Tadiar, *Remaindered Life*).

171 See McCormack, "Geography and Abstraction."

172 Ingold, *Being Alive*; Deleuze and Guattari, *On the Line*.

173 Menon et al., *Right of Passage*.

174 Foucault, *Power*; Deleuze, "Postscript on the Societies of Control"; Lorimer, *The Probiotic Planet*.

6. Decolonial Cartographies

1. McKittrick, *Demonic Grounds*, ix.
2. See Sundberg, "Decolonizing Posthumanist Geographies."
3. Büscher, "The Nonhuman Turn."
4. Simone, *Improvised Lives*.
5. Wynter, "Novel and History, Plantation and Plot."
6. The term *Adivasi ontology* is, of course, a shorthand. I am mindful that there is no singular Adivasi ontology, but for purposes of my argument, it has both analytical and political purchase.
7. A prominent deity in the Hindu pantheon, Shiva is also known as Pashupati or the lord of animals.
8. Ingold, *The Perception of the Environment*, 29; also see Kumar et al., "Minimal Ecologies."
9. Ingold, *The Perception of the Environment*, 37.
10. Ingold, *Being Alive*.
11. McKittrick, *Demonic Grounds*, 132.
12. Lainé, *Living and Working with Giants*.
13. Lainé, *Living and Working with Giants*.
14. Simone, *Improvised Lives*.
15. Ingold, *Being Alive*.
16. McKittrick, *Demonic Grounds*, 135.
17. Deleuze and Guattari, *A Thousand Plateaus*, 259.
18. Ingold, *The Perception of the Environment*.
19. This crucial argument was made by Sarah Whatmore almost two decades ago. See Whatmore and Thorne, "Elephants on the Move."
20. Ingold, *Being Alive*, 160.
21. Jayasinghe, "Sri Lanka Elephants Face Jumbo Threat."
22. McKittrick, "Plantation Futures."
23. Simone, *Improvised Lives*, 2.
24. Whatmore and Thorne, "Wild(er)ness."
25. Ingold, "Epilogue"; Ingold, *Being Alive*.
26. Ingold, *Being Alive*.
27. Deleuze and Guattari, *A Thousand Plateaus*, 326.

28 For an evocative and far-reaching account, see Keil, "Elephant-Human *Dandi*"; Keil, "On the Trails of Free-Roaming Elephants."
29 Rowntree, *A Chota Sahib*, 19–20.
30 Allen et al., "Field Evidence Supporting Monitoring."
31 Allen et al., "Field Evidence Supporting Monitoring," 193.
32 Wynter, "Novel and History, Plantation and Plot."
33 McKittrick, "Plantation Futures," 11.
34 Remmers et al., "Elephant (Loxodonta africana) Footprints."
35 Remmers et al., "Elephant (Loxodonta africana) Footprints."
36 Platt et al., "Water-Filled Asian Elephant Tracks."
37 Wynter, "Novel and History, Plantation and Plot."
38 Rodney, "Plantation Society in Guyana"; Behal, *One Hundred Years of Servitude*.
39 Deleuze and Guattari, *A Thousand Plateaus*.
40 Saikia, "Forest Land and Peasant Struggles."
41 Simone, *Improvised Lives*, 125.
42 In the neoclassical model, animals become, to use Jonathon Turnbull and colleagues' evocative phrase, "*Animal economicus*" (Kumar et al., "Minimal Ecologies").
43 Whatmore, "Mapping Knowledge Controversies."

Conclusion

1 Cf. Behal, *One Hundred Years of Servitude*.
2 "Assam Budget to Boost Beleaguered Tea Industry."
3 Oxfam, *Addressing the Human Cost of Assam Tea*.
4 De Castro, *Cannibal Metaphysics*. A quick search on the internet reveals that the term has been in circulation for a while.
5 Yusoff, *A Billion Black Anthropocenes*.
6 Cf. Hecht, "Interscalar Vehicles for an African Anthropocene."
7 Bonneuil and Fressoz, *The Shock of the Anthropocene*; Yusoff, *A Billion Black Anthropocenes*.
8 Patel and Moore, *A History of the World in Seven Cheap Things*; cf. Moore, *Capitalism in the Web of Life*.

9. Moore, *Capitalism in the Web of Life*; Malm and Hornborg, "The Geology of Mankind?"
10. Sanyal, *Rethinking Capitalist Development*; Inverardi-Ferri, "The Enclosure of 'Waste Land.'"
11. Kirksey and Helmreich, "The Emergence of Multispecies Ethnography."
12. See Ingold, "Anthropology beyond Humanity."
13. Also see Münster, "Lantana Invades Teak Plantations."
14. Barua, "Feral Ecologies."
15. Cf. Chakrabarty, "The Climate of History."
16. Oxfam, *Addressing the Human Cost of Assam Tea*; Saha, Bhue, and Singha, *Decent Work for Tea Plantation Workers*.
17. Cf. Wadiwel, "Chicken Harvesting Machine."
18. Behal, *One Hundred Years of Servitude*.
19. Behal, *One Hundred Years of Servitude*, 4.
20. Gohain, "Chronicles of Violence and Terror"; Misra, *The Periphery Strikes Back*.
21. Simone, *Improvised Lives*; McKittrick, "Plantation Futures."
22. Achtnich, "Accumulation by Immobilization"; Tadiar, *Remaindered Life*.
23. Sanyal, *Rethinking Capitalist Development*.
24. Stoler, "'The Rot Remains.'"
25. Tsing, "Earth Stalked by Man."
26. Cf. Stuesse, *Scratching Out a Living*; Blanchette, "Herding Species."
27. Hinchliffe et al., *Pathological Lives*; Gandy, "The Zoonotic City."
28. Achtnich, "Bioeconomy and Migrants' Lives in Libya."
29. Barua, "Infrastructure and Non-human Life."
30. Li, "After the Land Grab."
31. Agrawal, *Environmentality*.
32. Besky, "Exhaustion and Endurance in Sick Landscapes"; Saha, Bhue, and Singha, *Decent Work for Tea Plantation Workers*.
33. McKittrick, *Demonic Grounds*.
34. Bonneuil and Fressoz, *The Shock of the Anthropocene*.
35. Mbembe, *Necropolitics*.
36. Simone, *Improvised Lives*.

BIBLIOGRAPHY

"Abadh Bonanchal Dhangxat Badha Diya Babei Hatya Kora Hol Taufil'ok." *Ajir Batori* (Guwahati), August 5, 1994.
Achtnich, Marthe. "Accumulation by Immobilization: Migration, Mobility and Money in Libya." *Economy and Society* 51, no. 1 (2021): 1–21. https://doi.org/10.1080/03085147.2022.1987751.
Achtnich, Marthe. "Bioeconomy and Migrants' Lives in Libya." *Cultural Anthropology* 37, no. 1 (2022): 9–15. https://doi.org/10.14506/ca37.1.02.
Adams, William M. *Against Extinction: The Story of Conservation*. London: Earthscan, 2004.
Agrawal, Arun. *Environmentality: Technologies of Government and the Making of Subjects*. Durham, NC: Duke University Press, 2005.
Ahmed, Rekib, Anup Saikia, and Scott M. Robeson. "Tracks of Death: Elephant Casualties along the Habaipur–Diphu Railway in Assam, India." *Annals of the American Association of Geographers* 112, no. 6 (2022): 1–23. https://doi.org/10.1080/24694452.2021.1990009.
Aikens, Natalie, Amy Clukey, Amy K. King, and Isadora Wagner. "South to the Plantationocene." *ASAP Journal*, October 27, 2019. https://asapjournal.com/south-to-the-plantationocene-natalie-aikens-amy-clukey-amy-k-king-and-isadora-wagner/.
Aiyadurai, Ambika. *Tigers Are Our Brothers: Anthropology of Wildlife Conservation in Northeast India*. New Delhi: Oxford University Press, 2021.
"Alleged Encroachment in Nambor Reserve Forest by Rangajan Tea Estate." *Sentinel*, July 2, 2021. https://www.sentinelassam.com/north-east-india-news/assam-news/alleged-encroachment-in-nambor-reserve-forest-by-rangajan-tea-estate-545096.

Allen, B. C. *Assam District Gazetteers*. Vol. 5: *Darrang*. Allahabad: Pioneer Press, 1905.

Allen, Connie R. B., Lauren J. N. Brent, Thatayaone Motsentwa, and Darren P. Croft. "Field Evidence Supporting Monitoring of Chemical Information on Pathways by Male African Elephants." *Animal Behaviour* 176 (2021): 193–206. https://doi.org/10.1016/j.anbehav.2021.04.004.

Ambagudia, Jagannath, and Virginius Xaxa. *Handbook of Tribal Politics in India*. New Delhi: SAGE, 2021.

Ament, Rob, Sandeep Kumar Tiwari, Melissa Butynski, Becky Shu Chen, Noris Dodd, Aditya Gangadharan, Nilanga Jayasinghe, et al. *Protecting Asian Elephants from Linear Transport Infrastructure: The Asian Elephant Transport Working Group's Introduction to the Challenges and Solutions.* Asian Elephant Transport Working Group; IUCN WCPA Connectivity Conservation Specialist Group/ IUCN SSC Asian Elephant Specialist Group. Gland, Switzerland: Asian Elephant Transport Working Group, 2021.

Anand, Nikhil. *Hydraulic City: Water and the Infrastructures of Citizenship in Mumbai*. Durham, NC: Duke University Press, 2017.

Annual Report on the Administration of Land Revenue in Assam, 1874–75. Shillong: Assam Secretariat Press, 1875.

Antrobus, Hinson Allan. *A History of the Assam Company, 1839–1953*. Edinburgh: T. and A. Constable, 1957.

Antrobus, Hinson Allan. *A History of the Jorehaut Tea Company Ltd., 1859–1946*. London: Tea and Rubber Mail, 1947.

Appel, Hannah C. "Walls and White Elephants: Oil Extraction, Responsibility, and Infrastructural Violence in Equatorial Guinea." *Ethnography* 13, no. 4 (2012): 439–65.

Appel, Hannah C., Nikhil Anand, and Akhil Gupta, eds. *The Promise of Infrastructure*. Durham, NC: Duke University Press, 2018.

Arvidsson, Josefin, Mats Amundin, and Matthias Laska. "Successful Acquisition of an Olfactory Discrimination Test by Asian Elephants, *Elephas Maximus*." *Physiology and Behavior* 105, no. 3 (2012): 809–14.

"Assam Awards Rs 2,625-Cr Flyover Contract in Kaziranga." *NBM and CW* (New Delhi), September 20, 2019.

"Assam Budget to Boost Beleaguered Tea Industry: Indian Chamber of Commerce." *Sentinel*, July 18, 2021. https://www.sentinelassam.com/guwahati-city/assam-budget-to-boost-beleaguered-tea-industry-indian-chamber-of-commerce-547078.

Assam Legislative Assembly. *Assam Legislative Assembly Debates, Official Report. Ninth Session of the Assam Legislative Assembly, Autumn Session, Volume II, No. 41, 18th and 20th October 1960*. Shillong: Assam Government Press, 1963.

"Assam Poised for Industrial Growth." *Times of India*, April 23, 1992.

"Assam Refinery May Hit Ecology." *Times of India*, February 6, 1990, 20.

"Assam's Scheme to Aid Poor Farmers." *Times of India* (New Delhi), October 9, 1978, 14.

Athparia, R. P. "Karbi Folklore and Identity." In *The Anthropology of North-East India*, edited by T. B. Subba and G. C. Ghosh, 307–32. New Delhi: Orient Longman, 2003.

Bamber, M. Kelway. "The Cultivation of *Passiflora Fœtida* and *Mikania Scandens* to Keep Down Other Weeds." *Circulars and Agricultural Journal of the Royal Botanic Gardens, Ceylon* 4, no. 16 (1909): 141–45.

Banerjee, Sayan, and Ambika Aiyadurai. "'Everyday Conservation': A Study of Actors and Processes in an Elephant Conservation Project in Assam, India." *Human Dimensions of Wildlife* 27, no. 6 (2022): 536–53. https://doi.org/10.1080/10871209.2021.1970861.

Barbora, Sanjay. "Riding the Rhino: Conservation, Conflicts, and the Militarisation of Kaziranga National Park in Assam." *Antipode* 49, no. 5 (2017): 1145–63.

Barbora, Sanjay, and Sarat Phukan. "Mines, Plantations, and Militarisation: Environmental Conflicts in Tinsukia, Assam." *Environment and Planning E: Nature and Space* 6, no. 1 (2022). https://doi.org/10.1177/25148486221089820.

Barkaith, S. "Hastividyârnava." 1734. Edited by P. C. Choudhury. Guwahati: Publication Board, Assam, 1976.

Barker, George M. *A Tea Planter's Life in Assam*. London: Thacker, Spink, 1884.

Barooah Pisharoty, Sangeeta. *Assam: The Accord, the Discord*. New Delhi: Penguin Random House, 2019.

Barry, Andrew. *Material Politics: Disputes along the Pipeline*. Oxford: John Wiley, 2013.

Barua, Maan. "Affective Economies, Pandas and the Atmospheric Politics of Lively Capital." *Transactions of the Institute of British Geographers* 45, no. 3 (2020): 678–92. https://doi.org/10.1111/tran.12361.

Barua, Maan. "Animal Work: Metabolic, Ecological, Affective." Theorizing the Contemporary, *Fieldsights*, July 26, 2018. https://culanth.org/fieldsights/animal-work-metabolic-ecological-affective.

Barua, Maan. "Animating Capital: Work, Commodities, Circulation." *Progress in Human Geography* 43, no. 4 (2018): 650–69. https://doi.org/10.1177/0309132518819057.

Barua, Maan. "Between Gods and Demons." *Seminar India* 651 (November 2013): 75–79.

Barua, Maan. "Circulating Elephants: Unpacking the Geographies of a Cosmopolitan Animal." *Transactions of the Institute of British Geographers* 39, no. 4 (2014): 559–73. https://doi.org/10.1111/tran.12047.

Barua, Maan. "Feral Ecologies: The Making of Postcolonial Nature in London." *Journal of the Royal Anthropological Institute* 28, no. 3 (2022): 896–919. https://doi.org/10.1111/1467-9655.13653.

Barua, Maan. "Infrastructure and Non-human Life: A Wider Ontology." *Progress in Human Geography* 45, no. 6 (2021): 1467–89. https://doi.org/10.1177/0309132521991220.

Barua, Maan. *Lively Cities: Reconfiguring Urban Ecology.* Minneapolis: University of Minnesota Press, 2023.

Barua, Maan. "Lively Commodities and Encounter Value." *Environment and Planning D: Society and Space* 34, no. 4 (2016): 725–44. https://doi.org/10.1177/0263775815626420.

Barua, Maan. "Some Thoughts on the *Hastividyârnava* of Sukumar Barkaith." *Airawat: Souvenir of the Kaziranga Elephant Festival* 4 (2006): 32–34.

Barua, Maan, Shonil A. Bhagwat, and Sushrut Jadhav. "The Hidden Dimensions of Human-Wildlife Conflict: Health Impacts, Opportunity and Transaction Costs." *Biological Conservation* 157 (January 2013): 309–16. http://www.sciencedirect.com/science/article/pii/S0006320712003345.

Barua, P., and B. N. Das. *Kaziranga: The Rhinoland in Assam.* Gauhati: Forest Department, Assam, 1969.

Barua, Prafulla Chandra. *The Saga of Assam Oil: From Nahorpung to Numaligarh (1825–1999).* Guwahati: Spectrum, 1999.

Baruah, Bhaskar Jyoti. "A Tribute to Late Gangadhar Saikia." In *Gangey: Khyudhra Sah Khetiyokor Pitriswarup Gangadhar Saikiadewor Smarok Grantha*, edited by Pratim Saikia and Rohit Borgohain, 45–47. Golaghat: All Assam Small Tea Growers Association, 2018.

Baruah, Damodar. "Father of Small Tea Grower Revolution." In *Gangey: Khyudhra Sah Khetiyokor Pitriswarup Gangadhar Saikiadewor Smarok Grantha*, edited by Pratim Saikia and Rohit Borgohain, 127–32. Golaghat: All Assam Small Tea Growers Association, 2018.

Baruah, Ditee Moni. "The Refinery Movement in Assam." *Economic and Political Weekly* 46, no. 1 (2011): 63–69.

Baruah, Sanjib. *India against Itself: Assam and the Politics of Nationality.* New Delhi: Oxford University Press, 1999.

Baskaran, N., and Ajay A. Desai. "Ranging Behaviour of the Asian Elephant (*Elephas Maximus*) in the Nilgiri Biosphere Reserve, South India." *Gajah: Journal of the Asian Elephant Specialist Group*, no. 15 (1996): 41–56.

Bates, Lucy A., Katito N. Sayialel, Norah W. Njiraini, Cynthia Moss, Joyce Poole, and Richard W. Byrne. "Elephants Classify Human Ethnic Groups by Odor and Garment Color." *Current Biology* 17 (2007): 1938–42.

Behal, Rana Partap. *One Hundred Years of Servitude: Political Economy of Tea Plantations in Colonial Assam.* New Delhi: Tulika, 2014.

Behal, Rana Partap, and Prabhu P. Mohapatra. "'Tea and Money versus Human Life': The Rise and Fall of the Indenture System in the Assam Tea Plantations 1840–1908." *Journal of Peasant Studies* 19, no. 3–4 (1992): 142–72.

Bennett, Jane. *The Enchantment of Modern Life: Attachments, Crossings and Ethics.* Princeton, NJ: Princeton University Press, 2001.

Bennett, Jane. *Vibrant Matter: A Political Ecology of Things.* Durham, NC: Duke University Press, 2010.

Benson, Etienne. *Wired Wilderness: Technologies of Tracking and the Making of Modern Wildlife.* Baltimore, MD: Johns Hopkins University Press, 2010.

Berlant, Lauren. "Slow Death (Sovereignty, Obesity, Lateral Agency)." *Critical Inquiry* 33, no. 4 (2007): 754–80.

Besky, Sarah. *The Darjeeling Distinction: Labor and Justice on Fair-Trade Tea Plantations in India.* Berkeley: University of California Press, 2013.

Besky, Sarah. "Exhaustion and Endurance in Sick Landscapes: Cheap Tea and the Work of Monoculture in the Dooars, India." In *How Nature Works: Rethinking Labor on a Troubled Planet*, edited by Sarah Besky and Alex Blanchette, 23–40. Albuquerque: University of New Mexico Press, 2019.

Besky, Sarah. "Monoculture." In *The Anthropocene Unseen: A Lexicon*, edited by Cymene Howe and Anand Pandian, 277–80. New York: Punctum, 2020.

Bhattacharya, Nandini. *Contagion and Enclaves: Tropical Medicine in Colonial India.* Liverpool: Liverpool University Press, 2012.

Bhowmik, Sharit K. "Small Growers to Prop Up Large Plantations." *Economic and Political Weekly* 26, no. 30 (1999): 1789–90.

Biermann, Christine, and Becky Mansfield. "Biodiversity, Purity, and Death: Conservation Biology as Biopolitics." *Environment and Planning D: Society and Space* 32, no. 2 (2014): 257–73. https://doi.org/10.1068/d13047p.

Birney, Charles Folliott. *The Story of the Assam Railways and Trading Company Limited 1881–1951.* London: Harley, 1951.

Bist, S. S. "Elephant Conservation in India—an Overview." *Gajah: Journal of the Asian Elephant Specialist Group*, no. 25 (2006): 27–35.

Biswas, K. "Some Foreign Weeds and Their Distribution in India and Burma." *Current Science* 2, no. 11 (1934): 422–25.

Blanchette, Alex. "Herding Species: Biosecurity, Posthuman Labor, and the American Industrial Pig." *Cultural Anthropology* 30, no. 4 (2015): 640–69. https://doi.org/10.14506/ca30.4.09.

Bonneuil, Christophe, and Jean-Baptiste Fressoz. *The Shock of the Anthropocene.* Translated by David Fernbach. London: Verso, 2016.

"Bonoriya Hatir Upodrow'ot Raij Atankita." *Ajir Batori* (Guwahati), May 27, 1994.

Bor, Norman Loftus. "A Sketch of the Vegetation of the Aka Hills, Assam: A Synecological Study." *Indian Forest Records (New Series) Botany* 1, no. 4 (1938): 103–221.

Borkotoky, Namrata. "Brewing Trouble or Transforming Nature? Making of Tea Plantations' Environments in Assam, 1830s–1930s." PhD diss., Indian Institute of Technology Guwahati, 2021.

Bourdieu, Pierre. *Outline of a Theory of Practice*. 2 vols. Cambridge: Cambridge University Press, 1977.

Bradshaw, Gay A. *Elephants on the Edge: What Animals Teach Us about Humanity*. New Haven, CT: Yale University Press, 2009.

Brice, Jeremy. "Attending to Grape Vines: Perceptual Practices, Planty Agencies and Multiple Temporalities in Australian Viticulture." *Social and Cultural Geography* 15, no. 8 (2014): 942–65. https://doi.org/10.1080/14649365.2014.883637.

Brockington, Dan, Rosaleen Duffy, and Jim Igoe. *Nature Unbound: Conservation, Capitalism and the Future of Protected Areas*. London: Earthscan, 2008.

Bruce, C. A. *An Account of the Manufacture of the Black Tea as Now Practiced at Suddeya in Upper Assam*. Calcutta: G. H. Huttmann, Bengal Military Orphan Press, 1838.

Brühl, Paul. "Recent Plant Immigrants." *Journal and Proceedings of the Asiatic Society of Bengal* 4, no. 11 (1908): 603–56.

Bruinenberg, Hidde Peter. "Elephant Party in Addo-Park South Africa." YouTube, 2007, 2:26. http://www.youtube.com/watch?v=EyWd7ozjwbA.

Bull, Jacob, ed. *Animal Movements, Moving Animals: Essays on Direction, Velocity and Agency in Humanimal Encounters*. Uppsala: Uppsala University, 2011.

Büscher, Bram. "The Nonhuman Turn: Critical Reflections on Alienation, Entanglement and Nature under Capitalism." *Dialogues in Human Geography* 12, no. 1 (2021): 54–73. https://doi.org/10.1177/20438206211026200.

Campbell, A. "Notes on the Mode of Capture of Elephants in Assam." *Proceedings of the Zoological Society of London* 37, no. 1 (1869): 136–40.

Caro, Timothy M. *Conservation by Proxy*. Washington, DC: Island Press, 2010.

"Centre Modifies Kaziranga Highway Bypass." *Assam Tribune* (Guwahati), November 20, 2008.

Chakrabarty, Dipesh. "The Climate of History: Four Theses." *Critical Inquiry* 35, no. 2 (2009): 197–222.

Chakrabarty, Dipesh. *Habitations of Modernity: Essays in the Wake of Subaltern Studies*. Chicago: University of Chicago Press, 2002.

Chakrabarty, Dipesh. *Provincializing Europe: Postcolonial Thought and Historical Difference*. Princeton, NJ: Princeton University Press, 2007.

Chakraborty, Gorky. "Agriculture in Assam: Emerging Micro-trends." In *Changing Agricultural Scenario in North-East India*, edited by Bimal J. Deb and B. Datta Ray, 189–205. New Delhi: Concept, 2006.

Chakravartty, Anupam. "Controversial Kaziranga Elevated Road Project Goes for Public Scrutiny." *East Mojo*, September 4, 2021. https://www.eastmojo.com/assam/2021/09/04/controversial-kaziranga-elevated-road-project-goes-for-public-scrutiny/.

Chandler, David. *Ontopolitics in the Anthropocene: An Introduction to Mapping, Sensing and Hacking*. London: Routledge, 2018.

Chao, Sophie. "Children of the Palms: Growing Plants and Growing People in a Papuan Plantationocene." *Journal of the Royal Anthropological Institute* 27, no. 2 (2021): 245–64.

Chatterjee, Piya. "An Empire of Drink: Gender, Labor and the Historical Economies of Alcohol." *Journal of Historical Sociology* 16, no. 2 (2003): 183–208.

Chatterjee, Piya. *A Time for Tea: Women, Labor, and Post/Colonial Politics on an Indian Plantation*. Durham, NC: Duke University Press, 2001.

Chew, Matthew K., and Andrew L. Hamilton. "The Rise and Fall of Biotic Nativeness: A Historical Perspective." In *Fifty Years of Invasion Ecology: The Legacy of Charles Elton*, edited by David M. Richardson, 35–48. Oxford: Wiley-Blackwell, 2011.

Chief Engineer (Construction). "Northeast Frontier Railway (Construction Organisation) Notice: Pre-qualification of Contractors." *Times of India*, March 28, 2000.

Chief Engineer (Construction). "Northeast Frontier Railway (Construction Organisation) Tender Notice No. Con/2008/Jan/04." *Times of India*, January 17, 2008.

Choudhury, A. K. "Controversial *Mikania* (Climber)—a Threat to the Forests and Agriculture." *Indian Forester* 98, no. 3 (1972): 178–86.

Choudhury, Anwaruddin. *A Naturalist in Karbi Anglong*. Guwahati: Gibbon, 1993.

Circle Officer. "Submission of Report on Damage of Paddy Land Due to Indiscriminate Earth Cutting and Mining Activities at the Hills of Karbi Anglong." Letter No. Bkc 4 2014 to the Sub-divisional Officer, Civil, Bokakhat. Office of the Bokakhat Revenue Circle, Bokakhat, Assam.

Clifford, James. *Returns: Becoming Indigenous in the Twenty-First Century*. Cambridge, MA: Harvard University Press, 2013.

Collins, James. *Report on the Caoutchouc of Commerce: Being Information on the Plants Yielding It, Their Geographical Distribution, Climatic Conditions, and the Possibility of Their Cultivation and Acclimatization in India*. London: W. H. Allen, 1871.

Colombino, Annalisa, and Paolo Palladino. "In the Blink of an Eye: Human and Nonhuman Animals, Movement, and Bio-political Existence." *Angelaki* 24, no. 6 (2019): 168–83. https://doi.org/10.1080/0969725X.2019.1684708.

"Concern over Move to Open Quarry Near Kaziranga." *Assam Tribune* (Guwahati), January 6, 2006.

"'Conservation Should Take Priority over Development.'" *Assam Tribune* (Guwahati), November 28, 2008.

Conservator of Forests, Eastern Assam Circle. "Construction of Boundary Wall on NRL's Proposed New Township Land-Request for Suspension/Cancellation of the Land Acquisition in Favour of NRL for New Township Thereof." Letter from Conservator of Forests to Additional Principal Chief Conservator of Forests, fg.24/NRL/Illegality/GIT/EAC/, 2. Office of the Conservator of Forests, Eastern Assam Circle, Jorhat, Assam, August 20, 2015.

Conversion of NH-37 to 4 Lane Road Demand Committee. *Save Kaziranga National Park: Construct NH-37 in Its Original Alignment from Koliabor to Numoligarh.* Kaziranga: Conversion of NH-37 to 4 Lane Road Demand Committee, 2009.

Coole, Diana, and Samantha Frost. "Introducing the New Materialisms." In *New Materialisms: Ontology, Agency, Politics*, edited by Diana Coole and Samantha Frost, 1–46. Durham, NC: Duke University Press, 2010.

Cooper, Melinda E., and Catherine Waldby. *Clinical Labor: Tissue Donors and Research Subjects in the Global Bioeconomy.* Durham, NC: Duke University Press, 2014.

Correia, David. "F**k Jared Diamond." *Capitalism Nature Socialism* 24, no. 4 (2013): 1–6.

Coulter, Kendra. *Animals, Work and the Promise of Interspecies Solidarity.* London: Palgrave Macmillan, 2015.

Crooks, Kevin R., and M. Sanjayan, eds. *Connectivity Conservation.* Cambridge: Cambridge University Press, 2006.

Crosby, Alfred W. *The Columbian Exchange: Biological and Cultural Consequences of 1492.* Westport, CT: Praeger, 2003.

Crutzen, Paul J. "Geology of Mankind." *Nature* 415, no. 23 (2002): 23.

"Damages by Rogue Elephants." *Amrita Bazar Patrika*, December 6, 1901.

Das, Jyoti P., Bibhuti Prasad Lahkar, and Bibhab Kumar Talukdar. "Increasing Trend of Human Elephant Conflict in Golaghat District, Assam, India: Issues and Concerns." *Gajah: Journal of the Asian Elephant Specialist Group*, no. 37 (2012): 34–37.

Das, Karabi. "The Small Tea Growers of Assam: A Study of Their Monopsonistic Exploitation and Production." PhD diss., Indian Institute of Technology Guwahati, 2019.

Dasgupta, Keya. "Plantation Economy and Land Tenure System in Brahmaputra Valley, 1839–1914." *Economic and Political Weekly* 18, no. 29 (1983): 1280–90.

Davis, Janae, Alex A. Moulton, Levi Van Sant, and Brian Williams. "Anthropocene, Capitalocene, . . . Plantationocene? A Manifesto for Ecological Justice in an Age of Global Crises." *Geography Compass* 13, no. 5 (2019): e12438. https://doi.org/10.1111/gec3.12438.

Davis, Mark A., Matthew K. Chew, Richard J. Hobbs, Ariel E. Lugo, John J. Ewel, Geerat J. Vermeij, James H. Brown, et al. "Don't Judge Species on Their Origins." *Nature* 474, no. 7350 (2011): 153–54. http://dx.doi.org/10.1038/474153a.

Deb Roy, Rohan. *Malarial Subjects: Empire, Medicine and Nonhumans in British India, 1820–1909*. Cambridge: Cambridge University Press, 2017.

de Castro, Eduardo Viveiros. *Cannibal Metaphysics*. Minneapolis: University of Minnesota Press, 2015.

Deleuze, Gilles. *Foucault*. Translated by S. Hand. London: Continuum, 2007.

Deleuze, Gilles. "Postscript on the Societies of Control." *October* 59 (winter 1992): 3–7.

Deleuze, Gilles, and Félix Guattari. *On the Line*. Translated by B. Massumi. New York: Semiotext(e), 1983.

Deleuze, Gilles, and Félix Guattari. *A Thousand Plateaus: Capitalism and Schizophrenia*. London: Continuum, 1987.

"Depredations by Wild Elephants." *Assam Tribune* (Guwahati), July 17, 1994.

"The Deputy Commissioner of Durrang . . ." *Pioneer*, April 2, 1896.

"Derailed by Elephants." *Amrita Bazar Patrika*, July 17, 1901.

Dey, Arnab. *Tea Environments and Plantation Culture: Imperial Disarray in Eastern India*. Cambridge: Cambridge University Press, 2018.

Diamond, Jared M. "The Island Dilemma: Lessons of Modern Biogeographic Studies for the Design of Natural Reserves." *Biological Conservation* 7, no. 2 (1975): 129–46.

Diamond, Jared M., John Terborgh, Robert F. Whitcomb, James F. Lynch, Paul A. Opler, Chandler S. Robbins, Daniel S. Simberloff, and Lawrence G. Abele. "Island Biogeography and Conservation: Strategy and Limitations." *Science* 193, no. 4257 (1976): 1027–32.

Director, Kaziranga National Park. "Information Regarding the Incident That Took Place under the Eviction of Kaziranga National Park on 19-09-2016." Letter No. Knp/Fg.605/High Court's PIL No. 66/Pt-1 to Principal Chief Conservator of Forests and Head of Forest Force, Assam. Eastern Assam Wildlife Division, Bokakhat.

Director, Kaziranga National Park. "Opening of New Stone Quarries in Areas Adjacent to Kaziranga National Park." Letter No. Knp/Fg.65/Cm to Chief Conservator of Forests, Assam. Eastern Assam Wildlife Division, Bokakhat.

Director, Kaziranga National Park. "Siltation of Mori Diffalo River and Agricultural Field of Panbari Area Due to Crusher Plant." Letter No. Knp/Fg.65/C.M. to the Conservator of Forests, Hills, Karbi Anglong. Eastern Assam Wildlife Division, Bokakhat.

"Dispur Mulling Wildlife-Friendly Highway Near Kaziranga." *Sentinel* (Guwahati), April 18, 2016.

Divisional Forest Officer. "Geleki Stone Quarry-Closure." Letter No. B/Knp/2016/9019 to the Divisional Forest Officer, Karbi-Anglong West. Eastern Assam Wildlife Division, Bokakhat.

"The Drainage Problem." *Times of India* (Calcutta), August 15, 1924, 14.

"Drunk Animals—Marula Fruit Party!!" Posted by herbecgm on YouTube, 2010, 3:54. https://www.youtube.com/watch?v=7Le9ufN5uEc.

Dutta, Ananda Chandra. *Shade Trees, Green Crop and Cover Crop Plants in the Tea Estates of North East India.* Tocklai, Jorhat: Tea Research Association, 1977.

Dutta, Anwesha. "A Phenomenological Exploration into Lived Experiences of Violence in Northeast India." *South Asia: Journal of South Asian Studies* 44, no. 2 (2021): 201–17. https://doi.org/10.1080/00856401.2021.1852489.

"Elephant Corridors under Human Pressure." *Assam Tribune* (Guwahati), July 2, 2005.

"Elephant Hunting in Assam." *Pioneer* (Allahabad), January 22, 1873.

"Elephant Kills 5, Locals Live in Terror (India)." Statesman News Service, July 10, 2009. Accessed September 19, 2012. http://www.savetheelephants.org/news-reader/items/elephant-kills-5-locals-live-in-terror-40india41.html.

Elephant Preservation Act, 1879. Legislative/1879-04/File No. 147 (192). National Archives of India, New Delhi.

"Elephants Kill One More at Numaligarh." *Assam Tribune* (Guwahati), June 30, 2005.

"Elephants on Drunken Rampage Kill Three People." *Guardian*, December 3, 2010. http://www.guardian.co.uk/world/2010/dec/03/elephants-drunken-rampage-india.

Elton, Sarah. "Growing Methods: Developing a Methodology for Identifying Plant Agency and Vegetal Politics in the City." *Environmental Humanities* 13, no. 1 (2021): 93–112.

Ernwein, Marion. "Bringing Urban Parks to Life: The More-Than-Human Politics of Urban Ecological Work." *Annals of the Association of American Geographers* 111, no. 2 (2021): 559–76. https://doi.org/10.1080/24694452.2020.1773230.

Ernwein, Marion, Franklin Ginn, and James Palmer, eds. *The Work That Plants Do: Life, Labour and the Future of Vegetal Economies.* Bielefeld: Transcript, 2021.

Federici, Silvia. *Caliban and the Witch: Women, the Body, and Primitive Accumulation.* New York: Autonomedia, 2004.

Fishel, Stefanie R. "Of Other Movements: Nonhuman Mobility in the Anthropocene." *Mobilities* 14, no. 3 (2019): 351–62. https://doi.org/10.1080/17450101.2019.1611218.

Fleming, Jake. "Toward Vegetal Political Ecology: Kyrgyzstan's Walnut-Fruit Forest and the Politics of Graftability." *Geoforum* 79 (2017): 26–35.

"Flyover to Ensure Rhino's Safety." *Hindu* (New Delhi), July 28, 2003.

"Forest Department Incurs Loss Worth Rs 42 Crore." *Sentinel* (Guwahati), September 21, 1994.

Forest Range Officer. "Enquiry on an Installation of Stone Crushing Industry." Memo No. Kr/Crusher Machine/96/480, February 25, 1996, to Divisional Forest Officer, Bokakhat, Assam. Forest Range Office, Kaziranga Range, Kohora, Kaziranga.

Forest Range Officer. "Siltation of Moridifaloo River and Agricultural Field of Panbari Due to Crusher Plants." Letter No. Kr/48/07/1509-60, June 28, 2007, to Divisional Forest Officer, Bokakhat, Assam. Forest Range Office, Kaziranga Range, Kohora, Kaziranga.

Forest Survey of India. *The State of Forest Report 1993*. Dehradun: Ministry of Environment and Forests, Forest Survey of India, Government of India, 1993.

Forest Survey of India. *The State of Forest Report 1995*. Dehradun: Ministry of Environment and Forests, Forest Survey of India, Government of India, 1995.

Foucault, Michel. *The History of Sexuality*, vol. 1: *The Will to Knowledge*. New York: Penguin, 1998.

Foucault, Michel. *Power: Essential Works of Michel Foucault, 1954–1984*. Edited by James D. Faubion. New York: New Press, 2000.

Fowler, Murray E. "Toxicology." In *Biology, Medicine, and Surgery of Elephants*, edited by Murray E. Fowler and Susan K. Mikota, 415–29. New York: Wiley-Blackwell, 2006.

Gadgil, Madhav, and Ramachandra Guha. *Ecology and Equity: The Use and Abuse of Nature in Contemporary India*. New Delhi: Penguin, 1995.

Gadgil, Madhav, and Ramachandra Guha. *This Fissured Land: An Ecological History of India*. New Delhi: Oxford University Press, 1992.

Gandy, Matthew. "An Arkansas Parable for the Anthropocene." *Annals of the American Association of Geographers* 112, no. 2 (2022): 368–86. https://doi.org/10.1080/24694452.2021.1935692.

Gandy, Matthew. *The Fabric of Space: Water, Modernity and the Urban Imagination*. Cambridge, MA: MIT Press, 2014.

Gandy, Matthew. "The Zoonotic City: Urban Political Ecology and the Pandemic Imaginary." *International Journal of Urban and Regional Research* 46, no. 2 (2022): 202–19. https://doi.org/10.1111/1468-2427.13080.

Gandy, Matthew, and Sandra Jasper. "Geography, Materialism, and the Neo-vitalist Turn." *Dialogues in Human Geography* 7, no. 2 (2017): 140–44. https://doi.org/10.1177/2043820617717848.

Gauhati High Court. *In the Matter of W.P (C) No. 4860/2013, Sri Sunil Das and 7 Ors vs. the State of Assam and Others. An Additional Affidavit in Opposition Filed on Behalf of the Petitioners*. Gauhati High Court 35 (2014).

Gauhati High Court. *Numaligarh Refinery Ltd vs. Union of India and 7 Ors*. Gauhati High Court 4 (2018).

Gauhati High Court. *PIL (Suo Motu) 66/2012, 67/2012, and Wp(C) 648/2013 and 4860/2013*. Gauhati High Court 37 (2015).

Gauhati High Court. *Sri Sunil Das and 7 Ors vs. the State of Assam and Others. Writ Petition (Civil) No. 4860/2013*. Gauhati High Court 118 (2013).

Ghosh, Durba. "Small Tea Gardens—Silent Green Revolution in Assam." *Press Trust of India*, December 13, 1999.

Gibson, James J. *The Ecological Approach to Visual Perception*. New York: Taylor and Francis, 1986.

Gogoi, Debojit. "Ek Byatikrami Pratibha." In *Gangey: Khyudhra Sah Khetiyokor Pitriswarup Gangadhar Saikiadewor Smarok Grantha*, edited by Pratim Saikia and Rohit Borgohain, 121–23. Golaghat: All Assam Small Tea Growers Association, 2018.

Gogoi, Mayuri. "Kaziranga under Threat: Biodiversity Loss and Encroachment of Forest Land." *Economic and Political Weekly* 50, no. 28 (2015): 2616–17.

"Gogoi Meets Baalu, Discusses Road Development Issues." *Press Trust of India Limited* (New Delhi), November 20, 2007.

Gogoi, Ramen. "Axomor Bonanchal SULFA'k Eri Diya Hol Neki?" *Dainik Janambhumi* (Jorhat), October 1, 1994.

"Gogoi to Visit Kaziranga Today." *Telegraph* (New Delhi), July 15, 2012.

Gohain, Hiren. *Assam: A Burning Question*. Guwahati: Spectrum, 1985.

Gohain, Hiren. "Chronicles of Violence and Terror: Rise of United Liberation Front of Asom." *Economic and Political Weekly* 42, no. 12 (2007): 1012–18.

Gohain, Hiren. "Extremist Challenge and Indian State: Case of Assam." *Economic and Political Weekly* 31, no. 31 (1996): 2066–68.

Gohain, Hiren. "Once More on the Assam Movement." *Social Scientist* 10, no. 11 (1982): 58–62.

"Golaghat Villagers Move CM for Check on Tusker's Menace." *Assam Tribune* (Guwahati), June 13, 2009.

Goldman, Mara. "Constructing Connectivity: Conservation Corridors and Conservation Politics in East African Rangelands." *Annals of the Association of American Geographers* 99 (2009): 335–59.

Goswami, Shrutidev. *Aspects of Revenue Administration in Assam, 1826–1874*. New Delhi: Mittal, 1987. http://books.google.co.uk/books?id=YrvSLQhsM0EC.

Government of Assam. "The Assam Gazette (Extraordinary) Notification: The 31st May 1985." In *FRS 101/85/3*, edited by Government of Assam. Dispur: Government of Assam, May 31, 1985.

Government of Assam. "The Assam Gazette: 17 June 1964; Part IX Advertisements and Notices by Government Offices and Public Bodies." Shillong: Government of Assam, June 17, 1964.

Government of Assam. *Handbook of Government Circulars (from May, 2007 to August, 2009)*, vol. 5. Guwahati: Revenue and Disaster Management Department, 2019.

Government of Assam. "Major Projects and Activities under Assam Accord." September 7, 2021. https://assamaccord.assam.gov.in/portlets/major-projects-activities-under-assam-accord.

Government of Assam. "Problems Could Be Solved through Goodwill." In *Assam Information, April '91—March '92*, vol. 43, edited by J. P. Saikia, 47–49. Guwahati: Directorate of Information and Public Relations, 1992.

Government of Assam. *Report on Delineation of Nine Animal Corridors Connecting Kaziranga National Park to Karbi-Anglong*. Guwahati: Committee for Delineation of Corridors, Forest Department, May 4, 2019.

Government of Assam. "Small Tea Growers to Be Promoted." In *Assam Information, October 1992*, vol. 44, edited by G. K. Das, 39–40. Guwahati: Directorate of Information and Public Relations, 1992.

Government of Assam. *Statistical Hand Book Assam 2019*. Guwahati: Directorate of Economics and Statistics, 2020.

Government of Assam. *Tea Garden Land Ceiling Cases Pending at District Level*. Guwahati: Revenue and Disaster Management Department, 2014. https://dlrar.assam.gov.in/sites/default/files/Pending%20Tea-Garden%20cases%20District%20level.pdf.

Government of India. *Accord between AASU, AAGSP and the Central Government on the Foreign National Issue (Assam Accord)*. New Delhi: Government of India, 1985.

"Govt. Move Emphasises Threat to Assam Forests." *Times of India* (New Delhi), March 24, 1995, 1.

Graham, Steve, and Simon Marvin. *Splintering Urbanism: Networked Infrastructures, Technological Mobilities and the Urban Condition*. Abingdon, UK: Routledge, 2002.

Green, Annette, and Chris Sandbrook. "Beyond Connectivity: An Exploration of Expert Perspectives on Conservation Corridors." *Geoforum* 127 (2021): 257–68. https://doi.org/10.1016/j.geoforum.2021.11.002.

Greenhough, Beth. "Vitalist Geographies." In *Taking Place: Non-representational Theories and Geography*, edited by Ben Anderson and Paul Harrison, 37–54. Farnham, UK: Ashgate, 2010.

"Green-Kaziranga 2 Last." *Press Trust of India* (New Delhi), October 29, 2013.

Guattari, Félix. "On Machines." *Complexity: Journal of Philosophy and the Visual Arts*, no. 6 (1995): 8–12.

Guattari, Félix. *The Three Ecologies*. London: Continuum, 2000.

Guha, Amalendu. "Colonisation of Assam: Second Phase 1840–1859." *Indian Economic and Social History Review* 4, no. 4 (1967): 289–317.

Guha, Amalendu. "Colonisation of Assam: Years of Transitional Crisis (1825–40)." *Indian Economic and Social History Review* 5, no. 2 (1968): 125–40.

Guha, Amalendu. *Planter Raj to Swaraj: Freedom Struggle and Electoral Politics in Assam 1826–1827*. New Delhi: People's Publishing House, 1977.

Guha, Ramachandra. *The Unquiet Woods: Ecological Change and Peasant Resistance in the Himalaya*. Berkeley: University of California Press, 1990.

Guha, Ramachandra, and Joan Martinez-Alier. *Varieties of Environmentalism: Essays North and South*. New Delhi: Oxford University Press, 1997. http://books.google.co.uk/books?id=JCwSAQAAIAAJ.

Gureja, Nidhi, Vivek Menon, Prabal Sarkar, and Sunil Subba Kyarong. *Ganesha to Bin Laden: Human-Elephant Conflict in Sonitpur District of Assam*. New Delhi: Wildlife Trust of India, 2002.

Gurusubramanian, Guruswami, Azizur Rahman, Mridul Sarmah, Somnath Ray, and S. Bora. "Pesticide Usage Pattern in Tea Ecosystem, Their Retrospects and Alternative Measures." *Journal of Environmental Biology* 29, no. 6 (2008): 813–26.

Handique, Rajib. *British Forest Policy in Assam*. New Delhi: Concept, 2004.

Handique, Rajib. "Colonial Wasteland Grants and Their Impact on the Ecology and Society of Assam." *Proceedings of the Indian History Congress* 70 (2009–10): 733–40.

Haraway, Donna. "Anthropocene, Capitalocene, Plantationocene, Chthulucene: Making Kin." *Environmental Humanities* 6, no. 1 (2015): 159–65. https://doi.org/10.1215/22011919-3615934.

Haraway, Donna. *Staying with the Trouble: Making Kin in the Chthulucene*. Durham, NC: Duke University Press, 2016.

Haraway, Donna, Noboru Ishikawa, Scott F. Gilbert, Kenneth Olwig, Anna Lowenhaupt Tsing, and Nils Bubandt. "Anthropologists Are Talking—about the Anthropocene." *Ethnos* 81, no. 3 (2015): 535–64.

Harvey, David. *The New Imperialism*. New York: Oxford University Press, 2003.

Harvey, Penny, and Hannah Knox. *Roads: An Anthropology of Infrastructure and Expertise*. Ithaca, NY: Cornell University Press, 2015.

Hazarika, Lakshmi K., Mantu Bhuyan, and Budhindra N. Hazarika. "Insect Pests of Tea and Their Management." *Annual Review of Entomology* 54 (2009): 267–84.

Hazarika, Sanjoy. *Strangers of the Mist: Tales of War and Peace from India's Northeast*. New Delhi: Penguin, 1994.

Head, Lesley, and Jennifer Atchison. "Cultural Ecology: Emerging Human-Plant Geographies." *Progress in Human Geography* 33, no. 2 (2008): 236–45.

Head, Lesley, Jennifer Atchison, Catherine Phillips, and Kathleen Buckingham. "Vegetal Politics: Belonging, Practices and Places." *Social and Cultural Geography* 15, no. 8 (2014): 861–70.

Hecht, Gabrielle. "Interscalar Vehicles for an African Anthropocene: On Waste, Temporality, and Violence." *Cultural Anthropology* 33, no. 1 (2018): 109–41.

"Herd Kills Labourer." *Telegraph*, November 23, 2009. Accessed September 19, 2012. http://www.telegraphindia.com/1091124/jsp/northeast/story_11776063.jsp.

Hetherington, Kregg, ed. *Infrastructure, Environment, and Life in the Anthropocene*. Durham, NC: Duke University Press, 2019.

Hinchliffe, Steve, Nick Bingham, John Allen, and Simon Carter. *Pathological Lives: Disease, Space and Biopolitics*. Oxford: John Wiley, 2016.

Hodgetts, Timothy, and Jamie Lorimer. "Animals' Mobilities." *Progress in Human Geography* 44, no. 1 (2018). https://doi.org/10.1177/0309132518817829.

Hollinsworth, Victor M. "Assam." *Popular Monthly* 16 (1883): 100–106.

Hunter, W. W. *A Statistical Account of Assam*, vol. 1. London: Trubner, 1879.

"Hurt Elephant Falls Prey to Its Own Herd." *Telegraph*, November 20, 2008. Accessed September 19, 2012. http://www.telegraphindia.com/1081120/jsp/northeast/story_10136272.jsp.

"Illicit Liquor Attracting Wild Elephants." *Times of India*, January 6, 2011. Accessed September 19, 2012. http://articles.timesofindia.indiatimes.com/2011-01-06/mysore/28358168_1_illicit-liquor-wild-elephants-tamed-elephants.

Ingold, Tim. "Anthropology beyond Humanity." *Suomen Antropologi: Journal of the Finnish Anthropological Society* 38, no. 3 (2013): 5–23.

Ingold, Tim. *Being Alive: Essays on Movement, Knowledge and Description*. Abingdon, UK: Routledge, 2011.

Ingold, Tim. "Epilogue: Towards a Politics of Dwelling." *Conservation and Society* 3, no. 2 (2005): 501–8.

Ingold, Tim. "Materials against Materiality." *Archaeological Dialogues* 14, no. 1 (2007): 1–16. https://doi.org/10.1017/S1380203807002127.

Ingold, Tim. *The Perception of the Environment: Essays on Livelihood, Dwelling and Skill*. London: Routledge, 2000.

Ingold, Tim, and Elizabeth Hallam. "Making and Growing: An Introduction." In *Making and Growing: Anthropological Studies of Organisms and Artefacts*, edited by Elizabeth Hallam and Tim Ingold, 1–24. Farnham, UK: Ashgate, 2014.

"Inspect Industries around Kaziranga, MoEF Told." *Statesman*, April 22, 2012.

Inverardi-Ferri, Carlo. "The Enclosure of 'Waste Land': Rethinking Informality and Dispossession." *Transactions of the Institute of British Geographers* 43, no. 2 (2018): 230–44. https://doi.org/10.1111/tran.12217.

Ishikawa, Noboru. "Into a New Epoch: Capitalist Nature in the Plantationocene." In *Anthropogenic Tropical Forests: Human-Nature Interfaces on the Plantation Frontier*, edited by Noboru Ishikawa and Ryoji Soda, 589–94. Singapore: Springer, 2020.

IUCN. *World Conservation Strategy: Living Resource Conservation for Sustainable Development*. Gland, Switzerland: International Union for the Conservation of Nature and Natural Resources, 1980.

Jadhav, Sushrut, and Maan Barua. "The Elephant Vanishes: Impact of Human-Elephant Conflict on People's Wellbeing." *Health and Place* 18, no. 6 (2012): 1356–65. https://doi.org/10.1016/j.healthplace.2012.06.019.

Jadhav, Sushrut, Sumeet Jain, Nanda Kishore Kannuri, Clement Bayetti, and Maan Barua. "Ecologies of Suffering: Mental Health in India." *Economic and Political Weekly* 50, no. 20 (2015): 12–15.

Janiak, Mareike C., Swellan L. Pinto, Gwen Duytschaever, Matthew A. Carrigan, and Amanda D. Melin. "Genetic Evidence of Widespread Variation in Ethanol Metabolism in Mammals: Revisiting the 'Myth' of Natural Intoxication." *Biology Letters* 16, no. 4 (2020). http://dx.doi.org/10.1098/rsbl.2020.0070.

Jayasinghe, Amal. "Sri Lanka Elephants Face Jumbo Threat as 145 Die in Last Year." *Agence France Presse*, January 10, 2001.

Jegathesan, Mythri. "Black Feminist Plots before the Plantationocene and Anthropology's 'Regional Closets.'" *Feminist Anthropology* 2, no. 1 (2021): 78–93.

Jegathesan, Mythri. *Tea and Solidarity: Tamil Women and Work in Postwar Sri Lanka*. Seattle: University of Washington Press, 2019.

Johnsingh, A. J. T., S. Narendra Prasad, and S. P. Goyal. "Conservation Status of the Chila-Motichur Corridor for Elephant Movement in Rajaji-Corbett National Parks Area, India." *Biological Conservation* 51, no. 2 (1990): 125–38.

Johnson, Chris J., Oscar Venter, Justina C. Ray, and James E. M. Watson. "Growth-Including Infrastructure Represents Transformative Yet Ignored Keystone Environmental Decisions." *Conservation Letters* 13, no. 2 (2020): e12696. https://doi.org/10.1111/conl.12696.

Kalam, Tamanna, Hiten Kumar Baishya, and David Smith. "Lethal Fence Electrocution: A Major Threat to Asian Elephants in Assam, India." *Tropical Conservation Science* 11 (2018): 1–8.

Karlsson, Bengt G. "Resource Frontier." In *The Routledge Companion to Northeast India*, edited by Jelle J. P. Wouters and Tanka B. Subba, 382–87. London: Routledge, 2023.

Karmakar, Rahul. "Assam's Tea Country Where Lethal Liquor Takes Life." *Hindu*, March 2, 2019. https://www.thehindu.com/news/national/other-states/assams-tea-country-where-lethal-liquor-takes-lives/article26419679.ece.

"Kaziranga Bypass Plan Opposed." *Assam Tribune* (Guwahati), November 11, 2009.

"Kaziranga Extension Plan: State Govt Hampers Plan." *Sentinel*, June 29, 1994.

"Kaziranga'or Animal Corridor'ot Nixedhagya Jari Kori Bandha Korile Xokolu Nirman Karjya." *Dainik Janambhumi* (Jorhat), October 25, 2021, 2.

Keil, Paul G. "Elephant-Human *Dandi*: How Humans and Elephants Move through the Fringes of Forest and Village." In *Rethinking Human-Elephant Relations in South Asia*, edited by Piers Locke and Jane Buckingham, 242–71. New Delhi: Oxford University Press, 2016.

Keil, Paul G. "On the Trails of Free-Roaming Elephants: Human-Elephant Mobility and History across the Indo-Myanmar Highlands." *Transfers* 10, no. 2–3 (2020): 1–21. https://doi.org/10.3167/TRANS.2020.10020302.

Kenney-Lazar, Miles, and Noboru Ishikawa. "Mega-plantations in Southeast Asia: Landscapes of Displacement." *Environment and Society: Advances in Research* 10 (2019): 63–82.

Kikon, Dolly. *Living with Oil and Coal: Resource Politics and Militarization in Northeast India*. Seattle: University of Washington Press, 2019.

Kikon, Dolly, and Sanjay Barbora. "The Rehabilitation Zone: Living with Lemons and Elephants in Assam." *Environment and Planning E: Nature and Space* 4, no. 3 (2021): 1121–38. https://doi.org/10.1177/2514848620946973.

Kikon, Dolly, and Dixita Deka. "Strawberry Farms: Adopting New Crops in Northeast India." *Raiot*, June 1, 2022. https://raiot.in/strawberry-farms-new-crops-in-northeast-india/.

Kingsland, Sharon E. "Creating a Science of Nature Reserve Design: Perspectives from History." *Environmental Modeling and Assessment* 7, no. 2 (2002): 61–69.

Kirksey, S. Eben, and Stefan Helmreich. "The Emergence of Multispecies Ethnography." *Cultural Anthropology* 25, no. 4 (2010): 545–76. https://doi.org/10.1111/j.1548-1360.2010.01069.x.

Klinke, Ian. "Vitalist Temptations: Life, Earth and the Nature of War." *Political Geography* 72 (June 2019): 1–9. https://doi.org/10.1016/j.polgeo.2019.03.004.

Kolbert, Elizabeth. *The Sixth Extinction: An Unnatural History*. London: Bloomsbury, 2014.

Kumar, Siddharth Unnithan, Jonathon Turnbull, Oscar Hartman Davies, Samuel A. Cushman, and Timothy Hodgetts. "Minimal Ecologies." *Digital Ecologies*, February 23, 2022. http://www.digicologies.com/2022/02/23/siddharth-unnithan-kumar-et-al/.

Kumpf, Desirée. "The Organic Monocrop: Experimenting with Green Growth on Indian Tea Plantations." *Environmental Humanities* 15, no. 2 (2023): 1–18. https://doi.org/10.1215/22011919-10422256.

Kurmi, Milan Chandra. "Sorang Byaboxayir Douratmyot Tengani Bonanchal Nihshwexor Pathat." *Natun Dainik*, July 21, 1994.

Lahan, Parmananda, and Rajen N. Sonowal. "Kaziranga Wild Life Sanctuary, Assam: A Brief Description and Report on the Census of Large Animals (March 1972)." *Journal of the Bombay Natural History Society* 70, no. 2 (1973): 245–78.

Lahiri-Choudhury, Dhriti K. "Conservation of the Asian Elephant—1971–92: An Overview." In *A Week with Elephants: Proceedings of the International Seminar on the Conservation of the Asian Elephant (June 1993)*, edited by J. C. Daniel and H. S. Datye, 19–31. Bombay: Bombay Natural History Society, 1995.

Lahiri-Choudhury, Dhriti K. "Saving Elephants for Posterity." *IUCN/SSC Asian Elephant Specialist Group Newsletter* 6 (spring 1991): 18–19.

Lainé, Nicolas. "Conduct and Collaboration in Human-Elephant Working Communities of Northeast India." In *Rethinking Human-Elephant Relations in South Asia*, edited by Piers Locke and Jane Buckingham, 180–204. New Delhi: Oxford University Press, 2016.

Lainé, Nicolas. *Living and Working with Giants: A Multispecies Ethnography of the Khamti and Elephants in Northeast India.* Paris: Publications scientifiques du Muséum national d'Histoire naturelle, 2020.

Larkin, Brian. "The Politics and Poetics of Infrastructure." *Annual Review of Anthropology* 42 (2013): 327–43. https://doi.org/10.1146/annurev-anthro-092412-155522.

Latimer, Joanna. "Being Alongside: Rethinking Relations amongst Different Kinds." *Theory, Culture and Society* 30, no. 7/8 (2013): 77–104. https://doi.org/10.1177/0263276413500078.

Lemke, Thomas. "An Alternative Model of Politics? Prospects and Problems of Jane Bennett's *Vital Materialism*." *Theory, Culture and Society* 35, no. 6 (2018): 31–54. https://doi.org/10.1177/0263276418757316.

Lemke, Thomas. "New Materialisms: Foucault and the 'Government of Things.'" *Theory, Culture and Society* 32, no. 4 (2015): 3–25. https://doi.org/10.1177/0263276413519340.

Lewis, L. S. "Elephants at Work." *Strand Magazine: An Illustrated Monthly* 13, no. 77 (1897): 554–62.

Lewis, Michael L. *Inventing Global Ecology: Tracking the Biodiversity Ideal in India, 1947–1997.* Athens: Ohio University Press, 2004.

Lewis, Simon L., and Mark A. Maslin. "Defining the Anthropocene." *Nature* 519, no. 7542 (2015): 171–80.

Li, Tania Murray. "After the Land Grab: Infrastructural Violence and the 'Mafia System' in Indonesia's Oil Palm Plantation Zones." *Geoforum* 96 (November 2018): 328–37. https://doi.org/10.1016/j.geoforum.2017.10.012.

"Litterateur on Hunger Strike." *Telegraph* (Guwahati), July 29, 2015.

Lorimer, Jamie. "Non-human Charisma." *Environment and Planning D: Society and Space* 25, no. 5 (2007): 911–32.

Lorimer, Jamie. *The Probiotic Planet: Using Life to Manage Life.* Minneapolis: Minnesota University Press, 2020.

MacArthur, Robert H., and Edward O. Wilson. *The Theory of Island Biogeography.* Princeton, NJ: Princeton University Press, 1967.

Majumdar, Dilip. "Need to Intensify Base Metal Exploration Activities in Mikir Hills, Northeastern India." *Current Science* 99, no. 5 (2010): 1–8.

Malm, Andreas, and Alf Hornborg. "The Geology of Mankind? A Critique of the Anthropocene Narrative." *Anthropocene Review* 1, no. 1 (2014): 62–69.

"Man-Elephant Conflict Turns Grim." *Hindustan Times*, August 21, 2010.

Mann, Gustav. *Progress Report of Forest Administration in the Province of Assam for the Year 1874–75.* Shillong: Assam Secretariat Press, 1875.

Mann, Gustav. *Progress Report of Forest Administration in the Province of Assam for the Year 1876–77.* Shillong: Assam Secretariat Press, 1877.

Mann, Harold H. *The Tea Soils of Assam, and Tea Manuring.* Calcutta: W. Newman, 1901.

Mansfield, Becky. "A New Biopolitics of Environmental Health: Permeable Bodies and the Anthropocene." In *The Sage Handbook of Nature*, edited by Terry Marsden, 216–34. London: Sage, 2018.

Marder, Michael. "Resist Like a Plant! On the Vegetal Life of Political Movements." *Peace Studies Journal* 5, no. 1 (2012): 24–32.

Marx, Karl. *Capital: A Critique of Political Economy*, vol. 1. Translated by Ben Fowkes. London: Penguin, 1976.

Marx, Karl. *Capital: A Critique of Political Economy*, vol. 2. Translated by David Fernbach. London: Penguin, 1978.

Marx, Karl. *Capital: A Critique of Political Economy*, vol. 3. Translated by Ben Fowkes. London: Penguin, 1981.

Marx, Karl, and Friedrich Engels. *Manifesto of the Communist Party*. 1872. Reprint, Moscow: Progress, 1969.

Mbembe, Achille. *Necropolitics*. Durham, NC: Duke University Press, 2019.

McComb, Karen, Graeme Shannon, Sarah M. Durant, Katito N. Sayialel, Rob Slotow, Joyce Poole, and Cynthia Moss. "Leadership in Elephants: The Adaptive Value of Age." *Proceedings of the Royal Society B* 278, no. 1722 (2011). https://doi.org/10.1098/rspb.2011.0168.

McCormack, Derek. "Geography and Abstraction: Towards an Affirmative Critique." *Progress in Human Geography* 36, no. 6 (2012). https://doi.org/10.1177/0309132512437074.

McKittrick, Katherine. *Demonic Grounds: Black Women and the Cartographies of Struggle*. Minneapolis: University of Minnesota Press, 2006.

McKittrick, Katherine. "On Plantations, Prisons, and a Black Sense of Place." *Social and Cultural Geography* 12, no. 8 (2011): 947–63.

McKittrick, Katherine. "Plantation Futures." *Small Axe: A Caribbean Journal of Criticism* 17, no. 3 (42) (2013): 1–15.

Medhi, Shyam Bhadra. *Transport System and Economic Development in Assam*. Guwahati: Publication Board, Assam, 1978.

"Memorial Etched in Martyr's Blood—Column in Memory of Student Activist Unveiled in Guwahati." *Telegraph India*, June 1, 2009.

Menon, Vivek, Sandeep Kumar Tiwari, P. S. Easa, and Raman Sukumar, eds. *Right of Passage: Elephant Corridors of India*. New Delhi: Wildlife Trust of India, 2005.

Menon, Vivek, Sandeep Kumar Tiwari, K. Ramkumar, Sunil Subba Kyarong, Upasana Ganguly, and Raman Sukumar, eds. *Right of Passage: Elephant Corridors of India*. 2nd ed. Conservation Reference Series, vol. 3. New Delhi: Wildlife Trust of India, 2017.

Metzger, Jonathan. "The Moose Are Protesting: The More-Than-Human Politics of Transport Infrastructure Development." In *Planning against the Political*, edited by Jonathan Metzger, Phil Allmendinger, and Stijn Oosterlynck, 203–26. New York: Routledge, 2014.

Milroy, Arthur John Wallace. *Progress Report of Forest Administration in the Province of Assam for the Year 1934–35.* Shillong: Assam Government Press, 1935.

Milroy, Arthur John Wallace. *Progress Report of Forest Administration in the Province of Assam for the Year 1935–36.* Shillong: Assam Government Press, 1936.

Ministry of Environment and Forests, ed. "Ministry of Environment and Forests Notification, New Delhi, the 5th July, 1996." New Delhi: Ministry of Environment and Forests, Government of India, 1996.

Ministry of Environment and Forests. *Project Elephant (Gajatme).* New Delhi: Ministry of Environment and Forests, Government of India, 1993.

Ministry of Environment, Forest and Climate Change. *Borjuri P.P. Land Area Mine Plan.* New Delhi: Government of India, 2019.

Ministry of Environment, Forest and Climate Change. *Brief Summary of the Project: M/S M.P. Agarwalla.* New Delhi: Government of India, 2019.

Mintz, Sidney Wilfred. *Sweetness and Power: The Place of Sugar in Modern History.* New York: Penguin, 1986.

Misra, Tilottoma. "Assam: A Colonial Hinterland." *Economic and Political Weekly* 15, no. 32 (1980): 1357–64.

Misra, Udayon. "Assam Tea: The Bitter Brew." *Economic and Political Weekly* 38, no. 29 (2003): 3029–32.

Misra, Udayon. "No Tears for the Liberators." *Economic and Political Weekly* 28, no. 32–33 (1993): 1635–36.

Misra, Udayon. *The Periphery Strikes Back: Challenges to the Nation-State in Assam and Nagaland.* Shimla: Indian Institute of Advanced Study, 2013.

Mol, Annemarie. *The Body Multiple: Ontology in Medical Practice.* Durham, NC: Duke University Press, 2002.

Money, Edward. *The Cultivation and Manufacture of Tea.* London: W. B. Wittingham, 1878.

Moore, Jason W. *Capitalism in the Web of Life: Ecology and the Accumulation of Capital.* London: Verso, 2015.

Moore, Jason W. "The Capitalocene, Part I: On the Nature and Origins of Our Ecological Crisis." *Journal of Peasant Studies* 44, no. 3 (2017): 594–630. https://doi.org/10.1080/03066150.2016.1235036.

Moore, Jason W. "The Capitalocene, Part II: Accumulation by Appropriation and the Centrality of Unpaid Work/Energy." *Journal of Peasant Studies* 45, no. 2 (2018): 237–79.

Morris, Rosalind C. "Ursprüngliche Akkumulation: The Secret of an Originary Mistranslation." *boundary 2* 43, no. 3 (2016): 29–77.

Morris, Steve, David Humphreys, and Dan Reynolds. "Myth, Marula, and Elephant: An Assessment of Voluntary Ethanol Intoxication of the African Elephant

(*Loxodonta africana*) Following Feeding on the Fruit of the Marula Tree (*Sclerocarya birrea*)." *Physiological and Biochemical Zoology* 79 (2006): 363–69.

Moss, Cynthia. *Elephant Memories: Thirteen Years in the Life of an Elephant Family.* New York: Ballantine, 1988.

Münster, Ursula. "Forest Atmospheres: Ecological Nostalgia in a Teak Plantation." In *Soziale Ästhetik, Atmosphäre, Medialität: Beiträge aus der Ethnologie*, edited by Philipp Zehmisch, Ursula Münster, Jens Zickgraf, and Claudia Lang, 61–72. Münster: Lit Verlag, 2013.

Münster, Ursula. "Lantana Invades Teak Plantations and Turns Elephants Violent." Feral Atlas: The More-Than-Human Anthropocene, 2020. https://feralatlas.supdigital.org/poster/lantana-invades-monocrop-teak-plantations-triggering-elephant-aggression.

Münster, Ursula. "Working for the Forest: The Ambivalent Intimacies of Human-Elephant Collaboration in South Indian Wildlife Conservation." *Ethnos* 81, no. 3 (2016): 425–47.

Murphy, Michael Warren, and Caitlin Schroering. "Refiguring the Plantationocene." *Journal of World-Systems Research* 26, no. 2 (2020): 400–415.

Murphy, Michelle. "Alterlife and Decolonial Chemical Relations." *Cultural Anthropology* 32, no. 4 (2017): 494–503.

Myers, Natasha. "From the Anthropocene to the Planthroposcene: Designing Gardens for Plant/People Involution." *History and Anthropology* 28, no. 3 (2017): 297–301.

Nag, Sajal. *Pied Pipers in North-East India: Bamboo-Flowers, Rat-Famine and the Politics of Philanthropy (1881–2007)*. New Delhi: Manohar, 2008.

Naha, Dipanjan, Suraj Kumar Dash, Abhisek Chettri, Akashdeep Roy, and Sambandam Sathyakumar. "Elephants in the Neighborhood: Patterns of Crop-Raiding by Asian Elephants within a Fragmented Landscape of Eastern India." *PeerJ* 8 (2020): e9399. https://doi.org/10.7717/peerj.9399.

Nally, David, and Gerry Kearns. "Vegetative States: Potatoes, Affordances, and Survival Ecologies." *Antipode* 52, no. 5 (2020): 1373–92. https://doi.org/10.1111/anti.12652.

National Green Tribunal. *Rohit Choudhary vs Union of India and Ors (7 September, 2012), Oa 38/2011*. National Green Tribunal 15 (2012).

National Green Tribunal. *Rohit Choudhary vs Union of India and Ors (24 August 2016) Ma No. 787/2015 & 1006/2015 in Oa No. 38/2011*. National Green Tribunal 23 (2016).

"New Bridge over Brahmaputra Sanctioned." *United News of India* (New Delhi), October 1, 2009.

"NH Upgrade through Kaziranga Opposed." *Assam Tribune* (Guwahati), October 14, 2008.

Nicholls, Frank. *Assam Shikari*. Auckland: Tonson, 1970.

Nixon, Rob. *Slow Violence and the Environmentalism of the Poor*. Cambridge, MA: Harvard University Press, 2011.

Nongbri, Natasha. "Elephant Hunting in Late 19th Century Northeast India: Mechanisms of Control, Contestation and Local Reactions." *Economic and Political Weekly* 38, no. 30 (2003): 3189–99.

"Numaligarh Gears Up for Land War." *Telegraph*, June 28, 2007. Accessed August 29, 2013. http://www.telegraphindia.com/1070628/asp/northeast/story_7983299.asp.

Numaligarh Refinery Limited. *Additional Details Sought by Member Secretary on Proposal No. Ia/as/Ind2/134396/2018 Uploaded on 21.05.2020*. Numaligarh, Assam: Numaligarh Refinery Limited, May 29, 2020.

Numaligarh Refinery Limited. *Submission of Half Yearly Compliance Report on Environment Stipulation during the Period April '17 to Sept '17 of Ec for Nrl Township, Noc of Pcba for Nrl*. Numaligarh, Assam: Numaligarh Refinery Limited, November 27, 2017.

O'Connell-Rodwell, Caitlin E. "Keeping an 'Ear' to the Ground: Seismic Communication in Elephants." *Physiology* 22, no. 4 (2007): 287–94. https://doi.org/10.1152/physiol.00008.2007.

Officer-in-Charge, Rongmongwe Police Station. "Illegal Extraction/Excessive Extraction/Benami Transaction Etc." November 12, 2018. Rongmongwe Police Station, Karbi Anglong, Assam.

Ogra, Monica V. "Human-Wildlife Conflict and Gender in Protected Area Borderlands: A Case Study of Costs, Perceptions, and Vulnerabilities from Uttarakhand (Uttaranchal), India." *Geoforum* 39, no. 3 (2008): 1408–22. https://doi.org/10.1016/j.geoforum.2007.12.004.

Ollman, B. *Alienation: Marx's Concept of Man in Capitalist Society*. Cambridge: Cambridge University Press, 1976.

"One Killed in Elephant Attack." *Sentinel* (Guwahati), January 11, 2016.

Oriel, Elizabeth, Deepani Jayantha, and Amal Dissanayaka. "Plants Are Worldmakers: Spatial Knowledge of How Plants and Human-Plant Relations Mediate Human-Elephant Relations in Sri Lanka." In *Environment, Development, and Culture in South and East Asia: Local, Regional, and International Perspectives*, edited by R. Thakur. New York: Springer, forthcoming.

Oxfam. *Addressing the Human Cost of Assam Tea*. Oxford: Oxfam, 2019.

Pachuau, Joy L. K., and Willem van Schendel. *Entangled Lives: Human-Animal-Plant Histories of the Eastern Himalayan Triangle*. Cambridge: Cambridge University Press, 2022.

"Pachyderms Kill 2 More at Numaligarh." *Assam Tribune* (Guwahati), July 2, 2005.

Palmer, James. "Putting Forests to Work? Enrolling Vegetal Labor in the Socioecological Fix of Bioenergy Resource Making." *Annals of the American Association*

of Geographers 111, no. 1 (2021): 141–56. https://doi.org/10.1080/24694452
.2020.1749022.

Paramasivan, R. S. *Progress Report of Forest Administration in the State of Assam for the Year 1950–51*. Shillong: Assam Government Press, 1961.

Parikh, Kirit S. *Assam State Development Report*. New Delhi: Planning Commission, Government of India, 2002.

Parker, C. "The Mikania Problem." *PANS Pesticide Articles and News Summaries* 18, no. 3 (1972): 312–15.

Parks, Lisa. "Mediating Animal-Infrastructure Relations." In *Being Material*, edited by Marie-Pier Boucher, Stefan Helmreich, Leila W. Kinney, Skylar Tibbits, Rebecca Uchill, and Evan Ziporyn, 144–53. Cambridge, MA: MIT Press, 2017.

Patel, Raj, and Jason W. Moore. *A History of the World in Seven Cheap Things: A Guide to Capitalism, Nature, and the Future of the Planet*. London: Verso, 2018.

Payne, Katy. *Silent Thunder: In the Presence of Elephants*. New York: Simon and Schuster, 1998.

Platt, Steven G., David P. Bickford, Myo Min Win, and Thomas R. Rainwater. "Water-Filled Asian Elephant Tracks Serve as Breeding Sites for Anurans in Myanmar." *Mammalia* 83, no. 3 (2019): 287–89.

"PM Approves of Saikia's Moves." *Times of India*, July 7, 1992, 9.

Porcher, Jocelyne. "Animal Work." In *The Oxford Handbook of Animal Studies*, edited by Linda Kalof, 302–18. Oxford: Oxford University Press, 2015. https://doi.org/10.1093/oxfordhb/9780199927142.013.8.

Prasad, Soumya, and Christy Williams. *Extent and Distribution of Some Invasive Plant Species in Asian Elephant Habitats*. IUCN AsESG Wild Elephant and Elephant Habitat Management Task Force. Gland, Switzerland: IUCN—Species Survival Commission, 2009.

Principal Chief Conservator of Forests. "Gorh Ne Geleki?????" Letter No. Pccf/Ka/Wl/2016–17/1685 to the Divisional Forest Officer, Eastern Assam Wildlife Division, Bokakhat. Office of the Principal Chief Conservator of Forests, Diphu, Karbi Anglong, November 23, 2016.

Puzari, K. C., R. P. Bhuyan, Dutta Pranab, and H. K. D. Nath. "Distribution of Mikania and Its Economic Impact on Tea Ecosystem of Assam." *Indian Journal of Forestry* 33, no. 1 (2010): 71–76.

Rai, Usha. "Picknicking Dangerously with Assam Tuskers." *Times of India* (New Delhi), June 28, 1991.

Rai, Usha. "Refinery a Threat to Rhinos." *Times of India*, September 14, 1990.

Rajan, S. Ravi. *Modernizing Nature: Forestry and Imperial Eco-development, 1800–1950*. New York: Oxford University Press, 2006.

Rajya Sabha. "Scheme of Margin Money to Surrendered Militants." Latest PIB Releases, Press Information Bureau, Government of India, 2000. Accessed July 12,

2021. https://web.archive.org/web/20080404030044/http://pib.nic.in/archieve/lreleng/lyr2000/rdec2000/r13122000.html.

Ramsden, A. R. *Assam Planter: Tea Planting and Hunting in the Assam Jungle*. London: J. Gifford, 1945.

Rangarajan, Mahesh. *Fencing the Forest: Conservation and Ecological Change in India's Central Provinces, 1860–1914*. New Delhi: Oxford University Press, 1999.

Rangarajan, Mahesh. *India's Wildlife History: An Introduction*. New Delhi: Orient Blackswan, 2006.

Rasmussen, L. E. L. "Chemical, Tactile, and Taste Sensory Systems." In *Biology, Medicine, and Surgery of Elephants*, edited by M. E. Fowler and S. K. Mikota, 409–14. New York: Wiley-Blackwell, 2006.

"'Relocating Villages to Secure Jumbo Corridors Delicate Task.'" *Times of India* (New Delhi), January 31, 2016.

Remmers, Wolfram, Joao Gameiro, Isabella Schaberl, and Viola Clausnitzer. "Elephant (*Loxodonta africana*) Footprints as Habitat for Aquatic Macroinvertebrate Communities in Kibale National Park, South-West Uganda." *African Journal of Ecology* 55, no. 3 (2017): 342–51.

"Renewing Licenses to Make a Killing?" *Tehelka* (New Delhi), May 26, 2012.

"Reopens Lgd26." *Press Trust of India*, August 24, 2016.

"Reprieve for Kaziranga: Expansion of NH-37 Halted." *Assam Tribune* (Guwahati), August 18, 2008.

Rizvanovic, Alisa, Mats Amundin, and Matthias Laska. "Olfactory Discrimination Ability of Asian Elephants (*Elephas maximus*) for Structurally Related Odorants." *Chemical Senses* 38, no. 2 (2013): 107–18.

Rodgers, Dennis, and Bruce O'Neill. "Infrastructural Violence: Introduction to the Special Issue." *Ethnography* 13, no. 4 (2012): 401–12.

Rodney, Walter. *How Europe Underdeveloped Africa*. 1972. Reprint, London: Verso, 2018.

Rodney, Walter. "Plantation Society in Guyana." *Review (Fernand Braudel Center)* 4, no. 4 (1981): 643–66.

"A Rogue Elephant." *Amrita Bazar Patrika*, July 27, 1903.

Rosenberger, Robert. *Callous Objects: Designs against the Homeless*. Minneapolis: Minnesota University Press, 2017.

Rosengren, Sofia Mathilda. "Wastelands of Difference? Urban Nature and More-Than-Human Difference in Berlin and Gothenburg." PhD diss., University of Cambridge, 2020. https://doi.org/10.17863/CAM.57754.

Rosenzweig, Michael L. *Win-Win Ecology: How the Earth's Species Can Survive in the Midst of Human Enterprise*. Oxford: Oxford University Press, 2003.

Rowntree, John. *A Chota Sahib: Memoirs of a Forest Officer*. London: Tabb House, 1981.

Roy, Ananya. "Urban Informality: Toward an Epistemology of Planning." *Journal of the American Planning Association* 71, no. 2 (2005): 147–58. https://doi.org/10.1080/01944360508976689.

Roy, Ananya. "Why India Cannot Plan Its Cities: Informality, Insurgence and the Idiom of Urbanization." *Planning Theory* 8, no. 1 (2009): 76–87. https://doi.org/10.1177/1473095208099299.

"Rs 1cr Upgrade Pill for Kaziranga." *Telegraph* (New Delhi), October 11, 2012.

Saha, Debulal, Chitrasen Bhue, and Rajdeep Singha. *Decent Work for Tea Plantation Workers in Assam: Constraints, Challenges and Prospects.* Guwahati: Tata Institute of Social Sciences, 2019.

Saha, Jonathan. "Colonizing Elephants: Animal Agency, Undead Capital and Imperial Science in British Burma." *BJHS Themes* 2 (2017): 169–89.

Sahni, Ajai, and Bibhu Prasad Routray. "SULFA: Terror by Another Name." *Faultlines* 9 (2013): article 1. https://www.satp.org/satporgtp/publication/faultlines/volume9/article1.htm.

Saikia, Arunabh. "Will Assam Government's Ban on Using Molasses to Make Liquor Put an End to Hooch Deaths?" Scroll.in, March 5, 2019. https://scroll.in/article/915263/will-assam-governments-ban-on-using-molasses-to-make-liquor-put-an-end-to-hooch-deaths.

Saikia, Arupjyoti. "Coal in Colonial Assam: Exploration, Trade and Environmental Consequences." In *The Coal Nation: Histories, Ecologies and Politics of Coal in India*, edited by Kuntala Lahiri-Dutt, 63–78. Farnham, UK: Ashgate, 2014.

Saikia, Arupjyoti. "Forest Land and Peasant Struggles in Assam, 2002–2007." *Journal of Peasant Studies* 35, no. 1 (2008): 39–59.

Saikia, Arupjyoti. *Forests and Ecological History of Assam, 1826–2000*. New Delhi: Oxford University Press, 2011.

Saikia, Arupjyoti. "Imperialism, Geology and Petroleum: History of Oil in Colonial Assam." *Economic and Political Weekly* 46, no. 12 (2011): 48–55.

Saikia, Arupjyoti. *Jungles, Reserves, Wildlife.* Guwahati: Wildlife Areas Development and Welfare Trust, 2005.

Saikia, Arupjyoti. "Mosquitoes, Malaria, and Malnutrition: The Making of the Assam Tea Plantations." *RCC Perspectives*, no. 3 (2014): 71–76.

Saikia, Arupjyoti. "State, Peasants and Land Reclamation: The Predicament of Forest Conservation in Assam, 1850s–1980s." *Indian Economic and Social History Review* 45, no. 1 (2008): 77–114.

Saikia, Arupjyoti. *The Unquiet River: A Biography of the Brahmaputra.* New Delhi: Oxford University Press, 2019.

Saikia, Jatindra Nath. "Gongadhar Saikia: The Versatile Genius with a Towering Personality." In *Gangey: Khyudhra Sah Khetiyokor Pitriswarup Gangadhar*

Saikiadewor Smarok Grantha, edited by Pratim Saikia and Rohit Borgohain, 62–70. Golaghat: All Assam Small Tea Growers Association, 2018.

Saikia, Jyoti Prasad. *Stories behind a Hot Cup of Assam Tea: Listening to the Voices of Women Labourers in the Tea Gardens*. Dibrugarh, Assam: Centre for Women's Studies, Dibrugarh University, 2017.

Saikia, Meghali. "Tense and Aspect in Assam Sadri." *International Journal of Humanities and Social Science Invention* 9, no. 4 (2020): 6–13.

Saikia, Parag Jyoti, and Suraj Gogoi. "Bhupen Hazarika Setu and the Politics of Infrastructure." *Wire*, February 28, 2018. https://thewire.in/government/bhupen-hazarika-setu.

Saikia, Sabina Sehgal. "Corruption Main Issue in This Election: Saikia." *Times of India*, April 23, 1996.

Santiapillai, Charles. "The Asian Elephant Conservation: A Global Strategy." *Gajah: Journal of the Asian Elephant Specialist Group*, no. 18 (1997): 21–39.

Santiapillai, Charles, and Peter Jackson. *The Asian Elephant: An Action Plan for Its Conservation*. Gland, Switzerland: IUCN—the World Conservation Union, 1990.

Sanyal, Kalyan. *Rethinking Capitalist Development: Primitive Accumulation, Governmentality and Postcolonial Capitalism*. New Delhi: Routledge, 2007.

Sarma, Pranjit K., Bibhab Kumar Talukdar, Jayanta K. Baruah, Bibhuti Prasad Lahkar, and Nirupam Hazarika. "A Geo-spatial Assessment of Habitat Loss of Asian Elephants in Golaghat District of Assam." *Gajah: Journal of the Asian Elephant Specialist Group*, no. 28 (2008): 25–30.

Sarma, Ujjal Kumar, P. S. Easa, and Vivek Menon. *Deadly Tracks: A Scientific Approach to Understanding and Mitigating Elephant Mortality Due to Train Hits in Assam*. New Delhi: Wildlife Trust of India, 2008.

Secretary (Environment and Forests). "Letter from Secretary (Ministry of Environment and Forests) to Secretary (Ministry of Petroleum and Natural Gas)." January 18, 1994. Ministry of Environment and Forests, New Delhi.

Seetharaman, G., and Bikash Singh. "Assam Government's Move to Regularise Landholdings Can Improve the Fortunes of Small Tea Growers." *Economic Times* (New Delhi), October 15, 2017.

Sen, Ayanjit. "Drink Drives Elephant to Kill." BBC News, December 20, 2001. http://news.bbc.co.uk/1/hi/world/south_asia/1721442.stm.

Shafer, Craig L. *Nature Reserves: Island Theory and Conservation Practice*. Washington, DC: Smithsonian Institution Press, 1990.

Sharma, Chandan Kumar, and Prarthana Barua. "Small Tea Plantation and Its Impact on the Rural Landscape of Contemporary Assam." *International Journal of Rural Management* 13, no. 2 (2017): 140–61.

Sharma, Jayeeta. "British Science, Chinese Skill and Assam Tea: Making Empire's Garden." *Indian Economic Social History Review* 43, no. 4 (2006): 429–55. https://doi.org/10.1177/001946460604300402.

Sharma, Jayeeta. *Empire's Garden: Assam and the Making of India*. Durham, NC: Duke University Press, 2011.

Sharma, Jayeeta. "'Lazy' Natives, Coolie Labour, and the Assam Tea Industry." *Modern Asian Studies* 43, no. 6 (2009): 1287–1324.

Sharma, Kalpana. "Politics Threatens Assam's Rhinos." *Times of India*, September 22, 1990.

Shaw, R. C. "The Story of *Cuscuta* versus *Mikania* in Tyroon." *Two and a Bud* 14, no. 2 (1967): 95.

Siegel, Ronald K. *Intoxication: The Universal Drive for Mind-Altering Substances*. Rochester, VT: Inner Traditions, 2005. http://books.google.co.uk/books?id=6_nd2DZ-h-UC.

Siegel, Ronald K., and Mark Brodie. "Alcohol Self-Administration by Elephants." *Bulletin of the Psychonomic Society* 22, no. 1 (1984): 49–52.

Simberloff, Daniel, and Lawrence G. Abele. "Island Biogeography Theory and Conservation Practice." *Science* 191, no. 4224 (1976): 285–86.

Simone, AbdouMaliq. *Improvised Lives*. Cambridge, UK: Polity, 2019.

Simone, AbdouMaliq. "People as Infrastructure: Intersecting Fragments in Johannesburg." *Public Culture* 16, no. 3 (2004): 407–29. https://doi.org/10.1215/08992363-16-3-407.

Singh, D. M., Rathin Barman, and Bibhab Kumar Talukdar. *Report on Site Inspection in Karbi-Anglong Forest Areas Adjacent to Kaziranga Np Based on Complaints Received by Moef*. Kaziranga National Park: Forest Department, Government of Assam, 2010.

Sinha, M. K. "Elephant Migration in Kaziranga." *Tigerpaper* 8, no. 1 (1981): 16–18.

Sivasundaram, Sujit. "Trading Knowledge: The East India Company's Elephants in India and Britain." *Historical Journal* 48, no. 1 (2005): 27–63.

Somashekar, P. S. *Report on Rampant Mining in Karbi-Anglong Hills Adjoining Kaziranga Tiger Reserve, Assam*. New Delhi: National Tiger Conservation Authority, Ministry of Environment, Forest and Climate Change, Government of India, April 20, 2018.

Sonwalkar, Prasun. "Boundary Row Denudes Assam Forest." *Times of India* (New Delhi), May 9, 1989.

Spencer, Tom, and Sarah J. Whatmore. "Bio-geographies: Putting Life Back into the Discipline." *Transactions of the Institute of British Geographers* 26, no. 2 (2001): 139–41.

Srinivasaiah, Nishant, Vinod Kumar, Srinivas Vaidyanathan, Raman Sukumar, and Anindya Sinha. "All-Male Groups in Asian Elephants: A Novel, Adaptive Social Strategy in Increasingly Anthropogenic Landscapes of Southern India." *Scientific Reports* 9, no. 1 (2019): 8678. https://doi.org/10.1038/s41598-019-45130-1.

Star, Susan Leigh, and James R. Griesemer. "Institutional Ecology, 'Translation,' and Boundary Objects: Amateurs and Professionals in Berkeley's Museum of Vertebrate Zoology." *Social Studies of Science* 19 (1989): 387–420.

"State Govt Proposes Wildlife-Friendly Steps." *Assam Tribune* (Guwahati), November 17, 2013.

"State Tea Estates Possess 17,919 Bighas of Ceiling Surplus Land." *Sentinel* (Guwahati), February 11, 2017.

Stoler, Ann Laura. *Capitalism and Confrontation in Sumatra's Plantation Belt, 1870–1979*. Ann Arbor: University of Michigan Press, 1995.

Stoler, Ann Laura. "Imperial Debris: Reflections on Ruins and Ruination." *Cultural Anthropology* 23, no. 2 (2008): 191–219. http://www.jstor.org/stable/20484502.

Stoler, Ann Laura. "'The Rot Remains': From Ruins to Ruination." In *Imperial Debris: On Ruins and Ruination*, edited by Ann Laura Stoler, 1–38. Durham, NC: Duke University Press, 2013.

Stracey, Patrick Douglas. "Planning for a 'Project Elephant'?" *Cheetal* 18, no. 3–4 (1977): 32–34.

Stuesse, Angela. *Scratching Out a Living: Latinos, Race, and Work in the Deep South*. Berkeley: University of California Press, 2016.

Sukumar, Raman. *The Asian Elephant: Ecology and Management*. Cambridge: Cambridge University Press, 1989.

Sukumar, Raman. "Ecology of the Asian Elephant in Southern India. II. Feeding Habits and Crop Raiding Patterns." *Journal of Tropical Ecology* 6, no. 1 (1990): 33–53.

Sukumar, Raman. "The Elephant Populations of India—Strategies for Conservation." *Proceedings of the Indian Academy of Sciences (Animal Sciences/Plant Sciences)* suppl. (November 1986): 59–71.

Sukumar, Raman. *The Living Elephants: Evolutionary Ecology, Behaviour and Conservation*. Oxford: Oxford University Press, 2003.

Sundberg, Juanita. "Decolonizing Posthumanist Geographies." *Cultural Geographies* 21, no. 1 (2014): 33–47. https://doi.org/10.1177/1474474013486067.

Supreme Court of India. *T.N. Godavarman vs. Union of India (I.A. No. 4944/2019 in W.P.(C) No. 202/1995)*. Supreme Court of India. (2019).

Tadiar, Neferti X. M. *Remaindered Life*. Durham, NC: Duke University Press, 2022.

Talukdar, Bhupendra Nath. *Elephants in Assam*. Guwahati: Forest Department of Assam, Government of India, 2009.

Talukdar, Bhupendra Nath. *Hasti Katha*. Guwahati: Axom Bigyan Prajukti Bidya aru Paribesh Parishad, 2001.

Talukdar, Bibhab Kumar. *Multi-dimensional Mitigation Initiatives to Human-Elephant Conflicts in Golaghat and Adjoining Areas of Karbi-Anglong District, Assam*. Guwahati: Aaranyak, 2007.

Talukdar, Sushanta. "Quarrying Blocks Elephant Corridor." *Hindu*, July 4, 2005.

Tanti, Kamal Kumar. *Post-colonial Poems*. Translated by Shalim M. Hussain and Dibajyoti Sarma. New Delhi: Red River, 2019.

Tea Research Association. *Annual Scientific Report (1st April 1973 to 31st March 1974)*. Jorhat, Assam: Tocklai Experimental Station, 1975.

Tea Research Association. *Annual Scientific Report (1st April 1977 to 31st March 1978)*. Jorhat, Assam: Tocklai Experimental Station, 1978.

Tea Research Association. *Tea Encyclopedia Serials (No. 168/1: The Use of Herbicides for the Control of Mikania)*. Jorhat, Assam: Tocklai Experimental Station, 1970.

Thekaekara, Tarshish. "Living with Elephants, Living with People: Understanding the Complexities of Human-Elephant Interactions in the Nilgiris, South India." PhD diss., Open University, 2019. https://doi.org/10.21954/ou.ro.000102d4.

Thomas, Wilson. "186 Elephants Killed on Railway Tracks in Over 10 Years: MoEFCC." *Hindu*, May 14, 2021. https://www.thehindu.com/news/national/186-elephants-killed-on-railway-tracks-in-over-10-years-moefcc/article34558401.ece.

Thompson, Edward Palmer. "Time, Work-Discipline, and Industrial Capitalism." *Past and Present* 38 (December 1967): 56–97.

Thrift, Nigel, and J.-D. Dewsbury. "Dead Geographies—and How to Make Them Live." *Environment and Planning D: Society and Space* 18, no. 4 (2000): 411–32. https://doi.org/10.1068/d1804ed.

Tiwari, Sandeep Kumar, and P. S. Easa. "Documenting Corridors: The Process." In *Right of Passage: Elephant Corridors of India*, edited by Vivek Menon, Sandeep Kumar Tiwari, P. S. Easa, and Raman Sukumar, 34–38. New Delhi: Wildlife Trust of India, 2005.

"Traditional Elephant Habitat Affected in Deopahar." *Assam Tribune* (Guwahati), June 8, 2015.

Troup, R. S. *The Work of the Forest Department in India*. Calcutta: Superintendent Government Printing, India, 1917.

Tsing, Anna Lowenhaupt. "Earth Stalked by Man." *Cambridge Journal of Anthropology* 34, no. 1 (2016): 2–16.

Tsing, Anna Lowenhaupt. "Holocene Resurgence against Anthropocene Plantation." *Multitudes* 3 (2018): 77–85.

Tsing, Anna Lowenhaupt. *The Mushroom at the End of the World: On the Possibility of Life in Capitalist Ruins*. Princeton, NJ: Princeton University Press, 2015.

Tsing, Anna Lowenhaupt. "A Threat to Holocene Resurgence Is a Threat to Livability." In *The Anthropology of Sustainability: Beyond Development and Progress*, edited by Marc Brightman and Jerome Lewis, 50–66. New York: Springer Nature, 2017.

Vattakkavan, Joseph, Niranjan K. Vasu, Surendra Varma, Nidhi Gureja, and Ambika Aiyadurai. *Silent Stranglers: Eradication of Mimosa in Kaziranga National Park, Assam*. New Delhi: Wildlife Trust of India, 2005.

Vergès, Françoise. "Racial Capitalocene." In *Futures of Black Radicalism*, edited by Gaye Theresa Johnson and Alex Lubin, 72–82. London: Verso, 2017.

Verma, Nitin. *Coolies of Capitalism: Assam Tea and the Making of Coolie Labour.* Berlin: De Gruyter, 2017.

Verma, Nitin. "For the Drink of the Nation: Drink, Labour and Plantation Capitalism in the Colonial Tea Gardens of Assam in the Late Nineteenth and Early Twentieth Century." In *Labour Matters: Towards Global Histories. Studies in Honour of Sabyasachi Bhattacharya*, edited by Marcel van der Linden and Prabhu P. Mohapatra, 295–318. New Delhi: Tulika, 2009.

"A Visit to Kuch Behar, the Bhutan Duars and Assam." *Indian Forester* 11, no. 6 (1959): 251–61.

von Schnitzler, Antina. "Infrastructure, Apartheid Technopolitics, and Temporalities of 'Transition.'" In *The Promise of Infrastructure*, edited by Nikhil Anand, Akhil Gupta, and Hannah Appel, 133–54. Durham, NC: Duke University Press, 2018.

"VP Announces Assam Package." *Times of India*, January 3, 1990.

Wadiwel, Dinesh Joseph. "Chicken Harvesting Machine: Animal Labor, Resistance, and the Time of Production." *South Atlantic Quarterly* 117, no. 3 (2018): 527–49. https://doi.org/10.1215/00382876-6942135.

Wakefield, Stephanie. "Infrastructures of Liberal Life: From Modernity and Progress to Resilience and Ruins." *Geography Compass* 12, no. 7 (2018): e12377. https://doi.org/10.1111/gec3.12377.

Whatmore, Sarah. "Humanism's Excess: Some Thoughts on the 'Post-human/ist' Agenda." *Environment and Planning A: Economy and Space* 36, no. 8 (2004): 1360–63.

Whatmore, Sarah. "Mapping Knowledge Controversies: Science, Democracy and the Redistribution of Expertise." *Progress in Human Geography* 33, no. 5 (2009): 587–99. https://doi.org/10.1177/0309132509339841.

Whatmore, Sarah. "Where Natural and Social Science Meet? Reflections on an Experiment in Geographical Practice." In *Interdisciplinarity: Reconfigurations of the Social and Natural Sciences*, edited by Andrew Barry and Georgina Born, 161–77. Abingdon, UK: Routledge, 2013.

Whatmore, Sarah, and Lorraine Thorne. "Elephants on the Move: Spatial Formations of Wildlife Exchange." *Environment and Planning D: Society and Space* 18, no. 2 (2000): 185–203.

Whatmore, Sarah, and Lorraine Thorne. "Wild(er)ness: Reconfiguring the Geographies of Wildlife." *Transactions of the Institute of British Geographers* 23 (1998): 435–54.

White, Thomas. "Road Ecology." Ecologizing Infrastructure: Infrastructural Ecologies. *Society and Space*, November 30, 2020. https://www.societyandspace.org/articles/road-ecology.

"A Wild Elephant." *Amrita Bazar Patrika*, June 19, 1899.

"Wild Elephants in Assam." *Times of India*, January 11, 1904.

"Wild Elephants on Lines." *Times of India*, July 19, 1909.

"Wild Elephants Wreak Havoc in Golaghat Villages." *Assam Tribune* (Guwahati), July 21, 2005.

Wildlife Institute of India. *Eco-friendly Measures to Mitigate Impacts of Linear Infrastructure on Wildlife*. Dehradun: Wildlife Institute of India, 2016.

Wilson, Edward O., and Edwin O. Willis. "Applied Biogeography." In *Ecology and Evolution of Communities*, edited by Jared M. Diamond and Martin L. Cody, 522–34. Cambridge, MA: Harvard University Press, 1975.

Wolford, Wendy. "The Plantationocene: A Lusotropical Contribution to the Theory." *Annals of the Association of American Geographers* 111, no. 6 (2021): 1622–39. https://doi.org/10.1080/24694452.2020.1850231.

Wynter, Sylvia. *Black Metamorphosis: New Natives in a New World*. Schomburg Centre for Research in Black Culture, Institute of the Black World Records. New York: New York Public Library.

Wynter, Sylvia. "1492: A New World View." In *Race, Discourse, and the Origins of the Americas*, edited by Vera Lawrence Hyatt and Rex Nettleford, 5–57. Washington, DC: Smithsonian Institution Press, 1995.

Wynter, Sylvia. "Novel and History, Plantation and Plot." *Savacou* 5 (1971): 95–102.

Xaxa, Virginius. *State, Society, and Tribes: Issues in Post-colonial India*. New Delhi: Dorling Kindersley, 2008.

Yadava, M. K. *Detailed Report on Issues and Possible Solutions for Long Term Protection of the Greater One Horned Rhinoceros in Kaziranga National Park Pursuant to the Order of the Hon'ble Gauhati High Court*. Kaziranga National Park: Forest Department, Government of Assam, August 5, 2014.

Yusoff, Kathryn. *A Billion Black Anthropocenes or None*. Minneapolis: University of Minnesota Press, 2018.

Zaman, Rokibuz. "Villagers against KNP Flyover Project." *Times of India* (New Delhi), September 6, 2021.

Ziipao, Raile Rocky. "Infrastructure." In *The Routledge Companion to Northeast India*, edited by Jelle J. P. Wouters and Tanka B. Subba, 262–67. London: Routledge, 2023.

Ziipao, Raile Rocky. *Infrastructure of Injustice: State and Politics in Manipur and Northeast India*. Abingdon, UK: Routledge, 2020.

INDEX

AASU (All Assam Students Union), 69–70, 73. *See also* Assam Movement
abkaree. *See* excise tax
Adivasi, 49, 217, 230n173; and cartography 190–91; and dispossession, 122, 130, 143–45, 161, 179–80; and elephants, 18–20, 87–88, 91, 95, 97, 103–7, 138–39; lives, 31, 110–11, 199; ontology, 193, 195–96, 202, 203–4, 254n6; and simple reproduction, 124, 129; worker community, 2, 11, 15, 16, 29, 65, 67, 85, 109, 112, 117–19, 127, 141, 213, 215; workforce, 9, 86, 132–35, 206–7, 211; worldview, 186–89
affect, 17, 66–67, 68–72, 78, 101–2, 104, 106, 112, 118–20, 168, 210; ecologies, 113–17, 216; generosity, 196, 200; orchestration of, 160; politics, 95, 148, 203
agency, 20, 23–24, 62, 95, 97, 119, 152, 201, 203, 208, 213, 216; and conflict, 91; historical situation of, 18; of materials, 19, 99–102, 106, 111–12, 118–20;

ruination as, 53; vegetal, 122, 124–26, 130, 135, 142–44. *See also* other-than-human
alcohol, 18–19, 104–6, 118–20; agency, 101–2, 113–16, 117; consumption, 103; production, history of, 109–11; rice beer, 109–10, 218, 241n15; *sulāi*, 99–100, 107–12, 219
Anthropocene, 3, 21–25, 224n6; and capitalism, 61; and colonialism, 26–28; critique of, 25–26, 45, 62, 97, 208–9, 215–16; Eurocentrism of, 23–24, 27; and infrastructure, 66–67, 89, 95; as reverse déjà vu, 207–9; and scale, 32; South Asian, 17, 29–30. *See also* Capitalocene; Plantationocene
Assam Accord, 71–72, 73, 76–77, 127. *See also* AASU; Assam Movement
Assam Agitation. *See* Assam Movement
Assam Haathi Project (AHP), 4, 9–11, 12–13
Assam Movement, 18, 19, 69–71, 95, 121, 127, 135, 235n28. *See also*

Assam Movement (*continued*)
AASU; Assam Accord; militancy;
SULFA; ULFA

begār. *See* labor
Behal, Rana Partap, 29–30, 38, 45, 224n24
biogeography, equilibrium theory of island, 151–52, 165. *See also* SLOSS (single large or several small) debate
biopolitics, 22, 60, 91, 110, 192, 193, 195, 211, 214, 253n170; and conservation, 156, 167, 179–82; and political economy, 56. *See also* circulation; necropolitics
boundary object, 149–50
buffalo, 39, 41, 190

capital/capitalism, 24–25, 48, 61, 70, 81, 86, 127, 135, 141, 145, 187–88, 201, 203–4; accumulation of capital, 23, 52, 83, 122, 124, 126, 143, 183, 215; capitalist nature, 56, 79; colonial, 2, 9, 22, 30, 45, 47, 62, 69, 110; and conservation, 20, 160, 178, 181; and extraction, 79–80, 96, 149; lively capital, 34, 37–38, 126, 211; noncapitalist, 82, 212; and plantations, 26, 34–36, 43, 134, 179, 227n71; racial, 213–14. *See also* Capitalocene; need economy; plantation; primitive accumulation; surplus
Capitalocene, 24–25, 31–32, 201, 209. *See also* capital/capitalism
cartography, 5, 146; animal, 151, 176, 177–78, 197–201; counter-, 51, 195; decolonial, 20, 186–89, 191, 192, 193–94, 201–4, 215–16. *See also* track/tracking
Ceiling Act, 134; surplus land, 136, 145

cheap/cheapening, 43, 58, 110; nature, 25–26, 28, 33–34, 36–37, 48, 52, 56–58, 60–61, 78, 80–84, 143, 209. *See also* commodity; labor
Chromolaena. See *Eupatorium*
circulation, 34, 49, 51–56, 61, 63; and biopower, 183, 253n170; of biota, 16, 22, 52–53, 122, 124, 125, 130, 142, 144, 149, 213, 247n110; of commodities, 30, 39, 46; and infrastructure, 65, 77–78; of people, 48–49. *See also* mobility
coal, 33, 47
colonial/colonialism, 22–24, 25, 91, 99, 109–11, 132, 194–95, 197–202; administration, 6, 8–9, 34, 42–43, 45–46, 68, 109–10, 118, 168, 198; and Anthropocene, 26–28; as duration, 9, 14, 16, 27, 56, 130, 136, 143–44, 207; enclosure, 24, 186, 196; forestry, 5–7, 16, 41, 144, 190; governmentality, 215; hinterland, 43, 62, 69–70; history, 3–4, 15, 16, 23, 107, 109, 190, 205; hunting, 8–9; internal, 47; neo-colonialism, 18, 31–32, 62, 66–67, 68, 71, 94, 127–28, 142, 148, 169; petro-, 72–73, 94; plunder, 16–17, 30, 35, 46, 48; precolonial, 6, 111, 217, 219, 244n49; rule, 69, 80, 126, 130, 144, 213, 217, 218, 219; and transformation of landscape/fauna, 2–3, 61. *See also* capital/capitalism; decolonization; postcolonial/postcolonialism
commodity, 18, 25, 28, 30, 38, 46–47, 49, 58, 63, 77, 80, 100, 110, 122, 209, 211, 213–14; cheap, 25, 46, 58, 63, 77, 110, 122, 132–33, 202, 209, 211, 213–14; commodification, 46; living, 22, 42, 132; pro-

duction of, 127, 132, 202. *See also* cheap/cheapening; elephant

conflict, human-wildlife, 91, 97, 156, 195–96, 219. *See also* deforestation

connectivity, 20, 77, 79, 148–50, 151, 155–56, 164, 165, 166–70, 176–79, 181–84, 186, 191, 193, 200, 201, 214, 251n92; politics of, 158–63, 193. *See also* conservation; corridor; diagram; space

conservation, 3, 19, 20, 37, 86, 91, 162, 178, 181–84, 194–96, 203–4, 211; biodiversity, 122; connectivity, 148–51, 152–57, 159–60, 165, 176, 186, 214; elephant, 16, 18; and infrastructure, 166–70, 171–72; landscape, 149, 181, 202; of wildlife, 83, 164; revolution, 216. *See also* connectivity; deforestation

corridor, 20, 45, 93–94, 147–51, 152, 154–57, 158–66, 167, 169, 171, 172, 174–77, 178, 180–84, 186, 191, 193, 198, 202, 204; functional, 166, 176; structural, 166, 251n92. *See also* connectivity; conservation; deforestation; diagram; space

cosmopolitan ecologies, 53, 149, 213; flora, 55. *See also* ecology/ecologies

Dāngariyā, 186–87, 189–93, 194, 196, 203, 218. *See also* spirit

decolonization, 20, 185–204, 216. *See also* cartography

deforestation, 10–11, 17, 19, 46, 62, 99, 115, 121, 124, 127–29, 133, 139, 143–45, 148, 154, 181, 196, 212, 214; and militancy, 135–36, 203. *See also* conflict, human-wildlife; conservation; corridor; militancy; timber

déjà vu, reverse, 23, 136, 207–9

demonic grounds, 186–88, 192, 193, 201–2, 215

diagram, 5–6, 19–20, 28–30, 31, 33, 43, 48, 55, 58, 61, 152–53, 181–84, 186, 216; of connectivity, 19–20, 146, 147–56, 177, 193, 198, 201, 202, 214; of enclosure, 4–7, 19–20, 148, 179, 190, 193, 201, 214–15; unbound points, 7–11. *See also* connectivity; corridor; space

Diamond, Jared, 152–53

Doigurung Reserved Forest, 65, 76, 89, 90, 102, 103, 116, 124, 125–30, 134–35, 136–38, 189

duration. *See* colonial/colonialism

dwelling: alongside, 11, 20, 65, 103, 108, 120, 139–40, 196, 201, 203; animals and, 7, 10, 13, 33, 106, 144, 186–87, 193; politics of, 3, 29, 34, 161, 186–87, 197, 199, 210, 215–16. *See also* enclosure

ecology/ecologies: affective, 113–17, 119, 120; altered, 3, 11, 18, 24, 25, 62, 137, 150; crises, 25–26; and economy, 34, 209; effects of infrastructure, 66–67, 79–80, 88, 91, 95–96, 166; just, 28–29; of a Plantationocene, 16, 32–33, 51–52, 63, 96, 99, 149, 184, 211, 213–14; political, 15, 17, 31, 61, 73, 120, 124, 127, 148, 187, 211, 216; reconciliation, 171–72; science, 186; simplified, 22, 56–60, 122, 125–26, 142–44, 210, 211; world, 24–25, 26, 30–31, 34. *See also* cosmopolitan ecologies

elephant: bull, 8; bull herd, 4, 11–16; capture, 6, 8–9, 22; and

INDEX   291

elephant (*continued*)
  classification, 194–96; as commodity, 28; Control Scheme, 8; ethology, 7, 10, 12–14, 107–9, 111–12, 113–17, 210; hunting, 8–9; and infrastructure, 64, 66, 74–76, 166–67, 172–77; as infrastructure, 38–39, 42; and landscape, 11–16, 19–20, 46, 52, 55, 62, 87–97, 102–7, 119–20, 122, 125, 136–41, 144, 146, 181–82, 197–201, 207–8, 212; mobility, 65, 74–76, 77, 79, 87–94, 96–97, 130, 136–41, 148, 151, 158–63, 169–70, 172–75, 185–86, 189–93, 197–201, 215; *mukhna*, 4, 8, 116, 120, 219; *musth*, 41, 105, 219; as observant participants, 17; Preservation Act (1879), 6; reserve design, 154–57; smell, 107, 111, 176; SP04 herd, 4, 7–11, 12–14, 89, 120; taste, 107, 113–14; trade, 6, 39, 42; work, 39–43. See also *kheddah*; *matanga*; track/tracking
  enclosure, 2–3, 21, 27, 43, 45, 63, 156, 181, 184, 193, 197, 200; colonial, 24, 186, 196; of commons, 58, 143, 211; diagram of, 4–7, 10–11, 19, 148–50, 179, 190, 201, 202, 214; history of, 9, 15, 17, 24; of land, 25, 36, 200; model of, 5, 162–63, 166, 172. See also connectivity; corridor; diagram; dwelling
Engels, Friedrich, 25
environmental determinism, 152
environmental humanities, 26, 32, 208
environmentalism of the poor, 71, 95
ethnography: more-than-human, 17–18, 19, 210, 223n46; multispecies, 194. See also observant participation; tea plantation; track/tracking
Eupatorium, 52–53

excise, 108–10, 112, 119, 219, 241n15
excise tax, 109, 217
extraction, 16, 25, 28, 30, 35, 40, 41–42, 46–47, 57, 62, 67–69, 70, 77–86, 94–96, 117, 142, 167, 198–99, 210, 212, 214, 235n14

fences, 66, 121, 138, 161
Forest Department: colonial, 5, 217; competition with tea industry, 48, 197; and corridors, 156, 158–59, 161–63, 165, 167, 169–70, 176–77, 178–80; and deforestation, 128–29, 136, 246n80; and elephants, 6, 8, 90, 112, 116–17, 120, 161–63, 190; and evictions, 7, 14, 127; and leases, 6, 78, 82, 218; and plantations, 36–37, 54, 57, 59
forestry, colonial. *See* colonial/colonialism
Foucault, Michel, 56

Gandhi, Indira, 69
Gandhi, Rajiv, 71
Gohain, Hiren, 29, 30, 45, 71, 128, 142, 234n259
Golaghat, 75, 77, 84, 88, 89, 91, 111, 113, 123, 127–29, 130–32, 135, 141, 144, 147, 194, 207
grazing, 5, 15, 21, 37, 45, 159
Guha, Amalendu, 29, 30, 35
gustation. *See* elephant: taste

habitat fragmentation, 46, 148, 150, 151, 154–55, 156, 159, 164, 166, 168, 181–82, 183
habitus, 65, 66, 87, 90, 95, 96, 116, 118, 120, 172, 174–75

immobilization, 62, 145, 211, 253n170
indenture, 2, 9, 11, 21, 25–26, 28–29, 33, 35–36, 46, 48, 49, 52, 62, 77,

91, 102, 105, 109, 210. *See also* labor; plantation
infrastructure, 18–19, 31, 42, 46, 52, 53, 55, 63, 65–67, 68, 69, 78, 80, 87–89, 99, 102, 117, 122, 137, 198–99, 214; Bogibeel Bridge, 77–79, 83–84, 86, 89; colonial, 61, 73, 168, 171, 213; and conservation, 148, 149, 150, 166–68, 181; postcolonial, 69, 73, 76–78, 79, 116, 205, 212, 214; reconciliation infrastructures, 170–78, 183–84, 214; and violence, 62, 66–67, 72, 74–75, 86, 90, 91–94, 95–97, 101, 196, 203, 212. *See also* elephant; plantation; railways; roads
invasive species, 52, 122, 126, 232n205. See also *Eupatorium*; *Mikania*; weeds

Karbi Anglong, 77–78, 79, 80–81, 84, 85, 86, 158, 164, 165, 167
Kaziranga National Park, 73–74, 76, 79, 83, 84–85, 86, 89, 147–48, 150, 157, 158–59, 160, 161, 163–65, 167–74, 177, 178–80, 185, 205
Khamti, 193
kheddah, 42, 218
Krishak Mukti Sangram Samiti (KMSS), 161–62, 163

labor, 2–3, 26, 30, 34–43, 47, 48–50, 51, 52, 55, 56–57, 59–60, 61, 71, 102–7, 144, 145, 202, 204, 206, 208, 209, 210–11, 213, 227n87, 245n64; *begār*, 36–37, 217; and biopolitics, 110; cheap, 25–26, 28, 35, 36, 39–40, 51, 61, 132, 145, 202, 209, 245n64; child, 38; contract, 28, 33, 36; dead, 37–38, 132; *faltu*, 50, 62, 102, 135, 139, 211, 218; generational, 49, 211; labor-power, 36–37, 62, 82, 127, 132, 205; lines, 2, 9, 89, 206, 218; unpaid, 33, 34, 61, 132; wage, 2, 86, 87, 133, 140, 143, 145, 213. *See also* cheap/cheapening; elephant; indenture; plantation; reserve army of workers; surplus; tea plantation; vegetal work; work
land grab, 19, 45, 63, 122, 124, 134, 136, 138, 143, 145, 147, 211–12
lively capital. *See* capital/capitalism

Marwari, 79–81, 218
Marx, Karl, 25, 45, 80, 83, 143, 227n87
matanga, 194, 218. *See also* elephant
material politics, 18–19, 101–2, 112, 117–20, 208; vs. political matter, 19, 101, 144
matter. *See* material politics
metabolism, 22, 37, 96, 114, 126, 132, 211
Mikania, 15, 19, 53–56, 122, 124–27, 129–30, 137, 143–44, 197, 207, 213. *See also* invasive species; weeds
militancy, 17, 18, 63, 121, 127–28, 130–31, 133–34, 135, 142–43, 144, 203, 212. *See also* deforestation; SULFA; ULFA
mobility, 20, 66, 75, 96, 149–50, 156, 169, 171, 172, 174, 175, 176, 177–78, 181–83, 205, 207, 208, 213, 214, 253n170; hypermobility, 212; immobility, 88, 89; of labor, 52, 208. *See also* circulation; elephant; immobilization
monocrop/monoculture, 3, 5, 9, 11, 26, 28, 33, 48, 58, 63, 125, 140, 142, 201, 210, 213, 233n229

more-than-human, 29, 32, 34, 94, 161, 199, 222n33. *See also* ethnography; multispecies; other-than-human; work
multispecies, 22, 26–27, 29, 32, 120, 187, 209. *See also* ethnography; more-than-human; other-than-human

nature/society binaries, 5, 8, 28–29, 50, 62, 148–49, 197, 200, 201, 202, 208, 211
necropolitics, 19, 67, 91, 96, 97, 110, 117, 119, 120, 201, 208, 215. *See also* biopolitics
need economy, 82, 86, 95, 97, 102, 150, 178, 179, 180, 184, 186, 201, 209, 213. *See also* capital/capitalism
new materialism, 18–19, 99–102, 118, 208

observant participation, 17, 32, 120, 210. *See also* ethnography
oil, 33, 42, 47, 62, 64, 68–70, 72, 73, 77, 168; Numaligarh Refinery, 64, 66, 68, 69, 72–73, 74, 76, 84, 131, 165, 171, 185
olfaction. *See* elephant: smell
ontology, 18, 20, 23, 24, 25, 66, 67, 88, 95–96, 101, 109, 118–19, 187–89, 191–93, 195, 202–3, 210, 211, 215–16, 254n6
other-than-human, 9, 32, 83, 90, 120, 130, 187, 191, 222n33; agency, 18; denizens, 49, 62–63, 117; knowledge, 10, 187, 199; life, 17, 20, 27, 33, 34, 43, 63, 66, 88, 95, 140, 145–46, 156, 171–72, 188, 209–10, 214; mobilities, 96, 149–50, 167, 175, 212–13; resistance, 41; worlds, 117, 149.

See also agency; more-than-human; work

Panbari, 79, 84, 148, 157–60, 162–65, 175–77, 191–92, 197, 198, 202–3, 216
pesticide, 12, 60–61, 131, 133. *See also* pests
pests, 52; of tea, 58, 60. *See also* pesticide; tea plant; tea plantation; virulence
planetary change/transformation, 3, 5, 16, 17, 19, 23, 24–25, 29, 31–32, 33, 61, 62, 63, 142, 208–9
plantation: accumulation by, 124, 142–46; capitalist plantation complex, 35; economy, 37–38, 44–45, 52, 61, 82, 131–32, 188; and elephants, 41–43; as enclave, 56–57, 77, 144, 207–8; forestry as, 5, 9, 54, 58–60, 126; and infrastructure, 39–40, 46, 68–69, 72–73, 77; Labour Act of 1951, 61–62, 180; logics, 16, 19, 28–29, 31, 33, 38–39, 48–49, 52, 70, 94, 125, 141, 168, 201; and plants, 121–22, 126, 137–41; proto-, 43–44; and scale, 146; and time, 57; and virulence, 58–59, 131; workers, 1, 11, 21, 26, 32, 34–36, 38, 48–50, 55, 61–62, 65–66, 71, 77, 81–82, 85–86, 102, 109–10, 127, 135, 217, 218. *See also* labor; plantation multiple; reserve army of workers; small tea estate; surplus; tea plantation
plantation multiple, 17, 33–34, 61–62, 223n44, 226n64. *See also* plantation
Plantationocene, 2–3, 15–18, 19–20, 25–33, 35–37, 56, 61, 63, 67, 72, 78–80, 95, 97, 123–24, 130, 142–

294   INDEX

46, 148–51, 177, 178, 186–87, 188, 195, 203–4, 208–9, 210–16; as affective condition, 117; Assam's, 47, 62, 66, 68–69, 79, 148, 166, 184, 213; conservation in, 181–82; denizens of, 4; ecologies of, 16, 32, 53, 56, 60, 63, 96, 120, 149; elephants of, 55; habitability in, 9, 102, 189, 193; landscape, 12, 48, 88–89, 106, 132, 135, 192; materials of, 60, 61, 107–11, 113–14, 117–20; monocultures of, 39–40; political economy of, 82; spatialities, 43, 45, 47–48, 50–52. *See also* Anthropocene; Capitalocene

plants, 17, 19, 26, 34, 37–39, 51–52, 57, 122–24, 125, 126, 132, 140, 142, 144–46, 211, 213, 222n33, 232n205. *See also* tea plant; work

plot, 1, 3, 32, 50–51, 55, 56, 61, 121, 140, 141, 144, 146, 161, 188, 199–200, 201, 209

plunder. *See* colonial/colonialism

postcolonial/postcolonialism, 17–18, 25, 27, 29, 31–32, 33–34, 47, 48, 57, 60–63, 68–69, 96, 99, 118–20, 132, 136, 143, 182–83, 197–98, 203, 208–10, 215; ecology, 28, 32, 76, 213–14; fauna, 2–3, 9, 14, 89, 113; planning, 75; resource extraction, 79–80. *See also* conservation; need economy

primitive accumulation, 24, 35, 42, 43, 63, 143. *See also* capital/capitalism

protected area, 10, 11, 86, 148–49, 151–52, 156, 158, 159, 163, 172, 182, 184

quarry, 77–86, 87–88

race, 23, 25, 26, 27, 56, 61, 101, 194, 208; racial economy, 28, 34, 56, 60–61, 68, 111, 142, 212, 214

railways, 36, 40, 42, 46–47, 52, 68, 77, 84, 157, 168, 213, 214; train collisions with elephants, 46. *See also* infrastructure

raw material, 18, 25, 100

reconciliation ecology. *See under* ecology/ecologies

reconciliation infrastructures. *See under* infrastructure

reserve army of workers, 50, 62, 81, 82, 102, 133, 134–35, 211, 213, 218. *See also* labor; plantation; surplus

resistance, 7, 15, 18, 20, 29, 41, 186, 189, 190, 192, 193, 196, 200, 201, 202, 203, 215, 216

resource extraction. *See* extraction

resource frontier, 17, 19, 29, 46, 146

roads, 39, 45, 77, 78, 88, 96, 129, 143, 149, 157, 167–70, 171, 174, 175, 177, 198–99, 214, 217, 218; National Highway, 167–69, 171, 174, 177. *See also* infrastructure

Rodney, Walter, 26, 224n24, 235n24

rubber, 5, 43, 58

ruin/ruination, 15, 16, 34, 51, 53–54, 55, 62, 86, 105, 120, 122, 125, 130, 144–45, 168, 213, 214

scale, 19, 24, 25, 31, 33, 51, 63, 80, 121, 122, 126, 135, 141, 146, 150, 154, 202, 204, 208, 211

Sinha, Anindya, 9

slavery, 26, 29, 34, 35, 36, 37, 38, 51

SLOSS (single large or several small) debate, 152, 248n24. *See also* biogeography, equilibrium theory of island slow violence, 18, 32, 47, 56, 60, 61, 75, 77, 83, 88, 101, 102, 106, 116, 118–20, 130, 143, 146, 166, 167, 187, 196, 201, 212; of infrastructure, 66–67, 78, 90–91, 93–94, 95–97, 183. *See also* violence

small tea estate, 121–24, 131–33, 135–36, 139, 141, 143, 144, 145, 146, 180, 184, 211; growers, 121, 132–36, 141, 211. *See also* plantation; tea plantation

smell. *See under* elephant

Sonitpur, 2, 4–10, 11–16, 23, 27, 28, 34, 60, 89, 120, 199

space, 5, 28, 56, 67, 76, 82, 137, 158, 167, 184, 192, 201, 222n33; of animals, 10, 15, 203; binary, 2–3, 4, 28, 144, 148; extensive, 162–63, 166, 175, 181–82, 198; intensive, 162, 166, 175–76, 181–82, 184, 198, 202; inviolate, 148, 162, 164, 166, 176, 182, 184, 197; of ordinariness, 86, 96; production of, 34, 43–51, 183, 198; repurposing of, 61, 188. *See also* connectivity; corridor; diagram

spirit, 17, 20, 186–88, 189–93, 194, 200, 203, 215, 218, 222n33. *See also* Dāngariyā

stone quarry. *See* quarry

subaltern studies, 30

SULFA (surrendered militants of the United Liberation Front of Assam), 128–29, 131, 133, 134, 135, 141, 143. *See also* Assam Movement; militancy; ULFA

Sundarpur, 64–65, 107–19, 140–41, 185; Adivasi community of, 102–6, 127, 129, 133–35, 189, 191, 197; hills adjacent to, 78–79; landscape, 76, 87–91, 131, 186; quarries, 84; tea plantations in, 121, 123–24, 140–41, 180

surplus: capital, 21, 69; collectives, 43; land, 113, 132, 134, 136; population, 179, 180; value, 68, 79–80, 82, 83, 110, 111, 145, 201. *See also* capital/capitalism; labor; plantation; reserve army of workers

Talukdar, Bhupendra Nath, 75, 79, 199

taste. *See under* elephant

taxonomy, 5, 104, 188, 194–95, 202, 209, 229n126

tea plant, 38, 52, 124, 132, 135, 144; flush, 38, 57, 206; nursery, 38; plucking, 38, 55, 57, 61, 90, 126–27, 133, 136, 206; weeding, 55, 58, 60. *See also* tea plantation; weeds

tea plantation, 4, 8, 9, 12, 16, 28, 30, 33, 80, 89, 90, 102–3, 111, 113, 178; constricting economy, 47–48, 132, 181; ethnographies of, 31; expansion of, 21, 22, 25, 27, 35–36, 43, 63, 72, 136, 138–40, 179, 184, 206, 219; garden time, 57; industry, 34, 42; recruitment of labor for, 29; and virulence, 54–55, 58, 59, 126. *See also* ethnography; labor; pests; plantation; small tea estate; tea plant

timber, 5, 9, 26, 28, 32, 35, 36, 29, 40–43, 48, 53, 54, 57–58, 126, 128–29. *See also* deforestation

track/tracking, 1–4, 9–10, 19–20, 51, 78, 105, 124, 130, 137, 182, 186, 189, 194–96, 197–201, 202–3, 210, 214, 215, 218; *dandi*, 130, 139, 160, 197–99, 218, 255n28. *See also* elephant; ethnography

ULFA (United Liberation Front of Assam), 121, 127–28, 134, 142–43. *See also* Assam Movement; militancy; SULFA

underdevelopment, 16, 18, 61, 62, 67–68, 69, 71–72, 94, 97, 105, 120, 127, 142–43, 146, 148, 168, 171, 208, 212, 235n24

vegetal agency, 122, 124–26, 130, 135, 142–44
vegetal economies, 130–36, 145–46
vegetal geographies, 19, 123, 140, 182
vegetal places, 129–30
vegetal politics, 123, 136–42, 145
vegetal time, 135
vegetal work, 37–38, 122–23, 126, 132, 211. *See also* labor
violence, 3, 14, 19, 31, 62–63, 71–72, 85, 109, 124, 130, 133, 143, 146, 187, 199, 201, 210, 211, 212; colonial, 17, 26, 51, 192, 196; racial, 27. *See also* slow violence
virulence, 30, 34, 58–60, 122, 126, 129, 137, 144–45, 214. *See also* pests
vitalism, 18, 100–101, 118, 122, 144

Wasteland Grants, 35, 43
weeds, 52–53, 55, 56, 126; *Mimosa*, 52, 55. See also *Mikania*; tea plant
work: animal, 38, 41, 42; more-than-human, 34, 37; other-than-human, 16, 33–34, 37, 39–41, 52, 63; vegetal, 37–38, 122–23, 126, 132, 211. *See also* labor
world ecology. *See* ecology/ecologies

zone, 32, 45, 67, 77, 133, 168, 177; contact, 50; containment, 206–7, 214; No Development, 74, 84, 93, 165

INDEX   297